Cinematic Journeys
in Latin America

Cinematic Journeys in Latin America

Geography Through the Lens of Exploration and Discovery Films

RICHARD FRANCAVIGLIA

McFarland & Company, Inc., Publishers

Jefferson, North Carolina

LIBRARY OF CONGRESS CATALOGUING-IN-PUBLICATION DATA

Names: Francaviglia, Richard V., author.
Title: Cinematic journeys in Latin America : geography through the lens
of exploration and discovery films / Richard Francaviglia.
Description: Jefferson, North Carolina : McFarland & Company, Inc.,
Publishers, 2023. | Includes bibliographical references and index.
Identifiers: LCCN 2023031583 | ISBN 9781476692524 (paperback : acid free paper) ∞
ISBN 9781476649672 (ebook)
Subjects: LCSH: Latin America—In motion pictures. | Explorers in motion pictures. |
Quests (Expeditions) in motion pictures. | Action and adventure films—History and criticism.
Classification: LCC PN1995.9.L37 F73 2023 | DDC 791.43/628—dc23/eng/20230711
LC record available at https://lccn.loc.gov/2023031583

BRITISH LIBRARY CATALOGUING DATA ARE AVAILABLE

ISBN (print) 978-1-4766-9252-4
ISBN (ebook) 978-1-4766-4967-2

On the cover: Map titled South America, by W. & A.K. Johnston,
Edinburgh & London, 1895 (author's collection); *Embrace of the Serpent*
(Colombia/Venezuela/Argentina, 2015), aka *El abrazo de la serpiente*,
shown in center: Jan Bijvoet (Oscilloscope Laboratories/Photofest); *Aguirre,
the Wrath of God* (West Germany, 1972), shown: Klaus Kinski
(New Yorker Films/Photofest); *Anaconda* (1997), shown: Jon Voight
(Columbia Pictures/Photofest); *background*: film strip © StarLine/Shutterstock

Printed in the United States of America

McFarland & Company, Inc., Publishers
Box 611, Jefferson, North Carolina 28640
www.mcfarlandpub.com

Dedicated to
THE FILMMAKERS
who expand our horizons
and bring the past to life

Table of Contents

Preface and Acknowledgments

A Personal Journey into Film

This book was a long time in the making and involved many individuals who deserve my sincere thanks. It is a natural outcome of my life-long fascination with film, coupled with my interest in geography. The former was no doubt initially kindled by my aunt Faye Riffin's addiction to movies. In the days before television (1948), she'd take me to the small neighborhood movie theater in Cambria Heights (Queens), New York. Sitting there transfixed, we watched a wide range of films, some not entirely suitable for a five-year-old—for example, *The Red Shoes* and *Treasure of the Sierra Madre*. Over the years, my interest in film that began as recreational became more and more academic. Throughout much of my fifty-five-year career as a cultural-historical geographer, films increasingly impressed me as a significant source of popular information and misinformation about the places I studied.

I first became aware of their relevance to geography in 1965, when I took Professor Homer Aschmann's undergraduate level course titled "Geography of Latin America" at the University of California, Riverside. My specialty focus at that time was northwestern Mexico, as was Aschmann's. However, he knew all of Latin America rather well and served as a role model. In class one day, while he was discussing the forested regions of Venezuela, Aschmann mentioned the book *Green Mansions* by William Henry Hudson. Actually, I had seen the 1959 film of the same name a few years earlier, but did not know about the book. After class, Aschmann mentioned I should read it to gain a better understanding of Hudson's story. In retrospect, that was his subtle way of saying he liked the book better than the film.

Later that day, I checked out a copy of *Green Mansions* from the library, and read it along with my other studies. I quickly realized that it was a rather different story than the one I had seen on film; more nuanced, more detailed, and a lot darker. That experience started me thinking about how well other books and their resulting films compared. Addressing that subject properly involves comparing the two, but at that time this was virtually impossible because the film could only be seen at the theater during its initial run, or subsequently on television. Back in the 1960s, there were only three TV stations in most areas, and the movies one saw on TV were up to the station. If they felt like showing a particular movie—and if the antenna perched on top of your house, or the rabbit ears on top of your TV set, worked properly—then you could see it at home. However, in depth interpretation of the kind I had in mind—comparing the written accounts and stories in books with their counterparts on screen, or descriptions of geographical environments with those shown on screen—pretty much required having the

1

two versions of the story side-by-side. Having a book in hand was relatively easy, but obtaining the movie was quite another—something we take for granted today. Little did I realize that it would take me more than fifty years—and many developments in film viewing technology—to finally make the necessary book/film comparisons in this book.

In the meantime, I decided to become a professional geographer. By 1970, I had earned a doctorate from the University of Oregon and began my own teaching and research career. In the early 1970s, developments in video projection technology made it possible for me to use films in classes at Antioch College (Yellow Springs, Ohio), an innovative school that had a strong interest in communications and media studies. To my delight, the students seemed especially keen on film, no surprise given its growing popularity and their broader interests in communications. By the mid–1970s some of my Antioch students were actually making their own films in our "Reading the Landscape" class using recently developed hand-held video cameras. My colleague Don Myatt loved filmmaking, and we discussed the many special effects that were used to make movie scenes so memorable. Just a few blocks from Antioch, the Little Art Theater often showed great films—and still does to this day! At conferences, I met popular culture scholars such as Margaret King, whose ability to deconstruct films was inspirational, and geographer Karen Koegler, a passionate film buff interested in how places are depicted on screen. Occasionally, my film interests took me outside of academe as well: for example, one memorable consulting gig involved recommending film locations for the movie *Butch and Sundance: The Early Years*.

Throughout the 1970s, the blossoming of cable television was a boon to me and many other film lovers because new stations such as HBO offered films not seen on network TV. Moreover, advances in video cassette recording (VCR) technology now enabled me to play selected footage from my personal copies of televised films in class. By the late 1970s movie studios began selling VHS tapes of their feature films—a gold mine for those of us who wanted to bring the silver screen into the classroom. Those films having "Director's Cut" versions—that is, additional footage, or voice-over commentary—were especially valuable as one could learn more about how the film had been made. Throughout the 1980s, I increasingly used feature films in my geographical studies, showing selected footage in class on VHS tapes; I also discussed those films in several books that I subsequently published.

Although those films depicted places at various points in time, the realization that their stories could be compared to the actual process of exploration and discovery became clear to me in 1991 as I arrived at the University of Texas at Arlington (UTA). My dual position—Director of the Center for Southwestern Studies and the History of Cartography, and Professor of History and Geography—enabled me to work closely with the Society for the History of Discoveries and other organizations to develop public programs. I was in good company. My close colleague Gerald Saxon was Director of UTA's Special Collections and a fellow historian. Catherine (Kit) Goodwin was our Cartographic Collections guru and seemed to personally know each of the thousands of maps in our collection. Moreover, history professor Dennis Reinhartz was an authority on geographic exploration. Remarkably, all three were also avid film buffs! So, too, were my History Department colleagues Evan (Buzz) Anders and Jerome (Jerry) Rodnitzky.

At that time, the transition from VHS tapes to DVDs was occurring, and it helped revolutionize teaching as we could easily index scenes without having to rewind or fast-forward. DVD technology also made possible the snagging of images as stills for use in publications. Moreover, it resulted in the higher quality of both picture and sound. In one class, students and I compared the original written *Relación* of Spanish explorer Alvar Núñez Cabeza de Vaca (ca. 1485–ca. 1559) to the film version of his epic early sixteenth-century journey through portions of today's American Southwest and Mexico. Despite my Southwestern geographical specialty, anthropologist colleague Joseph Bastien—a former Jesuit priest—helped further kindle my interest in South America, regaling me with his exciting tales of field work in remote highland Bolivia.

My experiences at UTA were eye-opening, but my geographic interest in Latin America was greatly expanded on a trip to Ecuador in early January 1992. Although I had long been interested in that part of Latin America, my understanding to date had been based on vicarious experiences—classes, books, stories, and films. Now I was able to experience the real thing, thanks to an invitation from my wife's dear friend Ana Julia Rugel Hollis and her husband Patrick, who lived in Guayaquil. Their goal was to introduce us to their part of northwestern South America, which ultimately led to my passionate interest in that continent's physical and cultural geography.

In trying to better understand my deepening interest in Latin America, I realized that the many films I had seen over the years had left an indelible impression on my perceptions. In fact, for most of the major geographical regions south of the border, I could recall a movie that had depicted that locale and its action-packed history. These films included the aforementioned *Green Mansions* (1959); *Green Fire* (1954); and *Secret of the Incas* (1954) along with others that will also be interpreted in this book. Geographers do not usually make this kind of admission or confession about popular culture having a positive effect on their careers, but then again I have always appreciated the way places are depicted in varied sources—written (novels), recorded (songs) and the visual arts such as paintings. In a way, filmmaking is closely related to all those sources.

My point in recounting a very personal past in relation to cinematic Latin America is to underscore the trajectory that brought this book into being. I was at UTA when that marvelous invention called the Internet now made videos viewable to anyone anywhere in the world—provided they could get on-line. My seventeen wonderful years there provided me many new opportunities to interact with colleagues, including David Buisseret, Bart Lewis and Christopher Conway, all of whom were deeply interested in Latin American culture. Over the years, UTA also provided me ample opportunity to incorporate films into the curriculum in popular courses such as "History and Film" and "Images of the West." Under a grant obtained by the Houston Endowment, I helped produce and direct an educational video titled "Natural Encounters" that emphasizes the importance of maps as tools in teaching history and geography. In this book, I will discuss that experience where relevant.

After semi-retiring from UTA in 2008, I had more time on my hands, and could now more fully reflect on how words and images from the page become "the film version" that we experience on screen. Shortly after retiring and moving back to Oregon, I watched the compelling Alexander von Humboldt exploration-discovery film titled *Aire Libre* (1996) which had recently been released on DVD. At the time, I thought about reviewing it for *Terrae Incognitae—The Journal of the History of Discoveries*, and then writing an in-depth article about how it and other films work to convey pivotal events in the exploration of South America. However, other writing projects seemed more pressing, including two books about the Atacama Desert.

From 2010 to 2016, I accepted the invitation to lecture and teach classes in Religious

Studies at Willamette University (WU), making ever more frequent use of relevant films to enhance the experience. The 2009 travel-exploration-discovery gem *Journey to Mecca: In the Footsteps of Ibn Battuta* was one of the students' favorites, and mine as well. Concurrently, I developed a friendship with WU film professor Ken Nolley, who called to my attention the fine film on the Atacama Desert titled *Nostalgia for the Light*. Spanish professors Anna Cox, Patricia Varas, and John Uggen also had a strong interest in literature, cinema, and Latin American studies. Truth is, film was even getting more and more of my attention now—getting the upper hand, actually—as it was so rich in stories about exploration and discovery.[1]

Looking back now, I was fortunate to have firsthand access to the process of how people react to motion pictures by observing how my students responded to film footage in class. They also shared insights about how they became interested in film generally, and what they liked most, and least, about particular films. In other words, I literally had a captive audience whose reactions to films shed much light on how films affect viewers. In addition to learning from students and fellow faculty, though, I often found inspiration in friends outside of academe—including Tony Crowe, Roger Landers, and Stephen (Steve) Carlile—who shared fresh and unfettered perspectives about particular films. Steve also read the manuscript and provided helpful comments that improved it. Over many years, my wife Ellen has watched films with me, and her uncanny insight into the interpersonal relationships depicted on screen—no doubt reflecting her enduring interest in sociology—continues to amaze me.

Very recently (2019–2020), two developments in the journal *Terrae Incognitae* convinced me that the book project's time had finally arrived. The first was an insightful essay article by Carter Ringle titled "Fear and Loathing in the Americas: White Fanatics and the Cinematic Colonial Mindset," which focused on the deeper significance of historical characters in three of my favorite recent feature films that were set in South America.[2] The second was the publication of the "Special Issue on Exploring Latin America: Travelogues by Alexander von Humboldt, Archduke Maximilian, and James Bryce," which was edited by Richard Weiner.[3] That issue goes a long way toward rectifying the relative neglect of Latin American subjects in *Terrae Incognitae* over the last six decades. However, I felt more strongly than ever that the subject of how exploration figures in films about Latin America deserves more attention. *TI*'s Richard Weiner was supportive of this book project, and I thank him for his interest and guidance.

As sometimes happens, fate interceded with my plans to write articles related to the subject at hand. With the COVID-19 pandemic raging, and my philosophy being to never let a disaster sidetrack me, I hunkered down with my extensive personal library of DVDs, articles, and books on the subject. I soon found myself writing up a storm, which is to say expanding my vision from journal articles into this book. Although I plan to publish some additional articles that dig more deeply into subjects, this book is meant to be an incentive for future study by others. I see it having many possibilities, most inspirational being a textbook introducing students to Latin America through one of their favorite forms of entertainment. Hopefully, the public may be interested in the subject as well. In searching for a publisher, I recalled that McFarland had published *The Dinosaur Filmography*—a favorite in my personal library and one that can be read by scholars and film buffs alike. I thank their Acquisitions Editor Charlie Perdue for his faith in this book project.

As a film buff for the last sixty years, my most pleasant part of writing this book was selecting and re-watching relevant films in my personal film library, which consists of five-hundred plus DVDs. I hope that readers will not only appreciate my selections, but will also want to explore the films themselves, many of which are either still available for purchase, or for viewing on-line. To give readers a sneak preview of what they will encounter on screen, we have included some images from these DVDs. Although their quality is not as high as the originals, many of which are in color, they will provide a glimpse of the films' varied—and sometimes profound—content. Configuring these images and numerous other aspects of the book's digital production was made possible with the assistance from Lucas Knapp of Zum Computer Services. Assistance with the digitization of late-nineteenth century Arbuckles' images in my personal collection was provided by Craig Wheeler and Mark Bernt of Willamette University.

Ultimately, this book embodies my passionate interest in interdisciplinary scholarship. A strong supporter of this book project—Willamette University art historian and Women's Studies scholar Abigail Susik—reminded me that I seem at home in many disciplines. That is true, but geography is still my home base, and I thank fellow geographers such as Daniel Arreola, who has long shared insights about movies and their role in portraying Latin America. Also included is cultural geographer and long-time confidant Kit Salter, who in recent emails coined the term "placeography" for studies like mine that emphasize locales and their landscapes. Lastly, geographer W. George Lovell deserves thanks for his recent ground-breaking article titled "Latin America on Screen" (see Bibliography), which confirms that motion pictures are an indispensable element in the classroom. The book that you are about to read builds on Lovell's premise, but its purpose is even broader—to expand the definition of students to include the general reading public. After all, the same transformative cinematic experience awaits anyone of any age who is fascinated by geographies real or imagined. With that in mind, I would now like to begin our deeper journey into cinematic Latin America by sharing some insights on film itself and the varied ways it takes things from the page and moves them onto the screen as it portrays the geography of places in novel ways.

Introduction

*A Geographer's View of Latin America
and Observations about Filmmaking*

From about 1900 to the present, motion pictures played an increasingly important role in shaping peoples' understanding of places and their inhabitants. Building on and sometimes even superseding what was first written on the page as the historical record, or painted on canvas as scenery, the motion picture could seemingly bring things to life. Once content to read stories or view scenes as paintings or still photographs, the public could now discover the historic past or distant places as if they were personally there. The people that we called "armchair travelers" in an earlier era were now sitting in theaters and absorbing information about people and places in a new medium—a motion-picture projected onto the big screen. They would never look back, although today they are more likely to be gazing at small screens on personal devices.

Through the magic of filmmaking, sedentary people now vicariously experience places, whether deep in the mind of a character, in a familiar or foreign land, or even in outer space. The type of experience they have is largely up to the filmmaker, whose goal is to make viewers believe that what they are experiencing is really happening, or actually happened. Those experiences depend on settings; hence we say a film "takes place" somewhere. In this book, the setting is always Latin America, and many of the films discussed were actually filmed there. However, many others were filmed elsewhere—for example, in locales that looked similar enough to pass as authentic, or at fabricated venues such as Universal Studios in Hollywood or UK's Pinewood Studios, where set designers and builders literally created places masquerading as the real thing. If designed carefully, these sets could convince people into thinking that they are seeing real places—for example, a hacienda in Mexico—just as viewers can be convinced that they are watching the real past—perhaps the Mexican Revolution—come to life.

As geographers have known for decades, film is especially adept at depicting exotic places.[1] For many Americans and Europeans, films are as close as they ever get to the region covered in this book—Latin America—and consequently they know little about it. In 2019, this ignorance was satirized in the darkly comedic mystery film *Knives Out*, which features a wealthy Anglo-American family whose members are unaware which country their caretaker nurse Marta Cabrera is from. As the film progresses, one of them claims that she is from "Ecuador," another states "Paraguay," a third opines "Uruguay," and a fourth says "Brazil."[2] That family is evidently clueless about Latin America itself. They are not alone, for most in the audience would probably have trouble finding these South American countries on a map.

Within Latin America itself, our knowledge varies spatially. Although Americans often visit Mexico as tourists—no surprise given its proximity and attractive destinations—the number drops off rapidly in regard to the rest of Latin America. In 2019, which turned out to be the last "normal" pre-pandemic year, about 12.8 million American tourists visited Mexico. In that same year, a little over half of that number (7.9 million) visited the islands of the Caribbean, while only 2.8 million went to Central America, an important destination for eco-tourists. Meanwhile, only 1.87 million travelled to South America, as one might expect given the lengthy flights and increased ticket costs.[3] The distance-decay factor here is understandable but lamentable in that the distant parts of Latin America are fascinating and eye-opening. It is noteworthy that academic studies in the history of discoveries in Latin America show much the same pattern.[4] In this book, however, I hope to correct some of this imbalance by shedding considerable light on South America in addition to other, more familiar, parts of Latin America.

That said, a few other statistics are worth noting. Geographically speaking, the nineteen films covered in detail herein roughly represent the areal size of the region. Four are set in Mexico and Central America, which is now commonly called Mesoamerica, while the remaining fifteen are set in South America. If the latter seems an inordinately large percentage of films, it should be recalled that South America is about six times larger than the former—6.8 million square miles compared to about one million sq. mi (Mexico is 761,600 sq. and Central America 202, 230 sq. mi.). Despite my trying to rectify this oversight, even in this book South America gets shortchanged a bit.

Before going much further, something else needs to be addressed up front, namely the issue of film as a major source of conceptions—and misconceptions—about both history and geography, which are herein considered simultaneously as historical geography. As film-oriented geographers Tim Creswell and Deborah Dixon memorably characterized the distinction, it is the difference between the "real" and the "reel."[5] Concerning this tension between the actual and the film version, it is tempting to dwell on how accurately or inaccurately time and place are captured in any particular film. Regarding history, for example, we can compare the content of the films we watch to what the written record says transpired. Much the same can be said about geography: does the film accurately portray the location in terms of aspects such as topography, vegetation, and architecture, or has something substituted for them? In answering these questions, we might learn how and where the filmmaker represented or seemingly misrepresented the truth, and be tempted to judge the film on that basis. In that case, we might rate a film B+ on history and C- on geography and feel satisfied as arbiters of truth.

Although that type of evaluating may have some value, I shall take a different approach in this book. My main goal is to contextualize the nineteen films according to the type of story told and investigate each with the understanding that any film more typically deviates from the historical and geographical record. This deviation does not make a film wrong but rather a statement about the director's creative vision. Put another way, accuracy is far less of a concern to filmmakers than it is to many critics, including academicians. True, in some cases an eagle-eyed critic may spot an anachronism in a film—for example a soldier in ancient Rome wearing a wristwatch, or for that matter a much too modern map of Italy on a wall standing in for the Roman Empire. Both of these anachronisms are from *Spartacus* (1960), a film that is still highly regarded. Moreover, on occasion a filmmaker may deliberately introduce something out of place in time, as is the case in the controversial movie *Walker*, which is reviewed later in this book.

Because deviations from the accepted record often undergird a filmmaker's vision of what transpired, the film itself will be a testimonial to, or evidence of, that filmmaker's vision. Where possible, I will go behind the scenes to explore why this happened; at times I may even use the scriptwriter's or director's own words. I also use the original written narratives or artistic images that may have inspired a director—and show where and how they may have been modified to tell an even more compelling story. As will become apparent, sometimes these directorial inspirations even come from the work of other directors. As edgy filmmaker Quentin Tarantino brazenly claimed, "I steal from every single movie ever made."[6] With that in mind, I shall point out when some of the films covered in this book are derivative. Some films are even self-consciously so; for example two pay homage to the 1972 classic *Aguirre, the Wrath of God* by German director Werner Herzog.

It can be taken as a given that films deviate from the record—that comes with the territory—but even filmmakers attempting to accurately portray the history and geography of a place face many challenges. They have a story to tell, but must decide *how* to tell it. From the outset, they face a conundrum at the center of all storytelling, whether it occurs in the form of a spoken tale, written story, or a motion picture; namely, how to separate the teller from the tale. As noted during the annual UT Arlington Walter Prescott Webb lectures in 2005, which focused on the theme History and Film, "… although filmmakers often strive for accuracy, something usually compromises their ability to get their facts right (assuming, of course, that all the facts are known)." This usually happens "…because filmmakers often succumb to the temptation to tell *their own* stories."[7] Striving for truth may be a noble endeavor, but the creative impulses of filmmaking invariably involve subjectivity—and win out.

In reality, one can hardly blame a filmmaker for missing the truth hinted at above because information may be either elusive or contradictory. After all, historians themselves routinely challenge each other's sources and findings about the historical record. Moreover, geographers do the same as well regarding geographical facts. Although some sources may be more accurate than others, from the earliest days of geographic exploration, challenges arose, and conflicting reports were often produced. In the case of colonial Latin American sources, for example, information was originally created in the field or shortly thereafter, and then submitted to the Crown. This process involved filtering and sometimes outright censoring, and in any case there are often both unofficial (folk) accounts and official accounts of the same historical event.

Much the same can be said about visual illustrations—for example maps of places, or artwork depicting plants, animals, people, and geographical features—that may have accompanied reports. Some of these were wildly inaccurate despite claims they were true to life; truth is, explorers tend to view what they find through a lens colored by what they experienced earlier, for example a bison in the New World being drawn much like a cow from the Old World, albeit with a hump, as famously portrayed in Francisco de Gómara's *História General de las Indias* (1552).[8] In some cases these original illustrations became separated from reports and took on a life of their own. If these images were compelling enough, they were likely redrawn and enhanced, and sometimes corrected, through time as knowledge grew and publishing technology improved. In any event, as I shall demonstrate, filmmakers often find inspiration in these iconic images that further help bring a place, or narratives about it, to life.

With that issue of accuracy vs. inaccuracy addressed, I shall now move on to the focus of this book, which is how motion pictures treat the subject of exploration and discovery in Latin America—for example, early Spaniards exploring the Amazon basin in search of a lost city, or later archeologists discovering ancient ruins in Central America. To do so, I shall define two key terms that are involved in this process, always keeping in mind that they play out in time and space and in the human mind as well:

> *Exploration*—is the act of seeking out or searching for something, for example, a place.
> *Discovery*—is the act of coming to understand in more detail that which was encountered.

In the traditional sense, *exploration* involves traversing geographical space in search of something to discover, hence the "Age of Exploration" involved the expansion of empire(s) into new territory; however, more abstractly exploration also means seeking something to better understand it, as when one explores something (for example, a microorganism) to find answers to questions about it (say, its ways of reproducing). Similarly, *discovery* traditionally refers to better understanding something that has been encountered in geographical space; again, however, that something may not necessarily be geographical but can also refer to something more abstract, for example, discovering a cure for a disease.

Whereas exploration normally precedes discovery, those two processes can be interactive because discoveries often lead to subsequent explorations. In other words, both of them may be involved in the process of gaining knowledge, and therefore putting too fine a distinction on which-is-which may be more confusing than enlightening. With that caveat in mind, those who study these processes are increasingly using the hyphenated term exploration-discovery to indicate the close connection between both. I will do so as well. Viewed critically, this entire process is Eurocentric, but in this book I accept it as a given, as have filmmakers and others, including scientists.

Although the process of exploration is complex, and often involves many individuals, the person normally associated with it—the explorer—is usually emphasized. It is tempting, and far too easy, to generalize about the personality and/or mindset of any particular explorer. When examined carefully as a group, their character traits vary widely. Surprisingly, little has been written about this subject, an important exception being the in-progress multi-volume work titled *A Cultural History of Exploration*.[9] One of its contributors, historian of discovery Carla Rahn Phillips, suggests that varied psychological profiles or types, as revealed in personality and occupational testing, may be a profitable way to classify explorers; in that regard, a range of possibilities emerges, such as seekers, adventurers, missionizers, consolidators, traders, entrepreneurs, among others. As these types suggest, some explorers may be personally spearheading the exploration as the risk-takers we often imagine, while others may be part of a team or group and have considerable backing.

Historian Phillips further suggests that the emergence and dominance of the types mentioned above varies according to the time period in which they operated—for example, adventurers are more common in the early period (ca. 1500 to 1650) and consolidators more so in the period 1650 to 1800.[10] Of course, popular perceptions of explorers vary through time as well. Whereas early explorers were often regarded as heroic, especially when their exploits resulted in new territory being claimed and/or acquired, the tide often turns when they are examined more critically in later periods. Statues of them may be erected, only to fall when later generations scrutinize their accomplishments in a new light.

In this book, I will try to treat all explorers dispassionately. For the record, though, I shall state that geographic exploration-discovery often exacted a tremendous toll on those peoples and places that were "discovered" as a result of expeditions beginning about 1490. In the last three decades, scholars have increasingly focused laser-like light on that process, roundly condemning it. The purpose of this book, however, is to examine how several generations of filmmakers have depicted the exploration-discovery process over the last century. Whereas some filmmakers celebrated it and others condemned it, my objective is to avoid judgments and focus on how they used film as an art form to portray these geographical, and often cultural, encounters.

My seemingly hands-off approach is meant to supplement rather than substitute for the insightful critical work being done in film studies and other disciplines—studies clearly showing that filmmakers often objectify (which is to say treat like objects) the individuals and cultures they depict. Readers should understand that I am not a film studies scholar, but rather a scholar who studies film. As I showcase films that portray geographical exploration, I will write in a style that blurs the distinction between academic and popular writing. For the record, my ultimate goal is to show how filmmakers and their films portray exploration-discovery, regardless of any personal misgivings I or others may have about their subject matter.

That said, I should note that although films may objectify the world they are highly subjective, as evident in their very design. On screen, stories and their settings are almost invariably reshaped to not only reflect the filmmaker's creative impulses, but also to better elicit a response from the anticipated audience. Going from the real to the reel often results in five significant alterations, including the:

1. *compression of time*, so that actual events that took considerable time may be presented rapid-fire;

2. *simplification of complex events* into a more easily comprehended story, which often results in the omission of important facts;

3. *reduction in the number of people involved* into far fewer significant main characters, sometimes one or at best a few;

4. *tendency to moralize an event*, often by oversimplifying complex behavior into good and bad, so that the nuances may be lost;

5. *recasting of place or places*—including the topography and vegetation—may occur to make the geographic locale better fit the filmmaker's vision of the story's setting.

The above, while in some ways compromising reality, are more or less a given as a film develops from an idea or narrative, then into a scripted screenplay, then into the film itself being shot. There is a caveat about assuming films embody what was first written and then made it to the screen via the script. On occasion during the actual filming process, someone on the set—perhaps the actors themselves—may feel that different dialogue may be better than the script they are supposed to follow to the letter. Some directors resist such improvisation, for at this stage in the process it could inadvertently compromise the film by introducing something inconsistent with the plot. Others, however, are more open to it. As film viewers, we may be unaware that it even happened, unless someone who was on the set reveals it publicly. Finally, a film enters the editing stage, where a good editor may spot inconsistencies. Usually, editing is done to remove any superfluous or duplicative material but it is often a contested process. As suggested in the famous quote about fine film footage winding up on "the cutting room floor," editing can make or break an entire film. Sometimes it reveals a mistake that should have been corrected early on.

This brings to mind the short (27 minute) documentary film titled *Natural Encounters* that I scripted and directed for our university's "Cartographic Connections" website back in 2005.[11] That project had gone all the way through the editing process—we now had the final film in hand—when I realized there was an error in the narration. Faithfully following the script, the narrator's authoritative voice-over claims that Big Bend is "Texas's only National Park." However, I realized I had been thinking only about natural landscapes when I wrote that line, and had overlooked the San Antonio Missions National Park complex—which technically qualifies as well. The narrator was no longer available, so I asked the sound editor if he could change one word—from "only" to "own"—as that would correct the problem. That task seemed easy to me, as just a split second of the narrator's voice had to be deleted. For his part, though, the sound-man considered the film to be fine as is, and furthermore stated that no one would even notice. Nevertheless, as director I used executive privilege, and prevailed. It took some real doing, but he did a superb job, and now I could sleep better informing the world that Big Bend is "Texas's own National Park." No one was ever the wiser, until now.

That documentary film highlighted the role of nineteenth-century explorers in discovering patterns in the natural history of Texas, and I marveled at how harmoniously the visual film footage and narrative worked in explaining how explorer-discoverers went about their work. As omnipotent writer/director, I even cast *myself* in the role of a seasoned Mexican guide who helped the German explorer-geologist Ferdinand von Roemer (1818–1891) navigate the wilderness in the late 1840s. This part of the video called for some historical reenactment wherein the still-youthful Roemer and the grizzled guide find their way through a gap in the rocky landscape, emerging into a clearing at the base of a sandstone cliff. The scene was filmed on location in the colorfully-named "Penitentiary Hollow" portion of Lake Mineral Wells State Park and simulates the kind of rugged countryside traversed by Roemer as he made the first geological map of Texas.[12] There, with a leather bound note-book in one hand, the guide uses his other hand to point out the direction in which they should travel to find what Roemer is looking for. With this sweeping gesture, the audience can understand that the content of the expedition's notebook and the progress of the expedition were closely tied. In the process, the guide never says a word; in fact, no one does. As called for in the script, the narrator's voice-over describes the progress of Roemer's exploration in what had been part of Mexico about two decades earlier.

As intended, the scene featuring the guide accomplished several things. It underscored the importance of maps and field notes in exploration, in which they finally become a published map that accompanied Roemer's report. More importantly, though, it informed the audience that unnamed individuals, often locals who possessed considerable knowledge, helped make possible the discoveries of those whose names entered, and remained in, the historical record. At an artistic level, the scene summarized the film's trajectory of exploration (guided by a scout) leading to discovery (by the scientist). Looking back on this scene now, I see that it literally confirms the observation that films often go "from page to screen."

Making that film not only immersed me in filmmaking; it also helped me better understand the process of exploration-discovery itself. More to the point, it confirmed something that film historian Tom Conley discussed at a meeting of the Society for the History of Discoveries, namely, that the art and science of making motion pictures is similar to the endeavor involved in geographical exploration. In terms of making the unknown known, there are indeed some remarkable parallels between them. Admittedly, at first glance, it may seem that the action-oriented process of geographic exploration and the creative process of making films are completely different from each other. This too is based on the premise that we tend to think of exploration as "real" and film as "imitation."

However, as Conley astutely observes in his entry titled "Film and Exploration" in *The Oxford Companion to World Exploration*, "...exploration cannot be distinguished from simulation." For those accustomed to thinking of exploration and filmmaking as completely separate activities, Conley's claim may seem mind-boggling—until we realize that, as he puts it, "In both theme and form it can be said that exploration and adventure are indeed the essence of cinema at its very origins."[13] In other words, filmmaking is a *continuation* of the process of exploration, and has been since its inception.

How can this be? Deliberately using spatially expansive wording, Conley observes: "From the outset it was intuited that cinema embodied exploration because the spectator's eyes are led to wander about, decipher, and look all over the field of view projected on the screen." This explains why watching a film is so engrossing, for it involves two senses (sight and sound) working simultaneously, often overtime. It also explains why watching a film once may not be enough for many viewers, who often discover new things upon second, third, or even more viewings. With eyesight in mind, Conley concludes his analysis using another travel-related metaphor: "The viewer follows the itinerary of the lens that can record a multitude of things that often become perceptible only upon multiple and patient viewings."[14]

To Conley, this not only means that filmmakers are explorers, but that they also make discoveries as their films take shape. In a sense, viewers of a film are also discoverers, for they learn new things from the films they watch. That connection may explain why the public finds films about exploration-discovery to be so natural, and also why historians of exploration-discovery themselves have such an affinity for films that depict exploration. They may like or dislike those films, but feel compelled to watch them and discover how they portray the process of exploration, which always involves people encountering places, and often encountering other people (natives) as well.

Something else is worth mentioning here. Both endeavors—geographic exploration-discovery and filmmaking—are ultimately dependent on storytelling. As Stewart A. Weaver notes in the book *Exploration: A Short Introduction*: "to qualify as an explorer, one must not only find something new but write about it, publicize it, draw the attention of others to it."[15] In the case of filmmaking, that writing can literally be a screenplay, or even a later press release, but films about exploration often call on actual narratives of expeditions written by chroniclers themselves. Thus it is that film, which may seem separate from the written word and related images, almost invariably springs from that "paper" source, another subtle reference to the phrase "from page to screen."

Of course, a story may start out in one way, but wind up quite different as the filmmaker shapes it into their own creation. A film that closely follows the written record may be regarded as a documentary, and one that a filmmaker infuses with considerable imagination might be considered a drama. However, although distinctions between dramatic feature films and documentary films have been made since the early twentieth century, in reality the line separating them is often blurred. In this book, I will mainly focus on dramatized depictions of the past, as opposed to documentaries such as those intended for purely educational use. Nevertheless, I will mention films of both types where appropriate, especially those that blur the distinction between fact and fiction. In reality, every dramatic film contains some factual material, and every documentary contains something imagined by the filmmaker.

A film may be conceived in the mind, but customarily finds its way onto a page, or pages, that serve as a blueprint. As famed director Stanley Kubrick succinctly characterized this close connection, "If it can be written or thought, it can be filmed."[16] However, the distinction here is becoming blurred because we are now so accustomed to viewing film as such a powerful medium that it even affects the writing of fiction. As noted in an insightful on-line essay titled "Place Sets the Mental Agenda," popular culture guru Margaret King observed that "Novelist John Fowles described the written novel itself as a 'filmic form,' based on cutting, dialogue, and a series of settings envisioned as a film set."[17]

Above all, it is worth keeping in mind that film is a seductive medium, and its visual or graphic components are capable of stirring intense emotions. This power was first evident during the formative "silent" years of filmmaking, when the words spoken by actors had to be written on the screen because sound had not yet been integrated. Still, the moving picture alone could be so dramatic that even illiterate audiences could comprehend what was transpiring. Of later films with sound, director Alfred Hitchcock famously noted that "If it's a good movie, the sound could go off and the audience would still have a perfectly clear idea of what was going on."[18]

That may be true, but much would be lost because spoken dialogue and sound effects help make some films truly great. Would the confrontational scene between American prospectors and Mexican bandits posing as "federales" in the film *Treasure of the Sierra Madre* be as memorable without the grinning bandido's heavily accented and defiant "…Badges? I don't have to show you any stinking badges!"—or, shortly thereafter, would the bandits' off-camera beheading of Humphrey Bogart's character be quite as chilling without the grisly hacking sound of the machete accomplishing that horrifying act?

In film, music also plays a major role. Although at first largely a gap-filler in early silent films when a musician in the theater played a piano or an organ as the film was being projected, music transformed the film-going experience when deliberately composed musical scores could work hand in hand since the advent of sound ca. 1927. Of course, since the introduction of color film about a decade later, movies could capture landscapes and peoples as simultaneously either more real, or more fantastic, than those ordinarily encountered. As will become apparent, films about exploration are especially dependent on such technical effects because they can—like exploration itself—transport the viewer from the ordinary into the extraordinary.

Although films cover an incredibly broad spectrum of subject areas, how they depict connections between time and place can yield some insights about the filmmaker's visions of both. Of special interest in this book is the manner in which characters in films explore, discover and supposedly conquer geographic locales. Often, a filmmaker might depict this as an historic event, as when an explorer encounters seemingly "new" lands, such as the Americas in the late 1400s. Of course, these lands were known to Indigenous inhabitants well before the newcomers arrived, and that adds an exciting dimension to the experience; seen in that light, it becomes reciprocal, although how much so depends on the sensitivities of the filmmaker. These reciprocal discoveries are doubly interesting because they affect not only those discovered but also the discoverer as well. As French filmmaker/anthropologist Jean Rouch observed, "All the fiction films I have made were always on the same subject,—a discovery of the 'Other,' an exploration of difference."[19] In the Americas, the Other usually refers to Indigenous people, but as this book will make clear, Others of other races are involved as well.

In organizing the remarkably varied films covered in this book, history came to the rescue. This book places films about Latin American exploration-discovery into numerous topically themed and time-based categories. These begin around the time of early encounters between European explorers and Indigenous peoples; then address the trials and tribulations of colonial expansion, including the introduction of Christianity to the New World; and next cover the rise of the physical/life sciences (e.g., geology and botany) and the social sciences (ethnography and archaeology). In more recent times, the search for natural resources to exploit on a grand scale, and explorations in search of matters such as social justice, become major themes. That last period, our own time, is surprisingly rich in explorations and discoveries of a new kind—those involving a nebulous territory that lies beyond geography but is ultimately dependent on it, namely, the topography of the human imagination. As readers will see toward the end of this book, history increasingly yields to current issues, and the focus of what is explored may change. However, exploration-discovery continues unabated.

The nineteen films discussed in detail thus cover a breathtaking expanse of *space*—a good portion of the sprawling region called Latin America—and also of *time*— more than five hundred years. Although the subject of Latin American history in film is covered in Stewart Brewer's informative book *Latin American History Goes to the Movies*,[20] the objective in this book is to link history even more closely with geography. Why? Although history and geography are usually treated—and taught—separately, there are benefits to engaging them *simultaneously*. In my experience, people tend to learn history better when they can situate it geographically. Similarly, they learn geography more readily when places are linked to the past events that occurred there. This is not a new idea. As British explorer John Smith observed about four hundred years ago, "Geography without history is a carcass without motion, so history without geography wandereth as a vagrant without a certain habitation."[21]

How the geographical and/or cultural environment is depicted may also involve considerable liberties by filmmakers. Because they may even fictionalize elements of it in stories for greater impact, some readers may be put off by this. However, it should be recalled that all storytelling involves some exaggeration, some of it bordering on the supernatural. Rich examples of this in the form of magical realism characterize some Latin American fiction. As readers will see, some of this magic finds its way into exploration-discovery films as well. While on that topic, it should be re-stated that some of the films covered in this book are pure fiction, and many others are fictionalized accounts of actual events and places. Environments of all kinds may be depicted in stories involving many genres, including science-fiction, fantasy, and horror. As long as a film is set in Latin America and features exploration-discovery as a theme, no matter how fancifully, it is fair game in this book.

In the following brief chapters that comprise the body of this book, I will contextualize, summarize, and essentially review nineteen individual films about Latin American exploration-discovery in light of their themed time periods. In a few cases I will introduce other films to further contextualize those core films that get top billing. Although a few films made in Latin America for Latin American audiences will be covered in this book, most of them were actually made by, and for, outsiders living elsewhere. In particular, films made by North Americans and Europeans are studied here because those films have a broader international market, and hence have a greater cultural impact worldwide.

With geography in mind, I will now discuss the stage upon which these films take place—the sprawling region called Latin America. There is a caveat here, too: What we today call Latin America was originally known only by its parts—for example, the various European territories and Vice Royalties such as New Spain and Peru, and later as about two-dozen independent countries such as Mexico, Peru, Honduras, Chile, Bolivia, etc. At the same time, cartographers also used broader designations such as South America, Central America, and the Caribbean as they prepared and marketed their maps. As maps confirm, the name "Latin America" is a relative newcomer. It only dates from after political independence from Spain and was reportedly first used by the French traveler Michel Chevalier in the 1830s to strengthen alliances with what was called Latin Europe (i.e., where Spanish, Portuguese, French are spoken).[22]

Latin America as a region got more traction in 1856, when the term was officially used based on those romance language roots in order to emphasize that the region was not northern European in origin—partly in reaction to the expansionist filibustering expeditions from the United States. That naming was intended to generate political action, as based on the "Initiative of America: Idea for a Federal Congress of the Republics." Ironically, or perhaps cynically, the term was also embraced by France in the 1860s when Emperor Maximilian attempted to conquer Mexico—the premise being that France naturally belonged there based on the romance language connection. In reality, Latin America does contain some countries affiliated with northern European powers (for example, British Honduras and British Guiana, and Dutch Guyana).

For deeply rooted historical reasons, and also because it is such a large region, detailed maps showing all of Latin America on one sheet of paper are rare and often done for official purposes. For example, the U.S. Central Intelligence Agency (CIA) prepared one in the 1950s based a growing concern about communist infiltration into the area, but there appears to be little interest in such a map today. Only recently has "mapping Latin America" itself been conceptually studied in any detail, as evident in a ground-breaking anthology of the same name.[23] To provide sufficient detail, Mexico and Central America (often called Middle America) are often covered in one map; the Caribbean portion of Latin America is often included in Middle America as well. For its part, South America is usually covered on a separate map, although maps of its individual countries have been made since these areas' wars of independence from Spain. It is noteworthy that the vast nation of Brazil—the largest in geographic area and population in all of Latin America—never made the same type of spectacular violent break from Portugal, and the two countries have worked harmoniously to the present.

Because most readers may not be familiar with the geography of Latin America, I have included two maps of the region. The first is a current map of the political geography showing the locations of countries, many of which will be mentioned as locales where particular films take place. Most of these nations have been in existence since they gained independence from Spain by about 1825, the major exceptions being Cuba, which became a country in 1902 after the Spanish-American War, and Panama, which the USA appropriated from Colombia in 1903 to make way for the construction of the Panama Canal. Despite the *relative* stability of the region for almost two centuries, the boundaries of some of these countries have changed following border disputes with their neighbors, as depicted in a couple of the films discussed in this book. However, internal politics are quite another matter in Latin America: Within varied countries, revolutions have long impacted many facets of life, including filmmaking. The second map covers the region's physical geography, including the major mountain ranges, lowlands, and rivers. These physical features have long defined the character or sense place, and they often play major roles in films set in the region.

Map of the political geography of Latin America shows the location of countries described in the text. (courtesy University of Alabama).

These two maps reveal that Latin America stretches a great distance in a north-south direction. It extends over 6,000 miles (10,000 kilometers) and crosses the equator; therefore, when it is winter in Mexico, it is summer in Argentina, and vice versa. The climate and natural vegetation varies greatly throughout Latin America, and I will address some of that variation when interpreting the individual films. Regarding the lay of the land, the map showing the physical geography reveals that a mountainous backbone or spine runs roughly north-south through the entire region from the top to bottom, so to speak—from the present U.S.-Mexico border to the southern tip of South America. Although it is tempting to regard this long mountain range as one single chain, it splits into two or more separate ranges in many places. In some locales, the elevated land between them cradled civilizations that would later be depicted in motion pictures. Similarly, lowlands are important throughout Latin America, and include much of the Mexican state of Yucatan, the Llanos (plains) of Venezuela, and the vast Pampas of Argentina, Uruguay and southern Brazil. These, and the huge Amazonian lowlands, are the natural stages on which many films are set.

In addition to its remarkable physical geography,[24] Latin America's rich cultural geography begins with its Indigenous peoples and continues to grow and diversify as people from other parts of the world later migrated here. To these diverse Indigenous peoples, the equally diverse landscape was sacred and rich in symbolic meaning.[25] Far from being an empty wilderness as often described by later explorers, the early European arrivals found a land densely populated in many areas. Collectively, they lived lifestyles ranging from nomadic to densely settled and permanent. Agriculture was practiced throughout much of Latin America, with the exception of portions of northern Mexico and southern South America (viz. the south of Chile and Argentina).[26] That agriculture was based on many plants indigenous to the Americas, including maize, squash, beans, potatoes, and quinoa. Some crops were irrigated and others grown in *milpas*—patches where forests had been cut and burned. Fishing sustained many cultures living in coastal areas and along rivers.

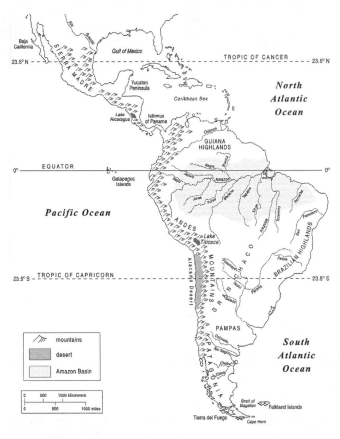

Map of the physical geography of Latin America identifies many of the geographic features discussed in the text. (courtesy University of Alabama).

Specializing in Latin America, geographer William (Bill) Denevan consulted studies by other geographers and anthropologists in order to estimate the Pre-Columbian population. His conclusion—about fifty million—came as a surprise to many who assumed Indians were present but scarce before the arrival of Europeans. Of these, about 17.2 million people lived in Mexico; 5.6 million in Central America; 3 million in the Caribbean; 15.7 million in the Andes region; and 8.6 million in lowland South America. The total figure could have been higher, perhaps up to 60 million. These numbers confirmed that Latin America was not only heavily populated, but that the indigenous people there had transformed large areas through their farming and other activities, including city-building in some locales such as the Valley of Mexico (Aztec), the lowlands of Yucatan (Maya), and the Andean highlands (Inca). More recently, ancient city-building cultures in the Amazon (e.g., Cotoca, Bolivia) have been added to the list.

Denevan's article coincided with the 500th anniversary of Columbus's arrival in the New World, as did several films about the event. Countering the popular belief that early Europeans who arrived in the western hemisphere found a primeval and undisturbed landscape, especially in forested areas, Denevan notes that this myth "was invented in the late eighteenth and early nineteenth centuries." There may be a good reason for their beliefs at that time, however, for as he further noted, the population of the Americas had been devastated by diseases introduced from the Old World: "By 1650, Indigenous populations in the hemisphere had been reduced by about 90 percent, while by 1750 European numbers were not yet substantial and settlement had only begun to expand."[27] With vegetation long flourishing after the near-collapse of the Indigenous population, small wonder vast areas were considered to be primeval wilderness never touched by mankind. For their part, early Europeans arriving in what is today Latin America left written reports about the large numbers of Native Americans, some of these explorers claiming that large cities once existed where none are evident today. These documents, along with reports by later explorers, ultimately found their way into published books and motion pictures, including documentaries and dramas.

Maps often appear in films about geographic exploration-discovery; they also subliminally influence filmmakers and audiences as well. A surprising number of films contain maps, sometimes subtly enough that the audience scarcely notices them, much less comprehends their symbolic value. My analysis of maps in these films will build on postmodern interpretations pioneered by cartographic historian J.B. Harley, whose work gained considerable attention about thirty years ago (1991). A productive period of cartographic analysis followed, though more recently (2019), cartographic historian Matthew Edney noted that the word "cartography" is so tied to colonial endeavors that it might best be abolished.[28] However, I think it is essential here because filmmakers were involved in depicting exploration-discovery using much the same cartographic conventions.

Using an analogy made by J.B. Harley, I would like to confirm that a map in a film can "...act as a visual metaphor for values enshrined in the places they represent."[29] For those places depicted on screen, maps can become part of the plot much like a character in a story. As in exploration, mapping is a natural part of cinema and difficult to separate from it. Again calling upon Tom Conley, this time in his book *Cartographic Cinema*, "a film can be understood in a broad sense to be a 'map' that plots and colonizes the imagination of the public it is said to 'invent' and, as a result, to seek and control." More explicitly, Conley continues: "A film, like a topographic projection, can be understood as an image that locates and patterns the imagination of its spectators."[30] If, as Argentine economist Ricardo Salvatore noted, "Map-making is a form of ordering the multiplicity of observable phenomena in a given space"[31]—then we might say that the given space can also be the motion picture screen.

Comparing images on screen with much earlier illustrations seen in antiquarian books and other sources, it becomes apparent that films about exploration-discovery have a pre-history, so to speak. In other words, they were influenced by works that predate filmmaking itself but greatly contributed to it. I shall next discuss a few graphic and cartographic images that likely influenced cinema around 1900, though were made years before. A map of South America from the popular "Wallis's New Game of Wanderers in the Wilderness" (London, ca. 1844) was part of this process by which the public came to anticipate the world that film would open to them. Published for Edward Wallis's series of adventure games covering the world, it subliminally endorsed Britain's expansion as an empire on which the sun never set, which included designs on Latin America. The gamer arrives in British Guyana in northeastern South America, and then explores the rest of the continent with native guides. In this game, they experience a virtually unexplored wilderness teeming with exotic wildlife in what is imagined to be largely *terra incognita*.

This game is worth a closer look. On its map, the physical or topographic regions are stylized and beautifully depicted as three broad categories or zones: in the northeast, a huge, river-laced zone is generally low-lying but punctuated in a few places by hills or mountains. It occupies about a third of the continent. This zone's deep green color symbolizes the dense foliage of the Amazon, and in one place a large serpent coils menacingly. The second, lighter-colored zone lies southward and appears drier. In one area, the buff color suggests a savannah or grassland over which large, ostrich-like birds such as the rhea roam. Toward the south of this zone, a man rides horseback across the plains chasing cattle, armed with a bola (boleadora) that he can throw to ensnare the legs of the fleeing animal. Popularly known as a gaucho, he is depicted on the Argentine Pampa. The last zone on the map is a stark, north-south running chain of mountains—the Andes—comprising the western rim of the continent.

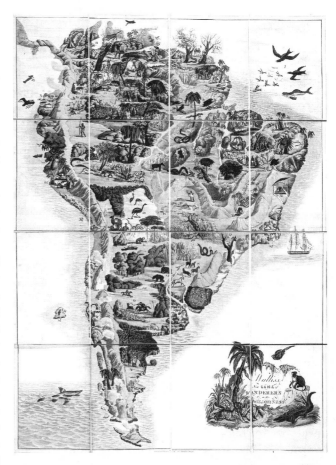

It is noteworthy that iconic figures like that gaucho riding across the Pampa and that serpent coiling in the jungle will emerge again and again throughout the nineteenth century, most famously perhaps in the popular Arbuckles' Ariosa Coffee Victorian Trading cards (ca. 1886). As they appeared in *Arbuckles' Illustrated Atlas of Fifty Principal Nations of the World* (1889) and also as individual cards, these images contained a wealth of visual information in the form of stereotypical scenes. On the cards for the

Map of South America from "Wallis's New Game of Wanderers in the Wilderness," London, ca. 1844 and subsequent editions. Although this game pre-dates filmmaking, it encourages players to imagine themselves on adventures to distant continents, and helped pave the way for adventure films like those described in this book (author's digital map collection)

nation of Uruguay and the Argentine Republic, the gaucho appears in much the form he took in Wallis's game, though in the latter he appears to be an Indian on horseback.

Especially evocative is the card for the United States of Colombia, so called from 1863 to 1886 when it was formally divided into those political sub-units; today it is known as the Republic of Colombia. On the left side of the card, agricultural activity thrives as workers harvest a crop, likely ipecauanha (*Caraichea ipecuanha*), which served as a source of powdered drugs used to cure ailments, including dysentery. On the right side, though, wild nature is illustrated in the form of a boa constrictor, its forked tongue jutting out of its wide-open mouth as the snake uncoils from a tree branch. The monkeys on the right side of the card appear to be agitated, possibly reacting to the snake and offering protection to their young. As will become apparent in my analysis of films on exploration-discovery, serpents like this one epitomized the dangers of Latin America's tropical regions. It is worth restating that Arbuckles' images became wildly popular at exactly the time that motion pictures were about to take the world by storm.

Arbuckles also produced booklets perpetuating the romance of exploration-discovery. A popular one—*Arbuckles' Album of Illustrated Natural History*—featured an entrancing image of a jaguar at river's edge with a rocky prominence looming above it. This image emphasizes both the beauty and the stealth of this large spotted cat whose range coincides almost perfectly with the geographical boundaries of Latin America—from extreme southern Arizona and south Texas all the way down to Argentina and Uruguay. In the accompanying text, Arbuckles almost academically claims that "this member of the cat tribe enjoys the distinction of being the largest and most formidable feline quadruped to be found either in North or South America." In other words, they

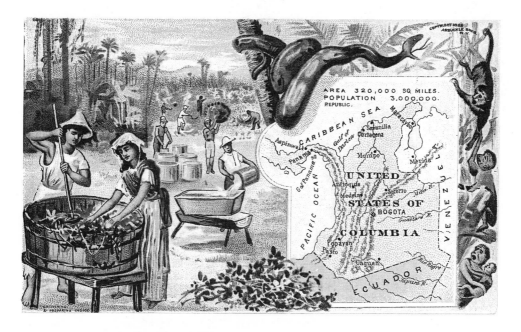

Arbuckles' Ariosa Coffee trading card for *The United States of Columbia*, New York, Donaldson Bros., Lithographers, 1889. The influence of such rich imagery about places on later filmmakers should not be underestimated as it confirms that considerable geographical information can be depicted in one frame (author's collection).

were man-eaters. I include it here because the position of the jaguar, and the rocks and vegetation depicted, appear to have influenced at least two of the Latin American films interpreted later in this book.

My premise that potent still images predating cinema helped stimulate that fledgling industry is evident in the works of the eccentric British-American photographer Eadweard Muybridge (1830–1904). As noted by photographer Byron Wolfe and geographer Scott Brady, Muybridge's famous still photos of a galloping horse in the late 1870s were seminal: "When shown in rapid succession his pictures form one of the simplest and earliest forms of animated cinema." More to the point here, Muybridge's manipulation of still photographs—including a series of spectacular landscape images of Central America—set a standard for later cinematographers hoping to bring places to life and awe the public in the process.[32]

As regards film itself, we can "read" a movie much like any other text, including a board game, trading card, photograph, or map. More specifically, using the "author-text-reader" model outlined by Christopher Lukinbeal and Laura Sharp, the filmmaker is the author, the film is the text, and the viewer is the reader.[33] In the typical film, viewers hear thousands of words and see even more images, but some stay with us while others are essentially forgotten. Regarding the former, many films contain one spoken (or thought) phrase that summarizes the entire plot. This type of line differs from a logline (i.e., a summary of the plot by an editor or others wishing to describe a film). Instead, it is embedded in the film itself as part of the

JAGUAR
(Felis onca)

This iconic image of a jaguar in its Latin American habitat is from *Arbuckles' Album of Illustrated Natural History*, featuring lithography by The Knapp Co., 1890. Images like this increased the public's interest in aspects of fauna and flora, and likely influenced filmmakers as they featured similar scenes in popular movies set in Latin America such as *Green Fire* (1954) and *Green Mansions* (1959) (author's collection).

dialogue or narrative. We might call these lines "synopsizers," for as they are spoken, they summarize what is transpiring. Although they may go right over the heads of some viewers, for others they provide a Eureka moment because they succinctly pull together many things that are happening on screen. The best synopsizers may even foreshadow what will happen later in the film—an example being found in *The Ox-Bow Incident* (1943) when Henry Fonda challenges the leader of a lynch mob who tells him to mind his own business. Fonda's reply—"Hanging's every man's business that's around"—resonates on many levels, including the personal and societal, underscoring the responsibilities of decent, law-abiding individuals in the face of mob rule.

Some of these synopsizers have become famous in their own right, as in the *Wizard of Oz* when Dorothy tells her bewildered pet dog: "Toto, I have a feeling we're not in Kansas anymore." Such lines may be surprisingly short, as in "I'll be back" (*The Terminator*) or more involved as in *Thelma and Louise* when an older/wiser Louise advises Thelma: "You shoot off a guy's head with his pants down, believe me, Texas ain't the place you want to get caught." With a line like that, the viewer comprehends that they will be on the run and determined to escape the long arm of the law that is generally unsympathetic to women who use lethal force to stop a rapist. In their attempt to find sanctuary in Mexico, these two fugitives will attain cinematic immortality by cutting a swath across the American Southwest.

Similarly, some visual scenes in a movie are so poignant or overwhelming that they become iconic. The silhouette of T.E. Lawrence on a camel in *Lawrence of Arabia*[34] is an example. The image itself is enough to bring to mind both Arabia's vast sand-covered landscape and the movie in which it appears. Another scene, this one from *Doctor Zhivago*,[35] is the family summer house in rural Russia transformed into a glistening ice-castle in winter, a perfect icon for a film that showcases Russia's climate extremes and sprawling landscapes. Those two examples might seem like "still" images, but they come to life when Lawrence urges his camel into action, and when the displaced Russian family arrives at the house. As I shall show, numerous films about exploration-discovery in Latin America have also been branded with such iconic images as well.

In filmmaking, an integration of images and words is essential. However, literature itself frequently inspires filmmakers as it can describe in words scenes that a filmmaker can later transform into an image on screen. In this regard, few discussions of twentieth-century Latin American literature fail to mention one of Latin America's most famous writers, Gabriel García Márquez (1927–2014), the Colombian journalist-turned-best-selling fiction writer, whose works "...redrew both the cultural map of Latin America and the contours of modern fiction...."[36] "Gabo," as he was affectionately called, considered himself a South American writer, perhaps because he recognized Colombia's unique geographic position in relation to the broader continent. As the Arbuckles' card showed, Colombia is the continent's northern gateway and the only south American country having two coasts, one facing the Atlantic (Caribbean) and the other the Pacific. Gabriel García Márquez described his nation's haunting landscapes in many of his novels, including his most celebrated—*One Hundred Years of Solitude*[37]—which was originally published in Spanish in 1967, English in 1970, and would soon affect filmmaking.

Several things about this novel are relevant here. First, it is his most epic literary work, autobiographical in part and based on his own family's life near Colombia's Caribbean coast.[38] It abounds in interesting characters, plots, and sub-plots—but has no visual images. Nevertheless, García Márquez uses words to create a highly visual sense of place. He masterfully captures the remarkable cultural diversity of coastal Colombia, with Native Americans, Spaniards, Black people, and mixtures thereof, as well as Jews, Gypsies, Middle Easterners—all vividly described and woven into the long and complicated story. Moreover, this novel is also an allegorical telling of the broader history of South American exploration, discovery, colonization, independence, and the more recent exploitation of resources by outside corporations.

The big question about *One Hundred Years of Solitude* involves one of the ironies of Latin American filmmaking. Despite being approached by many producers and directors, García Márquez himself emphatically insisted that it *never* be made into a movie—and this stipulation has been honored to the present. So incomprehensible is this to his many fans that an impressive and compelling faux movie trailer has actually been made about this epic, but non-existent, film![39] This trailer makes the viewer long to watch the film that never was. Of course, this author knew that as a blockbuster, the story's languid sense of timing would have to be changed, and likely compromised. Nevertheless, as I shall show, some scenes from that novel were so memorable that they influenced subsequent films about South American exploration-discovery.

For the record, though, it should be noted that some of Gabriel García Márquez's books have actually become movies. Among the finest of his books-set-to-film is *Love in the Time of Cholera*,[40] which is also a story about chronological time as well as geographical space. In the genre of a romance, its protagonist, Florentino Ariza, waits more than fifty years to consummate his relationship with Fermina Daza, whom he has loved since their teenage years. In geographic space and over the years, Florentino expands his horizons as the owner of a Colombian steamship line, but time binds him to Fermina and his first romantic encounter. This is no simple story of unrequited love, but rather a complex and highly allegorical tale of exploration-discovery. The movie superbly captures this story, but some well-respected critics savaged it when it was released in 2007. True, the book is better—a literary masterpiece—but the film is beautifully done. It should also be noted that the author himself is said to have given the screen version of *Love in the Time of Cholera* an enthusiastic "thumbs up" after watching it.[41] There is a moral here: although critics are entitled to their opinions, some are not quite up to critiquing the films they review. With his simple but eloquent evaluation, García Márquez put those haughty critics in their place.

My reviews of films in this book are unusual in that they generally guide the reader through the entire plot, with asides about the types of depictions of events, and in particular the cultural and physical geographic settings depicted. Moreover, my reviews will squarely address, and challenge, a premise that some reviewers use to judge a film, namely, whether it succeeds by faithfully adhering to the original written source or script. A reviewer's premise that a film should closely follow the original story may seem logical, but like all quests for accuracy, can be taken too far as well. For his part, García Márquez knew that the film *Love in the Time of Cholera* was not a literal translation of his novel, but he respected the filmmaker's vision. As film critic Daniel Fienberg recently observed, "…what works on the page can sometimes play as fundamentally silly and hollow on-screen…."[42]

Similarly, the "look" of the film in capturing places is dependent on the ways it depicts the geographical setting. In this case, the images employed in such films— regardless of whether they are maps or landscapes—can also be judged on how effectively they capture the originals. Again, however, there are limits to this kind of scrutiny, for it may be too short-sighted if it fails to take into account the filmmaker's intent to accentuate aspects of place or to exaggerate something that happened in the past. As will soon become apparent, artistic license is not only allowable but also desirable if it can enhance the desired effect. In judging films, one can look too closely, which is to say myopically, and miss the bigger picture.

ONE

Apocalypto

Exploration Before
European Contact

Exploration is normally assumed to be a process that accompanies European colonization, but that assumption fails to take into account exploration by Indigenous
peoples themselves long before Columbus arrived. As the Americas became populated by humans about 20,000 years ago—some claim much earlier—those entering it
likely forged ahead in hopes of exploring in order to discover new opportunities. Leading this advance into new territory must have been exhilarating and terrifying, but we
can only speculate based on the limited archaeological evidence left behind. It is possible that some pictographic designs constituted maps of sorts, but they were likely done
long after the fact. The lack of clear connections between these original arrivals and the
Native Americans present at the time of European contact in what is today Latin America—1492—clouds the issue of origins. Further complicating this are the creation stories
of many Native American peoples themselves, which often claim that they originated *in
situ*, rising from under the earth at those locations.

Nevertheless, many of the tribes presently occupying regions do recount more
recent journeys taken by their ancestors, a case in point being the numerous tribes in
today's Arizona, which was once at the northern fringes of New Spain. Although the
San Pedro River valley is normally considered to lie south of Apache country in terms of
current Native identity, something remarkable happened when elders and others from
varied tribes such as the White Mountain Apache and San Carlos Apache visited there
with anthropologists. Although the Apache are not homogeneous, those tribal members
recognized the landscape of the San Pedro valley and environs as part of their ancient
story-telling about the far-flung travels of their tribes. The anthropologists who conducted the study consider these to be "landscapes of a living past."[1]

Appropriately, the first film I would like to examine in detail features Indigenous
people front and center. Its place and time is Central America before the arrival of Spaniards. For the record, this area had been popularized in the United States and Europe
since as early as 1841, when John Lloyd Stephens' best seller *Incidents of Travel in Central
America, Chiapas, and Yucatan* revealed its archaeological treasures.[2] Stephens' energetic writing style, and the book's detailed illustrations, literally put this region on the
map.[3] Since then, it has been associated with archaeology and adventure.

When released in 2006, the film *Apocalypto*[4] created a sensation. Although it is
about the Indigenous past, it was not conceived by Native Americans at all, but rather
the American-born/Australian-raised actor Mel Gibson, and Iranian-American script

writer Farhad Safinia. Gibson had been associated with high-energy action films since his breakaway role in *Mad Max* (1979) and his blockbuster *Braveheart* (1995). The pair had recently collaborated on Gibson's controversial religious film *The Passion of the Christ* (2004), and both agreed that something new in action films was needed to keep that genre from becoming stale. For its part, the film *Apocalypto* that they co-wrote would indeed mark a departure from past films, although as I shall show, it does have a derivative quality in some scenes.

The script of *Apocalypto* showed considerable imagination in relating an epic journey, and the plot's intensity made it a hit with movie-goers, including those in Mexico. In limited showings, it fared well among Native Americans in Chickasaw, Oklahoma, who praised its Indigenous casting.[5] There is an underlying tension in this film that soon came to the surface: Although most audiences realized that *Apocalypto* is fiction, its attention to detail and elaborate sets strived for realism. Therein lies a clue to how it would be received. In a review written immediately upon the release of *Apocalypto* (December 6, 2006), Robert W. Welkos wrote what must have been the understatement of the year: "It is a fiction film—not a documentary—which may let down those looking for accuracy at every turn."[6] Within days, the criticism turned into a full-scale war of words, with claims about accuracy and inaccuracy coming from all directions, though mostly from scholars. In reviewing this film, I will discuss some of those let downs, as Welkos called them, which amounted to take downs by academicians displeased with Gibson's depiction of the Maya.

Cinematically speaking, several aspects of *Apocalypto* made it stand out. To begin with, the enigmatic title itself suggested doom and hinted at its being based on creation-destruction myths of the Maya. A rough translation of the Greek verb, however, is more hopeful, as Gibson had intended: it means "I uncover, or disclose or reveal." Second, the spoken language in *Apocalypto* was an approximation of ancient Yucatecan Mayan throughout. Gibson was no stranger to this technique as his *The Passion of the Christ* was filmed in ancient Aramaic, with subtitles for various audiences worldwide. This linguistic aspect further helps give *Apocalypto* an exotic and mysterious appeal, but more importantly, plumbed Gibson's belief that "hearing a different language allows the audience to completely suspend their own reality and get drawn into the world of the film." More to the point, as Gibson added, it also "puts the emphasis on the cinematic visuals, which are a kind of universal language of the heart."[7]

Third, the fact that the entire cast is of Indigenous origin or Latin American heritage gives *Apocalypto* an additional quality of visual authenticity. Moreover, many of their faces had never been seen before on film, a factor that added novelty to its seeming veracity. As a student of mine put it, the film seemed "surprisingly fresh." Lastly, the intense action and explicit violence in this film not only provided Gibson the opportunity to try some new techniques, but also shattered the popular myth of a peaceful idyllic America before the arrival of Europeans. Like *Mad Max*, which my fellow film buff Gary Falk claimed was "a monument to entropy," *Apocalypto* is essentially in overdrive from beginning to end. In keeping with the theme of this book, it represents a continuous journey into the unknown for its main characters, who are both amazed and terrified by what they discover as the film progresses.

Appropriately enough, the doom hinted at in the title is reflected in the opening words on the screen, a quote from philosopher W. Durant: "*A great civilization is not conquered from without until it has destroyed itself from within.*" This is a sobering note, in part because the envisioned audience resides in what they might consider a great civilization with film technology that can bring exotic places into movie theaters and living rooms. Unlike the people they are about to experience on screen, everyone viewing the film lives in relative safety and everything seems to be under control.

Apocalypto begins with a hunt in progress as a small group of men chase a wild animal through the jungle. The creature is difficult to recognize at first because only parts of it—flaring nostrils, shaggy fur, and shiny fangs—are shown. As the action continues the audience realizes it is a large hog-like animal that is highly agitated and fleeing the hunters—or is it the other way around? The shrieks of the animal, and the grunts and screams of the hunters, confirm this is life and death combat. At times the animal seems to be chasing the hunters, and lashes out at one, seriously injuring him. The hunters are armed with primitive weapons such as spears and bows and arrows, and these scenes reveal the danger involved in hunting wild animals without firearms.

Suddenly, however, the hunt ends as the huge tapir triggers a deadly spring-trap. The animal is killed instantly, impaled on sharp spikes protruding from this ingeniously wicked device. It is a very clever and deadly device, but might impress some in the audience as being a bit too clever and perhaps a bit too modern. In analyzing this film, historian Stewart Brewer calls it "a Rambo-style booby-trap"[8]—a hint that Gibson, like most filmmakers, is not above borrowing something from another movie when it works. In this film it works perfectly, bringing the action to a stop and now focusing it on the hunters themselves. Triumphantly, one of them cuts out the animal's heart, and shares it with the other victorious hunters. The scene is further recorded from a spidercam high above them, and the circle they form turns it into a stunning ritual. In directing the film, Gibson was banking on this pivotal hunting scene building rapport with the audience. It does that perfectly. Although they might be horrified by the spectacle, viewers no doubt secretly admire the hunters' bravery and skill. These hunters are part of the environment and dependent on it for sustenance. Like Mark Twain back in the 1870s, Gibson sees something noble in what was then called "primitive man." Ever the subversive, Twain noted that people who might be considered savage by modern civilization are actually more human than the modern Victorians who avidly read his irreverent books.[9]

In *Apocalypto*, the sentiment is much the same because Gibson humanizes the hunters. In the scenes that follow, the hunters banter about a wide range of things, including bullying one about his inability to impregnate his wife. This further disarms the audience, in effect personalizing and even universalizing the hunters as regular guys from anytime and anywhere. Much of it is the small-talk and locker-room conversation that Gibson seems to enjoy sharing on screen. It represents a marked departure from the lofty talk about the great creator that Indigenous people often spout in films. Although some critics considered this "frat house" banter rather too contemporary to be believable, Gibson wisely knew it would have an endearing effect.

The audience watching *Apocalypto* has little idea of the time period in which it takes place, except that it appears to be the stone age, judging by the hunter's weapons and their face-and-body painting. The hunters wear little in the way of clothing, and the lushness of the vegetation suggests a tropical setting. Much of their habitat is dense jungle, which adds to the sense of mystery. Gibson was fascinated by the lowland tropical Maya, an ancient civilization that was vanishing when the Spaniards arrived. That said, they have descendants living in this region today, suggesting their tenacity in the face of many challenges. Gibson admires that type of perseverance against the odds, and it shows in this film.

As the hunters carry their prize back to their village, they encounter a bedraggled group of people who ask for permission to enter their territory. Clearly frightened, the strangers are seeking a new home as they have been run out by a more powerful people who devastated their village. With this exchange, Gibson clearly establishes that this is no Eden, but rather a place of danger and instability. The hunters are led by Jaguar Paw (Rudy Youngblood) whose father Flint Sky (Morris Birdyellowhead) tells him that fear is the worst enemy and that one should never surrender to it. After letting the refugees pass by, the hunters return to their home village, which appears to be in complete harmony with the jungle setting.

The scenes that follow reveal more and more about the tribe's structure and their interpersonal interactions. It is a closely-knit community and based on not only hunting, but evidently a modest amount of slash and burn agriculture as well. Given the small number of people in the village, perhaps one hundred, it likely represents a band under the leadership of Flint Sky, with his son Jaguar Paw second in command. The village seems idyllic but tenuous based on what the fleeing people had experienced earlier. Suddenly, by complete surprise, the serene village is attacked by a group of ferocious warriors who are much more advanced in their craft than the natives. Led by Zero Wolf (Raoul Trujillo) whose dress and ornaments confirm he is in command, this predatory expedition is equipped with better weapons and armor. The contrast between the villagers and the warriors is striking, and suggests that they represent two cultures—one subsisting and the other plundering.

Torching the village as they advance into it, the warriors kill anyone who resists or tries to flee. Among them is a particularly sadistic miscreant named Middle Eye (Gerardo Taracena) who seems to enjoy barbarity for its own sake. As they sack the village, they quickly subdue and harness all the men, abuse some of the women, and leave the children behind to fend for themselves. In the process, Jaguar Paw's wife Seven (Dalia Hernández) and his young son Turtles Run (Carlos Emilio Báez) are lowered to safety into a deep pit using a long rope. On the way out of the devastated village, one of warriors suspects someone may be hiding in that pit, and cuts the rope, making escape impossible. He also throws some boulders down into the hole in hopes of killing anyone, but luckily they miss their targets. Now in shackles, Jaguar Paw has a very personal score to settle with Middle Eye, who deliberately killed his father Flint Sky and derisively calls Jaguar Paw "Almost" to signify he will never be the leader that his father was.

On a grueling forced march, and tied together by ropes around their necks, Jaguar Paw and what remains of his people are driven through country that is new to them. Along the way, they are marched along cliffs where one of the prisoners is cut loose by Middle Eye and falls to his death. It is a brutal act that confirms Middle Eye's villainous inhumanity. The wide-open sun-drenched vistas in these scenes contrast starkly with the dense shady jungle of their homeland. Filmed in part in Costa Rica and the tropical lowland south of Veracruz, Mexico, the scenery along this trek captures some of the feel of the interior of the Yucatan Peninsula, but is much more dramatic. This is another hallmark of film, which can slightly exaggerate topography or vegetation in order to accentuate the essential character of place. This usually involves close coordination between the location scouts and the cinematographer—all under the guidance of

In *Apocalypto* (2006), Jaguar Paw's tribe is forced from their jungle village into new territory along a river by their cruel captors. The camera angle accentuates the topography, and the horizontality of the figures lashed together emphasizes the long distances being traversed by these captives (Touchstone Pictures and Icon Productions).

the director. Although filmed in separate locales, they can be brought together through adept editing.

For their part, Jaguar Paw and his fellow prisoners have no idea where they are headed, and this uncertainty adds to a feeling of impending doom. Along the way, they and their captors encounter a little girl whose skin is covered with welts, evidently from smallpox. Played by María Isidra Hoil but nameless in the film, she is no ordinary child, but rather seems to have a sagacious air about her despite her sorry condition. Eerily, she begins telling the future, predicting the fall of Mayan civilization. Some of the warriors dismiss this, but some sense it as a powerful omen. For their part, Gibson and Safinia brilliantly use this oracle girl—who seems as much a specter as real flesh and blood—to foreshadow the trajectory of *Apocalypto*. It is worth noting that females have few speaking roles in this tersely scripted film, which in this regard is reminiscent of another tribal-centered film *Lawrence of Arabia*. Some may see this as misogynistic, but then again both films deeply explore the consequences of male hubris.

On this relentless march, the prisoners are led through a site ravaged by mining. Here, the white material extracted—limestone—is ground to a powder and heated to become quick-lime. It is a scene of devastation and Gibson wanted it to symbolize the rapacious exploitation of the environment. The film's archaeological consultant Richard Hansen notes that producing this material for city construction resulted in considerable deforestation—for use as firewood—in the ancient past.[10] One of the prisoners is somewhat optimistically making mental notes of where they are, saying that they will be able to "tell stories of a place stone-built." Like all explorers, voluntary or otherwise, he evidently intends to return home with some tales to tell about the journey. However, another prisoner ominously states that "the earth bleeds" in this area. Here, the prisoners see groups of evidently enslaved workers whose skin is covered with white dust, which gives them the appearance of ghosts or zombies.

Moreover, they also see withering cornfields ravaged by drought. This hints at the peril of relying on large-scale agriculture, which is a hallmark of supposedly advanced civilization. In Gibson's vision, a twin imbalance involving a climatic catastrophe—a major regional drought—coupled with overzealous exploitation of resources, has led this society to the brink of collapse.

Shortly thereafter, the prisoners finally arrive at a large city that has been hewn out of the jungle. Its bustling marketplaces are full of exotically clad and wildly body painted people, creating an aura of ethnic convergence. Many things are sold here, including fruit, slaves, and brightly colored birds. Now being paraded through the city streets, the prisoners will soon be slathered with bright blue paint that further distinguishes them from the teeming crowds. They are now reluctant explorers of a novel, chaotic, and terrifying environment—the city.

In these urban scenes, the people's remarkably different dress intrigues both the prisoners and the audience. Consultant Hansen notes that many of the costumes and body decorations were based on ancient Maya images. That said, some of the scenes have a decidedly "Oriental" quality that suggests the commerce of the ancient Near East. Given co-writer Safinia's Iranian background, which is to say familiarity with ancient Persia, it may have had a familiar feel to him. To some viewers, myself included, the women's' foreheads featuring a red ornamental dot may suggest India, where they are called *bindis*. There is no reference to them by archaeologists of the Maya, and their presence in the film underscores the observation that the place seems highly cosmopolitan in character. More broadly, the elaborate scarification on people's bodies in *Apocalypto* reveals more than a remarkable attention to detail. Those impressive scars also demonstrate that a type of branding—some of it painful—was experienced in this geographical locale at this time, its purpose being to indicate tribal identity and social status.

As their grueling forced march nears its end in *Apocalypto* (2006), the enslaved tribe enters a bustling Mayan city—the first they have ever seen. Although exhausted, they notice the people's different dress and the fact that their captors keep slaves. This film by Mel Gibson was noteworthy for its use of Indigenous languages and effective use of subtitles (Touchstone Pictures and Icon Productions).

Anthropologist Richard Hansen played a major role in the design of the impressive sets built for *Apocalypto* (2006), including the city's impressive pyramids which symbolize imperial political power and its abuses. In this scene, the prisoners in Jaguar Paw's tribe have now been body painted in bright blue by their captors—indicating their status as victims who will be sacrificed to the gods by priests atop the pyramid (Touchstone Pictures and Icon Productions).

In *Apocalypto*, the city's huge and impressive pyramids are symbols of power, or rather the abuse of power. These were not only based in part on Mayan designs from various periods but also involved some artistic license to create the impression or impact that Gibson was trying to achieve. Some of the city suggests an Aztec influence, as Gibson intended. Overall, the cityscape they encounter is staggering in that Gibson avoided using CGI (Computer Generated Imagery) in favor of actual construction. In an informative anthology book chapter dedicated to this film, archaeological consultant Hansen takes readers on a guided illustrated tour of that cityscape, from its shops to huge ceremonial pyramids. Of interest here is that a number of the buildings that had been constructed for the set were intentionally aged (weathered) to give them the look of dating from earlier periods, and now on the decline. Of even more interest is that during construction of the sets, every ceiba tree (*Ceiba pentandra*) on the site was avoided—much as the ancient Mayans may have done as these trees were sacred to them.[11]

In this city, Jaguar Paw and his fellow prisoners realize, to their horror, that people are being sacrificed atop the temples, whose steps are glistening red as fresh blood flows down them. In a methodical process, a priest oversees the stabbing and decapitation of those sacrificed. After the victims' still-beating hearts are ceremonially cut out of their bodies, they are held aloft to appease the gods. Simultaneously, the decapitated heads are sent bounding down the steep steps like soccer balls. Cinematically speaking, this nightmarish scene is right out of *Conan the Barbarian*, one of the truly great films made about brutal empires run amok. Like Conan, Jaguar Paw is at the very center of a drama showcasing a depraved world.

In short order, two of Jaguar Paw's people are sacrificed before his eyes, and he is next in line. However, a solar eclipse occurs just in time for the action to pause as the gods appear to be appeased. Momentarily, everything is plunged in darkness. It should be noted that among the many things that could irritate critics about this film, one was the short length of the eclipse itself—several seconds of total darkness—and the other was the presence of a full moon the next night (an astronomical impossibility).[12] To Gibson's credit, one can only imagine the audience sitting for about three-to-five full minutes of darkness, the timing involved in a real eclipse, or having enough knowledge of the night sky to find fault with this depiction. More to the point, as noted earlier, films compress time to keep the story moving, and may rely on effects that in this case emphasize the shape of the full moon to artistically balance the circular nature of the corona that accompanies a total solar eclipse.

Among the many things that infuriated critics, the scenes of human sacrifice were highest on the list. However, as archaeologist Hansen noted, they are based on the fact that Aztec influences found their way into the Mayan region of Yucatan toward the end of the prehistoric period, when the region was experiencing considerable environmental stress. To critics who claim the Maya were incorrectly depicted as "blood thirsty predators" by Gibson, Hansen cites numerous early Spanish accounts including members of the Francisco Mirones y Lezcano expeditions into the Yucatean interior. this Aztec-style blood-letting seems stereotypically violent and certainly shatters the myth of a peaceful idyllic pre–Columbian America.

On their way to this appointment with the priestly executioners, the blue-painted prisoners had been marched past ancient Maya murals similar to the Preclassic murals at San Bartolo, Peten, Guatemala. In one scene, Jaguar Paw gazes at them in horror and disbelief. Although those murals seem to perfectly capture the action underway, Hansen objected to them being used because they were from the wrong time period and hence out of place. However, to Gibson these murals serve the purpose of "…moving the film along by allowing the prisoners to realize their fate without additional scenes of conversation."[13] Needless to say, Hansen lost the argument. To Gibson's credit, those murals work perfectly as the camera pans the prisoners' death march along that mural, making the distant past seem to come alive.

Spared from sacrifice by the fortuitous eclipse, Jaguar Paw and his remaining fellow prisoners are taken to an area where they are given a chance to flee—provided they can avoid a fusillade of arrows shot and spears thrown at them. One by one his comrades are killed, but Jaguar Paw manages to outwit the spear throwers and archers, until shot through and through by an arrow in the back. He crumbles to the ground, and seems to be dead. However, as Zero Wolf's son comes closer to be sure he is dead, and kill him if he is still alive, Jaguar Paw springs to life and kills him. He has outwitted his captors. Enraged, Zero Paw now summons about a dozen warriors and leads the chase.

In some of the most intense on-foot action scenes ever filmed, Jaguar Paw runs for his life—and toward home. He stays ahead of them, and is even shot through the torso again by another arrow. However, he still keeps on running, the effect being that he is either superhuman or being assisted by supernatural forces. Now entering the jungle, he is more in his element, but with his pursuers slowly gaining, he climbs a tree and finds refuge there. The warriors pass below him and it appears he has outwitted them, but after a while Zero Wolf notices a drop of blood on the back of a warrior, and deduces it is from Jaguar Paw hiding up in the trees. Back they go, just in time for Jaguar Paw to hear a menacing growl—and see a huge black panther moving toward him along a tree limb. Jaguar Paw quickly reaches the ground and runs furiously with the panther in hot pursuit, followed as closely by the warriors. In one incredible scene that lasts only a few seconds, the black panther is about to overtake the blue-painted Jaguar Paw—at the same time a warrior is also closing in on him. That warrior now moves in directly behind Jaguar Paw, but is unknowingly in front of the panther, which changes its mind, or rather its target. In a flash, it takes down and instantly kills the warrior. The other warriors arrive and kill the panther, but it has provided Jaguar Paw the much-needed opportunity to put more distance between himself and his pursuers.

As he continues his headlong flight, Jaguar Paw arrives at a point where a river cascades over a high waterfall. As will become apparent time and time again in this book, waterfalls are frequently used in storytelling to signify major points in the plot. This is one of them, and it is spectacular. As Jaguar Paw sees the warriors closing in, he decides to take a leap of faith. With no other alternative, he jumps into the river and is carried over the towering falls. Death seems imminent, but then again nothing can stop Jaguar Paw from going home. He survives the fall and the warriors are amazed when he pulls himself out the water at the other side of the river far below them. He also defiantly yells back at them that he, not they, rule this area. Symbolically, this waterfall scene confirms that Jaguar Paw is a force of nature, and indomitable.

Now more determined than ever to catch him, the nefarious Zero Wolf orders his men to follow him on the same death-defying jump. When the cowardly Middle Eye tries to dissuade him, Zero Wolf kills him on the spot. Together, the remaining pursuers follow Jaguar Paw's lead and plunge over the falls. Several are killed, but Zero Wolf and

In this scene from *Apocalypto* (2006), a defiant Jaguar Paw (Rudy Youngblood) has momentarily escaped his captors by successfully plunging over a waterfall, a geographic feature often used in film to signify a change in the story's trajectory. Director Mel Gibson effectively used the jungle environment of southern Mexico and the Yucatán for this classic survival escape film set in Pre-Columbian times (Touchstone Pictures and Icon Productions).

a few others make it. Now followed closely by his pursuers, Jaguar Paw finds himself in quicksand that turns out to be a tar-like substance. Completely coated in shiny black, he now emerges and strikes terror in his pursuers as he appears much like a black panther himself, and hence in alliance with nature.

As the film progresses, Gibson gives the audience a crash course in jungle survival. In one scene, Jaguar Paw manages to locate and dislodge a large hornet's nest, which he tosses at the pursuers, who scatter amid cries of pain. In another, Jaguar Paw finds a deadly frog and extracts poison from it. Curling a leaf into a tube, he shoots poison darts at his pursuers, killing a couple more. Zero Wolf has let down his guard, and he is now in Jaguar Paw's territory. A gathering rainstorm signals the end of the drought, but the chase is still on and the action not letting up. In a scene reminiscent of the film's opening hunt, Zero Wolf is killed by the same kind of booby trap that killed the tapir. Jaguar Paw has triumphed over his people's adversary, but two more pursuers remain, determined to finish him off. Overall, this seemingly unending escape—men hunting a man—has few parallels in film history as it is so epic, although Cornel Wilde's 1965 African saga *The Naked Prey*[14] set the standard.

At this point, Jaguar Paw is more concerned than ever about the fate of his wife and child. To viewers, it may seem like an eternity since his village was raided, but evidently only a few days may have elapsed. Another rainstorm is now approaching, heightening Jaguar Paw's concern about them. Presumably they may still be alive in the pit, but it could fill with water and drown them in the process. Scenes now switch to her, still trying to get out of the pit as water begins filling it. Like Jaguar Paw, she is Ingenious and resilient but gravity is against her. Spectacularly, she goes into labor and their second son is born underwater as its level continues to rise.

Apocalypto now launches into one of the more surprising endings, or rather near-endings, in film history. Shifting focus back to Jaguar Paw, it shows him exhausted as two pursuers reach him at the edge of the forest near the coast in a downpour. They could finish him off at this point, but both the pursuers and pursued are distracted by what they behold. From the shoreline, all three exhausted men look toward the sea. The camera circles around them, momentarily showing all three from behind as they behold a stunning sight offshore in the distance—three Spanish ships making landfall, with men on boats about to land on shore.

This scene is striking indeed, and has much the same revelatory impact as the discovery of the Statue of Liberty's arm and torch in the finale of *Planet of the Apes*. Like that science fiction scene, this one provides a Eureka moment. It definitively reveals the time period as about 1500, and confirms the young girl's prophecy of people coming from afar who would "Scratch out the Earth. Scratch you out. And end your world." The audience may believe that the scene depicts Columbus' arrival in 1492, but Gibson wanted to more accurately depict the first arrival by Spanish ships under the command of Pedro de Alvarado in the Yucatan in 1511; however, Christopher Columbus did reach this general area earlier, on his fourth voyage in 1502.

Something else about this scene is surprising. Jaguar Paw is more concerned with the fate of his family than inter-hemispheric contact, and walks away as the two entranced warriors head toward the Spaniards. Arriving back at the ruined village in the nick of time, he saves his family. In the closing scenes, he and his wife view the Spanish ships from a hill above the coast. She asks, "What are they?" and he says, "They bring men." Entranced by the ships, she asks, "Should we go to them?" He states just the opposite: "We should go to the forest ... to seek a new beginning." This, in a sense, can be seen as Gibson's recognizing that the last place an Indigenous American might want to be is in an easily conquered locale such as a failing city, which Spaniards tended to conquer with surprising ease. It also reinforces the belief that the nuclear family is a key to survival, though of course life here was based on the interdependence of families and the clans they formed. We can only imagine what their fates might be, but history confirms that huge changes are in store for them and the entire region.

Ironically, some critics thought Gibson's arrival of the Spaniards was his way of "saving" the Indians for Christianity, though he vehemently denies this. In retrospect, Gibson's leaving the ending wide open to speculation about what might happen was viewed as brilliant by some, but it also encouraged others to fill in their own scenarios—based mostly on what they knew about his pro–Christian religious fervor and his politically incorrect personal beliefs (including his anti–Semitism). Ultimately, Gibson prevailed. The public loved *Apocalypto*, as did many critics, but some had a field day finding fault with it. Gibson's harshest critics saw this film as an endorsement of American attitudes that berated Indigenous peoples. In a scathing review titled "Maya Culpa?" Mark Stevenson panned the film as an insult to not only the Indigenous Maya but also to Latin Americans.[15] In another caustic takedown titled "Apocalypto and the end of the wrong civilisation," *The Guardian*'s Alex von Tunzelmann cited a litany of things—culture, violence, religion, and timing—incorrectly portrayed in the film. Many of these had been pointed out by academics, but von Tunzelmann found the film's ending to be particularly off-putting: "Apocalypto seems to have been made to argue that the Maya civilisation was evil and revolting, and that it was a jolly good thing that the Spanish turned up to conquer it." Sounding much like a historian but forgetting the film is fiction, Tunzelmann continued: "That view is hard to sustain if you know any of the basic facts about Mayan civilisation or the Spanish conquest." His verdict was that Apocalypto deserved a "'C'— grade as entertainment and a history grade of 'Fail.'"[16]

Interestingly, Gibson viewed the decadence and deceit portrayed in his fictional film as a metaphor for something much closer to home in time and place, namely the United States' misguided adventurism in the Iraq War (ca. 2002–03) as precipitated by the administration of then–President George W. Bush. As Gibson put it more generally, with environmental degradation, excessive consumption, and political corruption in mind: "People think that modern man is so enlightened, but we're susceptible to the same forces—and we are also capable of the same heroism and transcendence."[17]

In the context of films about exploration and discovery, *Apocalypto* serves as an interesting chapter in that it provides an Indigenous look at the arrival of the Spaniards, who will transform the geographic region from Indigenous American to Latin American. That transition involving Europeans was often a brutal process that played out in different ways in several key locations, as evident in the next three films to be discussed.

Two

The Other Conquest

An Indigenous View of the Encounter

Before discussing the next film, I shall set the scene by noting that the four voyages of Christopher Columbus were pivotal in Spain's encounters with the New World. They began in 1492, and by the time his fourth voyage had ended in 1504, had given Spain a much clearer idea of the challenges involved in the process of exploration and colonization. From early in the nineteenth century, when the American writer and diplomat Washington Irving published *A History of the Life and Voyages of Christopher Columbus* (1828), that explorer's name has become synonymous with exploration and colonization. Irving dramatized the story based on Columbus' original letters, and it was published as four volumes in England and three in the United States. No less an explorer than Alexander von Humboldt praised it, and Columbus became a household word in the English-speaking world as well as much of Europe.

Of the many challenges Columbus faced, first and foremost is the realization that an explorer, no matter how visionary, does not necessarily make a good colonizer. Some of this is made clear in a dramatic film by Ridley Scott titled *1492: Conquest of Paradise*.[1] In company—or competition—with two other films about Columbus released in 1992 for the controversial Quincentennial of the "discovery" of the New World, Ridley Scott's film tackles a complex subject. He portrays the Italian (Genoan) explorer as a man of singular vision who has to fight the establishment in order to prove that Asia can be reached by sailing west from Europe—thus avoiding direct conflicts with the Muslim world. As about four centuries of expensive and bloody Crusading had proven, the Islamic world would be impossible to re-take without allies in Asia. More than coincidentally, Scott would later direct what is arguably the best dramatic film ever made about the Crusades—*Kingdom of Heaven* (2005).

In *1492...*, Scott portrays Spain as freshly re-taken from Muslim rule in the *Reconquista* (re-conquest) and brimming with often violent energy. He suggests, and rightly so, that the reconquest could now be extended across the ocean to include the part of the world that Columbus hoped to reach—southeast Asia. The film portrays Columbus as religious, but sidesteps his fanatical zeal and his eschatological belief that the world would soon end—and that before that cataclysm would happen, all of its inhabitants should be converted to Christianity. That said, Scott does recognize that the people that Columbus mistakenly called Indios (Indians) provided an unparalleled opportunity for empire building.

Like all dramatic films, Scott's *1492 ...* takes liberties with the historical record in many places, as noted in a critical reviews by historians, including an insightful critique by scholars Carla Rahn Phillips and William D. Phillips, Jr.[2] However, as director, Scott's major goals involved keeping the story moving and the audience engaged. Along the way, *1492 …* simplifies historical complexities as it makes points about good and evil, and also provides the audience characters with whom they can identify or despise. It oddly downplays the actual cost Spain would have to pay to fund the voyage—much more than that involved in hosting two lavish balls (major events). It also involves strained dialogue between Columbus (Gérard Depardieu) and Queen Isabella (Sigourney Weaver) that borders on the flirtatious, if not flippant. A fine actress in her own right, Weaver seems ill at ease in this regal role, almost as if thinking: *Can you believe the over-the-top costume they've squeezed me into?* For his part, Depardieu cannot seem to escape his breezy persona as a French sex symbol who makes the Queen giggle like a schoolgirl. In reality, they were both pretty worldly, his experience as an explorer in the Old World being one of his credentials, and her extensive experience in governing recognized as involving skill and compassion despite her zealous Catholicism. The two had something else in common, similar ages: both were born in 1451 and died just two years apart (Isabella in 1504 and Columbus in 1506).

As Scott makes clear, Columbus was a savvy self-promoter who coupled the personal profit motive with loftier goals. As history would prove, it was a model that would transform the New World. Isabella was risk-oriented, and visionary, enough to bankroll his project. In retrospect, their discussions were among the most important in world history, and indisputably the most important in the history of the Americas. Scott's *1492 …* is remarkable in that it not only conveys some of the complexity involved in funding and implementing the first voyage in 1492 but also the three subsequent voyages—a considerable period of time and a tremendous amount of territory to cover. That is a formidable task for a filmmaker, but Scott tackled it and generally succeeded.

At the same time that Scott's film was released, the academic world was abuzz with sobering confirmation that Columbus' vision was in large part delusional. As Enrique Dussell tersely noted: "What Columbus actually saw and what he wanted to see were two different things. He categorically affirmed in his diary that he landed in Asia."[3] For his part, Scott demonstrates that Columbus's flawed vision may have succeeded in Spain's gaining a foothold in the Americas, but that he was not the talented official needed to manage the herculean task of bringing two cultures face to face, and having one smoothly colonize the other in the process.

By definition, colonization aims to do more than just expand territory; it also assumes that the new geographical areas appropriated will ideally look like, and behave in line with, the vision and expectations of the colonizers. The colonizers move in, and the natives adjust. We now regard such colonization as arrogant and short-sighted, not to mention brutal and exploitative, but it helped reshape the world. Although other empires had colonized parts of the world—for example, Greece, Rome, China, and the Islamic gunpowder empires—Spain now seized the opportunity to make it trans-oceanic. Shortly thereafter, other European powers would attempt to do much the same.

Because people already existed in the new lands encountered, they represented either an obstacle or an opportunity. If compliant, these indigenous people could provide a ready source of labor. If not, they could turn the colonizer's vision into a nightmare. Usually, the outcome was somewhere in between. Ambivalence was always involved. For example, Columbus soon began enslaving Indians but Isabella had him arrested for doing it. Regarding the imposition of authority over indigenous people, after Isabella's death the Spaniards would cynically clarify it in the *Requerimiento* (1510) as a choice: Indians would be left alone and free to live as they did originally, provided that they accepted the teachings of the Church and the control of Spain. Those refusing to comply so would be considered hostiles punishable by warfare and could be legally enslaved.

The film that will be interpreted in this chapter builds upon the legacy of Columbus, and is based on one of the most significant episodes in Latin American history—the Conquest of Mexico. It, too, is a fictionalized story, but relies much more clearly on historical records than the wildly speculative scenario presented in *Apocalypto*. The conquest of Mexico has been written about from several perspectives, most famously by William Prescott, the historian of Spanish America whose 1843 book titled *History of the Conquest of Mexico* is widely recognized as a classic. It not only brought Mexico's history into the American consciousness, but also set a new model for how history can be related in an engaging way by bringing to life the individuals involved.

The event in question is the Spaniards' arrival into the Aztec capital of Tenochtitlan—today's Mexico City—and its conquest by Hernan Cortés (1485–1547), who killed its emperor Moctezuma (ca. 1466–June 29, 1520) and thousands of his followers. Prescott was the first but certainly not the last to tell this inherently dramatic story to a broader audience; more than a dozen books on the conquest are currently available about it, and several feature films make reference to the conquest in one form or another. Whereas most such *entradas* (explorations inland) encounter new peoples and new places, the goal of this one was to conquer one of the most impressive civilizations in the New World—the Aztec empire, which occupied a densely populated valley in the center of Mexico surrounding its key or capital city, Tenochtitlan. By most estimates, the Aztecs numbered about 25 million. For perspective, Tenochtitlan—now called Mexico City—was the largest city in the world at the time. For that matter, it has since remained the largest city in the Americas and is still one of the largest in the world. The Spaniards may have conquered this locale but it still remains a major crossroads of the Americas with a rich Indigenous past, present, and future.

The film I have selected to place the Aztec Empire in cinematic context is titled *The Other Conquest*[4]—and with good reason: it tells the story of the conquest from the perspective of an Aztec who survived that event. The idea for the story took place in the mind of director Salvador Carrasco, a native of Mexico, when he was studying film in New York in the early 1990s. A specific date during his stay—August 31, 1991—was the 470th anniversary of the fall of Tenochtitlan. With a film project in mind, Carrasco began imagining what the event would have been like for an Indigenous survivor. Like the later film *Apocalypto*, it is not a retelling of one particular written document but rather crosses the line into fictionalized history. However, *The Other Conquest* employs a storyline that could be credible given the general trajectory of the conquest itself.

Carrasco was well aware that the conquest of Mexico had already been featured in popular film. For example, in 1947, the bestselling book titled *Captain from Castile*[5] was turned into a lavishly filmed epic of the same name. Actually, only the first half of the book made it to the screen, wherein events in Spain find the main characters becoming part of Cortés's expedition into Mexico. Upon arriving in coastal Mexico, Cortés (Cesar Romero) ignores repeated Aztec attempts to dissuade him from reaching Tenochtitlan. In one poignant scene, a young Aztec man named Coatl (Jay Silverheels) informs the duplicitous Spaniards that they are destroying his peoples' culture, but they ignore him. Beautifully filmed in Technicolor, Henry King's *Captain from Castile* had the blessings of the Republic of Mexico. It was entirely filmed there (even the scenes supposedly shot in Spain) and used many archaeological sites. It epitomizes, and was one of the earliest American films in, the postwar boom of American films made in Mexico.[6] King's film ends on the note that the arrival of Cortés was an important step in Mexico becoming a modern nation. Its conclusion features one of the most spectacular landscape scenes in any Latin American film. As Cortés and his troops near Tenochtitlan, behind them a sweeping vista includes a real volcano (Paricutin) sending a towering cloud skyward and casting a gloom. This ominous scene has long impressed filmmakers, and literally sets the scene for what would transpire in the film I shall now discuss in detail—Carrasco's *The Other Conquest*.

According to Carrasco, the story of what happened to the Aztecs belief system after the Spaniards arrived needed telling. Like director Henry King, he envisioned a film that would break boundaries and shine light on the Aztec culture. However, unlike King, whose film took shape and arrived on screen in about two years, Carrasco had no reputation, few Hollywood connections, and little money, so *The Other Conquest* took about ten years to make. Passionately believing in the story, Carrasco secured funding

In this spectacular scene from the film *Captain from Castile* (1947), Spanish conquistadors advance into the heart of Mexico, signaling the beginning of the end for Aztec domination. Director Henry King was lucky that the eruption of Paricutin coincided with the filming, adding elements of drama and foreboding to this depiction of conquistadors on the march (Twentieth Century–Fox Film Productions).

from unconventional sources, including Spanish opera singer Plácido Domingo. Like Gibson's film, Carrasco's would be based on archaeological sites that were associated with cultural conflict. As his film idea took form, Carrasco visited many sites throughout Mexico to find those that fit the developing story. His goal was to show how Indigenous traditions survived the heavy hand of the religious system introduced by the conquerors. In Carrasco's vision, most of it would take place at the edge of Spain's colonizing grip. As he put it: "We were looking for an intimate, timeless setting with distinctive architecture, far away from the metropolis, where clandestine rituals could have taken place without the Spaniards knowing."[7] The wording "could have" in his statement is important, for it confirms the conjectural nature of the story. Still, like good fiction, it can sometimes reveal a deeper truth than non-fiction.

At its very beginning, *The Other Conquest* features a logo, a transposed Aztec skull and a cross—which serves as a symbol for the two cultures that will interact in this film from beginning to end, where the logo appears again. Those two symbols in the logo are superimposed, suggesting fusion. The film itself opens with a brief synopsis of the crucial events of 1519–1520, wherein the brutal colonization of Mexico began under the leadership of Cortés. As recent archaeological study is confirming, Cortés was an astute observer of conditions who enlisted Indigenous enemies of the Aztecs to assist him in overthrowing their empire.[8]

The film's protagonist—Topiltzin—first comes on screen as a survivor of the massacre at the Great Temple in 1520. His name is especially significant, for Topiltzin Ce Acatl Quetzacoatl was a mythical or legendary God of the Toltecs about four centuries before this film takes place. For his part, the film character Topiltzin will also have a pivotal role. He is played by Damián Delgado, a slender athletic actor who is also a dancer. The latter is apparent in his expressive movements, bringing to mind a stealthy and graceful jaguar. At night, in a driving rainstorm, Topiltzin emerges from hiding under the body of a slain Indian. Despite the slipperiness of the steep masonry slope, he adroitly claws his way up and out to freedom. As he looks down at the base of the temple, he sees a dead Aztec woman. As a symbol, she may signify the mother goddess. Her presence foreshadows the plot that will be heavily female-centered. Although it is a gloom-filled scene of desperation, the audience will soon learn that Topiltzin is not only a survivor who can endure privation but also a cultural adaptor who can coexist with the Spaniards, largely by pretending.

The film now moves ahead in time (to 1548) and back across the ocean to Spain, where the last rites are being administered to an elderly priest named Fray Diego (José Carlos Rodríguez). These rites will signify "peace at last—the final journey ... to where all mortals go." This hints at the padre's turbulent life, which, though now ended, will be one of the threads that bind the film. The priests who give him these rites are surprised to discover hidden in his Bible the fragments of an Aztec codex recounting the conquest. The Aztecs chronicled much of their history using this technique, and the Spaniards, hoping to abolish that pagan history, destroyed much of it. The artwork is significant as it was made by Topiltzin, who will be at the center of the film and help recast the conquest from his perspective as well as Diego's—hence the film's intriguing title: *The Other Conquest*. In keeping with this bi-cultural emphasis, the film is in Spanish and Nahuatl, with English subtitles.

The focus now shifts back to Mexico twenty-plus years earlier (1519) as conquerors under the direction of Cortés march along steep trails hauling a large cross and cannons. Those implements symbolize the militant Christianity introduced by the

Spaniards into this part of the Americas, where spectacular pyramids marked the presence of a civilization about to be conquered. In one scene featuring a sweeping vista of verdant hills and temples—a clearly beautiful place—a Spaniard asks: "Are we supposed to destroy this?" It is a haunting question because it confirms that even these destroyers can see beauty, and can question themselves about what is going to transpire—at least when they are out of hearing range of their commanders. It is also Carrasco's way of reaffirming his love for his native land.

As an interesting subtext, the film notes that whereas the conquerors thought they were bringing "absolute truth" as regards religion, their mission was compromised from the beginning because "a conversion is never complete." Moreover, it may have unintended consequences. As the film puts it, even the Crusades (from Europe to the Holy Land) inadvertently "brought Muslim ideas into Christianity." One key element that these conquistadors carry into Mexico is a life-size statue of Mary holding Jesus. The statue is both exquisite and realistic—so lifelike that she almost appears to be a richly costumed but paralyzed actress. Although these Christian soldiers have been warned about the perils of worshipping idols, the care that they take with this one reveals their reverence. Carrasco picked the perfect icon. In modern-day Mexico it is recognized that the Virgin Mary has a localized counterpart—the Virgin of Guadalupe—who represents a fusion between the Madonna and the Aztec Mother Goddess Tonantzin. In retrospect, Carrasco's making this statue as important as any other character in this film was a stroke of genius. It, or rather she, will play a major role as this story unfolds. In fact, when Topiltzin first sees this statue, he envisions in his mind's eye the Aztec maidens he has sacrificed to the gods.

In the film *The Other Conquest* (1999/2000), Fray Diego (center) and a group of helmeted Spanish troops reach the Aztec interior of Mexico. Amazed by the beauty of the scene before them—with its lush valleys, stunning mountains, and Aztec temples—they skeptically ask "Are we supposed to destroy this?" As a tribute to his native Mexico, director Salvador Carrasco use authentic locations to showcase its landscapes and cultural history (Twentieth Century–Fox).

As the audience soon learns, Topiltzin is an illegitimate son of Moctezuma and he has a half-sister named Tecuichpo (Elpida Carrillo) who is Moctezuma's daughter. Further intensifying the drama, she also becomes the mistress of Cortés, who realizes that she is a key to having the Indians embrace this hybrid empire. For his part, Cortés (Iñaki Aierra) is passionately attracted to her, his aggressive rape of her in one scene mimicking his conquest of her empire. In this new role, she will have two identities. On the one hand, she is called Doña Isabel by many in recognition of her new role with Cortés, a name that subliminally links her to the Spanish queen that started the process of conquest in 1492. On the other, she is still known as Tecuichpo to her brother Topiltzin. Like him, she is straddling two empires.

In a pivotal event that takes place in 1526, a squadron of troops under the command of the brutal Capitan Cristóbal (Honorato Magaloni) encounters a clandestine ceremonial sacrifice of a willing young woman. Topiltzin plays a major role in such ceremonies, which are considered barbaric by the Spaniards. As portrayed by Carrasco, this shocking but reverent sacrificial scene is rich in symbolism and artistically filmed. Predictably, it outrages the Spaniards, and the encounter soon spirals into the slaughter of several Indians. Horrified by the violence, Fray Diego chastises his fellow Spaniards, exclaiming, "you've become just like them!" He further chides them by stating, "If only our soldiers had as much faith as the Indians do!"—but to no avail. Defiantly, the Spaniards burn Aztec codices and imprison the survivors.

Topiltzin survives by feigning his devotion to the Virgin Mary, and Diego believes he has found a willing convert. Topiltzin appears to be slowly evolving into a devoted acolyte, at least from Diego's perspective. Now given the Christian name Tomás, he is

In this scene from *The Other Conquest* (1999/2000), Spanish conquistador Hernando Cortés (Iñaki Aierra), Aztec priest-turned-monk Topiltzin (Damián Delgado), and his half-sister Tecuichpo (Elpida Carrillo) banter about the state of affairs under Spanish rule. By this time, Tecuichpo has become the mistress of Cortés and is now known as Doña Isabel. Soon, she and Topiltzin will challenge the religious and political expectations of both the Catholic Church and the Spanish Crown (Twentieth Century–Fox).

In a striking close-up from *The Other Conquest* that embodies filmmaker Salvador Carrasco's fascination with the deeper symbolic aspects of Aztec life, Topiltzin's brother Alanpoyatzin (Guillermo Ríos) drapes a serpent—likely a harmless Mexican bull snake—over his head in an ancient ritual. Serpents were regarded with ambivalence and even disdain by Christians at the time, but the Aztecs revered them as a manifestation of the god Quetzal as they symbolized both wisdom and the continuity of life (Twentieth Century–Fox).

sent to a monastery far from Tenochtitlan. Carrasco's choice of this name is quite appropriate, for Thomas is the disciple in the Bible who doubts the miracles attributed to Jesus. For years, Topiltzin keeps his ancestral faith alive through the cult of Tonantzin, which is centered on an Aztec Mother Goddess. Although he worships that Goddess, the statue of Mary has an increasingly powerful effect on him—an effect that seems to increase with the destruction of Aztec iconography.

In several important scenes, the fraying relationship between Topiltzin and his brother Alanpoyatzin (Guillermo Ríos) plays out. In a tersely written scene foretelling what will come, one brother tells the other, "we must adapt to survive," but is told "I don't adapt." Although they've come to blows at times, their rivalry is not quite as divisive as that between Cain and Abel. However, it does have a direct biblical outcome: Alanpoyatzin betrays Topiltzin to authorities in a way that recalls Judas Iscariot betraying Jesus to Roman authorities. In more peaceful scenes, the idyllic gardens of Xochimilco serve to suggest an edenic life, but this is the locale in which Alanpoyatzin strikes a deal with Spanish authorities. A close-up of Alanpoyatzin in a serpent's embrace—or rather embracing a serpent—confirms his allegiance to Aztec mythology. Shortly thereafter, Topiltzin is apprehended in a spectacularly rocky area full of twisted roots as his brother looks on a short distance away. Director Carrasco has an eye for scenery that helps compliment the many moods of this film. Like Judas, Alanpoyatzin is consumed by guilt when Topiltzin is dragged away by soldiers.

Throughout the film, the Virgin Mary and the Aztec goddess are juxtaposed. Statues of both are filmed to show the connection between these religious icons. Slowly, Diego himself will become convinced that they represent one and the same—the mother of God. It is blasphemous, of course, but Diego and Topiltzin are now both hiding secrets and developing a mysterious bond. In one dream-like scene, Topiltzin imagines himself about to sacrifice Mary by plunging a dagger into the statue's chest. For their part, Doña Isabel and Tomás have secrets and a bond as well. In a scene that likely shocked many viewers, brother and sister decide to perpetuate their royal lineage by conceiving a child. This brings to center stage a practice that has deep roots as far back as ancient Egypt but is incestuous and therefore banned in later times. Carrasco tries to de-eroticize these sex scenes as justified to preserve the blood line of the ancient Aztecs, but ironically it comes off as highly sensual, no doubt because it uses a number of cinematic techniques associated with soft-core pornography, including mood lighting and staged body positioning. Diego, who witnesses this forbidden yet awesome coupling spectacle, now feels that the original state of innocence he once knew has been lost. In a personal sense, though, by losing his innocence he is becoming more worldly, which is to say better able to understand the Aztec religion. Diego now seems to understand, but is unable to answer, Topiltzin's pointed question asked earlier in the film: "Why have you come to take away that which is ours?"

Just as his sister has two different names, and hence two identities, her brother also takes on a dual identity now that he is in his monastic role. As Tomás, he serves as a scribe. This is a brilliant device on the part of the director, who now has him reading and writing, and hence Europeanizing—to a point. Beneath it all, he is Aztec and longs for the old ways. In one place in the film, he tells Diego, "You have turned my people into ashes, [and] our truth went up in smoke." Diego does not respond, but now he is coming to understand and even admire the strength of Tomás' resolve.

In another scene in the monastery, Thomas More's 1516 book *Utopia* is shown, a reference to not only the search for the ideal community in the New World, but also a reminder that the similarly named Tomás is now a writer himself. Originally published in Latin, and making references to Americus Vespucci, its setting is an island off the coast of South America (likely Brazil), and social life there has aspects of a monastery. However, unlike anyone else in his monastery in Mexico, Tomás' linguistic skills include Nahuatl and reading/creating the symbolic languages in the codices. Seen in this light, Carrasco has masterfully created a savvy character who now understands both the European and Aztec mind.

Throughout, *The Other Conquest* is rich in such subversive metaphors and symbolism. For her part, Doña Isabel is subversive as well, telling Cortés that some things can only be said in Mexican. She does not say Nahuatal at this point but Mexican—implying that even his people's Castilian Spanish is undergoing the process of *mestizaje*. In one humorous passage earlier in the film, Doña Isabel translates a very long Spanish phrase into Nahuatl, and its brevity surprises the Spaniards, who sarcastically reply, "What a concise language!" A Spaniard may use such dismissive wording, but Doña Isabel knows better. The underlying message here is that the Spaniards are mincing a lot of words and still missing the point.

In religion, too, remarkable things are happening as the two systems have come face to face and are nearing a showdown. Fray Diego is central to this, and Topiltzin's Aztec ways are making him question his own. It works both ways. When Tomás becomes ill, Diego searches for a cure for him, realizing the power of indigenous medicine. In a sense, Topiltzin is slowly converting Diego to his indigenous religion, while Topiltzin is increasingly obsessed with the Virgin mother. In a climactic scene, Tomás transforms himself back into the primal Topiltzin, removing his clerical robe and donning his Indigenous garment as he risks all to remove the statue of the Virgin and escape with it.

In doing so, he removes the crown of thorns from her head and sets aside the baby Jesus, essentially universalizing her as the Mother of all mankind, not just Christians. He claims that there is only one Mary—which is to say she is as one with the Aztec Mother Goddess. He now has her in his possession but fate intervenes: he loses his grip on the escape rope, and falls to his death holding her. Hearing the commotion, Diego and others find them in this embrace. In one of the final scenes, Diego urges Cortés to come to the monastery in order to "witness the miracle of how two races can be as one through tolerance and love." The image of a devout Diego overseeing Topiltzin and Mary, finally together where they belong, is a haunting—but hopeful—way to end a film about the lasting consequences of colonial conquest. As film scholar Santiago Juan-Navarro observed, Don Diego has undergone a "conversion process," or more explicitly "a process of religious, political, and cultural negotiation with the indigenous Other."[9] As a bookend to the film, the last thing viewers see is that stylized logo for the film, the cross and an Aztec skull glyph superimposed.

Viewed in the context of Latin America's historical geography, *The Other Conquest* can be regarded as an exploration-discovery saga into the mindsets of two distinctly different cultures occupying the same space simultaneously. Although Carrasco positions

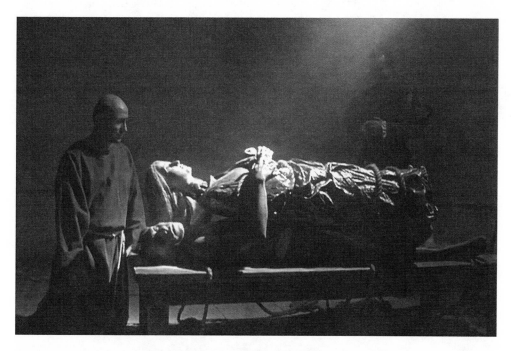

The concluding scenes in *The Other Conquest* (1999/2000) feature Fray Diego (José Carlos Rodríguez) standing over the life-like fallen statue of the Virgin Mary and the body of Topiltzin (Damián Delgado) who died during that tragic fall. The rays of light entering the scene diagonally onto the figures suggest a spiritual illumination of events. Fray Diego now realizes that Topiltzin died trying to unify the statue (and hence Christianity) with venerable Aztec ritual (that is, the Indigenous tradition)—a cinematic metaphor for the vibrant *mestizaje* (fusion of faiths and cultures) found in Mexico today (Twentieth Century–Fox).

the Indigenous and European representatives in a rather simplistic binary framework, he creatively portrays Diego and Topiltzin as two interpenetrating beings. Ingeniously, he uses their relationship as a metaphor for *mestizaje*, the potent crossing of Indigenous and imported races. Of course, that also serves as a metaphor for modern Mexico itself.

To further place this film in the context of the sixteenth century, the death of Fray Diego in 1548 coincided with ever growing concern about the treatment of Indians in Spain's New World possessions. As early as 1500, concerns began to be raised about the abuses involved in colonization, including the harsh punishment and enslavement of Indians by Columbus and other explorers. At that time, debate about whether Indians were human beings or not—and thus whether or not they had souls—was one of the most pressing issues facing both the Church and Crown. On the one hand, calls mounted for better treatment, but on the other, many felt that Indian sacrifices and even reports of cannibalism required a stern hand, including the use of military force against them.

By 1542, new laws had been passed protecting the Indians but enough disagreement and ambiguity remained that it led to the Valladolid Debate of 1550–1551. In that series of debates, Bartolomé de las Casas (the Dominican Bishop of Chiapas Mexico) argued for the fair treatment of Indigenous peoples. On the other side, the humanist scholar Juan Ginés de Sepúlveda argued that all intertribal and other violence amongst Indians themselves required the use of Spanish military force. At that time, some claimed that the annihilation of Indians to stop them from abusing and killing each other was reasonable. Nothing was formally decided at the time, but ultimately Las Casas' views increased in popularity. A main concern remained around Indigenous labor, which was needed to encourage and sustain colonization efforts. As an interesting side light regarding unintended consequences, officially abolishing Indian slavery inadvertently contributed to the opening of the African slave trade in the later sixteenth century—a scourge that would haunt the Americas for several more centuries.

THREE

Cabeza de Vaca

Exploration at the Margins of Empire

The film *Cabeza de Vaca*[1] is set in almost exactly the same time period as *The Other Conquest*, but far to the north under very different circumstances. It is the first film I will discuss that is based directly on a contemporary written source, or rather sources. Its namesake—the Spanish explorer Alvar Núñez Cabeza de Vaca (ca. 1490–ca. 1559)— was a treasurer on an ill-fated expedition by Pánfilo de Narváez that set out to explore the northern rim of the Gulf of Mexico in 1527. The expedition began with 300 men and almost from the start ran into trouble, much of it the result of poor judgment on the part of Narváez. After exploring portions of today's Florida, the setback-plagued expedition continued westward and continued to unravel; ultimately, only four men survived it, among them Cabeza de Vaca. Those survivors took almost nine years to finally make it back to Mexico. By accident, one might say, they explored a virtually unknown and lightly populated region that includes portions of modern day Texas and the American Southwest, as well as large section of northern Mexico.

Significantly, Cabeza de Vaca wrote a semi-official report to the Crown titled *La Relación* in 1542 that brings the region to light in a superbly written narrative form. Its second edition, more dramatically titled *Naufragios* (Shipwrecks) appeared in 1555 and is very similar, except for chapter titles and very minor rearranging in places. Additionally, a summary of the account titled *Joint Report* was presented to authorities by the survivors of the expedition upon their return to Mexico City in 1536 and commonly called Cabeza de Vaca's *Relación*. Re-published in varied English editions since the early 1900s—for example, *The Journey and Ordeal of Cabeza de Vaca: His Account of the Disastrous First European Exploration of the American Southwest*[2]—De Vaca's compelling tale finally reached the screen in 1991.

Directed by Nicolás Echevarría, the equally compelling film *Cabeza de Vaca* begins at the end of his epic journey in 1536, when he and three other bedraggled survivors arrived unexpectedly on foot in Culiacán on Mexico's west coast. The Spaniards there are surprised to see them because the entire expedition had vanished without a trace almost nine years earlier in far-away Florida. One of those incredulous Spaniards states that "It must have been hard, living among the savages." Almost as if raving mad, and exclaiming "ocho años" (eight years) after they learn how long they had been gone, Cabeza de Vaca (Juan Diego) and the others with him look more like wild men than Spaniards. The way Cabeza de Vaca almost wistfully points to the north, to what he calls "…these places … these lands," conveys the impression that he had some memorable experiences there. His wording leaves a lot to the imagination, and he begins relating his story. The film now flashes back about eight years to Florida in 1528, where this long journey began.

Before I continue interpreting the film, however, I feel obliged to contextualize the expedition that brought Cabeza de Vaca there in the first place. It had been ordered by Charles V who commissioned Pánfilo de Narváez to reconnoiter the Gulf coast from La Florida all the way to the Rio de las Palmas near present day Tampico, Mexico. Missing from the film are the first forty or so pages of the written account, wherein Cabeza de Vaca sailed from Spain in June of 1527 on that "Armada" of vessels carrying 300 soldiers and would-be colonists (including some women and African slaves). They arrived in Hispaniola, where they attempted to re-provision the ships but about 150 of the men stayed behind, apparently finding the pastures green enough there. The next stop was Cuba where Narváez ordered De Vaca—second in command—to take two ships up the coast to Trinidad for additional provisions. While there, a hurricane destroyed both ships and claimed 60 men and 20 horses.

Cabeza de Vaca was awed by the power of these storms which frequently plague the Caribbean. Like most Spaniards, he had never experienced a hurricane—a natural phenomenon that provided him the opportunity to integrate considerable drama into the storyline of his account. In the first chapter, he describes the wreckage left by the hurricane, noting that as they searched the marshy woods they "came upon the little boat of one of the ships lodged in some treetops." That description underscores the potency of the storm and leaves an indelible impression. As I shall later show, that small lifeboat would grow in size and later be re-imagined as a full-size sailing vessel. Wary of these hurricanes, the expedition on which Cabeza de Vaca would sail waited in Cuba until the next spring (1528) before continuing.

Despite this caution, when they set out again yet another storm hit, sending their vessels off course. Instead of returning to Cuba to resupply, as Cabeza de Vaca suggested, Narváez ordered the expedition to continue on to Florida even though water and other supplies had run low. Upon reaching the Florida coast on April 15, 1528, likely near present-day Tampa, Narváez conducted some initial reconnaissance. Evidently, the Indians' repeated mention of a place called "Apalache," where abundant gold and food could be found proved irresistible to Narváez. Over the objection of Cabeza de Vaca—who urged all of the ships to find safe ports first and the expedition to stay together as they might otherwise never find each other again—Narváez decided to split the expedition into two in order to reconnoiter to the north.

Cabeza de Vaca was conflicted. Rather than being branded a coward by Narváez, he reluctantly joined him and about 300 men and 42 horses. In his written account, De Vaca vividly reveals the disappointments encountered on this ill-conceived *entrada*. He also nicely describes the country, which was lightly populated but otherwise rather barren. According to his *Relación*, the Indians were alternately helpful and menacing. Regarding the latter, it was on this reconnaissance part of the expedition in La Florida that De Vaca learned firsthand about Indian arrows that could penetrate armor.

Cabeza de Vaca's written narrative continues on an increasingly grim trajectory. Near starvation, the group decided to head straight to the nearby Gulf and make rafts to sail west to the Rio Pánuco. Narváez figured it was about fifty miles to that part of Mexico—a gross underestimate as it was closer to 900 miles. Although a map attributed to Alonso de Pineda (1519) would have clarified the shape of the Gulf of Mexico,[3] and the great distances involved, Narváez was either unaware of it or thought he had a better understanding. To make matters worse, the carpenter had been left behind, so they had to build rafts as best they could. As they would soon learn, these were not very sea worthy.

It is here in Florida, at this sorry state of affairs, that the movie begins in earnest. Although De Vaca's written account does not openly criticize Narváez, perhaps to avoid offending authorities, the film savages him. According to many sources, Narváez singled out De Vaca for the toughest and most dangerous jobs. As they were trying to head west to Mexico the barges (as he called them) briefly come into shouting distance of each other, one carrying an exhausted De Vaca and other commanded by Narváez, who had the strongest men with him. In the written account, when De Vaca's group asks for some strong sailors for help, the offer is declined by Narváez: "He replied that it was no longer a time when one should command another; that each must do as he thought best to save himself; that that was what he was doing now. So saying he pulled away in his barge."

In the movie, however, although Narváez (Beau Melanson) says and does much the same, he adds the startling declaration: "Spain ends here!" This terse statement sheds light on Narváez's selfishness and arrogance, but goes much farther toward not only foreshadowing a crisis developing in Cabeza de Vaca's mind, but also the intentions of the filmmaker himself. In the film, a friar with Cabeza de Vaca tells Narváez: "Here ends your hope of salvation." As Narváez pulls farther away, he snidely adds the sarcastic words to the effect, have a good voyage. As is by now evident, the script was not only based on the historic written sources but also supplemented and embellished by a faster moving and highly dramatized script written by director Echevarría and Guillermo Sherman.

That cinematic statement "Spain ends here" beautifully symbolizes the geographical and political implications of Narváez' arrogance: the mission is now out of the hands of a European power and in the hands of fate. As it would turn out, it was those survivors who would make history, in the process immortalizing themselves and casting doubt on both the competence and character of Narváez. That same memorable cinematic quote about Spain ending is also a subliminal nod to Mexico's ultimate separation from Iberia and a hint that the plot (like that in *The Other Conquest*) will center on the relationship between freer thinking Spaniards and the Indians they encounter. It is at this point that Cabeza de Vaca's story takes flight as it develops into a highly original [Latin] American tale. Now free from the tyranny of arbitrary central authority, Cabeza de Vaca is ready to come into his own as one of the most remarkable explorers in history.

As Cabeza de Vaca's raft touches ground safely, he and the ragtag crew are thankful to be alive but beginning to take stock of their desperate situation. The sea has offered them only hazards, so they decide to walk ashore and begin exploring. Among them is Estevanico (Gerardo Villarreal), a slave called the Moor, who was born in North Africa. Being one of the more intrepid of the crew, Estevanico carefully walks into a forest, where he encounters an unsettling sight—a bloody, feathered effigy-like object hanging from a tree branch. Alarmed, the friar among them named Suárez (Farnesio de Bernal) wields his cross, proclaiming, "There's witchcraft at work here." Everything about this scene— its lighting, grisly imagery, suspense, timing—owes a debt to horror films. They soon discover blood dripping from a tree, where they spy a bloody bone dripping. In large boxes that the men recognize as from one of the other rafts, they discover the mutilated remains of their co-expeditionists. Horrified, Fray Suárez demands that their remains be burned. However, the others including Cabeza de Vaca protest, claiming it would be

The Mexican film *Cabeza de Vaca* (1991) depicts the epic journey of that sixteenth-century explorer on the fringes of New Spain. Shipwrecked on the coast of Florida, a group led by Cabeza de Vaca readies itself to explore inland. As the positioning of figures in this scene suggests, the man of African descent named Estevaníco (Gerardo Villareal) will play a significant role in the film—though he was only occasionally mentioned in the original historical records of the expedition (Concorde-New Horizons).

sacrilegious. The latter urges that they should flee—immediately. Fray Suárez has his way, and a funeral pyre is soon burning. At this point, hostile Indians attack and inflict serious casualties. The scene of the mortally wounded friar walking away, his back bristling with arrows, is simply unforgettable. Symbolically, he walks toward the light as an enveloping darkness closes in. This scene foreshadows the martyrdom that some religious figures would face as Spain sought to colonize the Indians. Although there was no such scene in the written accounts, director Echevarría uses it here to stunning effect.

The next scene finds the group, now captured by the Indians, being taken to communities near the shoreline. Held in cages, they are terrified as the Indians poke at and otherwise intimidate them. In the film, they are separated and Cabeza de Vaca is taken far away by canoe. Before he goes, he yells to his comrades: "To the Pánuco—Always to the West!" Even though no map is used in the film, that geographic direction serves as their goal; by individually heading west, they will not only complete the trip but also return to civilization. In this part of the film, Echevarría elected to have Cabeza de Vaca serve as the sole representative of the expedition.

Now beginning his life as a slave, he learns firsthand the indignities suffered by the Crown's captured Indians. It is here that a fictionalized character based on the mysterious short man called Mala Cosa (Bad [Evil] Thing) in the *Relación* appears. In the movie, Echevarría transforms Mala Cosa (José Flores) into an armless dwarf with a penchant for verbal abuse. The written account notes that Mala Cosa was a shapeshifting being who wandered through the region visiting local tribes and causing injuries and then healing them, and even appearing as either a man or a woman, but in the movie he is more tangible. Although short of stature, he wields considerable power despite— or perhaps because of—his physical condition. *Cabeza de Vaca* was not the first film to enhance and/or exoticize the appearance of indigenous people encountered, nor would it be the last. In the film, Mala Cosa is cast as Cabeza de Vaca's personal nemesis as he assigns him degrading tasks such as gathering shellfish, constructing shelters, hauling wood like a pack animal, and other hard work. Among these, Cabeza de Vaca has to hand-feed Mala Cosa, who is highly abusive and extremely ungrateful. In one scene, Cabeza de Vaca gently hand feeds Mala Cosa, who spits a mouthful of food into his face.

Unlike the Mala Cosa in the written *Relación*, the cinematic counterpart is in close alliance with a shaman or sorcerer who wields even more power. In one memorable scene, as the shaman draws a circle in the sand, Cabeza de Vaca tries to escape from

In *Cabeza de Vaca* (1991), the film's namesake explorer (right, played by Juan Diego) is imprisoned by and must serve the Indian dwarf called Mala Cosa (José Flores) who wields considerable power and exercises it mercilessly. Filmmaker Nicolás Echevarría made very effective use of locations along the coast of Mexico to depict this part of Spanish Florida in the 1500s, including its Indigenous villages (Concorde–New Horizons).

Mala Cosa by running wildly along shallow waterways and through dense, jungle-like vegetation. Simultaneously, this shamanic sorcerer has tied a lizard to a stake and harasses it, the lizard ultimately winding up closer to the stake as it tries to flee. Finally, the lizard winds up close to the stake and unable to move. For his part, Cabeza de Vaca continues his headlong flight, thrashing through reeds and splashing through shallow estuaries as he tries to put distance between himself and his captors. He seeks freedom by running as far away as possible—but unwittingly winds up back at that very location, face to face with the tethered lizard! Very powerful dark magic appears to be at work here, and it dramatizes Cabeza de Vaca's hopelessness.

So trapped, Cabeza de Vaca finally lashes out. He has reached the breaking point and has a full-blown, ideologically charged tantrum. This Spaniard's melt-down is pivotal and worth some closer analysis. Screaming at Mala Cosa that "I am more human than you!" he declares that he represents the King and God, and that Spain has dominion over all of the Indies. Suddenly, though, Cabeza de Vaca seems to realize that he is in the hands of God and that everything is happening for a reason, even if unimaginable to him. It is an epiphany, and confirms his deeper spirituality. It also underscores the power of his captors and above all his need to adapt rather than resist.

In another impressive scene that follows. Cabeza de Vaca witnesses the shaman make a large pictographic representation of a tall human figure, part of which is under-water. Significantly, the camera rises to reveal the outline of the figure and its position, its head underwater. The high camera angle suggests a cosmic view of what is occurring. The shaman then wades into the water and uses a long stick to spear the eye of the figure. A moment later, but far away, a hapless Indian man emerges from the water else-where grasping his face and screaming in pain from a serious eye injury. The injury is more than coincidental as it figures as a major turning point in the plot as the scene shifts to a village, to which the injured man returns, his howls of pain causing wide-spread consternation.

Despite considerable effort, the villagers are unable to help the wounded man, who appears to be sliding toward death. At this point, Cabeza de Vaca begins to help after entering into a trance, perhaps induced by peyote. In remarkable scenes, he becomes almost rubber-like as he swirls around seemingly possessed by a mysterious force. He then lays an open hand on the Indian's swollen eye and seems to pull out some-thing unseen but malignant. In the *Relación*, Cabeza de Vaca has a chapter on "how we became medicine-men," but the film positions him as the major healer. When the man quickly heals, Cabeza de Vaca is given his freedom. Now, sensing his power and perhaps regretting his mistreatment of Cabeza de Vaca, Mala Cosa is saddened at his depar-ture. In an insightful essay titled "The Spaniard and the Dwarf," Lauren Eisner notes: "The conquistador Cabeza de Vaca and the dwarf Malacosa [sic] are an unlikely pair, but Echevarría moves them through a series of stages in which they are both transformed."[4] In a sense, this film is about exploration as transformation of both the explorer and the explored.

That transformational scene of a now-free Cabeza de Vaca is literally pivotal as it occurs about half-way into the film and marks a sharp divide in the plot and geographic location. By this time, he has experienced something described in the *Relación*, but glossed over in the film. While deep in the Texas interior, he makes a transition, as noted by Alan J. Silva: "As Cabeza de Vaca becomes a participant observer, or 'goes native,' he gradually transforms the colonizing self of the Florida parts of the narrative into a middle phase between self and Other."[5] In this regard, Echevarría has done what many filmmakers do, namely compress both chronological time and re-arrange geographical space to keep the story moving.

Almost with a jolt, that pivotal scene opens with Cabeza de Vaca finding his way through a rocky desert wilderness, looking much like a prophet from the Bible. The weather soon takes a turn for the worst. As it begins snowing, he shivers uncontrollably, desperately trying to wrap himself in furs but losing the battle against the bitter cold. He will need a miracle in order to survive and the audience is about to witness one. In the *Relación*, Cabeza de Vaca mentions an Indian lighting a bush on fire, but that happened closer to the Texas coast. In the film, an Indigenous man is shown lighting a fire, but not in proximity to any vegetation. Instead, it depicts Cabeza de Vaca facing away from the camera toward the tree and himself summoning it to ignite by uttering the same words as the Indigenous man who sparked a fire moments before.

This is another example of the cinematic Cabeza de Vaca adopting, or perhaps even co-opting, a shaman's power. However, it also links the Spaniard to a similar event described in the Bible, namely Moses and the burning bush (Exodus 3). In that version,

Films treating the process of exploration and discovery often involve a transformation of the explorer. The scenes in *Cabeza de Vaca* that were shot in the interior states of Coahuila and Durango, Mexico, helped confirm his transformation into a shamanistic healer. In this scene, he appears much like a wandering biblical prophet holding a staff and clad in animal skins. This costume and arid mountainous setting are reminiscent of Moses in the wilderness. Importantly, this scene prepares the audience for miraculous events that will soon follow (Concorde-New Horizons).

God does the igniting and the fire is symbolic of a force that lights the way to salvation. In the film, this act saves Cabeza de Vaca's life. As the fire increasingly consumes the tree, he removes his makeshift mittens and embraces the warmth, having summoned and harnessed spiritual power to survive. This is yet another way that Echevarría casts Cabeza de Vaca as a towering religious figure.

Viewed metaphorically, the story of this small group's survival is always a balancing act between the self (Cabeza de Vaca) and the Other, both the Indigenous people and his vastly diminished rag-tag band of comrades. Throughout the story, Cabeza de Vaca is leading the men entrusted to him—whether they are physically present or not. Here, in this desert region, he is miraculously reunited with several comrades, including Estevanico, Alonso del Castillo (Carlos Castañón), Andrés Dorantes de Carranza (Daniel Giménez Cacho) and Esquivel. The latter had been on another raft but fate brought them together. In the *Relación*, this happens much earlier, and much farther east along the Texas coast, but director Echevarría sees something magical and spiritual in the desert itself, and stages that moving reunion here.

The film is more explicit in other matters as well. In a scene that film seems especially adept at depicting—bantering—the irreverent Esquivel is said to have eaten other comrades after they died. Still in charge, Cabeza de Vaca inquires to determine whether this is true. Ever the devious rascal, Esquivel cynically tells Cabeza de Vaca about the fate of an expedition member named Pantoja: "If your Lordship would like to see him again you can wait till I shit. Perhaps you'll recognize something." This is simultaneously irreverent and humorous, but then again is a metaphorical way of saying that this expedition can transform men into something not only unrecognizable but also objectionable.

Cannibalism in the wilderness of what would become Latin America, including here on the northern extremities of New Spain, has long fascinated Spanish explorers. It also titillated readers back in Europe, who had a deep fascination with the forbidden topics an expedition might encounter. For the record, Cabeza de Vaca's account appears to be the first mention of it in print, for it notes that some of the expedition's deceased members suffered that fate when consumed by their famished comrades. It further notes that Indians were horrified by this cannibalism, which they found inconceivable. This is all the more ironic because early on in the film, the captured members of the expedition are worried about being eaten by their Indian captors—never realizing that they might make a meal for their own comrades. At every turn in the tale of *Cabeza de Vaca*, both in the original written accounts and on film, it becomes increasingly apparent that the line between civilization and savagery is not only fine, but becoming more and more blurred.

Within a short time, all of the surviving expedition members wind up being prisoners again and are about to be killed when warfare breaks out between tribes. Estevanico helps free them, but Esquivel is among the casualties, and now only four survivors remain. In the film version of this survival tale, Cabeza de Vaca becomes fast friends with a young man named Ariano, whom he saves by miraculously removing an arrow point lodged deep within his belly. Ariano will later die and be beyond revival, and Cabeza de Vaca will be almost inconsolable with grief. Cinema specializes in delivering intimate scenes like these. From another victim beyond help, Cabeza de Vaca removes a round object they determine to be a Spanish musket ball. He is now experiencing a forensic clue—the foreshadowing of Spanish atrocities—a hint they are getting closer to home.

Although the *Relación* makes amply clear that Cabeza de Vaca is a devout believer in God, the movie makes him far more. The film not only recognizes his experiences as a faith healer, which he comments on in the book as something that endeared him and others in his group to the Indians. In the film, he is also able to perform actual miracles. Even though the *Relación* discusses him helping an Indian man seeming to be dead but who survived, a stunning scene in the film takes such healing a few steps further, and even changes the gender of the individual involved. The scene in question begins as a funeral procession passes by in a small pueblo, solemnly carrying the body of a young woman who died some time ago. The mourners are covered in a clay-like mud that harmonizes with the adobe architecture of this region. As Cabeza de Vaca interrupts the ceremony, he meticulously examines her body after slowly removing her shroud. At this point, a member of his group says, "There's nothing you can do." Nevertheless, he proceeds to perform arcane rites that result in his pulling a white, rounded, fist-size stone from under her hands. He tells the doubters that by looking into this stone, one can see she is alive. Within moments, she is seen walking out of the building, to everyone's amazement.

This sensational scene reveals that Cabeza de Vaca has become a geomancer able to read signs in objects from the earth, and it terribly frightens his group. They may be wondering: *Is this the kind of witchcraft that Fray Suárez had warned us about earlier?*

In this pivotal scene from *Cabeza de Vaca* (1991), a funeral procession in a desert pueblo provides the namesake explorer (center, with staff) with an opportunity to bring the dead back to life—as Jesus did with Lazarus. The dead woman lies under a blanket, and she is flanked by pallbearers whose skin is covered with dry mud or powder. The film sets captured the essence of Indigenous adobe architecture, confirming that the explorers had traveled far from the Florida coast on their way back to the Pacific coast of Mexico (Concorde-New Horizons).

For their part, Estevanico and the others are also shaken to the core because Cabeza de Vaca has done what Jesus did to Lazarus (John 11, 1–14), namely bring the dead back to life. Blissfully unaware of any potential conflicts with Judeo-Christian traditions, the entire village rejoices at the miracle. At about this point in the film, the four comrades begin wondering how they will relate their experiences if and when they finally return to civilization. The one who understands this best is Estevanico, but they all come to the realization that "We'd better stop talking about magic if we are going back to Christian lands."

The time spent among these seemingly more advanced tribes has an idyllic quality as well, at least in some scenes. One of his comrades now begins a relationship with a young woman, a reminder that encountering the Other often has a sexual dimension. Not a word is spoken as they engage in this intimacy, an ingenious way of confirming that some forms of communication transcend the barrier of language. For his part, Cabeza de Vaca remains steadfastly celibate and above earthly temptation—no doubt a reflection of his being the most spiritual of the group. The *Relación* shies away from such sensual subjects, but filmmakers often find them irresistible.

Toward the end of the film, the four survivors are shown trekking through a vast desert. They are heading toward the South Sea (Pacific Ocean) but losing their bearings. As the comrades straggle along, hope for their survival begins to fade. However, as if in a mirage, they are overjoyed to see four Spanish soldiers on horseback riding toward them. Alas, their joy turns to fear as the soldiers assume they are Indians, and start brutally rounding them up. Finally, they convince the Spaniards that they are the survivors of the long-lost expedition. Cabeza de Vaca is now dismayed to learn that the very Indians who had welcomed them into their villages so warmly are now being enslaved by the Spaniards. To make matters worse, they are being forced to build a cathedral, another reminder of the Church's role in the conquest. When Cabeza de Vaca challenges the commander, reminding him that his faith should not permit this slavery, he threatens to imprison him. Cabeza de Vaca has now come face to face with the reality of the Spanish conquest of Mexico, and he is appalled. When the commander demands to know on what authority Cabeza de Vaca speaks, he simply answers "faith."

In the movie, he and Estevanico now defiantly agree to tell the truth about what they have experienced. However, the others in the expedition begin to spin yarns about things such as golden cities and rivers of honey. When one of the Spaniards begin asking "Have you seen the golden cities?" one of the group says, "Yes." He then adds a sexually charged boast that he has personally "fucked Indians with three tits." Otherwise, he says they are just like other women—in other words, well equipped. The soldiers chuckle in a bawdy macho manner that can still be heard in the same region about five hundred years later. "Three tits?" Cabeza de Vaca exclaims incredulously, and then begins laughing at the absurdity of it all. When the bantering conversation begins conflating the "golden city, golden rivers, and golden women," they are asked, "Where? When? Tell us!" Their answer—"To the north"—is a reference to future expeditions such as the one involving Fray Marcos de Niza and Estevanico himself—the latter whose search for fabled cities would become part of the folklore of the American Southwest.

Regarding Estevanico, more properly or respectfully known as Esteban (or Estevan), ethnicity will always be a factor worth more scrutiny. This is further complicated by his evidently being a Moor, and likely Muslim who may have converted to Christianity. In the *Relación*, Cabeza de Vaca treats him dismissively and tolerably by turns, while in the film Echevarría treats him better, and seemingly downplays his racial difference. On the other hand, in that role he serves as an intermediary as he is both one of the explorers and yet always the Other. To his credit, Echevarría seems to sense that this slave of African descent has deeper insights than anyone else in the group of four survivors. If and when a dramatic film is made about Esteban's subsequent exploration to the north, it will hopefully take into account his complex identity and considerable accomplishments as what Dennis Herrick calls "The African Slave who Explored America."[6]

The film ends with a strange sight, several dozen Spanish soldiers escorting a huge (ca. fifty-foot tall) silver-colored cross through the desert. To facilitate its transport, the cross is being transported in a horizontal position. It is so large that it dwarfs the men carrying it, and the entourage brings to mind a metallic caterpillar moving slowly but steadily across the landscape. As it moves along, a distant thunderstorm over the mountains darkens the skies and sends down columns of rain. This scene has an apocalyptic quality—a fitting end to Echevarría's surreal vision of Christianity's arrogant but tenuous presence in a formidable landscape.

Although Echevarría absolves Cabeza de Vaca of all responsibility for the oppression of Indians, the *Relación* leaves things a bit more open-ended, and him not quite off the hook, at least according to literary critics. Among them, Alan Silva concluded: "Despite everything Cabeza de Vaca learns from the natives, he still maintains a certain ethnocentric and racist construction of 'difference' (Christian vs. Pagan) because he can only understand what he learns through a language that constructs 'knowledge' (of the Other) through categories of difference."[7] That said, Echevarría cuts him far more slack and provides him with a heroic trans-cultural identity.

In retrospect, this film takes some remarkable liberties with history and geography. Fully half of Cabeza de Vaca's journey took place along the northern Gulf coastal plain from Florida to Texas. It is a sweeping area that begins with lush vegetation and transitions into semi-arid grassland as one moves westward, and finally into true desert as we know the term today: areas with little or no vegetation. Topographically, the first half of his journey took him into remarkably flat country, especially for a Spaniard, and this may have been disorienting. After all, it was the Spaniards who named (or rather re-named) the Llano Estacado (Staked Plain) of west Texas, likely in light of the tall yucca plant stems that broke the monotony and made it easier to judge distances in an otherwise oceanic expanse of short grass. Of this entire vast area, Cabeza de Vaca's *Relación* makes clear: "We saw no mountains,"[8] Yet, because the film was shot along the coast in western Mexico, mountains often appear on the horizon. This discrepancy, of course, may be something only a geographer might find fault with, but it subtly compromises the agoraphobia-generating flatness of the landscape described in the first half of the *Relación*.

Of geographical interest here is that Echevarría's film neglects a significant aspect of the vegetation encountered by Cabeza de Vaca. Surprisingly, it does not mention, nor show the use of, the nopal, or prickly pear cactus (*Opuntia* sp.) as well as other cacti that Cabeza de Vaca comments on repeatedly in his writings. Columbus first commented on cacti, for they are as indigenous to the Americas as the Indios he described. Having first originated in South America about a million years ago, cacti proliferated throughout both continents.[9] Despite Echevarría's cinematic omission of these plants, Cabeza de Vaca says they sustained both the Indians and the travelers, their delicious fruits (*tunas*) reminding him of figs. As he makes clear, these cacti sometimes meant the difference between survival and starvation. For the record, the *Relación* appears to be the first published reference to cacti in all of northern New Spain, and hence all of North America. In Mexico's long history, they are so relevant that they now form a part of the nation's coat of arms—a branching prickly pear atop which an eagle perches with a snake dangling from its beak.

In the second part of the film, with his portrayal of magical realism ever intensifying, Echevarría wonderfully captures events and conditions that might seem impossible, but are transpiring before the eyes of the viewer. Even more down-to-earth scenes capture some remarkable views agreeing with the *Relación*—for example, that "Here we began to see mountains." *Echevarría* makes especially good use of the arid interior of northern Mexico, in which case Coahuila almost seems to double for the Holy Land in places. Moreover, as the film suggests, the cultural diversity increased, or rather intensified, in what the *Relación* now characterized as an "incredibly populous country."[10] Echevarría's depiction of the Indigenous people here, with their stone and adobe architecture and colorful body painting, conveys some of the enchantment we associate with the region today. Cinematically speaking, the depiction of Indians in *Cabeza de Vaca* appears to have influenced Mel Gibson's wonderful body decorations in *Apocalypto*.

Many who study the American Southwest and northern Mexico have long relied on the *Relación* as a source on the region's geography and prehistory. For their part, geographers and others such as Carl Sauer and Clive Hellenbeck nearly a century ago traveled in the footsteps of Cabeza de Vaca—or as close an approximation of those locales as possible given the four centuries that had elapsed. The *Relación*'s failure to mention the columnar cacti, especially the forty-foot-tall saguaro cactus (*Carnegiea gigantea*), seems to confirm that Cabeza de Vaca traveled farther east and south than the Sonoran Desert, and likely kept within the Chihuahuan Desert on this part of their travels. All in all, though, it was a remarkable journey indeed. On both the written page and on screen, there is a compelling quality to this desert region, part of its appeal being a testimony to trans-acculturation.

The journey's connections with Indians helped dispel some myths and mark an auspicious beginning to what we would later call ethnography. It also appears to mark the beginnings of outside observers engrossing themselves in Indigenous cultures. As Cabeza de Vaca himself said about his Avavares and Arbadaos Indians in Texas, "We always went naked like them." One might add: not entirely naked, of course, for few people ever have been that natural, but remarkably so for European Christians. In relation to their exposure to the elements, Cabeza de Vaca noted, "we shed our skins twice a year like snakes."[11] As opposed to their privileged lives in Spain, they learned to make things with their own hands and came to appreciate the simplest of pleasures. Being among the very first ethnographies of this part of the world, the *Relación* is all the more remarkable as it was put together from memory after those eight years had transpired.

Regarding chronology, it should be noted that the *Relación* states: "All of the Indians of this region are ignorant of time, either by the sun or moon; nor do they reckon by the month or year." This marked a startling difference from Europe, which was now becoming more and more engrossed with time and how to measure it. On the other hand, Cabeza de Vaca quickly added: "They understand the seasons in terms of the ripening of fruits, the dying of fish, and the position of stars, in which dating they are adept."[12] Small wonder that Cabeza de Vaca himself lost track of measurable time—hence his near disbelief that he had spent "ocho años" (eight years) when informed by Spaniards as his journey ended. For a filmmaker—who inevitably must live by the clock as a movie is made—Echevarría does a great job of helping the audience lose track of time along with Cabeza de Vaca as he moves through a seemingly timeless land. Although Echevarría's film about these experiences likewise romanticized that epic experience, it nevertheless captures some of the terror and magic embodied in the original accounts.

As historian David Weber concluded in *The Spanish Frontier in North America*, the most significant aspect of Cabeza de Vaca's expedition "…was that the four wanderers, in the course of becoming the first Europeans to cross the continent north of Mesoamerica, saw more of its inhabitants than any of their countrymen and thus excited further exploration." Weber also notes that the published accounts in Spain exaggerated de Vaca's original modest accounts and made "…tantalizing reference to lands to the north where emeralds could be found, and 'where there are towns of great population and great houses.'"[13]

Remarkably, four years after returning to Spain, Cabeza de Vaca headed back to the Americas, this time to South America, where he oversaw the colonization of the interior and its inhabitants. He was known to be sympathetic to the Indians there as well, likely too sympathetic, as it conflicted with the wishes of powerful landowners. He returned to Spain in chains, and died in poverty years later—but not before writing a remarkable account of the interior portion of South America.[14] It is to that vast continent that I shall now turn.

Four

Aguirre, the Wrath of God

Missteps in Sixteenth-Century Colonial Exploration

As noted in the discussion of the films *The Other Conquest* and *Cabeza de Vaca*, Spanish exploration in the New World occurred in the form of *entradas,* organized expeditions whose ultimate aim was conquest. From the earliest period of Spanish exploration in South America, written journals based on explorers' exploits offered glimpses of the obstacles that would be encountered and the fortune that could gained when sought-after places were finally reached. Among the latter were fabled locales such as a spice-rich valley (Valle de Canela or the Valley of Cinnamon) and the fabulously wealthy region and cities where gold reportedly abounded (viz. El Dorado). Although explorers in the northern part of Latin America were also searching for lost cities such as Cíbola at this time, the northern portion of South America had begun to lure explorers since Columbus first glimpsed the continent's northeastern coastline in 1498. Tentative explorations were made into the interior, but began in earnest in the 1520s.

Noteworthy among these were those by Francisco Pizarro (1471–1541) and his brothers (particularly Hernando Pizarro). These conquistadors advanced from the Pacific coast south-eastward into the Andes, culminating in the conquest of the Inca Empire in 1532. That empire was much larger geographically than the Aztec empire. It comprised much of western South America from present-day Ecuador southward into Chile and Argentina. However, it had only about half the population (ca. 12.5 million). Moreover, much of it involved mountainous country that was difficult to traverse. The heart of the Inca Empire was similarly associated with riches, in particular gold and silver, that made it irresistible.

That conquest of the Inca Empire was depicted in a play titled "The Royal Hunt of the Sun" and the 1969 motion picture of the same name. *The Royal Hunt of the Sun*[1] depicts the expedition leaving Spain in 1530, arriving on the sandy shores of Peru, and working its way up into the Andes to the Inca city of Cajamarca. However, for the most part it focuses on the tragic palace intrigue that resulted in the death of Atahualpa and the victory of Spain over the Incas. Not content with victory, the Spaniards used it as a springboard for additional exploration of the interior. The Pizarro expeditions permitted Spain to quickly expand its grip on the continent west of the line demarcated by the Treaty of Tordesillas (1494).

The region's physical geography was astounding. Unbeknownst to Pizarro, the Inca Empire sat astride the world's longest continental mountain range (ca. 7,000 km, or 4,300 miles). Subsequently, numerous expeditions fanned out across the northern and western parts of the continent, including several into the Amazon basin. At that time, these explorers were unaware that they were entering the world's largest river basin, and were about to traverse one of the world's longest rivers. The Amazon is also one of the world's most complex river systems, having 1,100 tributaries, including seventeen that are over 930 miles (1,497 km) long. Much of its vast basin was covered in dense jungle and impressive rain forests.

The first successful *entrada* that Pizarro dispatched to the Amazon was led by Captain Francisco de Orellana in 1540. Accompanying it was the Dominican friar Gaspar de Carvajal (1504–1584), who wrote a chronicle about it that was both documentary and riveting. Titled *Relación del nuevo descubrimiento del famoso rio grande que descubrió por muy gran ventura el capitán Francisco de Orellana* (Account of the recent discovery of the famous grand river discovered by very good fortune by captain Francisco de Orellana) it described previously unknown country. As the expedition explored eastward, it traversed the Amazon River and a number of its tributaries, and ultimately reached the Atlantic. In honor of this expedition, that river was briefly called the Rio de Orellana. In his chronicle, Carvajal claimed that a well-developed civilization existed there, and it featured an extensive system of roads and impressive monuments. In some places where Indigenous resistance was mounted, women fought alongside men. According to some sources, the King noted that women warriors were similarly described by Herodotus, and used their name "Amazon" for the river and the region.[2]

How such expeditions are immortalized in early writings and maps—and then on film—is of interest here. Like many original records, Carvajal's journal languished as later information superseded it. However, this "lost" account was rediscovered in the 1890s by Chilean researcher José Toribio Medina and subsequently published in English about forty years later.[3] Suddenly, a new window into sixteenth-century exploration opened. As fate would have it, Carvajal's account was read by the German filmmaker Werner Herzog,[4] and it is said to be the source of inspiration for one of the great films dealing with the exploration in the Amazon: *Aguirre: der Zorn Gottes* (1972), better known as *Aguirre, the Wrath of God*.[5] Closer to home, another possible source of inspiration for Herzog was the German explorer Ambrosius Ehinger, who explored portions of northern South America in the period 1529–1533.

Another source that inspired Herzog was early maps. By the mid-sixteenth century, the Amazon River was frequently simplified and stylized cartographically, one theme being its serpentine configuration, an evocative form that stimulated the popular imagination. The 1562 *Map of America* by Spanish cartographer Diego Gutiérrez, as masterfully engraved in Antwerp by Hieronymus Cock, exemplifies the almost reptilian cartographic treatment of the Amazon, with its stylized and symmetrically spaced islands emphasizing the river's snake-like shape.

For the record, the expedition reenacted by Herzog in *Aguirre, the Wrath of God* was a different one than that described by Carvajal, namely, the *entrada* mounted in 1560 by Pedro de Ursúa, as documented by Fray Pedro Simón about seventy years after the fact.[6] That later expedition, which proved to be far less successful but far more dramatic, was intended to be something of a safety valve. In Peru at the time, many ambitious and opportunistic men with titles were presenting problems for the Crown. It was hoped that the Ursúa expedition would give these opportunists something to do, and perhaps even discover riches in the process. Finding El Dorado was one of its stated goals. However, from this expedition, the Crown got far more than it expected, all of it the form of trouble. We know about this expedition largely from a later (1600s) manuscript written years after the event, and that passages from it further ensured that myth as well as fact would figure in later telling(s).[7] One thing is certain. In both a literary and cinematic sense, the Ursúa expedition had many elements guaranteed to hold audiences spellbound, among them madness, mutiny, mayhem, and murder. Ensuring this chaos was an expedition member who would become one of the most polarizing characters in Latin American history, namely the ambitious and headstrong Basque soldier named Lope de Aguirre (1510–1561).

A brief synopsis of that expedition will help readers better understand the plot of Herzog's film. Under the command of Don Pedro de Ursúa the expedition headed eastward out of the Peruvian Andes in search of the cities of Omagua and El Dorado. As it descended the mountains, it followed the Marañón River, a major tributary of the Amazon. The expedition encountered setbacks such as raging waters and recalcitrant Indians, and the soldiers becoming increasingly disenchanted. Trouble began in earnest as the expedition's command commenced to break down under the mounting dissension of Aguirre. Things went from bad to worse, and Aguirre assumed command. It soon became apparent that Aguirre was not only a tyrant but also had delusions of grandeur. In addition to executing several expedition members, he also renounced the King's claim to the areas being explored, and announced that he was now sovereign. A scathing letter written by Aguirre to King Philip II of Spain left no doubt about Aguirre's intentions. This, it should be noted, was a seminal event in Latin American history. Although internecine struggles characterized early Spanish *entradas*, the hijacking of one in defiance of the Crown itself was intolerable.

The story of Aguirre was the subject of Spanish language narratives, but the film *Aguirre, the Wrath of God* both visualized it and catapulted it into breathless action. Werner Herzog oversaw almost all aspects of this film's production. In addition to his title of producer-director, he also wrote the screenplay. Herzog was a newcomer at the time, but has subsequently become well-known for creating films depicting nature at its most stubborn, and visionary men at the edge of sanity.

The casting in this film was crucial, and Herzog oversaw that as well. Nominally in control of the expedition, its namesake Pedro de Ursúa (Ruy Guerra) personifies uncertainty and weakness. The expedition was composed of soldiers, civilians, and a friar. However, in the film Herzog included the friar Gaspar de Carvajal (played by Del Negro). Some historians might consider this inappropriate, but artistically speaking it involves real genius, for Herzog embeds a trusted authority and thus lends veracity to his story. The star of the film (Klaus Kinski) puts in a performance that is both mesmerizing and frightening. Viewers soon forget the incongruity of a blond, German-speaking Spanish conquistador running amok in sixteenth-century South America. To his credit, Herzog seems to stand back and respect Aguirre's wild trajectory. Viewers and expedition members alike cannot take their eyes off Kinski-as-Aguirre because he becomes increasingly more deranged and dangerous with each tortured league the expedition travels and with each foot of film shot.

As so chronicled, the story on film seems to have the quality of an edgy documentary. In this film we witness what Herzog later described in his famous "Minnesota Declaration" (1999): "There are deeper strata of truth in cinema and there is such a thing as poetic, ecstatic truth. It is mysterious and elusive, and can be reached only through fabrication and imagination and stylization."[8] To Herzog, truth may be found in varied dimensions and detour from strict rationality even to the verge of becoming a lie. In watching his films, audiences are asked to believe what is transpiring although it may seem at odds with scientific or objective truth. The key lies in winning the audience's trust as the film unfolds.

Filmed on location in Peru, *Aguirre, the Wrath of God* captures the perplexing topography, convoluted hydrography, and dense vegetation of the vast portion of South America lying east of the Andes. It opens leisurely, with a voice-over that sets the scene, a startling statement that it was the Indians who invented the legend of El Dorado in response to the Spaniard's first brutal encounters with them. That statement is prescient because Herzog's goal is to not only position man against nature, but also man against man.

The audience's first glimpse of the scenery reveals a dimly lit, mist-shrouded, mountainous region. Visually speaking, this opening scene is so disorienting that the viewer needs a few seconds to make sense of it. What at first appears to be a dark land-scape with a nearly flat horizon—but entirely rotated 90 degrees, which is to say tipped on its side—soon comes into focus as the dark mass of the mountain on the left, with its nearly vertical drop off to the right at which the cloudy sky hangs like a blanket. A closer look reveals an ant-like procession of people descending this nearly sheer cliff on a nar-row trail. The effect of this scene is stunning, for the trail seems to be dangling next to the sky. As the expedition works its way down this steep slope, viewers feel that they too are struggling to keep their balance.

These dizzying scenes were shot along the "Stairway of Death" at Huayna Picchu, Peru, and they reveal the toil involved in keeping items of civilization—including can-nons, palanquins (sedan chairs), and crates of material—from tumbling down into the wilderness abyss below. Some members are Spaniards and many are Indians, which is to say former Incas from the mountains now hauling loads like beasts of burden for the Spanish conquerors. In one scene, a cannon plunges into a ravine and blows up, per-haps symbolically suggesting that things are about to explode. The perilous vertical-ity of the trail not only emphasizes the expedition's daring descent topographically, but also symbolically as well. The expedition's descent will involve moral decline because a catastrophic breakdown in civil behavior is about to occur. The verticality soon yields to horizontality as the expedition reaches the Amazon River valley, where the country begins to open up into a series of hills but the rain forest and jungle becomes thicker.

It is here that Herzog assembles most of the important characters in one place for the first time—a portrait of Spanish explorers surrounded by dense vegetation and increasingly bickering among themselves. This group scene is worth a more penetrat-ing look. Given that motion pictures often accentuate action, the sedate, portrait-like nature of this scene is arresting. In composing it, Herzog built on a long artistic tradi-tion dating from the Renaissance in which people and their places in society are treated symbolically. At the center of this scene, a seated and almost slumping figure, wealthy nobleman Don Fernando Guzmán (Peter Berling) symbolizes the Crown's belief in the power assigned to its administrative leadership, in this case Ursúa's increasingly chal-lenged authority. The two figures flanking this throne-like seat are key to the expedition. Like most of the group they are standing, but of greater importance to the functioning of the expedition than the others. To the right, the robe-clad padre Carvajal (Del Negro) symbolizes the power of religion, in particular the Catholic Church. To the left stands the armor-clad Aguirre, never motionless for long and in fact already making demands.

A portrait-like scene from Werner Herzog's *Aguirre, the Wrath of God* (1972) centers on three symbols of Spain's power. The seated figure Don Fernando Guzmán (Peter Berling) represents civil authority. To the right stands the tall padre Gaspar de Carvajal (Del Negro), who represents religious authority. To the left, the armor-clad Aguirre (Klaus Kinski) represents the military, his posture and gesture suggesting urgency. Standing passively at the far left is Aguirre's daughter Doña Flores (Cecilia Rivera) (Werner Herzog Filmproduktion).

Almost encircling these three central figures are the expedition members who represent strength and discipline, at least ideally.

One figure in this scene seems out of place on a gritty expedition into the wilderness—a young woman almost regally dressed. Herzog included two women on the expedition—Aguirre's daughter Flores (Cecilia Rivera) and Ursúa's mistress Doña Inés (Helena Rojo). Symbolically, in this scene, Flores is standing behind her father, who has plans for her as he will bend the rules to suit his personal and familial gains. On this expedition, both of these women add an element of civility. In such male-driven adventures, the presence of women always adds an undercurrent of sexual tension, for they are widely considered weaker and more vulnerable, and objects of desire by an all-male crew. The fact that these women are closely related to the story's two major protagonists (Ursúa and Aguirre) further adds to the tension.

The jungle surrounding the figures in this scene will soon become a major character in the film. The decision of how to travel in an environment that seems to be trackless and full of obstacles such as dense, impenetrable vegetation is crucial. They soon conclude that their only option appears to be making rafts in hopes of navigating the river. Chopping down some tall trees along the river yields the logs they will need. The completed rafts will be essential to their success in getting down-river, but the problem of controlling those rafts has not been taken into account. As soon as they are launched, gravity takes over and sweeps them downstream toward the distant Atlantic Ocean. Along the way, the expedition witnesses the river's many countenances, from raging rapids in some places to stretches of quieter water in others.

In reality, filming took place on three rivers in Peru: the Urubamba, the Huallaga and the Nanay; they are tributaries to, and stand-ins for, the generic "Amazon." In this film and many others, waterfalls and rapids serve not only as breaks in the topography but also as junctures or turning points in the story. At one point where rapids defy it, the expedition loses several members who become trapped as their raft is unable to break free; on board, in-fighting claims several of them. Finally, in an effort to break the raft free, cannon fire has a disastrous outcome. Despite such setbacks, the expedition forges ahead. Traveling down the hazardous river and establishing camping places, they occasionally hack their way through dense jungle clothed in deep shadows.

Along the way, they encounter far less tame Indians; most are never actually seen in the film, though in a glimpse here and there they reveal two identities. Some simply gaze at the expedition mysteriously and then disappear, while others offer resistance in defense of their territory. In one terrifying scene, Indians snare expedition members, who are looped by the legs and sent spinning upward and left hanging upside down to be slaughtered.

The Amazon River plays a major role in *Aguirre, the Wrath of God* (1972). After constructing rafts, the expedition used the river system to explore the country encountered along the Amazon's course as it flowed toward the Atlantic Ocean. Filmmaker Werner Herzog used three tributary rivers to the Amazon in Peru—the Urubamba, the Huallaga, and the Nanay—to portray the river in its various countenances, from placid and easily traveled to whitewater filled with perils. In this scene, the expedition has easy going as the river widens after leaving mountainous territory (Werner Herzog Filmproduktion).

Their adversaries are virtually invisible, and silent as well, but lethal. In another later scene, an Indian couple bravely paddles out to one of the rafts. The man and woman are featured in close up views that have an almost ethnographic quality. He is dressed like the jaguar that he believes himself to be, and says he foretold the arrival of these men who create "thunder made with tubes." By this he means cannons, with which Aguirre is associated throughout the film. Meanwhile the Indian woman, who is dressed "immodestly" as the Spaniards often claimed, remains silent as a witness to what will soon transpire.

When the Indian man is offered the bible by Carvajal, he is expecting to hear the voice of God in it. Bewildered, he puts the book to his ear, shakes it, but hears nothing and swiftly throws it down in disgust. As noted by Stewart Brewer, Herzog here may be conflating this disobedience with an earlier incident in Peru in which Atahualpa himself had thrown down a copy of the *Requerimiento* in disgust—and paid the ultimate price for it.[9] In the film, Carvajal becomes enraged and the Indian is slaughtered for his defiance in rejecting the gospel. It is a brutal scene that underscores the religious fanaticism involved in these early colonial encounters. However, in keeping with what occurs in many dramatized accounts, this scene is based more on Herzog's imagination than any verified historical records of encounters in this far-eastern part of Peru. That said, it still epitomizes the zeal of colonization and the dire consequences of resistance.

In this scene from *Aguirre, the Wrath of God* (1972) an intrepid Indian (uncredited appearance) who has paddled out to meet the explorers is about to question how the bible literally contains the word of God—and pay the ultimate price for his skepticism. In making this film, Werner Herzog employed many Indigenous people from several tribes—a relatively new approach as many filmmakers used actors disguised as natives to play parts (Werner Herzog Filmproduktion).

Herzog effectively makes the point that these Indians were understandably suspicious of, and alarmed by, the intruders. However, the expedition members view them as one of the forces of nature that threaten from every quarter. These Indigenous tribes were subsisting in an environment that the Spaniards hoped to subdue. They practiced agriculture, but the soil was easily exhausted and they moved about to new areas where they felled trees, set fire to them, and raised crops such as manioc from the ashes. They were also skilled fishermen. Wary of outsiders and skilled at hunting game as well, they could just as easily turn their hunting skills on the invaders. To play these denizens of the rain forest Herzog hired members of two local tribes, the Aguaruna and Lauramarca. This casting added a level of authenticity heretofore unseen in dramatic films set in the region. Herzog himself had a great deal of sympathy for these Indigenous peoples, whom he viewed as endangered by progress.

Herzog also vividly re-imagines geographical boundaries in parts of this film. Although he envisions an abrupt divide between Andean and Amazonian cultures, recent archeological study reveals that the boundary between the advanced cultures of the Andean highlands and the more subsistence-oriented tribes to the east was not as distinct as it is often portrayed. The site of Kuelap in Peru's Utcubamba River Valley, with terraced cultivation of potatoes, spectacular funerary sculpture, and many shared customs is changing perceptions. As archaeologist Parker Van Valkenburgh puts it, "We used to think of the Andes and Amazon as being these two entirely separate worlds. But research is showing they were deeply interlinked."[10]

Another noteworthy aspect of this film is how the expedition confronts the natural world. Typically, explorers on the early *entradas* attempted to make some sense out of the natural history as knowledge about the locale could sustain them as well. In this film, however, Aguirre seems to view nature symbolically. For example, when he spies a sloth in the forest along the riverbank, he almost wistfully yet wryly tells his daughter that the sloth sleeps its life away. So identified, this animal appears to symbolize the cultural conflict between the explorers and the explored. In this regard, Aguirre may be comparing the torpid sloth to the Indigenous people, who are seemingly unproductive, at least compared to enterprising and agitated Europeans/Spaniards. Then again, Aguirre may be comparing the sloth to his misanthropic vision of humankind itself, which is to say its docility and blind compliance to established authority—at least according to his hypercritical standards and increasingly aggressive behavior.

As adventure films go, *Aguirre, the Wrath of God* is riveting, but I will only describe a few more of the most memorable scenes here. In one, the startled expedition encounters a European sailing vessel stranded high in the branches of a tree. Both the explorers and the viewer can only wonder about the miscalculations or natural forces that brought that vessel to grief, but it is a surreal reminder of failure that Herzog uses to foreshadow the fate of the Ursúa expedition. In keeping with the premise that literature impacts cinema, the scene may have been inspired by another sixteenth-century Spanish account that Herzog had read, namely, Cabeza de Vaca's *Relación*. In the previous chapter, readers will recall that Spanish explorer's reference to finding the small boat stranded high in the treetops after a Caribbean hurricane. However, given the vessel's imaginative increase in size in the film *Aguirre, the Wrath of God*, the scene may also owe a debt to an experience described by Gabriel García Márquez in *One Hundred years of Solitude*. In that work of fiction, the wreck of a Spanish galleon startles an expedition trudging through dense jungle far from the ocean, which "seemed to occupy its own space, one of solitude and oblivion...."[11] The haunting specter of an out-of-place vessel lingers in the mind years afterward, regardless of whether it was read about in a book, or viewed on film. In *Aguirre, the Wrath of God*, that surreal scene works beautifully and embodies an air of magical realism—a stylistic ingredient in twentieth-century Latin American literature that blurs the distinction between reality and imaginary. Ironically, some attribute the origins of magic(al) realism to German art in the 1920s.[12] Therefore, in Herzog's imagination, a surreal scene like this may have had artistic/visual roots closer to home; that, coupled with his avid reading of contemporary South American literature, such as that passage from the Gabriel García Márquez novel, may help explain this scene's presence in a film set on that continent.

In another memorable scene, a horse accompanying the expedition begins to become a liability, at least according to those in charge. As the men try to get the horse off the raft, it threatens to overturn it and pitch explorers and supplies into the river. With each step, the horse brings the raft closer to catastrophe. Finally, the horse is jettisoned, but the audience can only wonder what will happen to it in this jungle wilderness. The scene is poignant and symbolic: an animal meant to loyally serve the expedition is now useless, much like the mission itself. Watching this risky scene unfold, one wonders how it was even made without casualties. In the last view of the horse, the dumbfounded creature stands in water at river's edge, looking back forlornly and awaiting one of many fates we can only imagine. In scenes like this one, Herzog is a master at making the audience momentarily forget that cameras are running. Those with an eye toward cinema realize how masterfully the camera works in this film, almost like a silent member of the cast who is relentlessly revealing the damning actions and secrets of its (other) characters.

With no holds barred, *Aguirre, the Wrath of God* immerses the viewer in the action and drama of an expedition going awry. As astutely noted by Gregory A. Waller, "Herzog not only examines Aguirre's sense of history and theater, but also makes us recognize the camera's role as participant in this expedition and explores the camera's relationship to the forging of history...." In this film, history and geography are inseparable; the former is playing out on an indifferent stage of the latter, which consists of dense jungle rising from the relentless river system. Herzog bathes the entire film in a bluish-gray light that reduces visibility and emphasizes the claustrophobic quality of the environment.

The expedition itself represents a human society tenuously held together by a mission that is turning hopeless. To underscore this, Herzog had ingeniously assembled a diverse cast that included a slave of African descent, an enslaved Indigenous prince, and a native flutist. As Waller further notes, these non–Spanish men serve as "three representative examples of the non–European world whose presence helps to create the sense that *Aguirre* is a microcosm of New Spain in the sixteenth century."[13] That world was rife with political opportunism and chaotic transitions of power. After all, the seizure of the expedition from Ursúa by Aguirre, who had named Fernando de Guzmán as its nominal leader, cynically dramatizes the installation of a puppet. Padre Carvajal, who went along with these changes, can be seen as representing the Church's complicity in such events. Finally, with their numbers greatly reduced, the remaining members build one larger raft that will hopefully make it to the fabled place they seek. That, too, is destined to fail.

For their part, the Spanish women Doña Inez and Doña Flores exit the expedition unceremoniously. Much like the hapless horse, they will never witness the expedition's actual conclusion in which Aguirre is the last man standing, raving mad, making defiant declarations about his greatness to a group of wild monkeys that have swarmed aboard the raft. These animals may have some symbolic value as well, representing the sub-humanity that this expedition entails. Aguirre's most grandiose declaration—"I will found the purest dynasty the world has ever seen"—rings hollow.

Although Aguirre's cinematic mission is to find El Dorado, in reality he failed miserably, soldiering on, and working his way northward to Isla de Margarita, Venezuela, possibly by way of the Orinoco River. After seizing that island, Aguirre continued to defy the Crown but Spanish authorities caught up with and captured him in 1561. Convicted of treason, Aguirre was beheaded, then drawn and quartered. For good measure, his body parts were displayed in varied locales as a warning to would-be insurgents who might be tempted to defy the Crown.

Herzog's film was interpreted in a seminal 1985 article by historian of discovery Ronald Fritze in *Film & History*. Fritze astutely noted several ironies, one being that "although the real Aguirre had no interest in El Dorado, dramatically it is better to have him seeking the land of gold along with everyone else. What better way to emphasize a mad quest than to give it a non-existent goal?" Furthermore, the expedition's

In *Aguirre, the Wrath of God*, the camera assumes the role of a chronicler of an expedition that has failed. In the closing scenes, the film's deluded namesake explorer exclaims that he will found the greatest dynasty the world has ever seen in the Amazonian wilderness. His words are heard by no one but a group of monkeys that have swarmed aboard. The scene is filmed by the camera(s) circling the raft, creating further disorientation.(Werner Herzog Filmproduktion).

"... impersonality, invincibility, and implacable hostility only serve to give further emphasis to the basic insanity of the Conquistadors' perception of their world." Fritze also noted a marked departure from Herzog's original story, in which Aguirre and his men die fighting each other.[14] Being in complete control of the project, Herzog literally dictated the fate of the expedition.

Films are always a function of the filmmaker's own time(s) and place(s). Herzog was born in Munich, Germany, in 1942, and lived his childhood in the shadow of the Nazi regime. Some critics more or less naturally saw Aguirre as "a sixteenth century Hitler" in his film,[15] but the message may be more universal and complex. Fritze concludes with the disturbing thought that "in Herzog's mind, seeming madmen and outsiders may actually be closer to the reality of life than the rest of us while remaining as fully and frailly human as anyone." Based on something that Herzog hinted at in an interview, Fritze adds: "One almost wonders if he would have actually preferred to have made that point using Hitler (hence the Hitler parallels in *Aguirre*) but rejected that historical setting as too liable to serious misunderstanding" and instead preferred Aguirre as "...more distant and divorced from current emotion...."[16] One thing is clear: as an explorer himself into the mind of Aguirre, Herzog was free to shape the film's—and the expedition's—ending, leaving the viewer with a disturbing lack of closure. In retrospect, that open-endedness is one of the film's enduring strengths.

It is worth noting that despite Herzog's fascination with historical documents, he elected not to use any maps or depict mapmaking in this film. At first blush, that might seem an oversight, but given Herzog's motives, it was a wise choice. Maps above all convey a sense of authority and some knowledge of the countryside. In the case of this expedition, authority is always in dispute and the geography misunderstood. Moreover, mapmaking implies some overall plan and would run counter to Aguirre's swashbuckling opportunism and spontaneity. Seen in this light, the absence of a map is thus symbolic and metaphorical for an expedition that has not only lost its bearings, but is being taken farther and farther into unknown territory—geographically and psychologically.

Over the years, Aguirre has remained the quintessential madman, visionary but demented, ultra-violent and possessed. In the twentieth century alone, five Spanish-language historical novels were written about him. In Spanish-language films, Aguirre-inspired expeditions going awry in search of El Dorado include *El Dorado* (1988) directed by Carlos Saura,[17] and the recent 2017 *Oro* (Gold), a grim tale based on a short story by Arturo Pérez-Reverte.[18] However, Herzog's *Aguirre, the Wrath of God* is the most notable. It is seemingly timeless and now considered a classic. In retrospect, Herzog's film was highly revisionist and ground-breaking. When released in 1972, it was the first to present a Latin American expedition in disarray and bound for failure, and the first to resonate as an indictment of colonialism.

However, it should also be noted that Herzog, like Ursúa, got more than bargained for. As Aguirre, the temperamental Klaus Kinski frequently disputed Herzog's direction, claiming that he knew more about filmmaking than Herzog, and had given advice to far better directors with whom he had worked. Kinski would raise his voice and continue on these rants for hours. In one tape accidentally recorded when a soundman left a recording going, Kinski sounds like an enraged Hitler on a rant. For his part, Herzog rarely spoke but was smart enough to understand that some of Kinski's crazy energy should be channeled into the madman Aguirre. It worked. Behind the scenes, a film can embody emotion as intense as in reality—a reminder that making a film can be as much of an adventure as the adventure it is supposed to capture on screen. Sometime after the fact, and looking at things philosophically, Herzog admitted that there was considerable genius in Kinski—and that he even learned some things from working with him. In retrospect, he captured the essence of a madman on camera.

In the very personal introduction to his ground-breaking book *The Miraculous Lie: Lope de Aguirre and the Search for El Dorado in the Latin American Historical Novel* (2003), Bart Lewis wrote that one of his inspirations was watching "...the seething Klaus Kinski thrash his way through strangling Amazonic vegetation in Werner Herzog's 1972 film 'Aguirre, the Wrath of God.'"[19] Lewis's book—a masterful work in its own right—is the most definitive analysis of the Aguirre saga's transition from the original chronicles to those five historically-themed Spanish-language novels that were written about it. With good reason, Lewis calls Aguirre a "storied rebel." That term fits him perfectly, for it embodies the nearly mythic endurance and resistance that characterizes Latin American political history. With Aguirre as an inspiration, many rebels would follow, finally bringing to an end Spanish rule in much of Latin America by the 1820s.

FIVE

The Mission

Religious Expeditions in Eighteenth-Century South America

Although the subject of religion is central to several films already discussed (viz. *The Other Conquest*; and *Cabeza de Vaca*), it will be given even closer scrutiny in this chapter. For readers who may question if and how Christianity relates to the historical and geographical themes of this book, it should be noted that few calls for geographic exploration-discovery are more overt than the sentiment enunciated in the New Testament, namely the proclamation in Mark (16: 15–16) "Go ye into the world and preach the gospel to every creature." As noted earlier, religion was a catalyst from the very beginning of the Age of Discovery, one of the major goals of Columbus's voyages being to undermine Islam's grip on the world by ultimately re-taking Jerusalem as part of the Crusades. For Columbus, the riches of the Indies would bolster the Church's power to bring that re-conquest of the Holy Land to fruition.[1] Some early Portuguese explorations had much the same religious goal as well.[2] The Reformation (1519) soon presented the Catholic Church with additional challenges, but the fact that transatlantic exploration had begun a generation before under the aegis of Iberian powers was indeed fortuitous, and gave the Catholic Church a foothold in Latin America that remains palpable today.

One of the most storied, and controversial, aspects of exploration involved its role in seeking and discovering souls for conversion. In much of Latin America this involved the Indigenous people being sought out and ideally converted to Christianity. Rather than conquering empires, which had been accomplished by about 1535 and are featured in films such as *The Other Conquest* and *Royal Hunt of the Sun*, the more lightly populated areas now beckoned. The Indians in the vast lowland area east of the Andes in South America consisted of clans that were either nomadic hunters and gatherers, or sedentary agriculturalists. Since initial contact, military expeditions into Indian country had been the rule, and they were frequently accompanied by priests. Cabeza de Vaca had arrived here in 1540 and again was reminded of the corruption and abuse associated with the spread of militarized Catholicism. After much agitation, in 1652 it was finally decreed that the spread of civilization to the Indians should be accomplished by missions. As in much of Latin America, the goal was to bring these widely dispersed peoples together into self-sufficient settlements. The goal involved making religious conversion more effective and more humane, though that was not always achieved.

In his book *Frontiers of Evangelization: Indians in the Sierra Gorda and Chiquitos Missions* (2017), which compares missions in southern Mexico and this portion of South America, historian Robert H. Jackson noted that "To recruit new converts, the Jesuits organized expeditions they called *excursiónes* [sic], which often lasted for months." These Jesuit *excursiónes* aimed at what historian David Block calls "spiritual conquest" using "fluvial networks."[3] After briefly discussing several such *excursiónes* in the Paraguay River country, Jackson observes that some expeditions were disastrous. He provides an example of one in 1715 in which Indians not only killed Bartolomé Blendes, S.J., but also the natives who had accompanied him. This *excursión* had been attacked by Payaguaes Indians on an island in the Paraguay River. However, other tribes were more accepting. According to Jackson, "...many expeditions met little or no resistance and often returned with new converts." Thus gathered, they were clustered in mission settlements that became self-sustaining and productive—and an asset to Church and Crown.[4]

Jackson's study documents the notable concentration of such missions located in the region drained by the Paraguay River system. It is here, too, that the critically acclaimed film *The Mission* (1986)[5] takes place. Widely regarded as one of the finest feature films dealing with religion, it offers an especially vivid depiction of the exploration for human souls by missionaries in this rather remote but originally well-populated part of South America. The screenplay was written by award-winner Robert Bolt (*Lawrence of Arabia* and *Dr. Zhivago*), who based it in part on Philip Caraman's book *The Lost Paradise: The Jesuit Republic in South America*.[6] As that title suggests, that source offers a very sanguine picture of Guaraní Indian life under the Jesuits. In reality, the dynamic between Indians and the Church was often complicated and intense.

Adding to the drama here was the flashpoint that existed between two nominally Roman Catholic powers in South America, namely Spain and Portugal. Although interactions and conflicts between Indigenous and European peoples—and between those European powers themselves—occurred over about two centuries (ca. 1580 to 1780), one particularly troubled time period (ca. 1750 to 1757) is depicted on screen in *The Mission*. At this time, the religious power bases were changing as well. The Jesuits, who were such important allies to the Guaraní Indians, would be expelled by Portugal (and hence Brazil) in 1757 and by Spain (and hence the rest of Latin America) in 1767. This expulsion left the Franciscans, Dominicans and others in charge.

Superbly directed by British filmmaker-producer Roland Joffé, *The Mission* begins with a glimpse of an earlier time in which a lone Jesuit missionary worked his way along a river in search of souls to convert. Without a word being spoken on screen, this opening scene portrays that priest's failure in a cinematic spectacle that startles viewers. In the process of being executed by Indians, he is tied to a cross and sent plunging over a waterfall. The scene is so stunning that it served as the theme of the movie poster. That image froze the action, but on film the plunging water pulls the viewer down into the cataract with the crucified priest. In a close-up it is virtually impossible to freeze the action because it is so swift and the water so agitated, but the audience can make out the red gash of the stigmata inflicted upon him.

As only film can portray so vividly, it is a stunning and allegorical opening indeed for it contains a message that resonates on two levels. First, and most superficially, it underscores the challenges that men of faith will face here. Second, it reveals that the Indians have not only rejected the message but also used the same method of killing the messenger as that used by those who killed Jesus himself. In retrospect, it is one of the most visceral scenes in film history—a graphic representation of sacrifice and martyrdom, and hope and despair.

Promotional materials for Roland Joffé's *The Mission* (1986) feature the towering waterfall over which Indians send a crucified padre. However, this dizzying close up from the film personalizes that event, which will ultimately lead to other soul-searching expeditions into the interior of South America that result in the Guaraní Indians being missionized (Goldcrest Films).

Looked at more objectively, which is to say by deconstructing it, the scene is brilliant in that it manipulates geography, mythology, and history. The waterfall is more typical of the country proselytized more than a century earlier to the north along the Parapanema River, while the bulk of the movie itself takes place in more undulating—which is to say less rugged and less wild—topography farther down the Río Paraguay. The rivers in this film are part of the second largest river system in South America, the Paraná and Paraguay, which drains southward from the central part of the continent, ultimately reaching the Atlantic Ocean near Buenos Aires, Argentina, at the huge, funnel-shaped opening called the Rio de la Plata. As they reflect on this shocking opening crucifixion scene as the movie progresses, the viewer may sense that it represents not only a more primitive place, but also a more primitive time before effective communication between missionaries and Indians had been established. This scene helps prepare the viewer for what is to come, the unfolding of a story in which the Indigenous people come under the protection of the Jesuits as they cluster in mission communities.

As regards its plot, *The Mission* deftly uses two main characters, a mercenary named Rodrigo Mendoza (Robert De Niro) and the other a priest named Father Gabriel (Jeremy Irons). The former has a quick temper and strong libido, while the latter is a Jesuit priest who arrives hoping to gain the confidence of the Indians, which is to say be more successful than the padre who was crucified at the beginning of the film. Respectively billed as a man of the sword and a man of the cloth, they represent two potentially opposing forces (military and church) and more broadly or symbolically, evil and good. However, in this film, these two lead characters ultimately unite to fight the corruption of Empire. How successfully they achieve it will transpire over the length of the film, but both men are essential for setting the stage after the catastrophic opening scene.

The transition to a more successful missionary effort is made in the second major scene in the film, which is also striking and has no dialogue. In it, Father Gabriel arrives. He, too, works his way into the rugged back country but escapes the fate of his predecessor by diverting the Indians' attention in the gloomy forest. At first the Indians seem about to harm this priest as well, but he takes out his oboe and begins playing it. This lilting music enchants them, and they spare his life—thus beginning the process of successful proselytizing. This scene is not only a subliminal nod to the movie's haunting, and highly acclaimed, musical score by Ennio Morricone. More broadly, it also suggests that a new way of delivering messages to the Indians—one perhaps more universal in appeal than the written or spoken word itself—has proven more effective. On the other hand, the scene has a darker side as it unfairly portrays Indians as simplistic and easily won over by a pied piper. In fact, these Indigenous people had a rich culture, complete with a complex belief system, which was now being challenged by the universalizing impulse of Christianity. Small wonder many Indians resisted.

Thereafter, the Indians are introduced to Rodrigo when he accompanies Father Gabriel up the river. In order to reach the Indians, they must ascend steep cliffs, clawing their way up using their fingernails for traction and ropes to assist each other and haul supplies. Rodrigo is hauling his weapons of war, including his suit of armor, in a huge box-like parcel that he jealously guards. It is heavy and cumbersome, and he nearly falls several times. Finally, he reaches the top, exhausted. Seeing this armor in the parcel, and associating it with early Spanish *entradas*, the Indians are understandably frightened and threaten to kill Rodrigo. Refusing to let go of the parcel, Rodrigo is approached by an Indian who plans to take it from him. The Indian holds his knife to Rodrigo's throat and time seems to stand still. Father Gabriel does not intervene, leaving the choice up to Rodrigo. Although thoroughly exhausted, Rodrigo is determined to hang onto his possessions. Finally, he yields, and the Indian cuts the rope, sending the parcel tumbling into the river far below.

The cutting of that rope was symbolic, for it transforms Rodrigo from a hostile character like those in *Aguirre, the Wrath of God* into one who has surrendered to the Indians. When that parcel plunges into the river, Rodrigo's sins are washed away. Free of that burden, he breaks down crying, overcome by emotion. For the first time in his life, he has put his fate in the hands of God, and is overjoyed. In this scene, Joffé wisely

The Mission (1986) offers a Jesuit view of South American history. On a subsequent expedition into the wilderness in search of souls, a padre named Father Gabriel (Jeremy Irons) begins to gain the confidence of the Indians by playing a solo on his oboe—a haunting tune that becomes a key element in the film's acclaimed musical score by Ennio Morricone (Goldcrest Films).

used the roar of the waterfalls to great advantage, as they would drown out any conversation. Instead, Rodrigo's face tells it all. Over the space of about a minute, which can seem like a long time on film, his countenance changes from anger, to resignation, to joy, and then to euphoria. Watching this scene, the audience experiences what great acting and fine directing is all about. It is one of many scenes that make *The Mission* so memorable.

Not to be overlooked is this transformational scene's dependence on its geographic setting, which would have resonated differently if filmed on flat land and far from a river. Joffé brilliantly used both geographic features—the steep topography and the roaring waterfalls—to symbolize the challenges to be overcome in connecting with the Indians and overcoming Rodrigo's baser nature. Those two features resonate as symbols: Rivers have long played a role in spiritual rites such as baptism, and the towering cliffs that Rodrigo scales bring him closer to God (as in Moses on the mount). These geographic features not only aid in the transformation of Rodrigo, but also help shape the trajectory of the film. After experiencing this epiphany, Rodrigo becomes a priest. However, unlike the fictionalized padre Carvajal in *Aguirre, the Wrath of God*, Rodrigo would never again harm an Indian.

Few movies better reveal a film's director as an explorer encountering new geography and history. The on-location filming brought Joffé and his crew into the interior of South America, namely Colombia, Argentina and Paraguay, including the spectacular Iguaçu Falls featured in the opening scenes. Motion picture cameras had recorded these places before, but the cinematography in this film is noteworthy, tightly focused in a wide range of scenes from intense physical action to slower close-ups suggesting reflection. One later scene featuring Rodrigo lovingly playing with the Indian children stands out because not a word is spoken, nor needs to be. It is an idyllic scene and its filming has an impromptu quality, almost as if the camera accidently recorded it during a break from the more intense filming. That impromptu feel makes it seem real rather than staged. However, in the context of the film, this scene was pivotal because it reveals the formerly savage beast being tamed by the innocent children.

These trust-building scenes between the Jesuits and Indians depict an isolated backwater of Latin America living on borrowed time. In the film, Joffé carefully reconstructed the mission grounds and activities to capture the feeling of enclosure and protection of the Indians. The Jesuits had effectively colonized the Indians into a sedentary agricultural lifestyle. The buildings constructed in the compounds represent a combination of traditional ecclesiastical mission architecture with its vernacular adaptations to the tropical lowland environment, including pole construction and thatched roofs. With their attention to detail, the film's sets convey a sense of Indigenous order and productivity if not outright obedience. All seems harmonious and serene, which is to say that through Joffé's lens, the missions are idyllic. In particular, the mission San Miguel is an inspirational thing of beauty that, at least according to this film, represents the best of both worlds—humane European influences and Indigenous labor working in harmony. Some astute observers might see this as a metaphor for the film itself, or rather the film's vision of itself. The film's constructed environment suggests syncretism and an improvement in the lives of the Indians. In reality, however, such clustering by the Jesuits made Indigenous populations more susceptible to diseases. Nevertheless, the feeling prevails in this film that life was better inside the mission complexes than outside of them. Within these enclosures, the Jesuits protected the Indians from predation by

The sets for *The Mission* involved considerable research into Indigenous and early church architecture, and stressed the Jesuits' willingness to use native crafts as they pursued their peaceful "spiritual conquest." A visual centerpiece of the film was the beautiful Iglesia de San Miguel, whose traditional twin bell towers and baroque façade underscore Spain's religious presence in the wilderness along the Río Paraná (Goldcrest Films).

hostile tribes or other Spaniards and also offered stability from the vagaries of the physical environment, including drought.

The story soon takes a darker turn based on a real event that transpired in the early 1750s, when the Treaty of Madrid witnessed Spain ceding part of Paraguay to Portugal. The missions were ground zero in how that would play out. The question that swirls around this plot is which of the many forces vying for power in the region will win or lose. The major players include the Crown, the Church, and the wealthy *encomenderos*. The latter were the owners of the *encomiendas*, which consisted of land and Indians for their own use. Then, too, in parts of South America the *repartimiento* system—that is, Indian labor made available to landowners (and mine owners in some locales)— essentially conscripted the Indians. In this film, the Indians appear to be only pawns whose voices we never hear regarding their fates—a surprising directorial decision that silences them and, some critics claim, marginalizes them as well.

The outcome of negotiations will determine the fate of those Indians, who are fiercely defended by the Jesuits, and depicted by filmmaker Joffé as living an almost utopian life in the missions. Regarded with ambivalence by the Crown, however, these Indians are considered mere beasts of burden by the avaricious *encomenderos* and the even more predatory Portuguese *Bandeirantes*.[7] As historian James Saeger tersely observed, "the film makers assume Jesuit policies [to be] identical with Guarani [sic] interests, untrue historically and unconvincing on film."[8] As in *Aguirre, the Wrath of God*, this film also had to address its own labor-related issues involving the local Indigenous actors. However, because the Indians played a much larger role in the filming of *The Mission*, pay equity became a top concern, at times jeopardizing the production itself as local Indians (Waunanas) from local tribes portraying the Guaraní threatened to strike.

Returning to the plot of *The Mission*, into this quagmire of colonial-era politics strides Cardinal Altamirano (Ray McAnally) in 1752. His task is to oversee Spain's handing over of the seven missions to Portugal, although the money provided to those missions is but a fraction of their worth. The camera now moves indoors, and the film captures the darker drama of political intrigue. The tighter interior spaces suggest the limiting options being imposed by the negotiating parties. Strategically positioned during the negotiations are maps showing both the Jesuit-controlled area and the area according to the Treaty of Madrid. On one level, the latter map works to convey the authority of Europe over the region; after all, it supposedly indicates the good faith of opposing parties who have come to agreement. On the other, however, the Treaty map confirms the artificiality and even brazenness of outside influences over the everyday affairs at the mission, which the Jesuits see as working smoothly. In viewing the Jesuit map, Father Gabriel seems wistful. Regarding the other, he has his doubts about what is envisioned cartographically to be fair, but will likely play out quite differently on this now-sacred ground.

These indoor, almost claustrophobic scenes are pivotal to the entire plot of the film. In them, we witness the Jesuits going head-to-head with the authorities. With this in mind, some might see this standoff as an allegorical reenactment of the Liberation Theology (aka Theology of Liberation) as propounded by the Peruvian philosopher and Catholic theologian Gustavo Gutiérrez.[9] Films are always a function of the time in which they were produced, and *The Mission* is no exception. Liberation Theology was galvanizing both academic and public discourse in Latin America during the 1970s and 1980s—its emphasis on using the tenets of Christianity to help the region's poor Indigenous people fight against oppression by authorities. At that time, and in this film, it was difficult to determine whether these strategies were religious or political in nature as the two were so tightly bound. *The Mission* epitomizes this fusion. While casting it in the guise of a historical event, this seemingly modern religious/political philosophy was helping to transform present-day Latin America. Although a modern phenomenon, Liberation Theology had deep roots in the New World, perhaps as early as the Las Casas vs. Sepúlveda debates discussed under the film *The Other Conquest* (Chapter Two). Despite its playing out in the relatively conservative Reagan/Thatcher era of the 1980s, with its

In this dimly lit but moving scene from *The Mission* (1986), Father Gabriel (Jeremy Irons) ponders maps showing the changing balance of power, knowing that a treaty between Spain and Portugal will result in the end of mission life for the Indians he has come to love. Easy to overlook, maps in cinema serve many purposes, including setting the time period and depicting geopolitical developments (Goldcrest Films).

emphasis on individualism, Joffé's version of Liberation Theology resonated with the film-going public, including the students in film-related classes I taught, who naturally sided with the Jesuits and Guaraní rather than the Spaniards.

As *The Mission* progresses, the Guaraní Indians are thrust into the middle of this international drama between Spain and Portugal despite the efforts of the Jesuits to shield them from it. Although they have lived in relative peace at the missions until the above-mentioned economic interests threatened the area, they are now vulnerable as the stakes have been raised. As noted earlier, filmmaking often dramatizes and moralizes, and nuances are often lost in the process. This film clearly takes sides. In it, the Indigenous people symbolize innocence, the Crown represents crass incompetence, and the economic interests personify the evils of capitalism. *The Mission* culminates in the Guaraní War (1756), which resulted in disaster for the Indians. Those scenes are powerful indeed, for they involve the martyrdom of selfless characters such as Father Gabriel along with his followers. They also witness Rodrigo again taking up the sword to defend the Indians, an act by which he breaks his Jesuit vow but defends to the death the Indians he loves.

One scene spectacularly positions the pacifistic cross-wearing padre Father Gabriel and his flock being consumed by flames as the burning church looms in the background. Symbolism abounds in this scene, for Father Gabriel is essentially sacrificing himself—and literally going through hell as well—to protect those he loves. The cross is essentially the same feature that marked his predecessor's fate in the opening waterfall scene, and now it symbolically brings the film full circle. At the beginning, the cross represented the Indians' resistance to intrusion, and they used nature to rid them of the first padre and his religious philosophy. In the burning church scene toward the end of the film, however, the Indians had come to rely on that same cross for protection, and are now being consumed by man's inhumanity to man. Through its incredibly vibrant coloring and compositioning, this iconic image sears itself into the viewer's consciousness. Ironically, and tragically, Father Gabriel is the same music-playing priest whose life was originally spared by the Indians; now, however, he falls victim to the savagery of his own people: Europeans. Although the image is impressive as a still shot, the motion picture footage mesmerizes as the padre walks toward the viewer, who can almost feel the growing intensity and withering heat of the all-consuming fire. In still shots, it became one of the iconic images used to market the film.

As *The Mission* reaches its conclusion, and the Jesuit missions and their dreams lay in ruins, Altamirano speculates on the imperfect world we all inhabit. A few days after the mayhem has subsided, Indians scour the smoking ruins for anything salvageable, then slip off into the jungle. It is a sad, even sorry sight, but is leavened by some optimism as a biblical passage from John 1:15, appears on screen: "The light shineth in the darkness, and the darkness hath not overcome it." These words convey a message of hope, and perhaps re-cast the calamities just witnessed in 1750s South America as part of a more timeless and universal drama. Given what the audience has witnessed, the scene may seem rather odd, almost a let-down. On the other hand, Joffé may be making a statement here: *Granted, I've given the audience an imperfect ending, but then again it is an imperfect world in which we all live.*

In making *The Mission*, Joffé's goal was to tell a complex and ultimately political story in ways that would educate, entertain, and perhaps even enlighten audiences. The result is a film that begins as an adventure and evolves into a compelling drama. So tight is the storyline, and so beautifully photographed is the movie itself (which won the Academy Award for cinematography) that the audience may overlook the liberties it takes. A second and third viewing reveals that it oversimplifies and even vilifies various players in the political process, perhaps unintentionally. This, of course, is what film inherently tends to do, regardless of the filmmaker's intentions. Inevitably, when a film reaches its finale, the audience leaves the theater and the critics weigh in.

That review process did not take long, and the verdict was mixed. Although *The Mission*'s artistic merit was widely recognized, it received strong criticism on some fronts for its misrepresentation of South America's eighteenth-century frontier history. Over the years, the criticism has grown as academicians weigh in on issues of accuracy and cultural appropriation. Historian Saeger stated categorically that "Although *The Mission* strives to be politically progressive, it is compromised by its racism." According to Saeger, both the screenwriter and the director have simultaneously demeaned Guaraní culture and perpetuated the Black Legend.[10] The latter refers to the myth that Spain's presence was universally evil, when in fact many laws granting protection to the Indians were passed by the Crown. There is a note of irony here because Joffé elected to vilify Spain in order to empathize with the Guaraní Indians, only to be branded a racist for his portrayal of them. Criticism aside, *The Mission* is a beautiful film, rich in pathos, and one well worth watching for its fine acting, gorgeous cinematography, and its take on the thorny subject of Christianity in the far frontiers of Spanish and Portuguese Latin America.

As a postscript to *The Mission*, it should be noted that evangelization of South America's interior continued well into the twentieth century, albeit conducted largely by Protestant missionaries. In the 1956 evangelizing effort named "operation Auca," a Christian missionary family made contact with the Huaorani (Waorani) in the jungles of eastern Ecuador. As modern-day explorers in search of souls, they used aircraft to gain access to this remote area lying between the Napo and Curaray Rivers. The effort resulted in five missionaries being speared to death. In 2006, the Christian film *End of the Spear*[11] dramatized the event. Filmed on location in Ecuador, it used some of the exact locales, and descendants of the Huaorani peoples as actors, resulting in its documentary quality as well.

Six

Zama

Colonial Expansion and Its Discontents

As noted above, it may take decades for a written story to make it from the page to the silver screen. By the mid-twentieth century, South American literature was incorporating increasingly darker themes of seduction and desperation—two sides of a modernist coin circulating not only in Latin America but elsewhere as well. At this time, disquieting literary masterpieces such as Argentina's *El Túnel* by Ernesto Sabato (1948)[1] and *Zama* by Antonio di Benedetto (1956)[2] were being read in South America, sometimes in defiance of rigid right-wing regimes that censored such disturbing material. Significantly, both of the Argentine writers mentioned above are of Italian descent, another reminder of the European infusion of the new blood and ideas that accompany immigration. That connection might help explain some of the delightfully revenge-oriented absurdist themes that have also characterized Argentine cinema, including the mesmerizing modern-day crime drama *The Secret in their Eyes* (2009)[3] and the darkly comedic and razor-sharp *Relatos Salvajes* (*Wild Tales*; 2014).[4] Then again, Di Benedetto was also influenced by Russian writers such as Fyodor Dostoyevsky, so some of that gloom and cynicism in his writings may originate there as well.

Di Benedetto's novel *Zama* offers a case study in how geographic exploration figures in the plot of a fictional historical drama, and how cultural identity plays a role in the mix. That novel served as the catalyst for the recent film of the same name, which is a remarkable adaptation. The story begins in 1790 and much of it is set along an unnamed river that leads into the interior of the continent. It is likely the Paraná River in the vicinity of Asunción, but the author's keeping the specific geographical location vague is brilliant. He creates a disquieting sense of a place that can't be pinpointed and seems to float in space as well as time; thus the locale seems more universal rather than particular, a riparian outpost at the edge of civilization. Its protagonist—the fictional Don Diego de Zama—is a Corregidor or magistrate and thus employed by the Crown. Although a fictional character, Zama may have been based on a real Argentine Corregidor named Miguel Gregorio de Zamolla (1753–1819).

Since the beginning of colonization, race has been a factor in Latin America and it plays a major role in this story, as does one's actual place of birth. Zama is a Creole—that is, although of Spanish descent, he was born in the Americas. He is nominally white, but his status is lower than the Spanish-born *Peninsulares* who are in higher positions—what historian Benedict Anderson astutely called the "fatality of trans-Atlantic birth."[5] Zama himself is highly conflicted, ever-aware of his whiteness and self-consciously aware of the role that race plays in his dealings with others, including Indians and Blacks. At the same time, he is perennially aware of how his status as a Creole is compromising his success in a world where being born in Spain itself constitutes pedigree. Above all, he has a strong but ultimately deluded belief in how the Spanish colonial system *should* work, although success eludes him at every turn.

Using a term rarely heard today, Zama can best be described as *valetudinarian*, that is, someone who has an obsessive interest in his own condition, which is to say completely self-absorbed to the point of crippling neurosis. He is also a misanthrope, but there is another side to his character. The situation that this stifled Corregidor finds himself in is almost understandable, for he is trapped in a Kafkaesque plot that revolves around, and exposes, a corrupt, conformity-oriented system of privilege. This mechanistic system supposedly operates by rules but is in fact highly arbitrary. Zama longs to be with his wife and family who are now living farther west on the Pacific side of the Andes, but he is unable to get the promotion that will land him there. In the meantime, he sires a child with an Indian woman—a child that is not only a bastard who would have to struggle to be recognized as legitimate, but is also mentally challenged and unable to perform even simple tasks.

The Argentine film *Zama* (2015)[6] finally arrived about sixty years after the novel, and received rave reviews in most quarters. Directed by Lucrecia Martel, and beautifully filmed, it is an unvarnished portrayal of the Corregidor's bleak life in that small, almost nondescript river port on the Spanish frontier. The opening scenes find Zama (Daniel Giménez Cacho) gazing off into the river as he awaits news from afar. That image also

Directed by Lucrecia Martel, the 2017 Argentine film *Zama* presents a critical view of Spain's eighteenth-century frontier colonial outposts. In this iconic scene, the film's disenchanted namesake (played by Daniel Giménez Cacho) gazes out over the waters of the Rio Paraná hoping for news that will free him from his Purgatory-like assignment in the nameless colonial outpost (Bananeira Filmes LTDA).

became iconic in that it was used in the film's promotion. On the river, a small sailing vessel adds a visual counterpoint, suggesting a time when life moved at a slower pace.

In the film, Zama will occasionally strike much that same pompous pose in several other settings, all of them conveying his authority as one who watches over the place, and waits in vain to get out of it. In both the book and film, he is not only trapped in time but in geographic space as well. Although Bourbon reforms were finding their way into Spain's New World territories, life seemed to move at a snail's pace in outposts like the one he occupies. On screen, Zama moves slowly, sometimes fidgets, and perfectly portrays a man constantly awaiting the change that never comes. As he interacts with higher officials he is given glimmers of hope for a better position elsewhere, but is constantly thwarted by those superiors' failure to advance him. Periodically, he erupts in brutish rage, often at those below his status; this, too, comes to nothing.

Director Martel recreates Zama's world—a colonial townscape at the edge of nowhere—to perfection. Significantly, this cinematic townscape possesses none of the grand urban design and architectural amenities that one often associates with colonial Spain. It apparently has no plaza nor lavishly detailed baroque buildings such as churches and civic buildings. Their absence underscores the relative unimportance of the place, which some critics equated with purgatory. Moreover, although the buildings occupied by the higher-class Spaniards are of more solid construction, they appear to be in a state of near ruin, a visual touch that underscores not only the degeneracy of their owners but also makes the past palpable here. The place has been around for some time, though for how long remains a mystery. Few films have better captured the languor of everyday life in the late eighteenth-century frontier along the Río Paraná, or for that matter, any part of New World Spain. In Europe, change was happening at an increasing pace, and even reaching cities such as Buenos Aires and Asunción, but the backwaters experienced far less of it. In this setting, the cinematic Zama craves upward mobility but is restricted to aimlessly shuffling back and forth horizontally.

As the film progresses, Zama's everyday interactions with people in all walks of life are filmed in a languid style that perfectly matches his mounting disappointment. For him, the people in the outpost are objects of diversion or opportunity. His interactions with women provide a case in point. In one early leering scene, he observes some naked Indian women bathing in the river. A more self-disciplined man might keep walking, but Zama lies down in a concealed place along the riverbank in order to spy on them through the reeds. Noticing him, they angrily drive him away, his only shame being that someone in greater authority may be watching. Later, in another set of scenes that have overt sexual overtones, Zama takes elaborate steps to advance his status by seducing Luciana Piña (Lola Dueñas), the flirtatious and mercurial wife of the governor. To Zama, it is an exhilarating and risky challenge, but he is unsuccessful at that venture as well. In other scenes, he interacts with people from all classes as he performs his duties, always with only one goal, his own advancement.

As Zama attends to these errands, it is almost as if the camera were slowly ambling around town with him, capturing in intimate vignettes and fleeting glimpses a now long-vanished era. *Zama* is one of those rare films in which the characters seem to be real people, not actors—something especially hard to achieve in a historical film. The social stratification evident in this outpost is based on not only birthplace but also the aforementioned issue of race. The outpost's three social layers consist of white, brown, and black. Under Martel's deft directing, this becomes evident with few words being spoken. Whites control the place and move about at ease, Indians huddle in hovels at its margins, and those of African descent do all of the heavy lifting—literally as several of them heft ponderous furniture and other objects. Metaphorically speaking, this outpost mirrors the society of Spain's colonies in the Americas.

Some of the Indians in this imaginary outpost may have had real-world counterparts in the form of *criados*, those taken captive in the various wars. The women (*criadas*) in particular often found work indoors as domestic servants, while the men toiled in various jobs for their wealthy *patrones*. Many of these Indians became baptized Christians. That way, as an official Order put it, they could never "return to the heathen life, even if their relatives want them." They were, as historian David J. Weber succinctly observed, "neither savage nor Spaniard."[7] In this period (ca. 1780) some began earning wages, but society was still rigidly stratified by race. Being a mixture of Spaniard and Indian, *mestizos* had status somewhere between the two. For their part, Indians had higher status than those of African descent, some of whom mixed into the population. These *mulatos* may have composed about a third of the population in some parts of the region, viz. Buenos Aires. They could also be found in smaller communities as well. Blacks were frequently smuggled as slaves and sometimes dismissively considered to be trade goods. Although "race determined one's worth," as Weber added, an additional element in the population were miscreants of indeterminate heritage who "infested" the frontier areas. The scourge of Crown and locals alike, they plundered, pillaged, and raped their way through the countryside.[8] They owed allegiance to no one and kept areas on edge, as Zama himself would soon discover.

Zama is beautifully composed and rich in detail throughout, but it is the last

Filmed at the Barrancas de Empedrado in Argentina, where sedimentary bluffs face the Río Paraná, Lucrecia Martel's historically themed sets in *Zama* capture the essence of life in a frontier outpost ruled by Spanish-born elites but staffed by creoles who carry out colonial rule over Mestizos, Indians (seen here), and Black people. Filmed on a small budget, and reportedly completed in nine weeks, *Zama* is a testimony to creative literature-based filmmaking (Bananeira Filmes LTDA).

portion of both the novel and the film that I shall now discuss because it involves exploration of two types of territory—geographical and psychological. To finally achieve his goal, Zama joins an expedition in search of the Crown's nemesis, a mysterious outlaw that no one can identify, but whose name is known: Vicuña Porto (Matheus Nachtergaele). If Zama can bring that outlaw to justice, he believes that he will gain enough favor to finally succeed in being promoted to the coveted post in the province near Santiago de Chile, where he will be reunited with his wife and family (who never appear on screen). The quest for this outlaw is risky, as it means surrendering his title of Corregidor for the substantial promotion (and relocation) that a successful capture will certainly bring.

It is easy to downplay the significance of this third and last part of *Zama*, which is titled "1799." However, that is the part of the book and the film that vividly portrays traditional exploration, namely, the search for something of value in geographic space that brings explorers face to face with the unknown. Although the elusive criminal that Zama seeks is known by name, he has been seen by no one, though Zama thinks he has some clues to his identity. In both the book and the film, this expedition involves deciphering new terrain full of hazards such as trackless swamps, huge savannas, and hostile Indians. This expedition is looking for a man, but legends of wealth in the form of silver, or, more mysteriously, round coconut-size rocks containing valuable gems, are luring them as well. Spanish expeditions always involved considerable multi-tasking, and this one is no exception.

As the expedition proceeds, it is drawn deeper into not only unknown terrain but also into despair, becoming increasingly demoralized by Indians so stealthy that

This scene from *Zama* (2017) finds the film's namesake heading an expedition to find a wily outlaw in the wilderness consisting of tree-studded savannah. This tall grass country studded with distinctive chumba palm trees may seem idyllic, but in reality it is marshy and full of hazards. On this expedition turned manhunt, Zama's contingent is bedeviled by Indians who pop up lightning-fast from the tall grass, slay their victims, and immediately disappear (Bananeira Filmes LTDA).

the members regard them as "fantasmas" (phantoms). Stunningly filmed and making splendid use of widescreen, these scenes depict the expedition's progress into sweeping, *chumba* palm tree studded savannas, thickets, scrub forest, and marshes. It is here that film shines in creating a horizontal expanse of almost agoraphobia-inducing wilderness. Just below the surface, the entire environment is a saturated quagmire, seemingly floating on the water-table and symbolizing just how tenuous the expedition's foothold is. With each league away from civilization, the sense of peril becomes more palpable. The low-angle scenes in which red-painted Indians pop up lightning-fast from the waist-high grass, instantaneously snagging, dropping, and killing expedition members one by one, is pure terror, and perfectly captures the mounting horror of this trek.

As the expedition suffers losses and begins breaking down, it becomes clear that similar terror lurks within the ranks. Zama discovers to his horror that the sought-after Vicuña Porto has been among them, keeping a close eye on Zama, and waiting for this chance to rebel. In effect, Zama has taken the ultimate risk on this expedition, and has no escape. Porto now emerges to turn the tables on Zama and gain the upper hand. Alas, Zama has entered the darkest territory of all, where fate awaits him. His one bargaining chip, to reveal the location of the coconut-like stones that are said to be filled with gemstones, might prove of value to him as a ploy that can buy time. However, the defiant Zama decides not to cooperate, simultaneously garnering some power but sealing his fate.

That fate is horrific, and I reveal it here only because it is integral to the process of exploration and discovery in this story. For his refusal to disclose the source of the stones, the group urges that Zama be executed. However, Porto overrules them because, according to his reasoning, a man cannot be executed twice—once for being an informant to the Crown and the other for treachery to them. So he gives Zama a choice: "...a man can die before dying; he can endure a double death from a mutilation that annihilates him." Zama reasons that this is impossible; he can live if lucky enough even after being mutilated, but he does not realize that some fates can be worse than death. In a shocking scene, Porto chops off Zama's arms below the elbow. Almost demonically, Porto whispers to him, "Bury the stumps in the ashes from the fire. If you don't bleed to death, and you meet an Indian, you'll survive." The shocking scene of the mutilated Zama is the most explicit in the film.

In the book, Zama's last realization is part hallucination; he feels tourniquets being applied to the stumps and believes he has been rescued, stating, "I came back from nothingness. I wanted to rebuild the world." Opening his eyes, he sees not an Indian, but rather himself at age twelve: "Smiling like a father, I said, 'You haven't grown.'" With sadness Zama hears the reply, "Neither have you."[9] Remarkably, the film does not contain this conversation—only an Indian boy twice asking a barely conscious Zama, "do you want to live?" In the movie's last scene, a canoe bearing Zama is guided by Indians away from the camera and into the wilderness. In both versions, Zama is now at the mercy of the Indians he regarded so dismissively.

Geography plays an important role in *Zama*. Significantly, the story begins and ends at water's edge. It the opening scene, he anticipates the wide river conveying news that will change his fortune and reunited him with his family—news that never comes. At the end, he is paddled along a waterway by Indians who represent his only hope for survival. That waterway is no navigable river but rather an uncharted route only known by Indigenous people through an otherwise trackless wetland deep in the interior. That

In this haunting closing scene from Lucrecia Martel's *Zama* (2017), Indians manning a canoe silently pole their way through the sluggish waters of a meandering stream in the palm-studded savannah. Reposing in that canoe, Zama has become a victim of fate and his own arrogance, and is now totally dependent on the Indians for his survival (Bananeira Filmes LTDA).

interior, of course, is more than geographical but also psychological—another reminder that exploration-discovery is as much a psychological process as it is an actual physical endeavor. Zama will never return to the life he knew and is now in Tierra Incognita.

Where human hope ends, fate mercifully intervenes. The ending of both the book and the film confirm that exploration is always an adventure whose outcome—discovery—cannot be foretold. In the book's memorable last scene, Zama had come full circle in discovering himself. It offers a dramatic and allegorical reminder that exploration and discovery are difficult to separate, and that their trajectory can be circular rather than linear. Whereas the book is fairly explicit about Zama's inner thoughts at the end of the story, the movie is less clear. However, in both he is at the mercy of fate. *Zama* underscores the premise that stories about exploration-discovery turn inward with time and space, which is to say historically and geographically. In many of them, optimism and certainty are replaced by disenchantment and doubt.

In the service of this messaging, the movie's soundtrack works very effectively. Its surprising use of easily recognized twentieth-century music by the Brazilian duo Los Indios Tabajaras, including "Maria Elena" and "Harbor Lights" (Luces en el Puerto) adds a wistful note to the drama. The song "Siempre en Mi Corazón" (Always in My Heart) is another example. In addition to subliminally incorporating an Indian identity into the drama unfolding, these songs directly address the story's major themes. Symbolically, they are about romance and unattainability, or more to the point, longing and loss. They add a dimension of intimacy and immediacy—exactly the effect that Martel sought in this otherwise historically-themed film. A reviewer concerned about accuracy might find these songs too contemporary, but Martel knew better as they form a bridge between the historical characters and the modern audience.

At its core, *Zama* offers a grim view of modernity, an existential tale about a man incapable of adapting with grace—until fate does it for him. Such disquieting intro-spection was rarely encountered in eighteenth-century Spanish colonial America, but became increasingly common during the political dictatorships that flourished in the mid-twentieth century, when *Zama* first came into being. The story helps expose the workings of oppressive political systems, and thus uses writing, and filmmaking, as sub-versive forms of communication and resistance.

With good reason, Di Benedetto dedicated *Zama* "*A las víctimas de la espera*" (to the victims of expectation). In his time, there were many. For Di Benedetto, expectation and hope were being overwhelmed by the noise and alienation of modernity, but pol-itics would play an increasingly brutal role after the publication of his edgy and often disturbing novels. Ironically, in the 1970s Di Benedetto experienced firsthand the arbi-trariness of Argentina's governmental authorities when he was imprisoned and tortured for a year before being released. Although much younger than Di Benedetto, filmmaker Martel (born 1966) was well aware of the legacy of oppression by the political system during her country's "Dirty War" (1976–1983), which terrorized people and resulted in thousands vanishing after being rounded up by the police and military to become "The Disappeared" (Los Desaparecidos). In this context, the story *Zama* still resonates sev-eral generations after its original publication as a cautionary tale about the depravity of duplicitous government officials.

SEVEN

Aire Libre

The Humanization of Scientific Exploration and Discovery

During the later period of colonial rule, ca. 1750 to 1800, challenges to Spain's hegemony in much of Latin America were taking many forms and coming from all sides. In her provocatively titled book *Imperial Eyes*, Mary Louise Pratt notes that "two simultaneous and ... intersecting processes" in Europe—the emergence of natural history as knowledge and the focusing of exploration toward the interiors of continents—were having a profound impact on South America.[1] Pratt demonstrates that the natural historian became an important player in European exploration. Although the natural historian's goal was ostensibly scientific, it had immense economic and political consequences. Pratt's ground-breaking book urged audiences to take a more penetrating look at those who wrote (and illustrated) travel narratives based on their firsthand experiences.

The entire continent was fair game, but the proximity of South America's northern coast in the vicinity of Guyana and Venezuela made it an especially attractive point of arrival for northern Europeans. Closest to home, it was nevertheless wildly exotic country. A vivid and very early example of how tropical America could be visualized and verbalized by a northern European explorer involves the naturalist-illustrator Maria Sibylla Merian, who sojourned for two years (1699 to 1701) in Suriname (Dutch Guiana). This part of South America lured Europeans looking to make new starts, and Merian found renewed courage by escaping an oppressive marriage. Feeling a sense of freedom, she was emboldened to explore.

As an entomologist, Merian found Guyana's insect life fascinating. Besides being an observer on the cusp of science, she also had considerable artistic talent. In this new environment, she made many impressive watercolor paintings to illustrate her own written works as she documented the country beyond the capital city of Paramaribo. To further support herself, she provided illustrations to wealthy amateur collectors and scientists back in Europe. In addition to being accurate and superbly rendered, her illustrations were among the first to contextualize her subjects. For example, she depicted the iridescent blue butterfly *Morpho menelaus* on the castor oil plant. Its color is so striking that this butterfly would come to symbolize the unique beauty of tropical South America.

Some observers may have considered Merian's rendition to be a beautiful work of art, but she was clearly not satisfied. To her discerning eye, it did not capture the butterfly's distinctive coloring, which she characterized as "...looking like polished silver overlaid with the loveliest ultramarine, green and purple, and indescribably beautiful...." Despite using the smallest paintbrushes possible, and also the finest paper, she was unable to achieve the metallic effect seen in nature. In the end, Merian lamented

that "...its beauty cannot possibly be rendered with the paintbrush." Merian's admission is remarkable for two reasons, one technical the other historical: first, it candidly explains and even demystifies this artist's techniques in trying to capture nature; and second, it is a telling admission that exposes the Age of Exploration's quest for greater and greater fidelity in capturing images of living things in the field. That quest would intensify and ultimately lead to photography in the 1840s and its off-shoot—motion pictures— half a century later.

Also to her credit, Merian was among the first to situate natural history subjects into the broader landscape of South America, as seen in her stylized painting featuring creatures both along the shore and into Surinam's mountain-studded savannah. In a revealing passage, she noted that "all were observed by me in America and drawn from life, with only a few exceptions, which I have added based on the testimony of the Indians."[2] To Merian several centuries ago, and to some exacting filmmakers much later, verisimilitude in image-making mattered. Moreover, Merian's reliance on Indians is a recur-

Among the earliest scientific explorers in South America was the intrepid naturalist/artist Maria Sibylla Merian, who in 1699–1700 lamented that she was not better able to depict one of the tropical region's distinctive iridescent blue butterflies that she found in Suriname. Source: *Dissertatio de Generatione et Metamorphosibus Insectorum Surinamensium* (Amsterdam, 1719) (author's digital collection).

ring theme: as will become apparent in this book, to tell their stories most explorers and filmmakers have been (and continue to be) dependent on the input of Indigenous peoples, and filmmakers would depict this in the movies they made about the region.

The consequences of this scientific inquiry were enormous. Opening the door to continental interiors, scientists and natural historians exploring Latin America would play a major role in making that region accessible to the European and American imagination. By the mid–1700s, scientific expeditions probed deeper and deeper into the interiors, revealing a rich flora and fauna. The increasingly sophisticated readers who followed their explorations were dazzled by the exotic wildlife and fascinating customs observed by English, French, and German scientists.

As Merian had hinted at about fifty years earlier, an almost magical interior where spellbindingly beautiful butterflies—and riotously-colored and raucously-calling birds such as macaws and toucans—could not only dazzle and enchant explorers, but also unlock many scientific secrets. The Central American and South American tropics brought Europeans face to face with unique creatures such as the huge armadillo-like *tatou* and varied kinds of mischievous monkeys. Danger, too, was part of the appeal, with huge Boa constrictors, deadly poisonous snakes, ferocious caimans, and ravenous piranhas laying in wait.

Of the many scientists during the era, Alexander von Humboldt stands head and shoulders above all others. Born in 1769 to wealth in Berlin, Humboldt had a passionate interest in natural history. By 1790 he had attained an education that was both broad and specialized in certain subjects such as botany and geology. By all accounts Humboldt was a polymath, that is, learned in many diverse subjects in the arts and sciences. Moreover, he had a passion for field work that led to his making many original discoveries. Varied disciplines claim Humboldt to be theirs—an astronomer, botanist, chemist, geographer, physicist and the like—but in truth he was all of these and more. Humboldt was fluent in German and French but conversant in many languages, including English and Spanish. He had a penchant for making friends and building lasting relationships that, coupled with his love of travel, led a historian of exploration to claim "Humboldt was the most illustrious foreign traveler in the New World in the late colonial era."[3]

Among Humboldt's closest life-long friends was Aimé Bonpland, a brilliant French botanist who was four years younger and bristling with much the same passionate energy for studying nature in the field. Educated in Paris, Bonpland was a physician and natural historian of considerable talent. Although history has positioned Bonpland in Humboldt's shadow, as Stephen Bell astutely observes, he was a luminary in his own right and made many scientific discoveries.[4]

With that relationship in mind, I shall now discuss the Alexander von Humboldt-Aimé Bonpland-centered scientific exploration and discovery film titled *Aire Libre* (1996).[5] In it, Humboldt's relationship with Bonpland is explored as their expedition encountered northern South America in 1799. Not to be confused with the modern-day Argentine romantic drama of the same name, this Venezuelan film involves the famed Prussian explorer reflecting back on a portion of his life during which he makes numerous groundbreaking scientific discoveries—and personal discoveries as well. Since we know so little about Humboldt's inner psyche, portions of this film should be considered speculation rather than history. In fact, a disclaimer at the beginning of the film states that it is an "imaginary chronicle" that is "more dramatical [sic] than historical." However, as Mary Louise Pratt further observed, Humboldt himself was something of a dramatist as well, for he "…reinvented South America first and foremost as nature … a dramatic, extraordinary nature, a spectacle capable of overwhelming human knowledge and understanding."[6]

As a spectacle, nature might seem to be the perfect subject for a filmmaker. However, there was a catch: paradoxically, as Pratt continues, the nature that Humboldt experienced was "[n]ot a nature that sits waiting to be known and possessed, but a nature in motion, powered by life forces many of which are invisible to the human eye."[7] Whereas nature in motion may be relatively simple to capture on film, Humboldt added the challenge of capturing the essence of those mysterious life forces, which is to say making these otherwise invisible forces visible. Like the explorer he hopes to bring to life, the filmmaker must also plumb the *terrae incognitae* of what animates nature. In terms of cinematic expectations, director Luis Armando Roche had very big shoes to fill, not only portraying the world's most famous explorer and the secrets he and Bonpland uncover, but also capturing the spark that animates these explorers.

To Roche's credit, *Aire Libre* effectively portrays the expansive Humboldtian spirit of exploration in search of geographical and scientific discoveries. This film amounts to both a tribute and a paean, for Roche had long admired Humboldt's explorations. Emotionally invested in the project, he co-wrote the screen play with Jacques Espagne. Together, they ventured forth in creating an exploration-discovery story that—like Humboldt himself—embodies plenty of adventure and a great deal of cerebral reflection. Happily, they steered a course between those two poles and created a film that entertains, educates, and enlightens.

It is a challenge for a filmmaker to capture the sense of wonder that gripped Old World scientists in the New World while keeping as close to the scientific facts as possible. According to the journal entries of Humboldt and Bonpland, their encounter with nature made them feel like curious youngsters again. In viewing and reviewing this film, I found myself exploring the connection between two depictions of the past—the film version and the original sources such as Humboldt's written works—my goal being to determine where and how they converge and/or deviate. Until fairly recently, books such as the enthusiastic *South America Called Them* by Victor Wolfgang von Hagen (1945/1955) were standard, but a recent spate of scholarly works such as *Humboldt's Cosmos* by Humboldt aficionado Gerard Helferich (2004) have helped tell this intriguing story more objectively.[8] However, the most pertinent works are by Humboldt and Bonpland themselves, the *Essay on the Geography of Plants* being a fine example of their scientific teamwork.[9] Their account of the expeditions covered in *Aire Libre*—which were originally published as *Personal Narrative of a Journey to the Equinoctial Regions of the New Continent*[10]—inspired the screenplay, but only to a point.

Like a number of dramatic films made a generation or so ago, *Aire Libre* begins with a funeral, in this case Aimé Bonpland's in the Argentine. The year is 1858, and the next scenes shift to Germany, where the ninety-year-old Humboldt (played by Wolfgang Preiss in his last film role) is informed about the death of Bonpland. That sad news starts Humboldt reflecting on their travels together "some fifty years ago in the heart of terra incognita." On a map, Humboldt points out the part of the world that had brought him and Bonpland together. We see the map for only a few seconds but as the camera focuses on it, Humboldt points to a locale on a river seared into Humboldt's memory. In a close-up view, it is revealed to be the Río Orinoco. The authority with which he does this suggests that Humboldt himself not only played a role in exploration but also mapping; the two, of course, are often independent. More to the point, though, these brief glimpses of the map confirm that exploration and discovery are inextricably linked as well.

The film now shifts to the pair's voyage on the aptly named sailing ship *Pizarro*. After weeks at sea, that voyage culminates in a signature event in Latin American history, and the history of exploration-discovery as well: the landfall of the youthful Humboldt and Bonpland at Cumaná, Venezuela, in mid–July 1799. At that time, what we today call Venezuela was known as Nueva Granada, and the port city of Cumaná was the capital of the sprawling province of Nueva Andalucía which fronted on the northern coast of South America. It is important to note that Humboldt and Bonpland were especially focused on the South American continent itself, which straddled the equator and was known through previous exploration (especially French) to contain a wealth of geographic habitats. It should also be recalled that Spain itself had funded previous scientific expeditions to its colonies, including the recent Malaspina Expedition of 1789–1784 headed by Alessandro Malaspina and José de Bustamante y Guerra. However, the latter expedition focused only on the coastal perimeters of continents, not their interiors.

Although the arrival of Humboldt and Bonpland in Cumaná was unplanned because the *Pizarro* was forced to detour there due to medical problems on board, that proved fortunate as the adjacent area was perfect for natural history exploration. In the film, their arrival onshore is captured in an elevated shot that reveals both the shoreline and the tropical vegetation. The low-angle lighting gives this important scene an ethereal quality. In one sweeping take, the camera records the scientific European mindset encountering a seemingly unexplored tropical paradise.

From Cumaná, they will venture forth on excursions that resulted in many scientific discoveries. Humboldt was a luminary on this trip. He had been invited by Spain,

In this beautifully composed scene from *Aire Libre* (1997), explorers Alexander von Humboldt and Aimé Bonpland arrive on the north shore of South America—the beginning of an expedition that would greatly advance scientific knowledge. The scientific exploration of the tropics was of growing interest worldwide, and Venezuelan filmmaker Luis Armando Roche ably captured the spirit of the times (Bleu Blanc Rouge).

which was in the process of opening up its realm to scientists in hopes that exploration could stimulate discoveries that would in turn create economic opportunities. Alas, it was a bold diplomatic opening that would be a boon to natural history. However, it was one of the factors that would prove fatal to the Spanish Crown within a generation, for the liberalization advocated by outsiders such as Humboldt soon led to agitation for independence. That change haunts the story as the young Humboldt (Christian Vadim) himself experiences events that challenge his own sense of self—a persona that most historians regard as serious, dispassionate, and scientific despite his passionate humanism that was directed outward toward the politics of social change.

As noted earlier, dramatic films take some liberties with characters' roles, and *Aire Libre* provides many examples of this. In the film, the two explorers were primed for discovery, and just as soon as their landing boat touches the shore Bonpland (Roy Dupuis) begins collecting specimens. From almost the outset, their exploration and collecting was done with the assistance of locals. Humboldt's letters and journals support this, although the assistance provided was by a young Indian man they had met on board the *Pizarro* before they even landed. His name was Carlos del Pino and he later accompanied them on parts of the trip that drew them to this region in the first place—exploring the course of the Orinoco River. Humboldt's journals note the irony that their first

In Luis Armando Roche's film *Aire Libre,* naturalists Alexander Von Humboldt (Christian Vadim) and Aimé Bonpland (Roy Dupuis) began collecting a wide range of specimens new to science as soon as they reached the shore. This scene shows them examining seaweed and crabs, but they would soon head inland to determine the geographical relationship between two of South America's most important rivers—the Rio Orinoco and the Amazon River (Bleu Blanc Rouge).

and most lasting natural history contact in South America was a talented Indian. However, in the film, the local budding naturalist is a Latino named Pedro Montañar (Carlos Cruz) who puts his family life on hold in order to become their guide.

While on the subject of Indigenous peoples in this part of South America, it was originally (ca. 1500) within what anthropologists would later call the Circum-Caribbean region wherein highly advanced cultures based on intensive agriculture and substantial villages existed in close proximity to semi-sedentary tribes practicing slash and burn agriculture and skillfully fishing the waters. By the time von Humboldt and Bonpland arrived, however, this pattern had been drastically modified by introduced diseases, Christian religion, and a trade-based economy dominated by Spain. Adding to the cultural mix by the late 1700s was the large numbers of Africans originally imported by the Spaniards and the French. Although the lifestyle here was far from Edenic and the culture was much more than a simple Spanish-Indian duality, like most films *Aire Libre* creates the impression that it was virgin territory occupied by those two peoples. Dramatically speaking, however, that simplification is very effective, for by backdating the history it intensifies the primordial "feel" of this expedition.

Another cinematic liberty involves the compression of time so typical of dramatic films. Two years before the arrival of von Humboldt and Bonpland, an earthquake had rocked Cumaná and environs. About four months after they arrived, another temblor hit the city. According to their journal entries, Humboldt and Bonpland were awed by the destruction wrought by these *temblores*. However, the film creates the impression that one temblor happened shortly after they landed. Here, too, the director can be forgiven, for the camera-jiggling simulated action footage of the buildings swaying violently as colonial era architecture crumbles emphasizes the geological instability of the area—and perhaps even foreshadows the political instability on the horizon that will culminate in widespread revolution against the Crown. Film can pack many events into a short period of time, increasing drama and tension; an example of this the Leonid meteor shower that they astutely observed in close proximity to the earthquake. In a memorable scene, even before the dust settles Humboldt is actively noting the courses of the hundreds of meteors carpeting the night sky.

Throughout, *Aire Libre* rightly credits local Spaniards and Indigenous folk who introduced them to specimens new to science. In it, Humboldt praises earlier work in classification by Carl Linnaeus, and also alludes to the 1740s South American explorations of Charles-Marie La Condamine. However, he does not mention the work of the brilliant botanist Antoine-Laurent de Jussieu, who accompanied La Condamine and whose work resulted in the concept of families in classification systems that helped Humboldt immeasurably in understanding species diversity and distribution in South America. In scene after scene, Humboldt and Bonpland find and sketch specimens of the local flora and fauna, including a wide variety of tropical plants and animals such as snakes and parrots.

On this Venezuelan part of their South America trip, Humboldt and Bonpland traversed many diverse habitats, including the cooler, forested uplands in the east, and the sizzling hot *Llanos* (or grassy plains) inland from the coast. However, the film shows little of these, instead focusing on rivers, which were central to their major objective—trying to sort out the regional hydrography. Humboldt's goal was to determine how and where two rivers—the Orinoco and Amazon—meet. Decades earlier, La Condamine observed that the Rio Negro and Rio Casiquiare were key to this puzzle. In another example of how film compresses time, they seem to get to that task almost immediately, but in reality they embarked about four months later, after the rainy season ended.

As noted by geographer Karl Zimmerer, these investigations resulted in Humboldt's map of the Rio Orinoco system, which *El Libertador* Simón Bolívar (1783–1830) acknowledged was "a cartographic image that helped create the national territorial identity of Venezuela."[11] Although the film *Aire Libre* shows fleeting glimpses of Humboldt drafting this and other maps, it avoids dwelling on them; the audience does not literally see the contents of these maps despite their likely impact on director Roche and co-writer Espagne, who lay out scenes with broad horizontal stokes almost as if they are using the map as a guide. As on maps themselves, which may contain empty spaces—or "silences" as cartographic historians call them—the sparse use of maps in this cinematic adventure works to focus attention on the action taking place rather than the consequences of that action; that will come later in the film. Stated another way, in making this film Roche was less interested in portraying Humboldt as the recognized authority that he became than he is in depicting Humboldt as a budding explorer in the process of *becoming* an authority. Downplaying the actual mapping that Humboldt did helps this part of the film more open-ended and hence even more dramatic.

In both the movie and the original sources, Humboldt is always in charge, but Bonpland plays a major role as counterpoint. Humboldt is an astute observer and moves a bit more slowly and deliberately. Clearly the more enthusiastic of the pair, Bonpland is engaged with natural history and his senses appear to be running wild. By most accounts, Bonpland was stocky, but in the film he is muscular if not athletic. Humboldt too is up to the task, though in reality he had some health concerns. Insects in this area posed problems for all travelers regardless of their health. In one humorous scene, Bonpland is nearly driven mad by mosquitoes and buries himself in the sand, only to emerge scratching painful bites inflicted by other *bichos* (pesky insects) that live underground. In real life and in the film, Humboldt savored hearing about natural history from the locals, including reports of large boa constrictors. Despite the dangers, including the colorful and deadly coral snakes, the beauty of life here amazed them. This film's wonderful use of magnifying glass views of specimens being scrutinized further accentuates the act or process of discovery that accompanies exploration.

Among the local fauna commanding Bonpland's attention in the movie is the flirtatious and fiery Ana Villahermosa (Dora Mazzone), whom he meets shortly after his arrival. It is lust at first sight, and they make love with wild abandon, which Humboldt witnesses as if watching two animals mate. Alas, to Ana's dismay and Humboldt's relief, Bonpland chooses science over earthly pleasure and embarks on the expedition with Humboldt. In reality, Bonpland's most infatuating encounter took place elsewhere in northern South America, and it almost derailed that expedition. Nevertheless, the film captures not only Bonpland's passion for the local women, but also South America itself—a land to which he returned and married a local woman, living and studying nature for many years until his death. During those years, Bonpland often paid a steep price from petty political harassment and weathered occasional bouts with tropical diseases.

Throughout, *Aire Libre* nicely recounts the pair's earliest discoveries of unique flora, fauna, and other phenomena that had scientific and possible economic value. Among these were the rubber trees that would later become synonymous with the exploitation of the continent's interior river basins, especially the Amazon. Humboldt

In a delightful scene from *Aire Libre* (1997) depicting the close study needed to examine new specimens, Aimé Bonpland (Roy Dupuis) uses a magnifying glass—a subliminal reminder that the film itself relies on lenses to portray the act of exploration-discovery. Director Luis Armando Roche aimed for accuracy, but only to a point, stating that his film was a "dramatical" depiction of events (Bleu Blanc Rouge).

and Bonpland were well aware that medicinal plants could be found here, a case being quinine from the Peruvian chinchona tree, which had been discovered and used as early as the 1600s as an indigenous remedy for malaria. However, the native peoples themselves were interesting as well, for this era marked the beginnings of ethnography (later anthropology) and the fascination with anthropometry—the study of the dimensions of people's bodies, especially for comparative purposes between groups or races. The film's scenes showing Humboldt and Bonpland measuring the height of Indians are both revealing and delightful. Such scenes make abundantly clear their fascination with all life here, and serve as a reminder that early explorers were exploring people as well as places. When Bonpland applies red paint to his skin, and they both remove their shirts in the oppressive heat, there is a hint that they are tempted to go native. Scenes such as these help humanize these explorers, bringing them down a notch or two from their scientific perches.

In addition to a satisfying look at natural history discoveries, this film explores the intricacies of the socio-political environment. It depicts their making connections with local and regional government officials, one of whom (César Rivera, played by Dimas González) becomes their nemesis as he suspects them of subterfuge—either espionage or greed (seekers of El Dorado). It also effectively shows the importance of contacts in the Church being their guides. Humboldt's journals identify several of them. In the movie, a padre guides them through some difficult passages on the rivers, serving as a composite for the several priests that assisted them. Memorably, this priest has a sense of humor and irony, colorfully characterizing the location they seek as where "the waters mock the laws of gravity." Humboldt's writings frequently mention Padre Bernardo Zea, who accompanied them on the Orinoco expedition. He is depicted in this film as an important member of the expedition as he knows the territory much better than they do.

The cinematography along the Orinoco River superbly captures the explorers paddling their canoes through the Venezuelan interior. In this film too, waterfalls and rapids mark breaks in the storyline. In one scene, a canoe is upset, spilling the expedition's papers, which are collected and dried out in the sun. This scene provides director Roche the opportunity to showcase their copious notes and beautiful drawings, as well as depict the men working closely together to get the expedition back on track. Humboldt had nearly drowned at one of these patches of rough water, apparently the place he had pointed out on the map at the beginning of the film. That near-drowning is the most intense action scene in the movie, and it reveals how hard Bonpland had to work to resuscitate him. In this scene and in real life, Humboldt owed his life to Bonpland. The film's making this debt clear further rescues Bonpland from the perpetual shadow he had been in. Ultimately, the expedition was successful in that it also vindicated another Frenchman, namely the earlier-mentioned scientific explorer La Condamine. Humboldt and Bonpland definitively proved that La Condamine was right: the Casiquiare Canal (channel) at the juncture of the rivers really existed. In the broader scope of things, it also showed the fluidity of river systems such as the Orinoco and Amazon that tend to be considered separate entities.

Of the two explorers, it is noteworthy that Humboldt wrote very kinetically and visually, almost as if he were urging a painter to capture them on canvas. For example, at sunset after a powerful electrical rainstorm, he described the sun's appearance "...on a firmament of indigo-blue. Its disk was enormously enlarged, distorted, and undulated towards its edges. The clouds were gilded, and fasciculi of divergent rays, which reflected the most brilliant colors of the rainbow, extended even to the midst of the heavens."[12] Humboldt was among the first, but far from the last, to describe the majesty of South American sunsets in such vividly romantic terms. In a manner of speaking, though, Humboldt here also challenges filmmakers of the future who wish to capture some of this celestial magic as poetically. For his part, director Roche was up to the task as he portrays the environment with some of Humboldt's enthusiasm for it. This involves the effective use of close-ups of natural subjects as well as sweeping vistas with plenty of sky to remind viewers that Humboldt was interested in both the heavens and the earth.

This film is well titled. In vernacular Spanish "aire libre" (fresh air) also refers to new and unconventional lifestyle choices, what some refer to as "out in the open." Insightfully, it deals with themes such as seduction as exploration, and exploration as seduction. It almost choreographs the elaborate dance between the intellectual/cerebral and the sensual/carnal that characterized the nineteenth century. Sensuality and sexuality run like a strong current throughout this film. A few examples follow. Witnessing Bonpland and Ana copulating, the stoic Humboldt appears ready to make scientific observations; however, he also might be pondering why he knows so little about the female of his own species, or for that matter, a fellow male's being so swept away by sexual passion. In another scene, Humboldt is taken aback when the enthusiastic Bonpland describes how similar in appearance a newly discovered orchid is to a woman's

In various scenes, the film *Aire Libre* also makes very effective use of sweeping vistas—such as this one of the Humboldt/Bonpland expedition exploring the course of the Río Orinoco. Director Luis Armando Roche insisted on using authentic geographical locales and accurate watercraft to make the film as credible as possible. As in many films involving rivers, the rapids along this river spelled trouble for the expedition, and marked a turning point in the film's plot (Bleu Blanc Rouge).

vagina, which Humboldt has never seen until he assists Bonpland in delivering a baby. Elsewhere in the film, when Humboldt tells a group of adoring young women that pollen is the "sperm of plants," he seems clueless as to why they blush and laugh nervously.

One of the delightful mysteries in the history of science is Humboldt's sexuality, or lack thereof. In this film, Humboldt reflects on his own past to try to decipher how he intellectually immersed himself in the world and universe while denying himself the pleasures and heartaches that characterize romantic sexual relationships. For the record, he was remarkably discrete, leaving the world to wonder about his sexual orientation. For all we know, he might even have been asexual, but that is beside the point. Director Luis Armando Roche seems to respect this boundary, but recognizes the tension it causes. In one scene suggesting homosexuality, Humboldt very tentatively, perhaps lovingly, touches Bonpland's shoulder; they even swim in the nude together, but nothing sexual results from this. This is to the film's credit as Humboldt coming out would be too definitive and simplistic a solution to the mystery.

Aire Libre conveniently sidesteps one aspect of Humboldt's life that is a bit easier to uncover, namely, his tireless and very effective self-promotion. He not only underwrote the entire five-year Latin American exploration from his personal fortune but also spent as much or more promoting himself throughout his life. On screen and in popular culture, though, Humboldt's only obsession was knowledge, and he pursued it passionately and incessantly. Still, one wonders about any regrets he may have had. At the end of the film, the elderly and weary Humboldt prepares to die never having experienced earthly pleasures despite his many accomplishments. These include having shaped the trajectory of science, helping bring about political revolutions that literally freed people from chains, and leaving written masterpieces such as the book *Cosmos*, which owes a major debt to his explorations in South America.

The film *Aire Libre* focuses only on the Venezuelan part of the journey. Thereafter it continued westward into the towering Andes mountains, where Humboldt drew his profiles of the topography and sketched vegetation—work that is often considered the foundation of modern biogeography. Bonpland's observations contributed to this, but his work often goes uncredited. After the South American experiences, Humboldt was intent on seeing Spain's more northerly possessions as well. On his return to Europe by way of Mexico, he spent some time in Mexico City, making maps of New Spain for the Crown. These were based largely on maps in the archives there. His illustrations of and observations about Mexico's ancient ruins helped bring them to the attention of Europeans. On this return leg of the trip, the United States also beckoned. Before crossing the Atlantic, Humboldt visited Thomas Jefferson in Washington, D.C., in 1804, weighing in on maps of the western part of North America.

The work of Bonpland was similarly well respected, and emulated by subsequent explorers. Both left a great legacy. Interestingly, forty years later (1844) the free-wheeling American military explorer John Charles Frémont—a protégé of Humboldt—entered the wilds of Alta California, Mexico. On that reconnaissance, Frémont carried a copy of Bonpland's botanical studies, and named varied geographical features after his idol (e.g., Nevada's Humboldt River). At the same time, Frémont was busy revising Humboldt's map of the region, which became part of the United States after the U.S.-Mexican War (1846–48).

After their experiences in northern South America, the careers of Humboldt and Bonpland took different turns. Although Bonpland had been honored by Napoleon, he was the more introspective and locally focused of the pair, modestly dedicating the rest of his life to studying South America. Humboldt, on the other hand, was well-prepared to enter the world stage with a signature flair for the dramatic. As Humboldt put it in a letter to writer Caroline von Wolzogen in 1806: "In the forests of the Amazon River … as on the edges of the high Andes, I got the feeling—that, as if animated by a spirit from pole to pole, one single life has been infiltrated into stones, plants, and animals, as well as in the swelling breast of mankind."[13] *Aire Libre* succeeds in capturing this expansive spirit. To Humboldt, who concludes in the film that "our work lives on," it was all part of a continuing effort.

For his part, Venezuelan director Roche oversaw *Aire Libre* as an international effort between France, Canada, and Venezuela at a time when his country was in a difficult political transition between the right and left. Like Humboldt and Bonpland, who loved the place and its people even before the modern nation of Venezuela came into being, director Roche taps into a primordial spirit. In that sense, *Aire Libre* can be viewed as patriotic—a tribute to a country that is deeply loved and lovingly filmed on location—and whose exploration-discovery is now shared with the world through the magic of cinema.

For the record, *Aire Libre* was not the first film to address Humboldt. The 1980 film *Caboblanco*,[14] which is set in the fictional port of Cabo Blanco, Peru (but was actually filmed in the picturesque port town of Barra de Navidad, Jalisco, Mexico), gives Humboldt some recognition, albeit off-screen. Although the film was billed as the search for a sunken steamship off the coast of South America, much of it resonates as a Cold War era international spy drama involving German, British, and French operatives. Rounding out this international mélange is Gifford "Giff" Hoyt (Charles Bronson), an American expatriate trying to lead a quiet life as an innkeeper in the sleepy town. In one scene, Giff corrects a British operative who claims he is a scientist investigating the Humboldt Current that the famed scientist had discovered. To this seemingly authoritative statement, Giff responds that any scientist should know better: the current off the coast of Peru was not discovered by Humboldt, but rather named in his honor by subsequent scientists. Another delightful surprise in this film also involves geography: a pet parrot, which actually has a starring role throughout the film, is the only one that knows the latitude and longitudinal geographic coordinates of the treasure! This enjoyable film plays with many exploration-discovery tropes, most of which astute viewers will have a field day discovering. Of note is that critics tagged *Caboblanco* as a sorry remake of *Casablanca* (it does have some deliberate similarities), and it had very limited release in theaters in the United States, where it bombed. Thankfully, Europeans knew better, and it became a hit there, in the homelands of Humboldt and Bonpland.

EIGHT

Walker

Adventurism and Anachronism in Central America

In the nineteenth century, sweeping changes transformed much of Latin America, among the most profound being the expulsion of Spain, the creation of independent countries where provinces once existed, and the emergence of its neighbor to the north into a world power. Toward the middle of the century, the U.S.-Mexican War (1846–1848), followed by the Gadsden Purchase in 1853, had reduced the size of Mexico by about half. Among other things, this provided the United States with a southern gateway to the Pacific and the Orient. For most Americans, winning the war with Mexico was sufficient to fulfill claims of Manifest Destiny. However, some of them continued to eye lands south of the border with military expansion in mind. The more enthusiastic among these formed small private armies and acted on ambitions. Given Mexico's proximity, that still-young country seemed a natural for invasion by what historian Joseph Stout called "Schemers and Dreamers."[1] Latin American countries farther south beckoned as well to these enterprising and opportunistic explorers.

Called filibusters after the Dutch term for "free-booters," they often claimed to be freeing people from oppression by "despotic elites." As recent scholarship confirms, these filibusters were often idealistic and they hailed from all regions of the United States. Some were very well-educated professionals and highly charismatic. Disavowing the term "interloper," they considered themselves saviors of people in foreign lands. Some filibusters even claimed that they had been invited by important citizens of the countries they infiltrated. Ultimately, they had one thing in common: although they claimed to be freeing people from tyrannical governments, the new governments they created quickly degenerated into tyrannical regimes themselves.[2]

Noteworthy among these filibusters was the eccentric and eloquent William Walker (1824–1860). Born in Tennessee, he was highly educated and spent a year studying in Paris. A young man on the rise, Walker soon became well-connected in the Antebellum South. Although he had trained to be a doctor, he had other skills as well. At about five feet two inches tall and thin as a rail, Walker was undistinguished looking—except for his penetrating gray eyes. Like many Americans, he moved west to California in search of opportunity associated with the Gold Rush of 1848. In 1853, Walker became a household word when he brashly invaded northwestern Mexico with a small army and conquered, at least momentarily, the desert states of Baja California and Sonora. The American public loved such men of action, but the federal government was more ambivalent and disapproving. Although Walker had unified those two Mexican states under the name Sonora, his tenuous rule of that would-be empire lasted only about a year. Overstaying their welcome, he and his rag-tag army were thrown out, in part with the assistance of the U.S. military, to whom they surrendered. The film *Walker*[3] covers that episode briefly, but focuses on his next big move, the invasion of Nicaragua, a country far to the south in Central America, where Walker also hoped to take other countries as well.

As films go, *Walker* proved to be as quirky and controversial as its namesake protagonist. It was directed by Alex Cox, who hailed from England but studied film at UCLA. In 1984, Cox's film *Repo Man* had earned accolades for its gritty depiction of urban life. However, Cox now decided to tackle a more historical subject. At the time, Walker was a relatively unknown figure, though in 1860 Walker himself had published his accounts of what he called *The War in Nicaragua.*[4] By the mid-twentieth century, Walker had long faded into obscurity, and Cox aimed to resurrect him.

Cox first heard about the historical character Walker while in Nicaragua to observe elections in 1984, and then read more about him from an article in *Mother Jones* magazine, both of which hint at Cox's political activism. Fortuitously, Walker's book had been reprinted and annotated in 1985 by the University of Arizona Press. The screenplay was based in part on that source, but involved considerable imagination. The more Cox learned, the more convinced he became that Walker was the perfect subject for his next film. In the telling, Cox wanted to avoid glorifying Walker, who was "a pretty bad guy." As he added, "I didn't think he deserved [a] … normal, historical, respectful style." That proved to be an understatement.

By this time, Cox had fallen in love with Nicaragua, his zeal further ignited by its pro-communist government headed by Daniel Ortega, whom the left-leaning filmmaker found inspirational. A film about Walker as an interventionist would make quite a statement. Enthusiastic about the project, Nicaragua helped fund it. To prepare the screenplay, Cox hired Rudolph Wurlitzer, and they worked together on it as the project developed. Wurlitzer also wrote a book about the making of this film titled *Walker: The True Story of the First American Invasion of Nicaragua.*[5] The word "First" in that title was crucial because a second American invasion was currently underway in the 1980s.

In an unusual arrangement no doubt connected to the film's funding, two Nicaraguan officials reviewed the screenplay: Sergio Ramírez was Nicaragua's Vice President and also a novelist. The other, Ernesto Cardenal, was a poet. Those literary skills may help explain some of the film's almost poetic dialogue and its passionate, romantically patriotic portrayal of the country. As I will show, the pace of *Walker* varies from frenetic to languid, keeping the audience on its toes for what might come next. Cox leaves little time for reflection, though, and gets down to deadly serious matters very quickly, and those have everything to do with volatile politics.

Although the film begins with glimpses of Walker's occupying forces being routed from Mexico, it quickly moves to his trial in the U.S. for violating the Neutrality Act. Despite his arrest, Walker (Ed Harris) was considered a hero by many in the United States. Even though he is about seven inches taller than the real Walker, Harris proved to be perfect for the part of the grey-eyed Anglo-American zealot. The real Walker almost always dressed in black, and had the demeanor of an intense preacher, as does Harris throughout the film. Cock-sure of himself, Walker smirks when the California jury exonerates him. From the start, the film depicts Walker as having something of a dual personality[6]—a deeply introverted quality that contrasts with his flamboyant public persona. On the one hand, Walker personifies dedication. He has a sweetheart named

Ellen Martin (Marlee Matlin) whom he evidently adores and plans to marry; moreover, he also hopes to start a newspaper and become a respectable businessman. As in real life, Ellen is deaf and mute, so she communicates in sign language. Cinematically speaking, this emphasizes the complexities mounting in the communication between characters, and also hints at some of the same challenges between the director and the audience that lie in store.

Regarding communication, there is an underlying tension in Walker's relationship with Ellen, as evident in one humorous scene in which he communicates that he may have to cooperate with a Southern slaveholder to obtain funding. Obviously despising this slaveholder, whom she signs to "go fuck a pig," Walker is astounded by her unbecoming expressiveness. The slaveholder has no idea what she meant and Walker refuses to tell him. In another exchange, Ellen signs that she is fed up with Walker's obsession with "Manifest Destiny." He is nonplussed by Ellen's vehemence because his destiny is manifestly on the side of spreading far and wide the blessings of American democracy, even to those not willing to accept it. Truth is, quite aside from his domestic and journalistic plans, Walker intends to return to his risky filibustering, which Cox suggests is an irresistible addiction.

More practically, that adventurism will require considerable clandestine funding. In the next scenes, Walker is summoned to a meeting by the portly Cornelius Vanderbilt (Peter Boyle). Their surreptitious rendezvous in an isolated desert locale showcases the conflict between the idealistic Walker and the crafty Vanderbilt. As a confirmed leftist from Liverpool, Cox was looking for a despicable capitalist and found Vanderbilt irresistible. However, although that capitalist was involved in the intrigue of the time period, historians note that Walker appealed to Vanderbilt's assistants, and more to the point actually found funding support from Charles Morgan, a rival steamship magnate who was also developing routes to Central America. Cox was evidently unconcerned about such details.

In this memorable Walker-Vanderbilt meeting scene shot in the Sonoran Desert near Old Tucson, the lanky filibusterer meets with the toad-like transportation magnate—who brings to mind an Oriental potentate in a lavish tent, servants at the ready. With flies buzzing and Vanderbilt farting to prove his disdain for civility, Cox wants the audience to appreciate the seediness of what is transpiring. Vanderbilt personifies crass vulgarity while Walker seems to have loftier ambitions. Although both have geopolitical goals, Vanderbilt's is control over a shipping route across Central America that links his lines in the Atlantic and Pacific, while Walker's is the acquisition of territory for what he deems to be a higher purpose. A geography lesson is about to ensue as the conversation gets down to business.

When Vanderbilt asks Walker if the name "Nicaragua" means anything to him, Walker tersely responds, "Nothing at all." In reality, Walker was well-read and knew considerably more than Cox acknowledges. However, Cox wanted to position Vanderbilt as the know-it-all empire builder, and Walker as clueless. Conveniently, Vanderbilt has a colorful map of Central America positioned on an easel, and he uses it to lecture Walker and the audience about his strategy. Dismissively, Vanderbilt proclaims: "Nicaragua is a tiny, insignificant country somewhere to the south of here. But this worthless piece of land happens to control the overland route to the Pacific." This map gives the audience a glimpse of Nicaragua in light of Vanderbilt's empire building intentions. It also geographically situates Walker's next big expansionist move.

On the railroad tracks nearby, the transportation magnate's personal train

In this superbly composed scene from the 1987 film *Walker*, the story's namesake—lanky filibusterer William Walker (Ed Harris, left)—is introduced to the transportation magnate Cornelius Vanderbilt (Peter Boyle, seated) in the American Southwest. The easel-mounted map in the center of this scene depicts Vanderbilt's transportation route across Nicaragua—a prelude to the geography that Walker will encounter in that strategically-positioned Central American country (In-Cine Compañia/Industrial Cinematográfia/Northern/Walker Film Ltd.).

awaits, its plush private car and gilded locomotive lettered for what everyone called him—"Commodore Vanderbilt." With its locomotive's boiler hissing impatiently, the train provides a wonderful metaphor-charged symbol for American progress despite the fact that a railroad would not reach this area until about two decades later. This is just the first of many anachronisms that will follow, but it deftly serves to confirm the link between robber baron Vanderbilt and his transportation-related ventures. The idealistic Walker turns down Vanderbilt's offer to fund activity that will stabilize the country for business. Walker now heads back to civilization, but soon discovers that it is difficult to secure funding for his filibustering expeditions. After Ellen dies of cholera, the grief-stricken Walker reluctantly accepts Vanderbilt's proposition.

With the financing in place, Walker re-assembles his army and heads down to Nicaragua in 1855. He will, in effect, explore the area as he conquers it, a technique that Spaniards and others had long employed. Cox uses an on-screen map to chart, in a bright neon red, the course of Walker's ship as it travels south from San Francisco to Realejo on the Pacific shores of Nicaragua. From this point on in the film, Nicaragua takes center stage and is gloriously captured in spectacular footage by David Bridges. Location was uppermost in Cox's mind. As he matter-of-factly put it in an interview: "We made a film in Nicaragua that we couldn't have made anywhere else."[7] Through that lens, Nicaragua is both a beautiful and exotic place. Walker's personal notes reveal his enchantment with Nicaragua. The place filled his senses, as it did many of his troops. Nicaragua's air was like tonic, and its scenery breathtaking. Its coastal shorelines, expansive lakes, and volcanic mountains are stunning, and are Cox's tribute to this beautiful but war-torn Central American country. The invader's premise was somewhat romantic, but in a sense so was Cox's vision of the place.

After their arrival, which Cox depicts as not triumphant but rather comically as a shipwreck just offshore, Walker marches the troops toward what he calls the "small, un-regenerated hamlet" of Realejo. Here, Walker meets with local supporters of his invasion. Marching northward toward Rivas, his troops get their first glimpse of the beautiful landscape and the attractive women they've heard about through rumors. To get in top shape for the action scenes, Ed Harris led a company of the actors on what he jokingly called "a forced march" through ten miles of rural Nicaragua. It was grueling, and put them in the right frame of mind. As Harris made clear in interviews, this is a human story as well, and a lot of bonding goes on. Throughout the film, Walker is close to some of his men. One of them is Captain Hornsby (Cy Richardson), a man of African descent who seems the most loyal of all, and most hopeful for the democratic reforms that Walker espouses. For his part, Cox was fascinated by Walker's troops, who were called "The Immortals" as they defied death so readily for their leader and his cause. Surprisingly, with only a few hundred men, Walker was able to seize Nicaragua, and establish an upstart government in liaison with one important faction of the existing government, the "liberals," acting on Walker's behalf. To Cox, it was an act of betrayal and he wanted to set the record straight.

Through Cox's lens, some of the sights in the back country are peculiar indeed. In one scene, the troops encounter an itinerant artist sketching a large totemic idol in the

In the widely panned but brilliantly edgy film *Walker* (1987), the namesake's military expedition treks deep into Nicaragua, where it encounters an artist (uncredited) sketching a monstrous figure at the edge of the forest. Upon closer inspection, it appears to be a totem-like representation of a robber baron from the late-nineteenth century. This whimsical prop confirms director Alex Cox's disdain for capitalists in general, and Cornelius Vanderbilt in particular (In-Cine Compañia/Industrial Cinematográfia/Northern/Walker Film Ltd.).

jungle. It appears to be about eight feet tall, dark brown, bulbous, and rather grotesque; upon closer inspection, it is an ugly rotund man grinning like a contented Buddha or a gloating Cheshire Cat. As if encountering a significant archaeological feature—just the kind of thing that would have stopped Humboldt in his tracks and resulted in a drawing for posterity—the artist sketches it in his field notebook. For his part, Walker stares at the idol as if either awestruck or dumbfounded. The audience only sees this idol, and the sketch being made of it, for a few seconds, and may dismiss it as some bizarre archaeological curiosity. However, it is worth a closer look. Some viewers may think it resembles Jabba the Hutt from the *Star Wars* films (1977...), a nefarious being who plunders the universe—and they might be correct. A closer look reveals it to be a caricature of a predacious American robber baron, right down to the cigar in its mouth. To the left of this monstrosity, a snake slithers up a tree. This scene underscores how much Cox despised Vanderbilt and all he stood for. From that point on, attentive viewers realized that *Walker* was not going to be another run-of-the-mill, historically themed adventure movie. Throughout, Cox infuses an otherwise serious film with this type of edgy, off-beat satirical humor.

After their march inland carrying Cox's version of a flag that Walker designed for Nicaragua, they reach the deceptively sleepy town of Rivas, where they meet with surprisingly stiff resistance that claims many of the troops. Nevertheless, because he has inflicted substantial casualties there, Walker claims victory. From beginning to end, *Walker* is a violent film punctuated by quieter scenes of diplomatic interactions. That said, the mayhem is stylized and rendered almost artistically. Battle scenes full of

In this frenetic scene from *Walker* in which both the characters and camera are moving vigorously, the enthusiastic troops carry a flag for the proposed new ("regenerated") republic of Nicaragua. The film's director Alex Cox abhorred William Walker's historic invasion of the 1850s, and in this film drew parallels to the current (mid–1980s) U.S. invasion of Nicaragua under President Ronald Reagan, who sought to overthrow the communist-supported regime of Daniel Ortega (In-Cine Compañia Cinematográfia/Northern/Walker Film Ltd.).

slow-motion, blood-splattered action confirm Cox's near reverence for Sam Peckinpah's 1969 film *The Wild Bunch*.[8] That comparison is apt, for Peckinpah's film was also about American miscreants in Latin America, albeit much later (1910s) during the Mexican Revolution. Viewers who look closely will spot a remarkable sign that Walker and his troops pass. It reads SAM PECKIMPAH [*sic*] and is the type of inside joke that some filmmakers like to insert to keep viewers on their toes.

In his next move, Walker marches south with the remainder of the troops to the conservative stronghold of Granada, which is beautiful and strangely serene. Granada is the political center of the country and, surprisingly, puts up no resistance. Walker smugly fancies himself to be a conquering hero, liberating the people of Nicaragua and now controlling the capital. In one lush scene that mirrors Leonardo da Vinci's famous painting of the Last Supper, a banner hanging in the background welcomes him as Wilians [*sic*] Walker. For this conqueror who is sitting about where Jesus sat in the da Vinci painting, that sets an ominous tone.

As Walker soon discovers, Granada is ground zero for political intrigue. It is here that he becomes involved with an important and well-connected woman named Doña Yrena (Blanca Guerra). Although in real life Walker's relationship with her was the subject of some speculation, the film has him surrendering to Yrena's charms in a pivotal scene that takes place shortly after they meet. She meets alone with him and begins the conversation with politics, informing him that she can bring her enemies to their knees. Then, luring him into a private room, she does the seducing, coaxing him to kneel and perform oral sex on her. Clearly, Walker is unfamiliar with carnal love-making but evidently a quick learner, obeying her non-verbal commands. Metaphorically, he is now exploring the Tropics.

Upon entering the impressive capital of Granada with his troops, Walker finds the town eerily quiet and awaiting his arrival—a calm that will not last very long after the filibuster makes some ill-advised moves that enrage the opposition. In making the film *Walker*, director Alex Cox used this historic city to great effect. It was, after all, the actual location where the real William Walker formally took control of Nicaragua in the mid–1850s (In-Cine Compañia Cinematográfia/Northern/Walker Film Ltd.).

However, something else even more profound is happening. Through Yrena's seduction, Walker has become captive to the exotic Other, while tormented by the memories of his dead fiancée Ellen. In this film, Cox brilliantly uses sex as power, but not in the traditional sense of conqueror over the oppressed; rather, the conquered is getting the upper hand and hence gaining control through it. Yrena calls all the shots in this relationship, which is rather different than what transpired between the self-assured Cortés and the resourceful Tecuichpo in *The Other Conquest*. Yrena soon becomes Walker's mistress, bringing out his deep insecurities. Cox portrays him as an emotional wreck. Interestingly, Walker has again found himself with a woman who cannot understand what he speaks, as she supposedly knows no English, and he knows very little Spanish, at least in the film version.

Politically speaking, this nominally sexual relationship with Yrena has fatally compromised Walker's principles and derailed his ability to think coherently. In the film, she is a power-player in national affairs, but Walker's chauvinism and emotions keep him from recognizing this. Walker now holds a high position and seems to be pulling the strings, but is informed by his operatives that president Ponciano Corral is about to remove him. Enraged, Walker holds a mock trial and orders Corral's execution despite Yrena's pleas to spare his life. Alas, Walker ignores her pleas and has him executed in full public view. This act marks the beginning of Walker's downfall as Yrena turns the entire country against him. Although the cinematic Walker seems unaware of Yrena's real power, the screenplay and his actual accounts characterizes her as "A quick and minute observer, with all the gravity of the native race … fertile in resources for sending intelligence to her friends."[9] Imagine Walker's chagrin when he discovers—too late—that Yrena knew English all along. Although this sexual encounter may not have happened to the real Walker, it enables Cox to showcase Walker's faulty judgment and inability to communicate. After all, in Walker's short-lived nation of Nicaragua, English was the official language.

Cinematically speaking, *Walker* is a visual feast throughout, but the townscape of Granada is pitch-perfect as a stage for Walker's conquest. In scene after scene, its impressive but slightly rundown buildings and spacious plaza create the impression of former Spanish grandeur now slipping into decadence. A reviewer who visited the location in 1987 to cover the filming was charmed: "With its beautiful churches, broad central plaza and buildings with wide marble dance floors, Granada looks virtually untouched by the tumultuous events of the past decade."[10] In reality, the real Walker had burned down much of the town in the 1850s, but it had been rebuilt. On a technical note, the surface of the plaza was backdated by simply spreading a few inches of dirt over it. The infusion of capital through this film, which required construction of elaborate sets, employed many actors and extras; these helped give Granada's economy a much-needed boost. For Cox, the project amounted to a good cause as it boosted Nicaraguans' pride in their country struggling under the crippling economic sanctions and blockade imposed by the United States.

In this politically charged film, Walker's military invasion of Nicaragua starts out realistically enough but becomes hyper-dramatized as more anachronisms slip in. For example, people (including Walker himself) are excitedly reading issues of *Time* and *Newsweek* featuring him on the cover, though these magazines began publication in 1923 and 1933 respectively. Moreover, the otherwise period-perfect office setting features a desktop computer. In one memorable scene after the president's funeral, Doña

Yrena's horse-drawn carriage moves down a dirt road, only to be overtaken by a speeding Mercedes sedan that literally leaves her in the dust. When Walker seizes the steamships belonging to Vanderbilt in hopes of using them for expansion into other parts of Central America, the Commodore back in New York goes on a profanity-filled tirade; this too contains anachronistic language giving the impression that the future is converging on the past. Later, in a scene depicting the evacuation of Americans by the CIA (which was created after the Second World War), a helicopter arrives—about a century before it was invented. Being a Soviet chopper, it wasn't quite accurate for an American operation, but then again Cox was interested in creating effects, not authentic history or correct technology.

In that helicopter evacuation scene, Walker refuses to return to the U.S. despite Captain Hornsby's plea. On board the helicopter, the agitated Hornsby is killed by American machine gun fire, the suggestion being that a Black man is the Other to overly enthusiastic CIA agents. In these scenes, Cox portrays Walker as completely unhinged; in one over-the-top scene, as "doctor" Walker operates on a soldier, he removes small piece of the patient's flesh and eats it. This likely suggests that his megalomania is literally consuming those most loyal to him. To Cox, Walker's victories are literally pyrrhic. In one long, mesmerizing scene late in the film, truly spectacular footage shows the city of Granada ablaze as Walker strides through the raging conflagration. This image is so iconic that it was used in the movie's promotional materials, including the music CD, as well as the cover of Wurlitzer's book. It perfectly captures Walker's stand-alone, go ahead, character and propensity to use brutal force in achieving his ends. As in his earlier escape from Mexico, Walker seems immune from harm while others are slain all around him.

Signs and symbols in several languages abound in this film and are worth a deeper look. For example, the Nicaraguan flag especially designed and carried by Walker's troops to represent his new, or rather re-generated, country is only shown in reference to his invading maneuvers. Whereas Walker's flag was actually blue and white with a single star, Cox's was much different. More to the point, Walker's flag is never shown flying on any of the buildings during the almost two-year time his revolutionary government held sway. It is almost as if Cox does not want to glorify these symbols representing Walker's contemptible filibustering, but the historical record documents them in some detail. This is a subliminal clue that Cox edited and censored Walker and his escapades in order to preserve the integrity of a Nicaragua never really dominated by any upstart Yanqui.

As Cox intended, *Walker* drew attention to the current (1980s) civil war, in which the popularly elected socialist government Sandinistas and the U.S.-backed Contras were locked in mortal battle to gain control of the country. To Cox, it was just the latest of a long string of U.S. interventions aimed at keeping American-friendly officials in power and American banana companies in business. Harris relished the role of Walker, "who has incredible moral convictions but turns into such an evil person in the name of spreading democracy." Harris was impressed by Walker's bond to The Immortals under his command, as well as his passion for a cause. Harris's personal politics also played a role. He was against U.S. involvement and hoped the film might turn sentiment against it, thus stopping the bloodshed.[11] Of course, his being politically liberal, and hence simpático with Cox greatly helped. Although both Cox and Harris claimed the film was meant to promote peace and reconciliation—something that led to its backing by the Catholic Church—it clearly took sides, favoring the loyalists (and by extension the Sandinistas) and vilifying the insurrectionists (hence American-backed Contras).

In *Walker*, anachronisms become increasingly apparent as the film progresses, and they are used to suggest that Walker is increasingly losing touch with reality, as was the United States government under the zealous anti-communist president Ronald Reagan. Walker's even more ill-fated move to Honduras after his Nicaraguan debacle ended in his death by a firing squad in 1860. The real Walker had incurred the ire of Costa Rica and Honduras and they played a role in his demise. Even in that, though, Walker found immortality—at least for a while. As if on cue, his book *The War in Nicaragua* coincided with his execution, and helped keep his name in circulation as both a visionary and a martyr.

William Walker proved that timing matters. In an interesting retrospective about the making of *Walker*, Graham Fuller quoted co-writer Rudolph Wurlitzer: "When Alex [Cox] and I wrote the outline, we took the big decision to play with time, to see history returning, so that the reality of the film keeps shifting." Having made that decision, they noted something interesting happening: "As soon as we introduced the anachronisms, that opened the door for humor, irony, and surrealism." This, Wurlitzer contended, was key because "It was always important for this film to be funny—as well as serious and moving, with a progression into madness and horror."

However, although their premise was "If the anachronisms don't work, we'll know right away," they misjudged their impact.. As the quote above about humor, irony, and surrealism suggests, the audience was now juggling so many genres that things became confusing. Also, so many delightful anachronisms appeared that they likely gave the audience chronological whiplash, distracting from the trajectory of the historical story. Fuller noted that they had shot even more scenes involving anachronisms that never made the final cut. Among these was one in which Walker's beleaguered troops "…witness a ghostly procession of conquistadors in the jungle…."[12] In the context of this book, *that* would have been a striking scene, and one that could have grounded the film. However, it ended up on the cutting room floor, the premise being that "these dabs of the colonial past and future might have been too portentous, as if Cox had been trying to capture the hallucinatory quality of *Aguirre, Wrath of God* and *Apocalypse Now*."

Another thing that makes Walker such a strangely compelling film is its distinctive musical score by Joe Strummer, who decided to "keep it acoustic, much like 1850." That said, the fusion of wildly jazzy Caribbean and Brazilian samba seemed modern and edgy to viewers. On the other hand, the American folk sound of most of the score perfectly captures the type of cultural encounter underway between the troops and the locale. Songs like "The Unknown Immortal" and "Tropic of Return" make clear the vision and disillusionment of Walker's invasion. Despite the 1850 goal, its inclusion of that Latinized jazz decidedly helps move the film into the twentieth century, meshing harmoniously with the modern anachronisms. With occasional natural sounds such as crickets and waves reaching the shore, it is a haunting soundtrack for a disquieting film.

In the foreword of the 1985 republishing of Walker's *The War in Nicaragua*, Robert Houston made a prophetic observation about how one living in the present might view Walker's self-proclaimed actions in defense of democracy: "If now we address our rhetoric to fighting communism, then [in the 1850s] we addressed it to fighting ignorance, colonialism, the shameful inability of 'effete and decadent' races to govern themselves properly—anything that stood in the way of Progress." Houston added: "The ironies that have led us along a path from Nicaragua in the 1850s through … our habitual occupation of one Central American country or another, though Vietnam and to Central

America again in the 1980s, speak for themselves." He concluded, "There is no need for neon arrows to point them out. They will find you by themselves."[13] Houston wrote this two years before the movie *Walker* as released. For his part, Cox sounds a bit like Vanderbilt when he opined that Nicaraguans "...have always had this sort of geographical dilemma because they have this narrow strip of land that connects the Atlantic to the Pacific...."—a strategic asset but also a liability.[14]

Reading between the lines, it may be that Cox's conflation of the 1850s and the 1980s was too obvious, and perhaps simplistic. Intelligent audiences may have thought it amounted to overkill, if not condescension. Cox's neon arrows included everything from a helicopter to a new Mercedes Benz. Toward the end of the film, Walker himself seemingly alludes to things being disembodied from chronological time. For example, he asks Dr. Jones: "...when you were a little boy did you ever have a moment when you were sitting outside on the lawn and it was spring and you picked up a blade of grass or a beetle and you just watched it and it was whole and perfect and totally outside of time?" In this film, "outside of time" is apt indeed.

Another memorable quote is from Walker to his troops: "A great idea springs up in a man's soul, transports him from the ignorant present and makes him feel the future in a moment." However, perhaps the most relevant quote about time is from the real Walker himself, which he wrote in *The War in Nicaragua*: "...the army has yet [i.e., now] written a page in American history which is impossible to forget or erase. From the future, if not the present, we may expect just judgment."[15] To Walker, that America included the region we now call Latin America. In reexamining *Walker* in this light, it appears that critics in 1987 misjudged it based on their concern about how it treated the present. With thirty plus years hindsight, we can now see it as perfectly capturing for posterity Nicaragua at a crucial time in its twentieth-century history. It was Cox's love letter to a people under siege.

The very last scene in the film involves the firing squad that ended Walker's life. Some sources claim that he tried to make a speech in Spanish but was not permitted. By all accounts, he stood in front of an adobe wall as he faced his executioners, but in the film it is only Walker facing them on a beach. In the scene, which is done in silhouette with the sun behind the horizon, about six shots ring out simultaneously and Walker falls flat on his face into the sand. As the camera moves closer, Cox shows Walker prostrate, almost face down. He faces away from the camera as small waves lap against his lifeless body. In reality, however, one member of the firing squad moved forward, his gun barrel just a few inches from Walker's head. In what a biographer calls "a superfluous act of savagery," that unidentified gunman pulled the trigger and, as another biographer notes, "blew his face away...."[16] Given Cox's penchant for grisly and explicit gunshot violence, it is remarkable that the audience was spared this gruesome sight. Possibly, that carnage might have elicited some undesired sympathy for Walker, but then again it may suggest that Cox may have come to respect Walker enough to spare him that indignity.

In retrospect, Cox's enthusiasm for only going ahead in time from the 1850s in order to implicate his current political foes—rather than back in time to the implicate the colonial past as well—may have backfired. It kept the film from revealing a more universal story about the consequences of geographical expeditions resulting in political conquest. Many such factors appear to have had consequences for the film's bottom-line as well. *Walker* cost about six million dollars to make, but only brought in about a nickel for each dollar spent on it, a paltry $257,043. It fell victim to another financial reality.

Although Universal Studios was the distributor, they did little to publicize it and the film was rarely seen. Like Walker's undoing in Central America, this film proved Cox's professional undoing in Hollywood. He never made another film on this scale, though his 1991 Mexican production *El Patrullero* (The Highway Patrol Man)[17] proved he could still tell very compelling stories behind the camera. He continues to produce smaller independent films and teach college courses on film occasionally.

Not only was *Walker* a box office bust but also critics dumped on it because of the way it played fast and loose with history, and especially because it used anachronisms to the point of absurdity, if not distraction. Two of America's most respected film critics—Gene Siskel and Roger Ebert—each gave *Walker* zero stars. Given Cox's stature as a director, their decisive two thumbs down verdict was virtually unprecedented. Others were equally brutal. However, in a rare positive review, Vincent Canby wrote that "... *Walker* is something very rare in American movies these days. It has some nerve."

Most of the critics appear to have missed something profound about *Walker*. In a sense, it is two films in one. The first, a historical biopic about a misguided invader, could have succeeded if told straight. The second—a satire on misguided American policy as shown through a misguided American invader—could have been razor-sharp but was held hostage by the literalness of the anachronisms. Whereas I see *Walker* as those two films playing simultaneously, and working successfully, most reviewers and audiences do not think as stereoscopically or schizophrenically.

Of all the films reviewed in this book, *Walker* is the most difficult to find, though it went almost immediately to VHS tape, and then later (2008) as a Criterion DVD release. Truth is, critics had no way of knowing that it would become a cult classic for most of the reasons they panned it. *Walker* was wildly innovative; perhaps a bit too much so for critics' tastes, but nevertheless reveals considerable genius. In part because it took a high-profile political stance, *Walker* turned out to be too hot to handle, a searing historical/geographical parable about Latin America at the mercy of its neighbor to the north. That said, *Walker* is one of the truly essential Latin American exploration-discovery films—daring and memorable despite its flaws.

As a postscript to *Walker*, it should be noted that Ed Harris was not the first cinematic William Walker to run roughshod over Latin America. That distinction goes to Marlon Brando, who played the fictional Englishman Sir William Walker in *Burn!*[18] This 1969 Italian film directed by Gillo Pontecorvo was set on a fictional Portuguese Island in the Caribbean (Lesser Antilles) named Queimada (translated as burned) in the early nineteenth century. British intrigue plays a major role in a slave rebellion as the pyromaniacal Sir William Walker destabilizes the island by burning jungles, villages, and sugarcane fields. Brando jumped at the chance to play a Machiavellian white man ruthlessly manipulating Black slaves, nor was he a stranger to cinematic portrayals of revolutionary activity in Latin America, his most famous role being Emiliano Zapata in *Viva Zapata!* (1952).[19] As film historian Stewart Brewer philosophically observes in his discussion of such films: "Revolution and seeking for freedom through revolutionary violence has been endemic in Latin America throughout much of its history."[20] In a manner of speaking, it comes with the territory, and often proves irresistible to filmmakers—especially those who hope to shine a light on injustices.

NINE

Fitzcarraldo

The Foreign Entrepreneurial Capitalist as Explorer

As noted earlier of the film *Aguirre, the Wrath of God*, director Werner Herzog is a master at depicting obsessed characters. As Herzog himself discovered, few places on earth are better suited to making visions become reality—or reality become visions—than South America. That pertains not only to the early explorations of the 1500s, but those in the 1900s as well. Regarding the latter period, few films have better dealt with obsessive, exploitation-oriented exploration than Herzog's *Fitzcarraldo* (1982).[1] Set in the Amazon basin at the time of the great rubber boom of the late 19th and early 20th centuries, *Fitzcarraldo* is a period-piece with considerable panache. The rubber boom in the Amazon is one of the pivotal experiences in South American history and it comes alive in this quirky, but remarkably memorable, film.

Like the Spanish-born Lope de Aguirre four centuries earlier, the main character of this film—a mercurial, Irish-born entrepreneur named Brian Sweeny Fitzgerald but known to all as Fitzcarraldo—is a man with a unique vision that blurs the distinction between reality and fantasy. He, too, is played by Klaus Kinski, who seems custom-made for edgy parts. Kinski proved to be perfectly cast in this film; being white (and wearing a white suit), blond, and blue-eyed, he stands out in a world of dark-complexioned people. As Fitzcarraldo, he personifies the late nineteenth-century zealous capitalist whose goal is commercial development and profit. However, his greed is tempered by a softer side. As an avid music lover, Fitzcarraldo's main passion is bringing the opera to his part of the vast Amazon basin. Whereas many capitalists later gave away most of their fortunes after their deaths, Fitzcarraldo wants to spend it while living to see the opera come to the Amazon River town of Iquitos, Peru.

Therein lies the problem. He needs money to do so, but has a poor track record at raising it. His first effort, an aborted attempt to build a trans-Andean railroad, ended in failure. His second attempt, as a producer of commercial ice for massive public consumption in the sweltering tropics, seems destined to meet the same fate as, and is reminiscent of, the whimsical ice factory endeavor in the novel *One Hundred Years of Solitude*. In that novel, the eccentric Buendía family plans to construct buildings in the tropics out of ice to make the region more habitable, and Fitzcarraldo's scheme borders on that type of zany impracticality. When a detractor derides Fitzcarraldo as a "Conquistador of the useless," he feels even more compelled to plunge ahead. On the brighter side, Fitzcarraldo's beautiful and enterprising paramour Molly (Claudia Cardinale) has unswerving faith in him, stating on his behalf that "it is only the dreamers who move mountains." Molly is worldly and adept at making money. She runs a successful bordello in Iquitos. To tweak a phrase, Molly is a madam with a purse of gold.

The film begins with a frenetic and disheveled Fitzcarraldo, accompanied by a composed and unflappable Molly, arriving in Manaus, Brazil, on a small boat whose wheezing motor has broken down, so he paddles it furiously. They have come all the way from Iquitos, a journey of more than 900 miles (ca 1,500 km), evidence that Fitzcarraldo will do anything to experience an opera. Arriving too late as the opera house doors have been closed, Fitzcarraldo nevertheless talks his way in just as the performance begins. The opera is grand and the setting palatial, for Herzog shot these scenes at the opulent historic opera house in Manaus. After speaking with the haughty Manaus opera house manager, Fitzcarraldo becomes even more resolved to make Iquitos into much the same kind of cultural center. Fitzcarraldo may seem like a fanciful figure, but Herzog based him on the colorful Peruvian entrepreneur Carlos Fermin Fitzcarrald (1862–1897), who aspired to be one of the region's major rubber barons in the 1890s.[2]

The film now shifts to Iquitos, where Molly knows the town's movers and shakers, and arranges a meeting between them and Fitzcarraldo. They are not impressed with Fitzcarraldo's operatic obsession, but Molly narrows down the possibilities to the cynical and powerful rubber baron Don Aquilino (Brazilian actor Jose Lewgoy), who has so much money that he relishes squandering it just for the thrill. Moreover, he develops a liking for Fitzcarraldo, taking him under his wing in hopes of inspiring him. Unbeknownst to Fitzcarraldo, he is about to become an early twentieth-century explorer.

On what amounts to the first stage of Fitzcarraldo's explorations, Don Aquilino personally takes him deep into the back country where he has large land holdings. Toiling Indian porters convey the rotund, sedan chair–seated Aquilino, while a perspiring Fitzcarraldo charges ahead on foot, fascinated by the secrets of the densely forested interior being revealed to him on this journey. In this scene, Fitzcarraldo points to a tree and asks Don Aquilino if it is a rubber tree. Authoritatively, Don Aquilino answers "Yes," giving its scientific name "*Hevea brasiliensis.*" Dismissively, the cynical Don berates the Indians' beliefs that this is "the tree that weeps." However, Fitzcarraldo is captivated by their efforts that result in heavy, dense bales of latex and ultimately huge sums of money. As a visual device, the branching pattern carved into the tree trunk by the Indians to permit the white liquid latex to flow out by gravity is noteworthy. Reminiscent of the dendritic pattern of a river system as seen from the air (or on a map), it may be a subliminal reference to the fact that rivers play a key role in this film. This first phase of Fitzcarraldo's exploration results in an epiphany: the exploitation of rubber may provide him a way to reach his goal.

Back at the rubber factory owned by Don Aquilino, Fitzcarraldo's zeal intensifies when he learns about remote parcels farther in the interior that are inaccessible because they are effectively isolated from river transport to outside markets. Even tales of head-hunters and cannibals lurking there do not deter Fitzcarraldo. As with many adventure stories, a map further piques his interest. Hanging on the wall of Don Aquilino's office, it was purportedly prepared just before the border troubles of 1896 brought expansion to a temporary halt. Like a professor teaching an inquisitive student, Don Aquilino uses the map to inform Fitzcarraldo about the region. Fascinated by the map, Fitzcarraldo focuses his attention on one part of it that will play a major role in the film—the part that shows the location where two rivers running parallel to each other almost touch at one point. One of them (the Pachitea) is navigable through an infertile

This scene from Werner Herzog's tropical resource exploitation film *Fitzcarraldo* (1982) shows the film's namesake deep in the Amazonian jungle experiencing firsthand the tapping of rubber trees by natives. Fitzcarraldo (Klaus Kinski) wears this white tropical suit throughout the film. To viewers, the striking dendritic pattern on the tree trunk carved by workers to drain the latex may also serve as a subliminal cartographic reference to the configuration of river drainages—a major theme in this film (Werner Herzog Filmproduktion).

wilderness, and the other (the Ucayali) reaches into the promising lands but is not navigable due to an area called the Pongo das Mortes, a punishing stretch of rapids feared by the Indians. For the record, those two rivers actually exist in the Amazon basin, but their courses are not as depicted in the story. As Herzog mentions in the foreword of his informative book titled *Fitzcarraldo: The Original Story* (1982), he selected those rivers "...only for their sound." Similarly, the stretch of rapids is actually based on the less menacing-sounding Pongo de Manseriche, which located many miles away on the Río Marañón.[3] By writing the script himself, and overseeing all aspects of production, Herzog was in charge from beginning to end, including place-naming.

Returning to the story, when Fitzcarraldo asks Don Aquilino how accurate the map is, he replies "...pretty good...." This answer might normally cause some concern for anyone putting their trust in a map, but not to the visionary Fitzcarraldo. To him, it is sufficient to trigger a plan. As he observes, "the two rivers almost touch each other." By crossing the narrow divide between them, he could collect and trans-ship the baled rubber to markets, thus generating enough capital to start full-time production in the interior.

In reality, that divide between the rivers is called the Isthmus of Fitzcarrald,[4] and it interested Herzog even more than the aforementioned Carlos, after whom it was named. Fitzcarraldo's enthusiasm is likely to distract the viewer from the deeper messages embedded on this map, so I will now deconstruct it for readers. On one level, it is possible to see something of Herzog's inner psyche reflected in the positions of the rivers on this map. In a design sense, there is something sensual about their configuration. To those familiar with anatomical drawings, it has an almost uterine quality, the river courses suggesting fallopian tubes making a dual sinuous arc that further suggests the anatomy of the female body. Subliminally, this nominally topographic or hydrological configuration suggests fertility or fecundity, a theme that runs through Herzog's perceptions of the tropical Amazonian region of South America.

When the map's cultural content is viewed closely, those Indigenous people pictured on it add to the impression that not only this country, but also the people inhabiting it, qualify as primordial. In an insightful essay deconstructing this map, Richard John Ascárate observes that it "…assumes a cultural and historical surplus value far out of proportion to its brief time on-screen."[5] Created for the film by a Peruvian artist, this map is highly anachronistic for one supposedly made post–1896. Chronologically speaking it contains some mixed messages. Although its use of hachuring (from the French, to chop) is credible to indicate topography at that time—it is, after all, a scientific device from the mid-nineteenth century before contour lines were adopted by mapmakers— the map's depictions of nature and Indigenous people are not. As drawn, they are notoriously retro, long obsolete on scientific or governmental maps in 1896 and much more like those images on maps from two or more centuries earlier. A case in point is the anteater, another creature native to South America, with its long tongue extended. Other animals such as a sloth, crocodile, and monkeys add to the menagerie, suggesting several symbolic possibilities; the crocodile (of which South America has two varieties) suggests danger, while the sloth may signify torpor, but collectively the entire lot showcases an abundance of exotic tropical life.

Then, too, the images of anthropophagi generally, and cannibalistic native women in particular, are retro indeed. They are strikingly similar to—and clearly derived from—works by northern European illustrators such as Hans Staden's *Warhaftige*

In the historically themed film *Fitzcarraldo* (1982), a treaty map on the wall at the rubber factory provides Don Aquilino (right, José Lewgoy) with an opportunity to lecture Fitzcarraldo (Klaus Kinski) on the local geography, but the latter eyes the closeness of the two rivers at the bottom of the map and begins to develop geographic plan to get the rubber to market. Closeups of the map's content reveal its vivid illustrations of tropical animals and cannibalistic natives—symbols often found on much earlier European maps of the region. (Werner Herzog Filmproduktion).

Historia (1557) as later appearing in works by Theodor de Bry (1592) and Jan van der Straet (1638). Enigmatically, these flesh-devouring inhabitants were copied and drawn by the same unnamed Peruvian mapmaker, and Herzog evidently assumed they simply reflected a South American view and added to the authenticity. This is somewhat surprising given Herzog's interest in historical documents. Ascárate notes the irony here, for it may be that the mapmaker was unaware of the post-colonial critique connection, and/or putting one over on Herzog. For his part, Fitzcarraldo makes no comment about these seemingly fiendish peoples on the map, though when asked point blank earlier by Don Aquilino, "Have you ever seen a shrunken head?" he answers, "Yes. I mean no. Sort of...." As Ascárate wryly concludes of modern audiences who may have missed the connection between these people and the enduring tropes of colonial exploitation: "Have we seen these exotic others sometime, somewhere, before? Confronted with such a question, our only response may be that of Fitzcarraldo: 'Yes. I mean, no. Sort of....'"[6]

Fitzcarraldo is not one to trouble himself with such arcane connections. Excitedly carrying an armful of navigational maps back to Molly, he asks her to bankroll the project. Fancying himself to be an explorer, he exclaims, "we're going to do what nobody has ever done!" She agrees, and the second phase of his explorations is about to commence. In short order, Fitzcarraldo secures permission from the Peruvian government to develop the lands. In that scene, the doubting administrator who authorized it asks him a penetrating question: "Do you know what you are doing?" Tellingly, Fitzcarraldo doesn't even answer. Unfazed, he acquires an old steamboat and commences to refurbish it with money from Molly. Fittingly, he re-names it the *Molly Aida*.

The restoration of the vessel by scores of local workers is featured in numerous scenes; these provide a remarkable documentary record of the actual work that Herzog had to do in order to give the *Molly Aida* its historic feel for the rest of the film. One of the more memorable involves Fitzcarraldo showing Molly the work in progress, including a carpenter transforming a large piece of wood into the statue of a woman that will crown its prow. In this scene we see Fitzcarraldo's growing dependence on two feminized characters—Molly and the steamboat (traditionally referred to as she) personified by the maiden taking shape. Hand-carved for the film, this stunning statue features a native woman partially enveloped by a serpent. There is something visceral about this figurehead, a sensual woman in such close proximity to a deadly reptile, yet she seems to be invulnerable and even poised. Compared to Molly, who is usually dressed in white, the maiden is almost riotously polychrome. Like the map, this maiden is only seen for seconds but leaves a lasting impression.

There is an interesting cross-cultural back-story associated with "the carved Amazonian female figurehead," as Herzog relates in his book titled *Conquest of the Useless: Reflections from the Making of Fitzcarraldo*. As this symbol-rich icon was being fastened to the ship, a Campa Indian asked if she was dead, and was told "no, she is made of wood." When the Indian then asked if the snake was made of wood as well and told yes, he asked "how was it possible that the snake had crawled up and looped itself around her?" Herzog was well aware that the boundaries between the real and the imagined were being stretched when his European and American production was reshaping the cultural and historical geography of the indigenous peoples—as evidenced by his own vivid hallucinations at times.[7]

Returning to the film, Fitzcarraldo is bristling with self-confidence as the *Molly Aida* is christened, and now intends to prove that "I shall move a mountain." The

As the recently purchased steamboat is brought back into working order, Fitzcarraldo (left, Klaus Kinski) and his mistress Molly (right, Claudia Cardinale) discuss a figurehead that will be made by a local wood carver (unnamed, center). Later in the film, the completed figurehead for the steamboat *Molly Aida* is only seen for a few seconds, but is rich in regional symbolism—an Indigenous woman with a serpent wrapped around her (Werner Herzog Filmproduktion).

expedition to find that spot in the river adjacent to the isthmus gets underway after Fitzcarraldo hires a nervous Dutch captain, a surly Indigenous pilot, and a crew of about twenty listless locals. Keeping his strategy secret as the steamboat plies the river through denser and denser jungle, Fitzcarraldo states: "I am planning something geographic." Like his statement about moving mountains, it may sound like a metaphor but will prove to be an understatement.

Now underway, they have little trouble steaming upriver many miles. Along the way, they make a stop at the river terminal site of Fitzcarraldo's stillborn Trans-Andean Railway. This sojourn is pivotal, but to my knowledge film reviewers have overlooked it. In it, a dedicated station master of African descent (named Othelo in some sources and played by veteran Brazilian actor Grande Otelo; born Sebastião Bernardes de Souza) is overjoyed to see Fitzcarraldo again. For his part, Fitzcarraldo is surprised that Othelo has stayed on, now has a young family, and has remained loyal though unpaid. They embrace but Othelo is in for a shock. He has waited for the dream of the railway to be fulfilled, but Fitzcarraldo has long given up on it. On his brief tour of the site by Othelo, Fitzcarraldo is amazed to discover that the railroad's buildings and a locomotive and passenger car have been so well-maintained. In a brilliant soliloquy, Othelo proclaims that he has kept the jungle from consuming the site and even had to fight off Indians to keep them from looting it. However, Fitzcarraldo reveals that he has stopped only briefly to have his crew salvage rails for a project that he has in mind—but will not reveal to anyone. Othelo is beside himself as he sees the rails being taken up, and pleads with Fitzcarraldo not to take them out from under the locomotive in hopes that it will move across the mountains someday. Fitzcarraldo relents to a point, keeping Othelo's dream alive by permitting the rails to remain under the locomotive. With the work done, Fitzcarraldo and his crew continue their journey as Othelo bids farewell. Rarely is the collateral damage inflicted on workers by visionaries—in this case, Fitzcarraldo—so poignantly portrayed. This part of the film deeply personalizes the consequences of the Amazon's boom-bust cycles of commercial development.

Still possessed by his present vision, Fitzcarraldo never looks back. As the steamboat continues its journey, it enters virtually unknown territory, and tensions mount as Indians appear. The crew threatens to mutiny, but Fitzcarraldo momentarily restores order. To their surprise, the Indians now begin felling trees into the river behind them, effectively blocking their return to civilization. Panicked, the entire crew deserts, leaving only Fitzcarraldo, the captain, pilot, and cook on the vessel. Fortuitously, Fitzcarraldo had taken his wind-up phonograph, and he uses it to broadcast operatic music, which seems to soothe the Indians, who softly play flutes. As an aside, one wonders if Herzog's premise here was used a few years later in the filming of *The Mission* (1987), wherein oboe music helps a missionary bond with the Indians. In any event, it works in both movies. From the cook, who understands the natives' language, Fitzcarraldo learns that these Jívaro Indians have been waiting 300 years for the return of a white God who will be their savior. The Indians soon begin slinking aboard by the dozens, causing consternation. However, as if fate had dictated the entire scenario, Fitzcarraldo decides to capitalize on the situation by segueing into that role as white savior. To everyone's surprise, it works. They are now simultaneously in command of, and yet at the mercy of, the Indians.

Fitzcarraldo is a story, an expedition, and a film being inexorably drawn into unknown territory, some of it topographical and much of it psychological. As they continue onward, Fitzcarraldo scrutinizes the landscape for the place where the rivers

In this scene from Les Blank's documentary film *Burden of Dreams*, a jittery Fitzcarraldo (Klaus Kinski) is the center of attention as he ponders his next move after Indians (uncredited) board the *Molly Aida* uninvited. Perhaps in response to his earlier playing of opera music on a phonograph, they are softly playing flutes. At this very moment, the enterprising Fitzcarraldo is developing a plan to involve the Indians in his scheme of transporting his steamboat across the divide separating the two rivers (Les Blank and Flower Films).

should nearly touch. The captain informs him that the map they are using "is not precise" but Fitzcarraldo is undeterred. With map in hand, he soon spots that point, exclaiming, "This is it!" At this point he makes clear what "something geographic" meant. He takes a sheet of paper and confidently drafts a sketch map. Ingeniously, this map demonstrates to the crew, and the audience, exactly what he intends to do. He will defy geography itself by hauling the entire steamboat over that ridge, using the Indians as laborers. The captain is incredulous, saying it can't be done, but the Indian pilot thinks it is a fine idea. To everyone's amazement, all of the Indians agree.

Cinematically speaking, Fitzcarraldo's hand-drawn map works on several levels, confirming that it is he who is now the geographic authority and in complete charge of a ground-breaking expedition. In other words, he will put into action that which was only a subliminal conception in the map on Don Aquilino's office wall. The kinetic process of his drawing the map on board the vessel confirms that he will transform that very place. For Herzog, this map-making is in a sense autobiographical, because as filmmaker he will do much the same as what Fitzcarraldo now envisions. In this third phase of exploration, Fitzcarraldo is simultaneously exploring the environment and dominating it; this is exactly what happens when an explorer becomes a conquistador. Herzog was impressed that the real Fitzcarrald did just that by bringing a vessel to this point and hauling it overland to an adjacent river—but more or less as a publicity stunt. Moreover, that vessel was much smaller, only thirty tons, and was carted in pieces to the adjacent river.

In making this movie, Herzog was seemingly as possessed as his protagonist, for he decided that a much larger steamboat—over three hundred tons—would be used. Moreover, the vessel would be taken across in one piece, a feat that involved expertly trussing-up the interior of its hull so that it would not break in half. In filming this event, Herzog would use the real thing, not smaller scale models. This was in the time before the widespread use of CGI made such feats feasible, but even if that digital technology had been available, Herzog wouldn't have used it. Genius and madness combined here to produce an actual exploitation event—surveyors plotting lines through the jungle-covered slopes, workers actually felling forests and using dynamite to sculpt a deep gouge atop the hill, after which the steamboat itself was hauled, by hand and using the vessel's steam winches, over the divide. Those sections of railroad track came in handy as he used them for part of the boat's skid-way over the steep ridge. The effort was Herculean, and likely the most incredible engineering feat ever filmed in a dramatic movie. Herzog wanted the real thing, and that is what he—and the audience—got. In a sense, he was defying Hollywood directors, with their storehouses of visual tricks, and giving the audience his far more authentic version rather than a mere simulation. In reality, Herzog purchased three steamboats and used them in different scenes shot at varied filming locations in Peru over a four-year period.

Most discussions of *Fitzcarraldo* end with the scenes of the boat being hauled over the mountain, but other subsequent ones are notable as well. The morning after the night of wild revelry celebrating the engineering feat, the crew of the steamboat *Molly Aida* discovers that their vessel is nowhere to be found. They soon discover why she has vanished. During the night, several Indians cut the ropes holding her fast, and she drifted downstream—right into the jaws of the perilous rapids at the Pongo das Mortes. This, we learn, was done to appease the gods, who were angered by the boat being hauled to that river, thus denying them (and the rapids they oversee) the right to get even for such disobedience.

In making the film *Fitzcarraldo*, director/producer Werner Herzog was not content with the prospect of using miniature ship models. Instead, he decided to haul a real steamboat over the divide between two rivers—a dangerous and harrowing process that took a toll on the film crew, extras, and the environment. In Les Blank's documentary film *Burden of Dreams*, the environmental impact is evident in the felled trees and scar cut deep into the reddish-orange lateritic (iron rich) soil of the Amazonian tropics, (Les Blank and Flower Films).

Herzog, it seems, was willing to give those gods the opportunity to see how they would treat a real vessel. The scenes in which the huge boat careens defenselessly down the river are truly as spectacular as those involved in taking the boat overland. The film crew was on board to capture these wild scenes, and cameras also recorded it from the riverbanks. These comprise some of the most hair-raising maritime footage in film history. Contrary to how Hollywood would have done it—with a large ship model in a big tank of agitated liquid glycerin—this too is the real thing. Before our eyes, the vessel takes a severe beating, but manages to stay afloat and limp its way back to Iquitos, proving Fitzcarraldo's strangely circular vision of river navigation.

The film's concluding scenes are equally visionary, for they depict the arrival of a grinning Fitzcarraldo as members of the opera also arrive in separate vessels. In full costume, they present a surreal entourage much like an apparition traversing the river as music blares and the singers perform their parts. Unlike their uninvited arrival as nobodies in Manaus at the beginning of the movie, Molly and Fitzcarraldo are now triumphant. The beaming Molly watches proudly as Fitzcarraldo fulfills his dream of an opera in the hinterland. True to his vision, both he and Iquitos are vindicated.

This is a happy ending, but while this film was being made it could have been scuttled several times by unforeseen circumstances. The varied setbacks occurred almost from the start, and included irresolvable issues involving the Aguaruna Indians that forced a change in location from Santa María de Nieva to Río Camisea—several hundred miles distant. Then, too, the environmental damage and risk to life and limb while *Fitzcarraldo* was underway were astounding. Even back in the late 1970s, the outcry by environmentalists and workers' rights advocates was deafening, and such scenes could simply not be filmed today. Several people were seriously injured in making *Fitzcarraldo*. The environmental damage was evident in the deep scar cut into the orange-colored lateritic soil of the Amazonian tropical soil, though time has pretty much healed that wound.

As noted in the book *Burden of Dreams*, which accompanied Les Blank's fascinating documentary film about the making of *Fitzcarraldo*, even the close calls were ominous. For example, "…yesterday a huge tree was cut down for the film and it nearly wiped out the whole production crew and director in a single blow when it landed where it was not supposed to…."[8] In one of the most revealing takes in that documentary, Herzog throws his entire body into depicting the real goal of the movie—to transform geography. As he passionately describes the proximity of those rivers, and how Fitzcarraldo will use them to fulfill his dream, Herzog uses his arms to depict each one—in effect transforming himself into a map. He leaves no doubt that he has put his entire body and soul into making this film.

Making *Fitzcarraldo* involved a number of major production setbacks that would have derailed a less dedicated filmmaker. Its initial filming progressed so slowly that

As seen in Les Blank's eye-opening behind-the-scenes documentary film titled *Burden of Dreams* (1982 and 2000), the then-young director Werner Herzog uses his hands to characterize Fitzcarraldo's geographic vision to unite the two rivers—a gesture that blurs the distinction between body language and mapmaking. In other footage, Herzog brings his hands closer together until his index fingers almost touch as if he is pointing out the geographically themed plot of this film (Les Blank and Flower Films).

time took a toll on the actors and the budget. After forty percent of it had been filmed, actor Jason Robards (in the lead role as Fitzcarraldo) developed a debilitating case of amoebic dysentery and had to pull out of the film. Mick Jagger, who was playing Fitzcarraldo's eccentric sidekick, pulled out due to musical performance commitments. Whereas Herzog had tired of Robards' increasingly finicky demands and negativity, he was sad to lose Jagger, who was upbeat and enthusiastic about the project. Undeterred by these setbacks, Herzog decided to start over and forge ahead. When filming resumed, he dropped the Mick Jagger character completely and gave the temperamental Kinski the lead role abandoned by Robards. The filming progressed, but tensions remained high.

Most involved in the filming recall that Herzog's relationship with Kinski was strained to the breaking point. Some claim that Kinski was making life hell for those around him, including the Indigenous actors. As Herzog was well aware, this type of conflict between production company and locals had happened about a decade earlier in the making of *Aguirre, the Wrath of God*. The stories surrounding the making of both Peruvian based films merge in later tellings. In one version of the off-screen drama unfolding, a tribe's chief reportedly offered to kill Kinski. However, Herzog had an alternative. Fed up, he is said to have brandished a pistol himself and warned Kinski that if he did not cease and desist, two things would happen in quick succession. He would fatally shoot Kinski, and then turn the weapon on himself.

Beginning with *Aguirre*, Herzog had learned a lot from Kinski—including how to harness the actor's high-energy tantrums and channel them into memorable scenes. Truth is, though, suicide was not far from Herzog's thoughts during the filming of *Fitzcarraldo*. According to Les Blank, "he expressed his intention to end his life if he failed to complete the filming."[9] For his part, Kinski wasn't willing to go to the brink with Herzog. The temperamental actor backed down and the film got back on track. All told, *Fitzcarraldo* took four years and cost fourteen million dollars to make. It received favorable reviews, some of them wildly enthusiastic. A bit more restrained but recognizing its genius, critic Roger Ebert called it "…imperfect but transcendent."[10]

Even today, *Fitzcarraldo*'s powerful messaging about the rubber boom resonates in the hazy zone between history, folklore, and cinema. Recently, South American explorer Wade Davis described the mesmerizing "flash of wealth" that characterized the rubber boom in early twentieth-century Manaus, "where opulence reached bizarre heights." As examples, Davis noted: "Rubber barons lit cigars with hundred-dollar bank notes and slaked the thirst of their horses with silver buckets of chilled French champagne…" and "their wives, disdainful of the muddy waters of the Amazon, sent linens to Portugal to be laundered."[11] Those scenarios may have been recorded in the historical record, but the way Davis characterizes them is right out of Herzog's unforgettable film—almost word for word. That, of course, is a tribute to a great film.

Those who criticized the film tended to do so on ethical or ideological grounds. Some critics thought the prospect of Indians being charmed by opera played on a phonograph regarded those scenes as preposterous. Similarly, those scenes depicting Fitzcarraldo as a god were regarded as condescending. However, Herzog was evidently less concerned with cultural sensitivity than getting the story told on film. To the film's (and filmmaker's) credit it has been noted that Herzog and crew promised the Indians that they would help them obtain legal rights to their lands—a promise that Les Blank notes was honored.

Making *Fitzcarraldo* also revealed Herzog's deeper attitudes about the tropical jungle interior of South America. Whereas Kinski opined that this region is "erotic" and rich in life, Herzog thought otherwise and was clearly ambivalent about it. On the one hand, he caustically characterized it as "unfinished country," and cursed it as a "land of obscenity and overwhelming fornication." On the other hand, he says it left him "full of admiration; I love it—but against my better judgment."

While in the midst of filming *Fitzcarraldo*, Herzog stated that "I shouldn't make movies anymore. I should go to a lunatic asylum." And yet, out of the many he made, this film stands out as his most profound statement about what it is to be human, and especially what it is to dream. As Herzog concluded "This [film] might be the inner chronicle of what we are: otherwise we would [simply] be cows in the field."[12]

In retrospect, Herzog became obsessed with this film and that is evident throughout. One can only be amazed by his genius or madness: if the tales about its filming are true, few films have ever brought a filmmaker closer to the brink than this one, but then again none have better captured the grit of entrepreneurial madness unleashed on the tropics. Philosophically speaking, Herzog achieved something remarkable with *Fitzcarraldo*. In obliterating the distinction between reality and simulation, or nearly so, this eccentric movie reveals the intimate connection between exploration and filmmaking as enterprises. It also confirms that a filmmaker can be as visionary, and as possessed, as any (other) explorer.

As cinematic explorers, filmmakers can be just as persistent as the actual explorers they depict. Like a number of real explorers, Herzog couldn't resist returning to South America for one more big adventure. As the filming of *Fitzcarraldo* was wrapping up, Herzog became fascinated by Bruce Chatwin's novel *The Viceroy of Ouidah*—which centers on the mercurial Brazilian rancher Francisco Manoel da Silva, who rules over a portion of the vast *sertão*. This seasonally dry region of northeastern Brazil is rolling to rugged, and features scrubby vegetation (*caatinga*) consisting of thorny bushes and cacti. After an intense drought, da Silva's fortunes collapse and he turns to mining, but that fails as well. Desperate, he becomes an outlaw who engages in African slave trading, sailing to Dahomey and returning with his human cargoes—until the Portuguese outlaw Brazilian slavery in 1888. With its man-against nature (and vice versa) theme, *The Viceroy of Ouidah* was just the kind of twisted tale that Herzog couldn't resist. Like Aguirre and Fitzcarraldo, da Silva is based on a real character (Francisco Félix de Sousa).[13]

After making *Fitzcarraldo*, Herzog was now ready to tackle anything. He grabbed the rights to Chatwin's novel, and wrote the screenplay for the adventure-packed 1987 film titled *Cobra Verde*.[14] When it came to casting the sociopathic da Silva, Herzog did not have far to look. Kinski, with his impeccable credentials at playing risk-taking South American madmen, was selected. That decision was a tribute to Herzog's tenacity and ability to get the ultimate out of the wildly confrontational Kinski. In addition to causing problems on the set (the original cinematographer quit in disgust), Kinski provided advice on film locations to Herzog, recommending photogenic portions of Colombia. Herzog agreed. For authenticity, part of *Cobra Verde* was also filmed in Ghana, West Africa. It is a bizarre and gripping film with considerable cachet, but not quite the equal of Herzog's first two South American epics. *Cobra Verde* marked his last collaboration with Kinski, who died in 1991. By outliving Kinski, Herzog got the last laugh, creating a fascinating documentary film in 1999 titled *My Best Fiend* [sic], which preserves for cinematic posterity some of Kinski's now-legendary ill-tempered outbursts.[15]

TEN

Green Mansions

Exploring the Geographical
Dimensions of Fantasy

By 1900, South America's resources were being exploited at an increasing rate that delighted capitalists but alarmed natural historians. Among the latter was William Henry Hudson, the Argentine-born son of American emigrants who had settled in the Southern Cone in hopes of finding opportunity. Growing up in a rural part of Argentina south of Buenos Aires where the temperate grassland of the Pampa yields to the Patagonian steppes, Hudson developed a lifelong interest in natural history. As a young man, he explored and became familiar with the local habitats and published works on the ornithology and natural history of the region. He is still warmly regarded in Argentina as a national treasure. By century's end, however, Hudson had married a British woman and moved to England but never lost his love for South America. His 1885 book *The Purple Land that England Lost*[1] recounted a freer and more open life he remembered. In 1904, Hudson published his full-length adventure novel titled *Green Mansions: A Romance of the Tropical Forest*,[2] for which he is best known. Rich in descriptions of the rain forests of northern South America, it is a wistful and cautionary tale about nature in its many forms, including human nature.

A close reading of *Green Mansions* reveals that it achieves what most works of regional fiction hope to, namely, portrays a place intimately, and in as much detail, as if it were one of the characters in the story. Hudson loved South America and hoped to share it with a larger audience. He had already written fictional tales with plenty of adventure and an attention to detail, but was now prepared to take a leap into a relatively new genre. As a literary tale, *Green Mansions* fuses adventure and fantasy, especially romantic fantasy. Hudson biographer David Miller agrees with British journalist/ novelist Ruth Tomalin's 1954 assessment that "whether romance or poignant metaphor, *Green Mansions* is like no other tale; it pierces the heart; and it is unforgettable." However, Miller digs deeper into four varied stylistic elements that make this story come to life, and I shall weave them into the discussion throughout this review. Before doing so, however, I would like to provide a brief synopsis to contextualize the story in its Latin American setting.

The tale told in *Green Mansions* is revealed from two perspectives—a narrator (a British official stationed in South America) and a protagonist named Abel Guevez de Argensola. Mister Abel, as he is called, has fled after his involvement in a failed attempt at revolution in his native Venezuela. Soon, though, it becomes Abel's story, and he tells it in the first-person. Although the exact time during which the story takes place is never revealed, it is clearly set in the mid- to later nineteenth century, after independence when nation-wide revolutions were common. With a price on his head, the revolutionary Abel realizes he can simultaneously escape and act on a long-held dream: "Since boyhood, I had taken a very peculiar interest in that vast and almost unexplored territory we [Venezuelans] possess south of the Orinoco, with countless unmapped rivers and trackless forests; and in its savage inhabitants, with their ancient customs and character, unadulterated by contact with Europeans."[3] He is in no hurry and in little danger as he works his way along the Orinoco toward Guyana, where he encounters a sparsely populated country. Here and there are scattered villages, some "Christian" and others Indian. His journey has an ethnographic quality as he comes in contact with various tribes. Along the way, he hopes to find gold as he spies Indian jewelry containing some, but soon realizes that to be an illusion as his prospecting turns up little.

In the movie version of *Green Mansions*,[4] which was released in 1959, Abel's introduction to the region is far more action-packed and quickly timed. He is played by the tall and lanky Anthony Perkins. With the military in hot pursuit, Abel barely escapes capture by jumping into a river and hopping aboard a passing steamboat. On this leg of his journey he briefly discusses his misfortunes and aspirations with a nameless priest (Michael Pate). Arriving at an outpost along the river, he obtains a treasure map along with some supplies. We never see the content of the map but it symbolizes Abel's greed. Upon leaving the outpost, he hires two natives to take him deep into the interior. In their canoe, he imperiously points the way toward the treasure using the map, En route, they encounter a serpent slithering across a sandbar toward them, and give it wide berth. This part of his journey ends abruptly when he defiantly shoots his pistol at a feathered warning sign that other hostile Indian tribes have erected. Fearing retaliation,

In the 1959 film *Green Mansions*, the explorer Abel Guevez de Argensola (Anthony Perkins) faces dangers such as serpents and unfriendly tribes as he travels into the interior of northern South America. In this scene, after his canoe capsizes, Abel unwittingly reaches the shoreline as a jaguar prepares to pounce on him from above. In basic design and content, this scene brings to mind images popularized decades earlier in books such as *Arbuckles' Illustrated Album of Natural History*. Although he is in extreme peril at this point, an Indian will soon save Abel's life by killing the lunging cat in mid-air (Metro-Goldwyn-Mayer).

the Indians jump out of the canoe, which capsizes, toppling Abel and his belongings into the river.

The film's action is only just beginning. As Abel swims ashore, he is not aware that a jaguar has been stalking him. Like the jaguar in the Arbuckles' cards discussed earlier, this impressive man-eating cat is positioned above the river on a rocky outcrop. As I shall show later in this book, this is a scene not from the Hudson novel, but rather one clearly inspired by another earlier film titled *Green Fire* (1954). As in that earlier film, the scene culminates in the jaguar pouncing and being killed just in the nick of time—in mid-air—its lifeless body falling to the ground.

This cat scene in *Green Mansions* was an invention of Hollywood perfectly suited to an action-adventure film. In it, the jaguar was dispatched by an Indian named Kua-ko (Henry Silva) who saved Abel by spearing the cat. Kua-ko then takes Abel to a village that is ruled by his father, chief Runi (Sessue Hayakawa). The much taller Abel towers over these Indians, but their superior numbers and their formidable weapons give them the upper hand. Abel tries to convince the angry tribesmen that he means them no harm—to prove it, he offers them a sack of gifts—but they are clearly hostile and only calmed down when chief Runi intercedes on his behalf. In reality, actor Hayakawa is Japanese-American, but at this time filmmakers and audiences tended to be satisfied with any ethnic-appearing actor filling the role—even if Anglo American and complexion-darkened with make-up.

The film creates the impression that Abel was unprepared for what he would encounter in the region, and would be at the mercy of Indians whose language he could

In this scene from *Green Mansions* (1959), Abel (Anthony Perkins) is the center of attention as he is surrounded by hostile Indians. Although much taller than the tribesmen who hold him captive, Abel is outnumbered and will have to prove his mettle to the chief—another common theme in adventure films. With arm extended, Chief Runi (Sessue Hayakawa) urges calm to defuse the tense situation. Despite their exotic appearance, villages like this were filmed on elaborate outdoor sets near Los Angeles (Metro-Goldwyn-Mayer).

not understand. However, in the book, Abel was better prepared, revealing that he had actually learned two native languages, and was now ready to "...penetrate to the interior in the western part of Guyana, and the Amazonian territory bordering on Colombia and Brazil...." where authorities would have no interest in his arrest.[5] For Abel, traveling into this remote country is an adventure in itself. He becomes ill with fever, is nursed back to health by the Maquiritari tribe, and after a few weeks is able to begin traveling again, in search of excitement. As he put it in the book, "...I wished only for action, adventure— no matter how dangerous; and for new scenes, new faces; new dialects."[6] Although he reveals that one of his objectives is to find gold, which will be helpful in mounting a counter-revolution someday, he never does any significant prospecting. Instead, he discovers unique Indigenous cultures and dark secrets about humankind. In the book and film, Abel is less interested in understanding or sympathizing with the natives, and in the movie version he is downright defiant when confronted by them.

In a sense, the novel *Green Mansions* did for South America what Joseph Conrad's book *Heart of Darkness* (1902)[7] did for Africa, namely takes the reader deep into an interior region in order to expose human depravity. Not so coincidentally, both books have a tropical setting and were written about the same time; moreover, both feature narrators fascinated by the geography of remote places that are barely known. In both novels the quest takes the explorer into a land that could be as unsullied as Eden or as hopeless as Hell. As Abel travels deeper into the verdant wilderness, he comes in contact with another tribe, the Parahuari, and briefly settles there as he learns the ways of the people. The sojourn also enables him to explore the tropical rainforest that excites his interest, and lures him into discovering its many wonderful and terrifying secrets.

As a gifted chronicler and imaginative writer, Hudson masterfully portrayed his protagonist as both a man-on-the-move and a scientific explorer. In reality, Hudson himself was both, so Abel is semi-autobiographical. Like Conrad, Hudson used the landscape to set the story's mood. Although Hudson's stories frequently feature landscapes as settings, their use in *Green Mansions* goes far beyond that. According to literary historian David Miller: "The natural or geographical context particularly forms an imaginal richness, however, in *Green Mansions*; corresponding to the complexity or richness of the novel as whole." Miller concludes that "...Hudson manages in this book to bring together his major concerns, with the paradisial and with 'darkness,' and in such a way that his imaginal world is present in both its diversity and integrity."[8]

A closer examination of landscape in the book *Green Mansions* is in order in this chapter because Hudson's writing was prescient in light of a new form of entertainment—the motion picture—which was still in its infancy when this book was first published. In the beginning pages of the book, for example, Hudson infuses key passages with it. In one, he uses words to lead the reader's view toward a mountain that will play a key role in the story. As if giving clues to a future film location scout, he observes, "Beyond the stream and the strip of verdure that fringed it, and the few scattered dwarf trees growing near its banks, spread a brown savannah sloping upwards to a long, low, rocky ridge, beyond which rose a great solitary hill, or rather mountain, conical in form, and clothed in forest almost to the summit. This was the mountain Ytaioa, chief landmark in that district."

Almost if anticipating color film, Hudson then adds "As the sun went down over the ridge, beyond the savannah, the whole western sky changed to a delicate rose-colour that had the appearance of rose-coloured smoke blown there by some far-off wind, and left suspended—a thin brilliant veil showing through it the distant sky beyond, blue and ethereal." This future cinematic experience would have sound as well: "Flocks of birds, a kind of troupial, were flying past me overhead, flock succeeding flock, on their way to their roosting-place, uttering as they flew a clear, bell-like chirp; and there was something ethereal too in those drops of melodious sound...."[9]

Although Hudson's hyper-detailed writing style appears to emulate Alexander von Humboldt's journals written and published a century earlier, it is different in several ways. Hudson's is even more explicitly graphic and embodies a sense of action and urgency. In writing *Green Mansions*, Hudson unashamedly takes nature to a higher level, as it were. He asks the reader to believe the unbelievable, and thus uses nature as the gateway into a far more uncharted realm—the human imagination. Hudson's *Green Mansions* was timely indeed as it was published just as a new breed of explorers—filmmakers—were now longing to bring to the screen the action and drama on the printed page.

At this point in Hudson's novel, and the movie as well, the story takes a remarkable fantasy-like turn that challenges Abel's understanding of reality. Importantly, it marks the point where exploration in geographical space becomes exploration into the human mind. On one of Abel's trips into the forest at the foot of Ytaioa, he becomes aware that he is not alone but rather in the presence of a spirit, which he first mistakes for the call of a bird. Given Hudson's background in ornithology, it is no surprise that birds figure heavily in this story, both as the real birds that Abel encounters, as well as symbolically, at critical points in the plot.

Reflecting on his early experiences in his book *Idle Days in Patagonia*, Hudson devoted an entire chapter titled "Bird Music in South America." In one passage he notes that "It was a pleasure simply to wander on and on for hours, moving cautiously among the bushes, pausing at intervals to listen to some new note; or to hide myself and sit or lie motionless in the middle of a thicket, until the birds forgot or ceased to be troubled at my presence." In comparing bird calls in South America with those in England, Hudson concluded that "The South American forest has more the character of an orchestra, in which a countless number of varied instruments take part in a performance in which there are many noisy discords, while the tender spiritual tones heard at intervals seem, by contrast, infinitely sweet and precious."[10]

In *Green Mansions*, a particularly sweet and precious tone emanates not from a bird, but from a forest sprite. Its call is different from any he has ever heard, purer and almost angelic. This sprite slowly reveals itself to him as the story's central character, a mysterious nymph-like girl named Rima who is seemingly part human and part forest creature. As Jason Wilson noted in a pamphlet provocatively titled *W.H. Hudson: The Colonial's Revenge*, Rima is a deeply symbolic character, beginning with her name that reveals her character. Wilson claims that: "Rima is Spanish for rhyme; in the novel she stands for frail[ty], natural harmony, the long-lost original language of the mind that fuses a woman's voice, bird song and music." He continues that, for Hudson, "Poetry was primarily a biological activity, not a cultural one; it was emotional overflow, the sheer pleasure of being alive." In this interpretation, Rima represents a transcendent force with which Hudson felt a deep kinship. His South American roots always conflicted with the constraints of British culture, and they found some release in developing Rima as a tangible character.[11]

This is an intriguing premise, but David Miller rejects it as too reductionist, arguing instead that "Considered in relation to other factors—such as her harmony with nature, and her 'sublime' language—Rima's 'un-totalised' characteristics help to protect a fundamental mystery to her personhood...." In one mind-bending passage, Miller observes: "Abel speaks of the way that nature's discrete phenomena are in some sense brought together in Rima's being and her language, but also transcended by her and her speech; and in speaking to this, he comes close, at least, to showing authentic understanding, so that in speaking authentically of Rima, he has also spoken from (or disclosed) some part of his own authentic personhood."[12] Academic bantering aside, both Wilson and Miller make astute and compelling observations about this complex novel and its even more complex characters. To Abel, Rima's language is essentially untranslatable and therefore she is ultimately unknowable. And yet, through their relationship he ultimately comes to understand himself better.

As the story *Green Mansions* develops on the written page and on the screen, Rima becomes Abel's inspiration and obsession. However, before this happens, she becomes his protector. Shortly after he first encounters her in the forest, he is bitten by a deadly coral snake. For a while he is a near death, but Rima magically heals him. The presence of a venomous snake is unusual in a Hudson novel, but it serves a purpose here. First, it provides him a chance to showcase the region's fauna. Although many species of coral snakes are found in the Old World as well, in the New World their geographical distribution coincides with sub-tropical and tropical regions. Hudson thus uses this snake to underscore the dangers awaiting explorers in Latin America. Secondly, because snakes possess a mysterious and mythic quality, and can symbolize either good or evil, it was more or less natural for Hudson to incorporate one into the developing storyline of a novel that deals with such profound issues.

As in literature generally, snakes serve a symbolic purpose in the story *Green Mansions* because they personify ambivalence. Described as sublime by some—beautiful and almost magical—they can also signify danger and betrayal. In the novel, Abel reveals some of this ambivalence regarding the coral snake, which he was about to kill but paused because it was "...famed for its beauty and singularity as for its deadly character." That beauty is of special note here for it distinguishes the genus as well as the region. Almost as if he was describing a polychromatic serape, Hudson goes on to expound on the snake's beautiful coloring as "brilliant vermilion, with broad jet-black rings at equal distance round its body, each black ring or band divided by a narrow yellow strip in the middle." To him, it appeared as "an artificial snake made by some fanciful artist...." Even its eyes impressed him as "living gems."[13] In the book and the film, Abel succumbs to its beauty, and pays the price for the enchantment. And yet, that very situation enables Rima to demonstrate her power to overrule natural forces. At another level, the presence of a female and a snake in a paradise-like setting harkens back to the Bible, as does the name Abel itself. Elsewhere in the book *Green Mansions*, Abel describes the mottled landscape as appearing like a huge snake—"...I could see it stretching leagues and leagues away through forests and rivers, across wide plains, valleys and mountains, to lose itself in the infinite blue distance"—and also describes "anaconda-like lianas" that hung like cables from the trees.[14]

In both the book and on film, Rima is the most important, and enigmatic, element in *Green Mansions*. In the film version, and even more so in the book, Rima seems a likely prototype for Neytiri, the fetching humanoid alien in James Cameron's 2009 blockbuster sci-fi film *Avatar*.[15] Both are, in a sense, mysterious and ethereal, and both of them treat the environment with respect. Like the rainforest type environments that both of these nymphs inhabit, they too are quite vulnerable. And as in both the book and the film *Green Mansions*, it is humans, not nature, who will be their undoing. *Avatar* is patently science fiction, but *Green Mansions* reads—and can be viewed—as a real fantasy-inspired adventure story, that is, something that could conceivably happen here on earth. In both the book and the film, one wonders whether Rima is real or a figment of Abel's imagination. In other words, Abel may be on two expeditions simultaneously, one into a remote part of Latin America and the other into the depths of his own mind.

An important character in the story—an elderly man of uncertain ethnicity named Nuflo—is known to Rima as her grandfather; he has raised her as she never knew her parents. For several reasons we cannot fathom, Abel instinctively mistrusts Nuflo, and the feeling is mutual. At this point, it is worth pausing to note a seeming paradox in *Green Mansions* and perhaps much fantasy literature and film as well. Despite her inherent attractiveness, Rima is not sexualized in this story but rather emotionalized, triggering deep feelings in Abel that seem to transcend the physical. In summarizing the influential essay by Jean Laplanche and J.B. Pontalis titled "Fantasy and the Origins of Sexuality," film studies scholar Linda Williams observes that "...fantasy is not so much a narrative that enacts the quest for an object of desire as it is a setting for desire, a place where conscious and unconscious, self and other, part and whole meet."[16] Use of the terms "setting" and "place" in that sentence epitomize the geographical and psychological territory that Abel has entered, and which Rima inhabits. The rainforest embodies a timeless setting, but in *Green Mansions* and *Avatar* the clock is ticking as forces underway are threatening both Rima and Neytiri.

The story *Green Mansions* is not directly concerned with preserving the environment *per se*, but rather preserving Rima. As Abel learns more about Rima's past, he comes to realize that she is the sole survivor of a race of beings much like people but different indeed as they are more highly developed. One might say she is the last of an endangered species whose habitat has not been lost yet, but whose fellow beings have been exterminated by intolerant people, including other Indigenous peoples. The Parahuari are her nemesis, ultimately killing her because she possesses magical powers and has been deemed a witch or sorceress. To Abel, superstition is the enemy of not only Rima, but also of humankind. In both the book and the film, this darker characterization of Indigenous peoples hangs like a toxic cloud but nevertheless does not sugar-coat the Amerindian past, which provided examples of such brutality long before the arrival of European exploration and colonization.

The book *Green Mansions* was both well-written and well received, but the film version was neither a critical nor box office success. Regrettably, it missed the mark, falling short of the magical story that Hudson penned. In one sense, the filmmakers were not able to achieve the balance between the real and the fantastic that Hudson the writer achieved so well. Following up on something that I noted earlier, it could also be that this story, like *One Hundred Years of Solitude*, is essentially un-filmable because the written word is revealed at the reader's own pace whereas film moves inexorably at the filmmaker's. Compared to Hudson's prose, this film progresses at a much more rapid pace, with little or no time for reflection. In other words, one of the things that film normally does so well—compressing time—works against it here.

However, failure of this film to dazzle audiences may also lie in a series of more mundane causes, namely casting. The fact that director Mel Ferrer was married to

Audrey Hepburn—the popular actress cast as Rima—may have been one of them. In the book, Rima is a young girl, likely pubescent but probably half the age of the thirty-year-old Hepburn. Moreover, Hepburn's speech is somewhat distracting, and either the director or a voice coach should have asked her why a South American forest nymph was speaking English with a Pakistani or East Indian accent. Additionally, the chemistry between Abel and Rima seems a bit off in some scenes. For these and other reasons, *Green Mansions* is considered Hepburn's only failure. For his part, Perkins was a fine actor who could depict earnestness, but in this film seems strangely miscast, his acting almost wooden at times. The following year, though, he reached the pinnacle of his career in Alfred Hitchcock's *Psycho*.

Overall, the film version of *Green Mansions* seemed doomed by a litany of factors, including miscasting, reticent directing, and dialogue that is a bit too literal. It performed poorly at the box office, losing about a million dollars. Critics were not impressed despite its fine use of widescreen and a well-composed musical score. To its credit, some of the memorable scenes featuring Abel entranced by the forest setting have a truly magical quality in keeping with several of Hudson's passages. Interestingly, Ferrer went to South America in search of forested locations, but they proved much denser and darker than what he had in mind. In a manner of speaking, those forests were too real for the surreal effect Ferrer wanted to capture, so he used sets instead. It was a wise decision as they helped give those forest scenes their magical quality.

The heart of the story *Green Mansions* involves the relationship between explorer Abel (Anthony Perkins) and a mysterious sprite named Rima (Audrey Hepburn) who uniquely communicates with nature but is in extreme danger from those who misunderstand her. Cinematically speaking, Rima appears to be a likely prototype for Neytiri in James Cameron's blockbuster *Avatar* (2009). Hepburn was the wife of director Mel Ferrer, who hoped to film the enchanting forest scenes in South America, but found that environment too gloomy and not quite enchanting enough. Wisely, he opted to film these almost magical scenes on specially-designed sets (Metro-Goldwyn-Mayer).

On the other hand, the screenplay by Dorothy Kingsley did away with most of Abel's narration, leaving the actors to tell the story that flowed so beautifully from Hudson's pen as Abel's deepest thoughts. Moreover, the story itself, which was essentially archaic by the time the film version was released, needed considerable care in making it to the screen as viewers' expectations and preferences had changed. The book is in part a romance, but the movie veers very heavily in that direction. The inclusion of a wistful ballad-like song "Green Mansions," while sung very nicely by Perkins, is a nod to the romantic musicals that were so popular in the 1940s and 1950s, and hence distracting. In the book, Abel can and does play the guitar and sing, but only as a way of amusing the Indians—not serenading Rima.

Green Mansions is still an engaging read for those who like adventure stories set in exotic locales. For that matter, it is a very watchable film as it showcases some truly spectacular landscapes in Colombia, Venezuela, and Guyana, including the stunning Kaieteur Falls. As opposed to the book, rivers play a much greater role in Ferrer's film. Abel's river escape and steamboat trip, as well as his canoe journey with Indians are examples. As noted of *The Mission*, waterfalls can play an important role in a film, but in *Green Mansions* they are over-used to the point of distraction in scenes of intense emotion and drama. Moreover, filmmaking techniques can also exacerbate this. In *Green Mansions*, the interaction between actors playing out in the foreground is all too obviously on a soundstage, while the spectacular Kaieteur Falls behind them is obviously film running in the background.

Having returned to the enduring theme of landscape, I would be remiss if I did not point out that the film *Green Mansions* was visually flawed by some missteps in location selection. For example, throughout the book, Hudson uses the characterization "desert" to refer to unpopulated forested wilderness—not arid lands with little or no vegetation. In one passage in the book, Abel urges Rima, "Come, let us go to the summit together to see from it the desert beneath us—mountain and forest, mountain and forest."[17] This moving journey for Rima, which lies within the broader trajectory of Abel's journey, is an emotional one that brings them to the ruins of the long-abandoned settlement Río Lama. Along the way, she learns that she is the last of her people. Rima now knows that Nuflo (Lee J. Cobb) was one of the men who played a role in the destruction of Río Lama. Now, her betrayal by mankind seems complete; needless to say, and she is completely devastated.

However, misinterpreting Hudson's use of the word "desert"—the journey in the book was through a wilderness of trees—this crucial scene was filmed at Vasquez Rocks at the southern edge of the Mojave Desert. This barren, rocky locale is quite spectacular and very distinctive, but therein lies the problem. It is so unique and so photogenic that it had appeared in many Westerns for at least a generation, first in movies and then on TV. For viewers half expecting the Lone Ranger and Tonto to arrive at any moment to console Rima at Río Lama, the spell was broken. And therein lies an important lesson: To be successful, an exploration-discovery oriented film needs to seamlessly integrate landscape and plot.

As both a novel and a film, *Green Mansions* provides a look into the mind of an explorer-discoverer. However, by emphasizing Abel's romantic attachment to Rima, the movie downplays Abel the geographic explorer. In some stories, that might work, but not in this one. The movie's ending reinforces this, showing him wistfully advancing toward an ethereal Rima, with whom he joins hands after she has apparently risen from

In consulting the W.H. Hudson's 1904 novel *Green Mansions*, the film's scriptwriter misinterpreted the meaning of the word "desert," which at that time meant the "green desert" of the Amazonian forest where few people lived. In this scene from the film, Rima (Audrey Hepburn) literally finds herself in Vasquez Rocks at the southern edge of the Mojave Desert—a location that proved rather distracting because so many western movies and TV shows had been filmed there (Metro-Goldwyn-Mayer).

the ashes like the legendary Phoenix. However, in the book he literally carries Rima's ashes in an urn on a grueling trek back to civilization across eastern Venezuela, fleeing the region while plunged into the depths of emotional despair about mankind. On that trip, Abel traverses the spectacular brooding topography of the Guyana Shield (Guiana Highlands), where towering mesas locally known as tepuis loom ominously. He returns to civilization at Georgetown (British Guyana) a changed man who, at last, finally unburdens his soul by relating his entire melancholy story through the narrator.

As David Miller noted of the novel, that very darkness—the fourth theme he identifies—was one of *Green Mansions'* essential elements as literature. It runs through the book like a treacherous river. From almost the beginning, the novel reveals Abel's inexorable moral and psychological descent—a rare example of an explorer documenting his own journey from the geographical to the cerebral. We see him change from an idealistic revolutionary to a world-weary cynic as this story unfolds. Toward the very end of the novel, Abel has been transformed into an almost demonic character who has turned Indians against each other out of spite, and even slain a snake without mercy; after all, there is no Rima to protect nature and him any longer. As Miller concludes, "Abel's descent into 'darkness'—into the anti-paradisial—is far more terrifying in effect than anything disclosed of the Indians."[18] In excluding his revelation from the film's conclusion, much of the original story's soul was forfeited in favor of a happy Hollywood ending.

As a postscript to this review of *Green Mansions*, it should be noted that the rainforests of South America would be featured in other films. *The Emerald Forest* immediately comes to mind.[19] Said to be inspired by the published story *Wizard of the Amazon*, this 1985 film by John Boorman was set and filmed in Brazil. It, too, involves an outsider (an engineer) coming into the region on one mission and becoming involved in high drama involving avaricious outlaws, nefarious tribes, and considerable magic. A big difference, though, is that the engineer's own family is caught up in the drama. Controversy surrounds the actual source material for *The Emerald Forest*. The film claims it is a "true" story based on the plight of a Peruvian man and his family, but one suspects that it owes some debt to either Hudson's original book, or its later filming; perhaps both were inspirations. The subliminal clue to that connection lies in the title of Boorman's film, in which Emerald=Green, and Forest=Mansions, as Hudson himself stipulated in the subtitle of his novel: "a romance of the tropical forest."

ELEVEN

The Lost City of Z

Obsession and Exploration

A fairly recent American film—*The Lost City of Z* (2016)[1]—is a biopic about the controversial early twentieth-century British explorer Percy Fawcett (b. 1867). It is based on a written biography of the same name by David Grann (2009).[2] The film's director, James Gray, also wrote the screenplay about the exploits of this high-profile geographer who was frequently in the headlines from the time of his first expedition in 1906 to his last in 1925. These expeditions focused on the interior of South America where the borders of Brazil and Bolivia meet. The fact that Fawcett went missing on the latter expedition, and was never found, only adds to the mystery. By some accounts, Fawcett became so obsessed with exploration-discovery that it ultimately cost him his life. As discussed in this chapter, that dramatic premise makes for good storytelling and compelling filmmaking.

Filmed in part in the Sierra Nevada de Santa Marta National Park region of Colombia, *The Lost City of Z* has the look and feel of a classic adventure film with plenty of excitement, pathos, and history loosely woven together. Under this veneer, however, it is more focused on the personal costs and social consequences of exploration. The story's premise is seemingly straightforward: Fawcett's mission involves doing right for Britain, which has been called upon by an international commission to objectively determine the boundaries between Bolivia and Brazil. The cinematic Fawcett (Charlie Hunnam) possesses the cartographic skills needed and demanded by the Crown, and he has the stamina to confront the many challenges involved in mapping South America's tropical interior. Both countries are flexing their muscles and on the verge of war, and therefore much is riding on the outcome of the expedition. Britain's reputation is on the line, as is Fawcett's.

As with many explorations into South America, including Humboldt's, a major goal is deciphering the hydrography of river systems, which is a key to comprehending the geography. Fawcett's partner on the expedition is Henry Costin (Robert Pattinson). Shortly after their arrival in South America, Fawcett receives a letter from his wife Nina containing verses from "The Explorer" by Rudyard Kipling.[3] This 1898 poem emphasizes the point that exploration is a noble activity, but also ramps up the pressure on Fawcett to succeed. Fawcett reads aloud a few lines for Costin. One of those lines—"Something hidden, go and find it"—becomes the mantra of this film.

Cinematically speaking, they have arrived in South America at the time of *Fitzcarraldo*, when the Amazonian rubber boom was reaching its crescendo, so the stakes were high for both countries and the world economy as well. Echoes of the Herzog film

Fitzcarraldo emerge in the *Lost City of Z* as Fawcett and Costin find their way to the booming rubber town of Fazenda Jacobina, where an opera is underway, its lush and colorful performers contrasting with the lush but monotonous green of the jungle. Here, they meet a rubber baron (menacingly played by Franco Nero) who ominously tells them that no one who has embarked in search of the river's source has ever returned. The baron then tells them he wants to ensure that the status quo should remain in effect. To make his point clear, he issues a thinly veiled threat that their exploration should do nothing to jeopardize his prosperity. In a sense, this nefarious baron is the beneficiary of the corrupt colonial system whose machinations were portrayed in *The Mission*.

Although they briefly appear on screen, maps are at the center of the explorations portrayed in *The Lost City of Z*. For example, a large map that Fawcett holds as he and Costin take a train enabling them to reach a jumping-off place in Bolivia contains only an empty white space where they are headed. The immensity of the unexplored area becomes apparent as the map is spread open. Fawcett and Costin are tasked with surveying the "Río Verde," but have to fill in the blanks—literally. After their expedition begins in earnest, Fawcett opens his notebook to a map and shows it to the Indian guide he has just hired. The map indicates the course of the Río Verde, but seeing that its upper reaches are incomplete, an Indian guide uses his finger to trace the river's course to its headwaters. The challenge becomes more apparent as the Indian has indicated that more than half of the river's length remains to be traversed and charted. For good measure, the Indian states, in Spanish, that "…I know all of the river."

Cartographically speaking, this scene shot in very low lighting is far more complicated than it first seems. At one level, it is a nod to the fact that Indigenous peoples participated in the mapping of seemingly blank interiors, sometimes unwittingly assisting colonial exploration. At another level, though, it has a personal dimension, underscoring how dependent the outsider Fawcett will be on his trusted Native insiders' knowledge. However, in addition to this aspect of knowledge involved in mapping exploration, the issue of *authorship* is on display here as well. The Indian is not only able to read a European map, but also able to create one himself. In this scene, Fawcett's partially drawn map is being supplemented if not superseded by the Indian's input. However, the fact that this Indian only indicates the course of the river with his finger—and never formally draws it himself—suggests that his input will never be formally credited. That, alas, was often the case, though exceptions occurred, for example when American explorer John Charles Frémont credited their input as he mapped the Great Basin.[4] In the context of South America, a recent article by Juliet Wiersema titled "The Map of the Yurumanguí Indians" confirms that the erasure of earlier inhabitants has a long tradition.[5] In many exploration-discovery films, the Indigenous cartographic input is non-existent, and its inclusion in *The Lost City of Z* is long overdue.

In his book on the British search for El Dorado in South America, historian of exploration D. Graham Burnett insightfully notes how important these Indigenous informants were. As he observed: "Where Amerindians would not go, European explorers could rarely penetrate." He also notes the huge gap between Indigenous and colonial thinking. It became apparent to astute explorers that the landscape possessed a spiritual dimension to the native inhabitants. As Burnett observed: "the encounter with Amerindian spirit landscape was an inescapable part of any penetration into the interior, and the dynamics of that encounter were essential to the process of exploration." He concludes that "the terra incognita of the interior, though sparsely populated with

Amerindians, was seen by Europeans as thickly colonized by Amerindian spirits."[6] Seemingly unaware of the importance of such negotiations, Fawcett forges ahead into the interior, often brandishing a rifle as well as his map-drafting instruments; he is, after all, a mapmaker but also a military man—and not above the use of force on natives.

Fawcett has an epiphany on the first of several expeditions that he would make to the area. Somberly, he declares that "I have come to believe that mapmaking should be a secondary interest." We soon learn why Fawcett has changed his focus and his mission. According to the native guide, there is a lost city in the wilderness near the Brazilian-Bolivian border that once lured the conquistadors to their doom. The city, of course, is a version of El Dorado; in fact, that name resonates through the entire film as both a myth and a possibility. Accompanying one scene, a folksy song asking, "Have you ever seen a land like golden El Dorado…?" touts it as a land of gold and silver. The fabulous lost city in question is called Zed, but made all the more mysterious by being shortened to "Z" in some circles.

Nowhere mentioned is the fact that the British had only recently given up on their own colonial impulse to dominate this part of South America. In fact, renowned British explorer Richard F. Burton (1821–1890) was transferred there and based in Rio de Janeiro for two years in the late 1860s. More explorer than bureaucrat, he reconnoitered portions of the interior, publishing *Explorations of the Highlands of the Brazil*. Burton's highly detailed two-volume work described the mining regions in that country's

As this dimly-lit scene from James Gray's *The Lost City of Z* (2018) suggests, explorer-cartographer Percy Fawcett (Charlie Hunnam) was quick to use a rifle on his early 1900s expeditions into South America's "green desert," the then-common term for the Amazonian forest. To capture the essence of the rain forest, considerable shooting was done in the vicinity of the Rio Don Diego in Colombia's Tayrona National Park. With expedition partner Henry Costin (Robert Pattinson) seated in the shadows, Fawcett takes aim—an all-too frequent event that, according to the real Fawcett's critics, resulted in needless casualties among Indians (Plan B Entertainment).

interior, and discussed the region's river system and its potential role in increased development. It also related his experiences documenting mysterious archaeological features, further contextualizing them with an "Historical account of a large, hidden, and very ancient city, without inhabitants, discovered in the year 1753" that had been published by Brazil's Instituto Historico e Geographico in 1865.[7] Typical of Burton's works, it also described the fabulous gold and diamond regions (which he claimed were only barely developed) and also documented in vivid prose his epic rafting trip down the Rio São Francisco; such accounts motivated expeditions well into the twentieth century.[8] In this work, however, Burton reveals his darker racist side, repeatedly denigrating Brazilians of African descent, who were enslaved there until about two decades later (1888). In terms of espousing social justice, Burton was well behind Humboldt.

For his part, Fawcett regards non–European peoples with ambivalence; they can either assist his efforts or thwart them but are otherwise inconsequential. As regards his mission, he is depicted as altruistic to his core in this film, having no interest in the lost city's riches, but rather its meaning to world civilization. As the film progresses, Fawcett learns more about the supposed city, and unearths tantalizing artifacts in the field, becoming more and more convinced that Zed is the holy grail of all archaeological sites. Moreover, it is located in the Americas, not the Old World commonly considered the cradle of Western Civilization. Fawcett hoped to continue his search for the Lost City but the Great War intervened. In one scene that takes place during the war, Fawcett is depicted as taking seriously a fortune-teller's prediction that he is destined to discover the lost city. By some accounts, Fawcett really did have an interest in the occult, so this scene is plausible.

After the war, the film resumes with Fawcett getting back to his explorations in earnest. At a formal meeting of the Royal Geographical Society (RGS) in London, he announces the goal of his next planned expedition, claiming: "It is now my firm belief that Amazonia is far more than the green desert which many of us have supposed." It will be recalled that W.H. Hudson similarly used the term desert for such lushly forested areas in *Green Mansions* and it was well understood as referring to any unpopulated and unpromising area. When Fawcett adds that "I am proposing that Amazonia contain [sic] a hidden civilization…" laughter ensues as a detractor mentions conquistadors and El Dorado, but the undaunted Fawcett continues, "…one that may very well predate our own!" This bold claim precipitates near rebellion in the ethnocentric audience, but current recent (2022) digital reconnaissance in Amazonian Bolivia indicates the presence of tall earthen pyramids and urban forms that now vindicate Fawcett.

In this film, the Royal Geographical Society is portrayed as stodgy and solidly affiliated with the conservative establishment, which is to say it is aristocratic, sexist, allied with business interests, etc. In his presentation, Fawcett has his work cut out for him as the uproar continues. Now even more emboldened, he goes on the offensive: "We are currently discussing exploration," he reminds them, adding "It is the conquistadors and we who have been destroying Amazonia." With everything now on the line, he adds, "I have seen with my own eyes evidence of this civilization." He ultimately prevails at the meeting when he is supported by naturalist James Murray (Angus Macfadyen), at least for the time being. Murray will soon accompany Fawcett on an expedition into the tropics—and be way out of his league in that environment.

The film succeeds well in portraying Fawcett as a progressive with whom audiences increasingly identify, as he seems to be an environmentalist and believer in the greatness of earlier if not present-day Indigenous peoples. Moreover, he is interested in evidence, not popular sentiment. Fawcett claims that a Portuguese soldier's 1753 map located in the archives substantiates this claim. It should be noted here that this is a reference to the Manuscript 512 in the National Library of Brazil, which was "rediscovered" in 1839 and is controversial in its own right. In the film, it is Fawcett's wife Nina (Sienna Miller) who locates this document; in fact it is she who longs to join the explorers but is denied by both her husband and the RGS. Ironically, this film seems to be making a pitch for feminism but perpetuates the mistaken belief that there were no women explorers anywhere in the world at this time. There were, although they were admittedly rare in Latin America.

This film's cinematography was praised with good reason. The jungle exploration scenes are particularly well done. Although they include ample footage bathed in the gloomy bluish-gray lighting that typifies adventures set deep in the jungle, they are interspersed with well-lighted scenes that sparkle. The scenes of villages are very convincing as they are based on historical illustrations, including historical photos from some early twentieth-century expeditions into the region. In this region, housing consisted of branch and thatch construction that nearly blended in with the tropical environment. Fawcett's arrival into a village as tribal members encircle him is especially effective. An especially photogenic landscape in the vicinity of Colombia's Sierra Nevada de Santa Marta—a favorite location for filmmakers—lends some authenticity to this historical exploration-discovery story.

As in many films featuring explorers finding their way into back country, rivers play an important role in this one. Quite aside from their importance in boundary creation, they provide the filmmaker an opportunity to highlight the hazards involved in penetrating continental interiors. Director James Gray uses them effectively to signal

In *The Lost City of Z* (2016), locales throughout Colombia were used to depict the Amazonian interior of South America. The village scene sets created in the vicinity of the Rio Ancho rain forests near the Sierra Nevada De Santa Marta were especially photogenic. In this scene, Fawcett's expedition enters an Indigenous village and is greeted by inquisitive natives. At these locales, expeditions like Fawcett's were resupplied and were provided considerable geographical information (Plan B Entertainment).

changes in the plot. The scenes involving trouble in whitewater rapids when James Murray becomes deranged on their raft underscore the role of such geographic features in plots about explorations in trouble. Filmmakers such as Werner Herzog used them to great advantage in his two South American epic, so Gray was in good company filming here decades later.

As the film progresses, Fawcett's sense of urgency is heightened because the American explorer Hiram Bingham III has discovered the lost city of Machu Picchu in highland Peru. That discovery touts the accomplishments of the Incas, while Fawcett believes an even greater civilization existed father east. Some years later, on his last exploration into the area (1925), Fawcett is joined by his son Jack (Tom Holland), who was but a lad when his father first began exploring the region but is now a strapping young man. As they reach the area, the remains of the rubber boom are now palpable reminders of the bust suffered by that industry over the last two decades. However, as always, the depiction of Indigenous population remains ambivalent; by turns, they prove helpful and put up armed resistance. A scene in which Fawcett surrenders to the Indians rather than fighting them showcases the difference in stature between the tall explorer and the much shorter Indians who have the upper hand due to greater numbers and better knowledge of the environment, and is reminiscent of Abel in the same quandary in *Green Mansions*.

Before setting out on his last expedition, Percy Fawcett claimed to be concerned about both British Imperialism and American militarism in the area, although the film downplays the fact that well-placed Brits and Americans helped bankroll it. An added irony is that when the final expedition went missing, it is said that about one hundred lost their lives on that fruitless search for answers, despite Fawcett's own insistence that no rescue be attempted due to the dangers involved. However, speculation remains that Fawcett himself may have deliberately gone native, consumed as it were by his passion for the lost city.[9]

As in many adventure films, whitewater rapids figure in crucial events in the plot of *The Lost City of Z*. In this scene from the second expedition, the naturalist James Murray (Angus Macfadyen) becomes uncontrollable on the raft, and his antics threaten to careen it onto the rocks. Disillusioned with Murray, Fawcett sent him back to civilization—an action that embarrassed Murray, who retaliated by threatening Fawcett's reputation and career (Plan B Entertainment).

In touching scenes from *The Lost City of Z*, Percy Fawcett and son Jack explored the South American interior together in 1925. Seen here interacting with members of an Indigenous tribe (uncredited), Percy Fawcett (Charlie Hunnam, center) and Jack (Tom Holland, right) are intending to take photographs for posterity—a subtle reminder that explorations become known only after they are recorded; even more subtle is the message about film's importance to audiences watching this movie (Plan B Entertainment).

The last exploration scenes in this film are particularly well done, as they show Percy and his son Jack amongst the Indians. Here, too, the villages constructed for these scenes are very convincing and underscore Fawcett's dependence on them for everything from information to sustenance and protection from other tribes. In a clever use of still photography, the father and son team shoot pictures among and of the natives; the use of black and white here effectively historicizes the expedition and gives this part of the film a documentary feel. These are poignant images—the last taken of the explorers, who will soon vanish and become part of the region's local folklore and front-page news on the international stage. Above all, the acting and direction in *The Lost City of Z* highlights the bond between Percy and Jack, confirming the familial investment in this multi-generational exploration saga.

By now it should be clear that exploration-discovery stories often involve the experience of transforming the explorer-discoverer. In extreme cases such as the filibusterer William Walker, they claim the life of the explorer, who never returns to his native land but is effectively consumed by the place that had emotionally consumed the explorer. This loss enhances the story as it emphasizes the sacrifice involved. In a sense, the failure of an explorer to return adds an element of tragedy, but only to a point. Without such tragedies, exploration itself would be far less romantic. Ultimately, those who suffer the loss of the explorer also suffer from a lack of closure, as is evident in how Fawcett's wife Nina responds to the staggering loss of two.

The film's last scene is particularly moving and it takes place back in England. In it, Nina—who never gives up hope that her husband and son will be found—visits the headquarters of the Royal Geographical Society. There she learns that a Brazilian had reported seeing her husband and son, and even provided as proof—a brass compass used on the expedition. That compass is another cartographic element that helped chart the expedition, but here plays several symbolic roles almost simultaneously. First, it is a trope for exploration itself and deeper than that, geographic authority in general. In that role it is an artifact symbolizing the European search for, and objectification of, new lands. Secondly, and far more personally, it is a talisman that can sustain Nina's faith in her husband's survival. By handing it over to Nina, the RGS is effectively burdening her with hope and yet empowering her with a key of sorts that can unlock a mystery. After all, Nina hoped to be on that expedition and now has one of the essential objects of exploration herself.

In an almost magical closing scene, Nina walks past the flickering fireplace and out of the building into the fading evening light. With her back to us, she walks away almost surrounded by vegetation, and it appears that she too has entered the tropical regions as the light subtly intensifies. It is an ethereal scene so artistic—a grieving woman facing the light and entering primordial nature, occupying only a fraction of the darkened screen—that it suggests a new journey of exploration is about to begin. In a sense, it has something in common with a similar scene in *Cabeza de Vaca*, wherein the mortally-wounded Fray Súarez walks away from the camera through the darkened jungle, toward the light and into martyrdom.

An interesting postscript to this discussion of *The Lost City of Z*—which received considerable critical acclaim but did poorly at the box office—was how much controversy it generated. Shortly after its release, articles such as Eliza Berman's "The True Story Behind the Lost City of Z"[10] began appearing. Of special interest here is how it was savaged by John Hemming (b. 1935), noted explorer, historian, anthropologist and past president of the Royal Geographical Society. Hemming, who has extensive field experience in South America, caustically commented on the hype generated by the film's publicity, and Fawcett himself, in the April 1, 2017, issue of *The Spectator*.[11] In this no-holds-barred review article, Hemming claimed that portraying Fawcett as a great explorer was an insult to other real explorers, adding that Fawcett was in reality a racist, a "nutter" and a dangerous incompetent who never discovered anything but cost many lives in the process. Hemming also singled out the film's poor and inaccurate depiction of the Indigenous tribes. This take-down of a fellow explorer is a reminder that filmmakers depicting heroic feats of exploration can encounter challenges even more daunting than swollen rivers, dangerous animals, and rebellious film crews—namely, knowledgeable film critics.

Interestingly, Fawcett's early expeditions are said to have influenced his friend Sir Arthur Conan Doyle's popular 1912 science fiction novel *The Lost World*.[12] In Doyle's fantastic story, the mythical Professor Challenger discovers a locale in the remote South American interior where dinosaurs still roam. For its part, *The Lost World* has been filmed many times[13]—e.g., 1925, 1960, 1992, and 2001 as a fine BBC/A&E version[14]—but never on location in South America, much less in the stunning part including the spectacular plateau-like Mt. Roraima that so intrigued Doyle. Remarkably, the 1992 Canadian version changed the actual location of the adventure to Africa![15] This transposition is a reminder that adventure films emphasize the exotic, and often take liberties with the physical and cultural environment. As a stand-in, the rocky landscape of Zimbabwe was used, but failed to capture the almost surreal topography described by Doyle. Truth is, the tepuis of the Guiana Highlands represent one of South America's truly astounding iconic environments. Recently, they were showcased in the superb documentary film

Explorer: The Last Tepui.[16] The harrowing scenes in that film depicting climbers scaling the perpendicular cliffs remind us that adventure and danger still await intrepid explorers.

In retrospect, the almost surreal landscape of South America's interior highlands is in fact the same haunting country experienced by the traumatized explorer Abel toward the end of W.H. Hudson's novel *Green Mansions* (1904). In addition to Fawcett's early expeditions, it is likely that Hudson's novel also influenced Doyle's book; both focused on discoveries by fictional explorers who are desperately romantic and wind up disenchanted. Both novels were popular, selling well on both sides of the Atlantic. In the early twentieth century, adventure and romance were on the minds of many, and South America held a special appeal; for that matter, it still does—especially to those seeking new experiences in out-of-the-way places. The takeaway here is that writers not only influence other writers, but also influence filmmakers as well—who in turn may influence would-be writers in an endless cycle of inspiration and imitation.

Twelve

Secret of the Incas

Romanticizing the American
Explorer-Archaeologist

We now turn to a film that depicts the archeological treasures of the Andes. In the early twentieth century, Yale University professor of history Hiram Bingham III (1875–1956) was one of the American upstarts also bent on exploring South America for its rich archaeological content. Although not an archaeologist by training, Bingham had a strong interest in the history of Latin America, especially South America. As a noted Hispanicist, he had traced the military engagements of Simón Bolívar in Venezuela and Colombia, and written reports based on that field work and his searches in the archives. Summarizing Bingham's work on that assignment, historian Jordana Dym notes that he traveled to recover the past in a venerable tradition she characterizes as "Go, See, Map, Return, Disseminate."[1]

Bingham was also interested in civilizations, especially those that had vanished. In 1911, he published a popular book titled *Across South America*,[2] in which he documented his 1909 travels in Brazil, Argentina, Chile, Bolivia and Peru. Bingham's trek took him coast to coast—Atlantic to Pacific—through some of the most interesting landscapes on the planet. At the end of that journey, Bingham describes the archaeology and history of the Incas, who once ruled western South America from Ecuador to Argentina. However, he does not mention Machu Picchu by name in it because it was yet to be discovered, or rather re-discovered by him on a subsequent trip funded by Yale and the National Geographic Society.

The date of that later discovery—July 24, 1911—represents a hallmark in Latin American archaeology, and the event would be recounted many times in print. To my knowledge, the tome by James Bryce titled *South America: Observations and Impressions* (1912) appears to be the first popular book that mentions Machu Picchu, as follows: "There are striking ruins not far off [from Cuzco, Peru], such as those at Ollantaytambo and Pisac, and lower down the Vilcamayu Valley at Macchu [sic] Pichu [sic] and Rosas Pata, as well as others still more distant in the high country between here and Lima." In a footnote, Bryce cites recent research "...by my friend Professor Bingham ... [who also] ... discovered, in 1911, an Inca building at a place on the river Pampaconas fifteen days' journey north of Cuzco and only two thousand feet above sea-level."[3] Bingham's explorations were leading to a better understanding of how far Inca rule had extended. Bingham published his findings in a preliminary report to the National Geographic Society in 1912, and in an illustrated article titled "In the Wonderland of Peru" in the April 1913 issue of *National Geographic* magazine.[4]

Oddly, the Spaniards had somehow missed finding Machu Picchu. According to later research, it had been built ca. 1450 as part of an Inca palace and estate under emperor Pachacuti (aka Pachacutec) (1438–1472) and was abandoned at the time the Spaniards arrived in the 1520s. Vegetation soon encroached and the site was "lost," at least to Europeans. For his part, Bingham initially speculated that Machu Picchu presented the founding site of Inca culture and served as a fortress. That idea of it as the site of origins, and its being subsequently lost, only added to its popular appeal. The fact that it is located in the upper reaches of the Urubamba Valley at 2,340 meters above sea level—a valley that the Spaniards called Valle de Yucay and is popularly known as "Sacred Valley" today—ensures the site's ongoing attraction. The combination of mystery, history, and spirituality has proven irresistible, making Machu Picchu one of South America's most iconic locales.

Another factor in the site's attractiveness is its so-called "discoverer," for Bingham himself epitomized the professor as a man of learning and a man of action. As noted by Argentine scholar Ricardo Salvatore, Bingham was independently wealthy, assertive, and thought of himself as the "second Pizarro." More importantly, he was one of many early twentieth-century scholarly intellectuals from the United States whose "disciplinary conquests" were in line with North American economic and political interests in "their" hemisphere, per the nearly century-old Monroe Doctrine (1823).[5] In terms of the creativity involved in making such characters come to life on screen, Bingham would later serve, in a rather roundabout way, as an inspiration for one of the most endearing and recognizable characters in film history—the peripatetic archaeological explorer-discoverer Indiana Jones, who will be covered in more detail in the next chapter.

Bingham himself had an illustrious career that spanned five decades. Many years after first documenting Machu Picchu, an aging Bingham was present at the 1948 dedication of a new highway to it that was named in his honor. A lot had been smoothed over by then, for Bingham and Yale University had originally laid claims to the artifacts during a time when discoverers took home most of what they found. Peru was now elated that its patrimony was staying put. The much-publicized event in 1948 also brought the site back into the public eye. Shortly thereafter, Bingham published his popular book *Lost City of the Incas*, which further helped whet the public's appetite for archaeological adventure. It became so popular that it was reissued over the years by numerous publishers.[6]

It should be noted that the archaeology of this part of South America was of intense interest to Europeans as well. Through the 1920s and 1930s, imaginative writers and illustrators there became fascinated by ancient Incan ruins. For example, beginning in 1929, Belgian writer Hergé (pen name of Georges Prosper Remi) wrote a series of popular comic books based on the adventures of a boy named Tintin. One of these—*Tintin—Le Temple du Soleil* (aka Tintin and the Temple of the Sun)—was later made into a French/Belgian/Swiss film that few in the Americas ever heard about, much less saw.[7]

The subject of this chapter, however, is how Hollywood portrayed the exploits of an American explorer who discovers Incan archaeological treasures high in the Andes. In 1953, a feature film titled *Secret of the Incas*[8] was announced as part of the line-up of Paramount films. As the studio had promised, it was released with much fanfare on the big screen a year later. *Secret of the Incas* is a fictionalized film account of archaeologists exploring Machu Picchu, and the original screenplay by Sydney Boehm and Ranald

MacDougall took many liberties in creating the story and its characters. They also took liberties with time as well, and set the film in the present (the early 1950s) when Machu Picchu was fairly well known, but still had an aura of romance.

To its credit, *Secret of the Incas* showcases the real Machu Picchu. In fact, it is not only the first American feature film shot on location there, but reportedly the first shot in Peru as well. Of note is this film's well-meaning if somewhat gratuitous attempt to portray Indigenous culture as rightful possessors of sites and artifacts. Another first, or nearly so: two consultants from the University of Peru were involved in the project, which helps ground it to some extent. The musical score and songs by Peruvian coloratura soprano Yma Sumac reflect the combined Indigenous/exotic music that characterized adventure and romantic films in the 1950s.

Secret of the Incas featured two opposing characters, both of whom are knowledgeable about Andean archaeology and bent on discovering Incan artifacts for two very different reasons, fame vs. fortune. The first, a mild-mannered professor of archaeology named Stanley Moorehead, is played by the relatively sedate Robert Young, known for his solid portrayals of rather cerebral and professional characters. Moorehead's goal is science for science's sake, that is, knowledge, which in turn brings him professional respect and considerable public recognition. He has a university position and travels widely, these ventures being well funded enough for him to afford a team to help excavate archaeological sites. Moreover, he is welcomed by the Peruvian government as he agrees to abide by all laws pertaining to antiquities.

The second character, a younger and more opportunistic explorer named Harry Steele, was played by the consummate virile leading man-of-action Charlton Heston. For the record, Heston not only starred in *Secret of the Incas* that year, but also in another South America-set film *The Naked Jungle*,[9] which had been released a few months earlier. That film focused on the trials and tribulations of a conflicted cocoa plantation owner. Of the two films, *Secret of the Incas* was far better received. To critics, and perhaps the public as well, Heston proved better at playing a more complex and likable character than *The Naked Jungle*'s brooding, misogynistic, monomaniacal *patrón* who battles an army of voracious fire ants.

Thanks to the screenwriters' sense of humor and the fine direction by Jerry Hopper, Heston's witty, lightning-fast wisecracking throughout *Secret of the Incas* perfectly matches Harry Steele's alpha-male swagger. Originally from California, Harry is streetwise and culturally aware, fluently speaking three languages—English, Spanish and Quechua. However, his main motivation seems to be financial gain, and he might best be called a mercenary archaeologist. Adding a bit more depth to the character, Harry has been known to consort with even more materialistic and nefarious operators who deal in stolen artifacts. Although largely fiction, this story is based on the finds made by Bingham and the factual premise that for every honest and ethical archaeologist, there are many opportunistic plunderers who pilfer artifacts in hopes of selling them on the black-market.

Shot in Technicolor, *Secret of the Incas* opens with sweeping panoramic shots of two separate vehicles on their way to Cuzco, a modernizing city with a venerable Incan past. On one of the vehicles—a speedy, bus-like railcar ("*autocarril*") common in Peru— is the self-assured Harry Steele. On the other vehicle—a stake truck loaded with Indian workers on their way to Cuzco from La Paz, Bolivia—is a mysterious woman named Elena Antonescu (played by Nicole Maurey). Harry and Elena barely glimpse each other at a rural railroad crossing in the Andes where their vehicles almost collide. However, as if fated, they soon meet in Cuzco, where Harry conducts historic tours. Beguiled by each other, Elena informs Harry that she is fleeing communist oppression in Bulgaria and hoping to first reach Mexico undetected, and then slip into the United States.

The plot develops rapidly. At the museum in Cuzco, Harry discovers that the broken half of a stone artifact he has acquired at Machu Picchu is a perfect match to the broken artifact on display. Harry will do anything to quickly reach Machu Picchu and search for its prototype, a long-lost Inca artifact—a sunburst pattern gold shield encrusted with hundreds of precious gems. For her part, Elena will do anything to get to America. Harry also happens to be a pilot, and steals a plane from a Bulgarian agent who is pursuing Elena. Together, Harry and Elena fly not to Mexico, as she had hoped, but to Machu Picchu. After landing as close as they can to Machu Picchu, they use a small raft along a river, and then hike the remainder of the way on narrow and increasingly rugged trails. The scenery is stunning and helps give the viewer a sense of the remoteness and beauty of the area.

When Harry and Elena arrive at Machu Picchu, they discover that an archaeological investigation is underway. This displeases Harry, who hoped to have the place to himself in order to find the golden sunburst. Harry soon discovers that the American

Jerry Hopper's *Secret of the Incas* (1954) was reportedly the first American film shot on location in Peru, and it showcased the spectacular Inca site of Machu Picchu. In this scene, the fedora-wearing opportunistic adventurer-archaeologist Harry Steele (Charlton Heston) is accompanied by Elena Antonescu (Nicole Maurey) a Bulgarian refugee seeking asylum in the U.S. by way of Peru. Cinematically speaking, Harry is the likely inspiration for the later Spielberg character Indiana Jones (Paramount Pictures).

archaeologist Stanley Moorehead is there, excavating for other antiquities under the scrutiny of a Peruvian official and a taciturn tribal elder named Pachacutec (Michael Pate). Named after the early Inca emperor, he conveys considerable authority. Upon meeting Moorehead, Harry quips, "Dr. Livingstone, I presume," which Moorehead takes seriously and tries to correct. Of course, the idea of a man named Stanley being confused with one named Livingstone is a delightful inside joke, just one of the many gems in a witty script full of double and sometimes triple entendres. As Stanley and Harry banter about Inca archaeology, and Harry obliquely mentions the gold sunburst, Moorehead says it should be considered nothing more than a legend. "A legend?" Harry skeptically asks. Condescendingly, Moorehead replies that it is safe to assume that any such artifact made of gold would have been melted down for its monetary value long ago. Although not easily distracted, Moorehead is clearly smitten by Elena, and soon proposes marriage to her. Moorehead and Harry are now rivals on at least two levels, professional and personal.

Interestingly, although this film was said to be inspired by Bingham's archaeological discoveries, it does not mention them nor him. It is possible, perhaps even likely, that Moorehead is subtly standing in for the original discoverer Bingham. However,

The plot of *Secret of the Incas* (1954) intensifies in this scene set in one of the chambers excavated at Machu Picchu. Under the watchful eye of tribal elder Pachacutec (center, Michael Pate), free-wheeling Harry Steele (right, Charlton Heston) meets bookish archaeology professor Stanley Moorehead (Robert Young) and their competitive bantering begins. Very loosely, Moorehead appears to have been inspired by the famous American academic historian/ archaeologist Hiram Bingham III. This scene confirms Peru's interest that the patrimony of its Indigenous people be respected in the excavation of the Inca site (Paramount Pictures).

although Moorehead is visibly older than Harry, he is not old enough to have discovered the site almost forty years earlier. The screenwriters were also vague about the discovery of Machu Picchu, and unaware of its age. Harry tells Elena elsewhere in the film that Machu Picchu had been "lost for over a thousand years" before it was discovered—an enthusiastic claim for a site that we now know was created in the mid–1400s. Put graciously, although *Secret of the Incas* may have had some educational value in 1954, it has far less today—but is still very entertaining.

The scenes of Indigenous people arriving at the site in anticipation of the treasure being found are noteworthy; most are local extras, marking a departure from many films of the period when even extras were often white actors wearing costumes. Additionally, the use of the original site for these scenes adds a dimension of realism reminiscent of *National Geographic* magazine, which was also publishing in color at this time.

In keeping with many movies set in exotic places at this time, it featured a musical score that fused modern Latin-flavored orchestral and Indigenous folk songs. A centerpiece of the latter was the Peruvian folk singer Yma Sumac, whose wildly exotic album *Voice of the Xtabay* had topped the charts in 1950. In ancient lore, Xtabay is a gorgeous Maya/Yucatecan woman whose seductive songs lure men to their deaths. One might say Xtabay is a Latin American ancestor of the *femme fatale* in the modern era's film

In Jerry Hopper's *Secret of the Incas*, the archeological excavations underway are of intense interest to the region's Indigenous peoples. In anticipation of the archaeological team finding a long-lost ancient artifact—a golden sun disk that can help restore the cosmic order—the region's Indigenous colorfully-dressed people flock to the site. Machu Picchu provided a remarkable, amphitheater-like setting for the filming, and the weather cooperated (Paramount Pictures).

noir. However, although two songs from that album made it into the *Secret of the Incas*, Sumac's Xtabay persona—called Kori-Tica in the film—was far more benign though still intriguing. She performed her songs while wearing lavish costumes very loosely based on Andean Inca styles, and her lyrics supposedly recounted ancient stories about sun gods and other mythical figures and historical events. These, including her mimicry of wild tropical bird calls that showcased her stunning soprano voice, lent an air of folkloric authenticity to the film.

The plot of the film depends on a mounting tension between the traditions of the Indigenous people and the success the outsiders will have in finding the lost secrets of the past. Cutting to the chase, the university-trained archaeological team under Moorehead discovers the sunburst, but it is nothing more than a stone, rather than a gold, object. Naturally, this find sorely disappoints the Indigenous people who have flocked to the stunning site high in the Andes in hopes of experiencing the re-discovery of a splendid lost cultural treasure. However, Harry refuses to accept Moorehead's findings and does some ingenious sleuthing on his own. After piecing together clues about which way light beams reflect toward the treasure, he discovers the real gold sunburst in all its bejeweled beauty. Almost simultaneously, Harry has to confront an old partner who wants to steal the treasure himself. A scuffle ensues and the man falls to his death. Harry

In this triumphant scene toward the end of *Secret of the Incas*, the tribe is elated when the ancient disk is returned to the site, and lifted skyward by Pachacutec (Michael Pate). In recognition of the momentous event, Kori-Tica (Yma Sumac) sings and dances joyously. Peruvian folk singer Yma Sumac is an Indigenous portrayer of Andean stories set to music, and she gave the film the exotic look and feel audiences expected of adventure films in the 1950s (Paramount Pictures).

is saddened, but not for long. He is now free to travel anywhere he pleases with the treasure, but instead returns it to the Indigenous people, becoming a hero in their eyes. The audience-pleasing scene in which the golden disk is lifted high above the ruins of the ancient site by Pachacutec—thanks to Harry's efforts—is triumphantly joyous.

That said, modern viewers are likely to be put off by a key premise of this film, namely, that Indigenous people await cultural salvation from either an American archaeologist or an American fortune-hunter. However, few American viewers in 1954 saw anything amiss about such seemingly selfless acts. The plot's premise seemed to square with the idea that the United States was serving the role of protector against nefarious forces, and it might take a rascal to keep things on course. In this sense, Harry seems to be as much a secret agent who not only trips up the communists and frees a damsel in distress from their clutches, but also helps to restore a nation's patrimony (in this case Peru's) by outwitting mercenaries bent on stealing the archaeological treasures.

Naturally, in the process Harry has also redeemed himself in the eyes of Elena, with whom he will depart at the end of the film. Before they do, however, he pulls out a small golden artifact he has found somewhere along the way, and gives it to Elena as a present—confirmation that at least a bit of his roguishness will remain. As the film ends, Harry has beaten Professor Moorehead on all three counts: he can be heralded as a hero by the Indians and the archaeological community by returning the prized sun disk; he can keep some treasure himself for his efforts; and he can walk away with the woman that they both adore—a fitting finale at a time when men of action with nerves of steel ruled the silver screen.

Secret of the Incas did well at the box office and would influence other archaeology-themed adventure films well into the future. It is also credited with increasing tourism to Peru generally, and Machu Picchu in particular. More than four decades later, it inspired another film, the similarly titled *Secret of the Andes* (1998).[10] Produced by the Argentine company Semana Mágica, it represented a more recent corporate trend: Argentine-American partnership. Like *Secret of the Incas*, it centers on the search for a lost gold Inca object, in this case the Golden Disk of Huáscar, which has great spiritual value. Half of the disk is in a museum in New York City, but the other is still lost somewhere in the Andes. Uniting the two halves has long been the goal of archaeologists. The film's story was written by two Argentinians—Alejandro Azzano and Bernardo Nante. About ten years earlier, Azzano had served as the Argentine executive for production on *The Mission*. He has an abiding interest in storytelling, and the off-beat plot of *Secret of the Andes* reflects this.

In *Secret of the Andes*, the science of archaeology meets its match in the form of Indigenous magic. American archaeologist Brooks Willings (David Keith) is working in the field but having trouble with his crew excavating the site. An evil sorcerer is part of the problem, as is an unethical rival archaeologist, and the dig seems doomed to fail. There is also a good shaman who represents the positive side of Indigenous spirituality. As in many films, a padre represents traditional religion, which meets it match here. Compounding Willings' troubles is the unexpected arrival of his wife and their ten-year-old daughter Diana (Camilla Belle) who had been expelled from school in New York City because of her eccentric behavior. However, it soon turns out that Diana is in the right place at the right time, for she possesses magical powers. After embarking on an expedition with the good shaman, she ultimately helps find the missing half of the disk—thus saving her father's reputation and career.

Secret of the Andes was shot on location in far northwestern Argentina, a highly photogenic region where the Andes Mountains rise from high desert country punctuated by tall cardón cactus plants. In a number of memorable scenes, the landscape has a surreal aspect and gives this film a special look complementing its underlying theme of science meeting magic. The colorful village of Jucaitambo (in reality, the picturesque, historically designated town of Molinos in Salta Province) is central to much of the action. The wonderful, haunting Andean flute musical score is part of this film's appeal.

Films depicting anthropology and archaeology in South America often wrestle with how to portray Indigenous people and their spirituality, and *Secret of the Andes* is no exception. The film received marginal reviews and is rarely mentioned today. However, it is worth a second look—and serious study—for the way in which its plot employs Indigenous culture and magic in light of Christianity. Indigenous women in this film recognize Diana's power and help her in making the disk complete, evidently approving of its being taken to New York City to join its other half. Of note here is the daughter's real dual identity: actress Camilla Belle is Brazilian and American. More typically, such films involve pure White Saviors who help the Indigenous people reconnect with their past—a point I will say more about in the conclusion of this book.

As is evident in the films dealing with lost civilizations and their artifacts, antiquity has become an obsession in popular culture. For the record, the oldest known city in the Americas is not the elusive one that Percy Fawcett sought, nor even those associated with the Inca that Hiram Bingham popularized, but rather a less-well-known pre-Inca site in the desert of Peru north of Lima. Named Caral, its ruins date from about 4,000 BCE. Now a UNESCO Heritage site, Caral is rich in large earthworks and artifacts such as mummies. However, here as elsewhere in South America, the dramatic struggle between preservation and pillaging continues, as does the tension between well-meaning preservation-oriented outsiders and locals bent on economic development that can benefit their families.

Thirteen

Indiana Jones and the Kingdom of the Crystal Skull

Orellana's Revenge

As noted earlier, an account by Friar Gaspar de Carvajal of Francisco de Orellana's expedition into the Amazon was influential in shaping narratives well into the future, including the film *Aguirre, the Wrath of God* (1972). In the early twenty-first century, George Lucas and Steven Spielberg reprised Orellana's exploits in the fourth part of the Indiana Jones franchise—*Indiana Jones and the Kingdom of the Crystal Skull* (2008).[1] The character Indiana Jones was created by George Lucas, and first appeared in *Raiders of the Lost Ark* in 1981.[2] Lucas and Jeff Nathanson wrote the story featured in *Indiana Jones and the Kingdom of the Crystal Skull*; the screenplay was written by David Koepp. Played by Harrison Ford, the peripatetic archaeologist Indiana Jones was clearly based in part on Harry Steele in *Secret of the Incas* (1954), which played on TV in the late 1950s and early 1960s. It is no coincidence that Indiana Jones wears the signature brown leather jacket, tan pants, and three-day stubble that Charlton Heston sported in 1954. Alas, Harry Steele was not a professor, and so it is possible that Lucas infused a bit of Hiram Bingham, or rather Stanley Moorehead, into the Jones character—a natural, given their association with Machu Picchu in *Secret of the Incas*.

Like that 1954 archaeology-centered film, this Indiana Jones sequel supposedly takes place in the 1950s, when modern-day explorers were combing South America and Cold War intrigue abounded as communism began to infiltrate political systems worldwide, and especially in Latin America. As opposed to *Secret of the Incas*, however, *Indiana Jones and the Kingdom of the Crystal Skull* deliberately has a retro quality because director Spielberg was also trying to capture the magic of old B-grade sci-fi movies of his youth. In a sense, it brings Indiana Jones face to face with a rich ancient culture in Latin America—a region that had been mostly overlooked in the earlier films. Readers wondering why I've included a film that seems more in the realm of popular culture than serious exploration-discovery history should gird up for what follows, and recall that this book is about how Latin American exploration-discovery figures in a wide range of films. Therefore, fiction—and even science fiction—are fair game.

Audiences who've watched the Indiana Jones franchise develop from the early 1980s know that its plots seemed to become more and more complex and mind-boggling with each new movie. *Indiana Jones and the Kingdom of the Crystal Skull* is no exception. As a Hollywood action film,[3] it attempts to keep its audience enthralled to the point that images come at so rapid a pace that few viewers can really follow the intricacies of the plot. Some might claim that the flow of this Cold War–set action film is a veritable torrent, much of it done purely for thrills—or a future ride at a theme park. However, beneath its frenetic pace and intense action, there lies a compelling premise linked to the earliest of South American exploration narratives such as those by Gaspar de Carvajal—namely, that a city of gold lies somewhere in the Amazonian interior of that continent, and those who find it will be enriched beyond their wildest dreams.

The plot is complex but can be distilled as follows. While on an archaeological dig in New Mexico, Indiana Jones is abducted by armed Soviet infiltrators and taken to area 51 in Nevada. There, Jones is ordered to help them find a mummified alien corpse that he helped the Air Force identify in the Roswell UFO incident ten years earlier (1947). Led by a fanatically zealous agent named Irina Spalko (Cate Blanchett), the Soviets believe the mummy has supernatural powers in mind control. As the mummy is located, Jones escapes, only to be arrested as a Soviet agent by his own (American) government. Although Jones is cleared, he is placed on leave by his college. Near campus, Jones meets a young man named Mutt Williams (Shia LaBeouf) whose mother Marion (Karen Allen) is an archaeologist and former colleague who is being held captive in South America. He also learns that a former colleague named Harold Oxley (John Hurt) has discovered a crystal skull in Peru and believes it to be related to similar skulls found at Akator—a lost city that Jones believes to be mythical. For the record, Akator is supposedly located in the area where the borders of Brazil, Bolivia, and Peru meet, as described by the German journalist Karl Brugger in his sensational—and highly disputed—1976 book *The Chronicle of Akator*.[4]

How they reach this conclusion about Oxley's discovery of the crystal skull is worth some discussion here as it employs a series of remarkable cartographic images. As Jones thumbs through an old book about Francisco de Orellana, complete with images of the explorer, he realizes that a clue lies in the references to an extinct language called Keoma. Jones deciphers the text, stating that it means "follow the lines." In a synopsizing statement, he explains: "Leave it to Oxley to write a riddle in a dead language: *Follow the lines in the earth only gods can read which lead to Orellana's cradle guarded by the living dead*." In a Eureka moment, Jones exclaims: "He's talking about the Nazca lines!"

These lines really do exist, and they were etched across the landscape in parts of arid western South America by pre-Columbian peoples millennia ago. When seen from the air, such geoglyphs (literally earth carvings) comprise patterns that can stimulate the imagination. These geoglyphs are sometimes in the form of geometric designs, while others replicate the outlines of animals or people. The Nazca lines are the most famous of these. As noted by archeologist Gonzalo Pimental, some of these geoglyphs may have served as route markers or sign-posts in the desert.[5] In this context, the cinematic explorer Jones appears to be on the right track. Now energized, he exclaims: "Oxley's telling us the skull is in Nazca, Peru!" In quick order, he and Mutt are on the way to Peru, their flight indicated by a vintage airliner whose course is shown on a map of South America. In this on-screen mapped journey, several images of the aircraft appear almost simultaneously, in effect superimposed from several angles as the aircraft progresses from north to south, flying over Cuzco, Peru—the city out of which Harry Steele operated in *Secret of the Incas*. In addition to the red line indicating their travel, these shots of the plane from several perspectives turn what could have been a two-dimensional experience into seeming 3-D—a brilliant way of transforming map reading into a highly kinetic experience.

Their landing at Nazca is significant as Jones' first foray into Latin America, and the two explorers, one aging and the other young, strike quite a pose near the center of the sleepy town. In Nazca, Jones and Mutt learn that Oxley had been in a psychiatric hospital in Arequipa, where he left marks scrawled on a wall indicating the connection between the Nazca lines and the lost city. This too is a cartographic device. Using other clues left by Oxley, Jones has concluded that the term "cradle" also refers to a grave in that language, so they begin searching for a crypt. Jones and Mutt soon find the armor-clad body of Conquistador Francisco de Orellana—conveniently in a musty chamber not far from Oxley's cell. That stunning, rather gothic scene borders on horror and is noteworthy for the surprises that it reveals. Whereas one might hope to find a suit of armor belonging to a conquistador, finding his mummified body inside it is a decided bonus. Moreover, Orellana's face had been covered by a gleaming gold mask, adding a startling touch to the conquistador's appearance. This, Jones figures, was made by the Indians to symbolize the conquistador's obsession with the wealth embodied in El Dorado.

Making their discoveries complete, or nearly so, Jones and Mutt also find the impressive crystal skull, which Jones immediately determines has been made using far advanced technology. A word about this spectacular artifact so central to the story is in order. First, no crystal skull has ever been found in any ancient archaeological site. They began appearing in the nineteenth century, and are associated with the French invasion of Mexico by Maximilian. The earliest crystal skulls were small, but they got larger through time. The life-size skull in the movie is like those from the early twentieth century. Most are claimed to be of Aztec origin, and a few Mayan. Recent scientific analysis confirms that they are fakes dating from no earlier than the nineteenth century. That said, they proved irresistible to Spielberg, who in this film expanded their range into

In a dimly lighted scene from Steven Spielberg's *Indiana Jones and the Kingdom of the Crystal Skull*, the film's namesake (Harrison Ford) and Mutt Williams (Shia LeBeouf) make a spectacular archaeological discovery—the mummified body of conquistador Francisco de Orellana, including the mask that Indians used to symbolize his greed for gold. Shortly thereafter, Jones and Mutt find the fabled crystal skull, which will prove to be a key for revelations made later in the film as they search for a lost city in the Amazonian region (Lucasfilm Ltd,. and Paramount Pictures).

South America. Interestingly, the distorted shape of the skull in the film mimics some of the techniques that western South American tribes used to elongate the shape of the cranium in ancient times (e.g., Paracas culture). Cinematically speaking, it is a wonderful touch given Indiana Jones' supposedly discovering it in Peru. There are some clever inside jokes in this film, so when Jones holds the skull and says that it was made with far advanced technology, he just might be referring to the techniques involved in making such a fascinating movie prop.

With the stunning crystal skull in hand, Indiana Jones and Mutt have much to celebrate. However, their luck runs out at this point as they are again captured by the Soviets and taken to a camp in the Amazon. As their propeller-driven plane flies north-eastward, the flight uses the Nazca lines, as indicated by the map that now appears on screen. The maps in this part of the film are quite impressive as they superimpose airplanes, boats and other means of transportation involving the journey to the lost city. Like the vintage airliner earlier in the film, the steamboat on the Amazon is from the earlier part of the twentieth century, and shown near the river city of Iquitos, Peru, perhaps Spielberg's nod to the "Molly Aida" in *Fitzcarraldo*. Despite the seeming mystery about where they are ultimately headed, the Soviets evidently know their whereabouts on the way—and so does the audience, thanks to these maps.

En route to the lost city hidden somewhere deep in the Brazilian interior, more wild action scenes ensue. The dangers of tropical America, in particular South America, are showcased in this part of the film. In one scene, Jones up to his neck in quicksand is a sight to behold, especially because the only way he can be saved is by grabbing onto the only thing he detests—a snake! Whereas the film *Green Mansions* had used a serpent to suggest danger, this one appears in a comedic role. In another scene, Mutt is surprised by a monkey and feigns terror. In this film, Spielberg throws the book of tropical tropes at the audience. However, this type of comic relief later changes to horror as millions of ferocious fire ants—for which South America is famous—form a seething mass that chases down and subdues a Soviet agent; the horror is complete when they pour into his

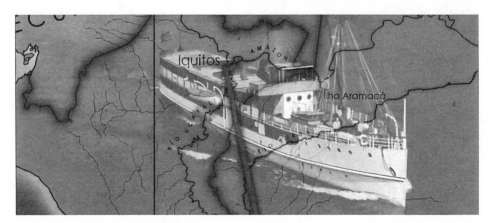

Throughout, the film *Indiana Jones and the Kingdom of the Crystal Skull* (2008) makes very effective use of cartographic images in varied formats. In this scene, a stylized map over which a steamboat traverses the Amazon near Iquitos shows the route traveled by the explorers, and may also be a subtle nod to Herzog's film *Fitzcarraldo*. By its very nature, film makes it possible for maps to transcend the static printed page and become part of the kinetic action (Lucasfilm Ltd. and Paramount Pictures).

In a humorous scene from *Indiana Jones and the Kingdom of the Crystal Skull* (2008), the film's namesake (Harrison Ford) is rescued from quicksand by companions Marion (Karen Allen) and Mutt Williams (Shia LeBeouf). They toss him the nearest thing available—and the only things he truly detests—a snake! Serpents have long been a trope associated with the Amazon, and director Steven Spielberg relied on them to keep the plot moving (Lucasfilm Ltd. and Paramount Pictures).

mouth and begin to consume him from the inside out while simultaneously pulling him underground. The convergence of genres in this scene—adventure, sci-fi, and horror—blurs the thin line that usually separates them.

In yet another film where waterfalls mark critical points in the plot, this one features a series of cataracts that serve as an important landmark that signals they are getting closer to the lost city. With the Soviets in close pursuit, they again escape along with Mutt's mother Marion and race, hell-bent, through jungle and along cliff-faces and over those towering waterfalls. After plunging about 150 feet, they come out unscathed—not only once, but several times. Although Marion's skilled driving and daring maneuvers places a woman in an exciting and welcome role, Spielberg's excessive use of action borders on the downright distracting in this part of the film. In her article sub-titled "lust and the frenzy of the visible," Linda Williams notes that certain scenes can be "…felt in the bodies of viewers…."[6] That essay was a brilliant interpretation of pornographic films, but it can be applied to the action film genre as well.

Williams persuasively argues that action-packed movies like this one challenge the long-held belief that film as we know it evolved solely from individual images effectively made to move before our eyes. Although 32 frames per second create the feeling of smooth action, there is more at work here, including the inherent ability of our brains to make still images seem to move due to the retention of retinal images. Williams suggests that for the last two centuries the proliferation of images has resulted in "…a bewildering array of subjective, physiological bodily effects and sensations produced within the bodies of observers."[7] To paraphrase what is happening, we ourselves have evolved (so to speak) to feel deeply within what Williams calls the "e-motion" of the motion picture images presented to us on the screen.

As nicely summarized by James Kendrick: "Action films are built around a core set of characteristics: spectacular physical action; a narrative emphasis on fights, chases and explosions; and a combination of state-of-the-art special effects and stunt work."[8] Additionally, intense exploration-discovery sagas on screen often depend on geographical features—gaping chasms, waterfalls, quicksand—which are woven into the story at critical points. In his numerous action films, Spielberg frequently uses them to great effect. However, after viewing this film, some might question how far this can be pushed. Heroes surviving plunges off waterfalls to elude their pursuers have now become clichés. In discussions with students, some claimed that although Spielberg knows how to deliver a body-rattling experience, and does so here, it was done with such gusto and predictability that it detracted from the plot. That said, there is no doubt that exploration-discovery narratives naturally lend themselves to highly-kinetic filmmaking.

Returning to the plot of this film, after Jones and his team survive all the hazards in getting there, the lost city that they've been seeking is finally at hand. Akator is impressive indeed, but might puzzle archaeologists. Although pyramids were constructed in western South America, the architecture of this lost city, with its prominent step-faced pyramids, appears to be stereotypically Mesoamerican. Of course, most viewers are likely not aware of that discrepancy. Besides, it comes with the territory as films often take such geographical and archaeological liberties. Then again, archaeological research currently under way is confirming that pyramids were constructed in the Amazon lowlands about a thousand years ago, though they were made of earth and likely looked rather different than their Mesoamerican counterparts.

For their part, the bedraggled explorers soon gain access to the heart of Akator by entering a large chamber housing the remains of thirteen crystal skeletons, one of which is missing the very skull that the intrepid archaeologists are carrying. At this point, as the frazzled audience is catching its breath, the pieces are about to come together. Jones comments that this site is filled with ancient artifacts from all over the

In Steven Spielberg's blockbuster *Indiana Jones and the Kingdom of the Crystal Skull* (2008), the lost city is discovered hidden deep in the Amazon. Interestingly, this city features spectacular pyramids more typical of those found in Mesoamerica and Mexico, but here they too suggest an ancient advanced culture that once existed before European conquest. As noted in the text, the geographic trajectory of this film—from Peru to the Amazon—essentially recreates the journey of the expedition of Francisco de Orellana (Lucasfilm Ltd. and Paramount Pictures).

world—Mesopotamia, Mesoamerica, China, etc. Seemingly as a professional courtesy, he exclaims, "They were archaeologists!" Once the skull is returned to its skeleton, an act that symbolizes the journey's end, a powerful force is activated and the city begins to disintegrate as a large flying saucer emerges. At this point, the sinister Irina—who tries to assimilate all the knowledge emanating from the force for large-scale mind control over the free world—is herself overwhelmed and destroyed by the force. In an increasingly rapidly rotating vortex, the city now completely disintegrates as water rushes in to reclaim the site. The explorers have discovered that these beings have vanished into the "space between spaces," suggesting their omnipresence. Soberly, Jones concludes that although searchers had long pursued the site for gold, that quest was misguided: to these wiser beings, the gold was a metaphor for *knowledge*, which was their real treasure.

Exploration-discovery sagas can have various outcomes, and this one ends in the solving of a riddle. Additionally, it enables Jones to reunite with Marion, marry her, and now appreciate their son Mutt. One might almost think that Jones has come full circle and is ready to hang up his signature fedora, which Mutt is now eyeing enviously after the wedding. However, Jones scoops up the hat, dons it, and now leaves with Marion on a well-deserved honeymoon. The message is that Jones, as the consummate serial explorer-discoverer, is not done yet. He is ready for the sequel—which finally arrived about fifteen years later (2023).

It is time for some additional reflection on, and contextualization of, this film—which is an exploration-discovery saga in structure, albeit one easy to dismiss as pop culture and little more. Of note is the way it tackles place as well as time. In it, the characters are searching for clues that play out in geographic space. As with all of the films in this franchise, *Indiana Jones and the Kingdom of the Crystal Skull* takes place in many geographic locales that ultimately fit together like the pieces of a jigsaw puzzle. Of note here is its Latin American connection. In a number of later novels based on the Indiana Jones character, of which there are about twenty so far, he traveled to Latin America as early as 1936; only in this film, however, is that region the main focus. Significantly the part of South America that lies between the heart of the Inca Empire and the eastern portions of Amazonia is the focus. Much of this cinematic territory comprises the very area where, about five centuries ago, expeditions were launched to find treasure in El Dorado. Cinematically speaking, Werner Herzog put it on the map with *Aguirre, the Wrath of God*.

Interestingly, *Indiana Jones and the Kingdom of the Crystal Skull* is the only film in the franchise in which none of the action scenes were filmed outside of the United States, reportedly because Spielberg wanted to be close to his family. Thus, he filmed the extensive Amazon basin scenes in the vicinity of Hilo, Hawaii, rather than use the real thing. Overall, it passes fairly well because Hawaii's biggest island has the requisite topography and vegetation to simulate the upper portions of the Amazon, provided that the cameras are pointed in the right direction. On the other hand, scenes such as the real Nazca lines of Peru were filmed from the air and later interspersed with the action footage, as were shots of spectacular waterfalls such as the impressive Iguaçu Falls, which straddles the Brazil-Argentina border. In a sense, this film's overabundance of scenic spectacles is in keeping with its overabundance of action scenes.

Although *Indiana Jones and the Kingdom of the Crystal Skull* did very well at the box office, it understandably received mixed reviews for some of the reasons hinted at above. At the time of its production, its professed attempt to mimic the feel of vintage 1950s films was compromised somewhat by heavy use of CGI in places. To ardent Spielberg fans, it seemed a letdown as they expected more from less—exactly the opposite of what this film delivered. In addition to these unfulfilled cinematic expectations was another issue that began to surface in popular culture at this time. The adventure film hero traversing the wilderness in search of the ancient past—the very theme that made *Secret of the Incas* feel so natural in 1954—still worked but was wearing thin.

By 2008, when this Indiana Jones in Latin America saga finally arrived on screen, new themes of exploration—for example, in search of social justice, environmental protection and the like—made it seem just a bit out of step. It feels even more so today. That said, *Indiana Jones and the Kingdom of the Crystal Skull* perpetuated the romance of South American exploration-discovery history. It and others in the franchise certainly helped shape a generation of video games in which exploration-discovery ranks very high. As noted in the Introduction to this book, these have venerable roots in geographically-themed board games such as Wallis's Adventures, which were popular in the mid-nineteenth century well before the advent of film—which they appear to have influenced if not anticipated. If present trends continue, exploration-discovery sagas are likely to have an even more promising future in electronic games, for the big screen is no longer their only venue.

For readers who may be wondering why I titled this chapter "Orellana's Revenge," it has to do with a primitive form of justice. Although the real Francisco de Orellana was an inspiration to Werner Herzog, whose original script for *Aguirre, the Wrath of God* included prominent reference to him, his name never made it into that 1972 film. Alas, Orellana's name had pretty much been lost to popular history until resurrected for *Indiana Jones and the Kingdom of the Crystal Skull*. Now, if one searches for Francisco Orellana on line, a plethora of websites and images associated with the Lucas/Spielberg film pop up. One of them literally resurrects the conquistador as depicted in the film, in effect reconstructing his exploits much as Indiana Jones would have. This includes his supposed burial location in a Peruvian desert not far from the mystical Nazca lines and his association with all the artifacts from the film, including the golden artifacts and crystal skulls—and of course the lost city in the Amazon basin. According to this imaginative information, Orellana is said to have been mummified by Indigenous people of the Peruvian desert, a premise that adds a certain archeological credibility to the story. By filling in the back-story for the filmmakers, these sites such as "Fandom"[9] help keep Orellana on the radar and the franchise alive. In the Indiana Jones version, Orellana cuts quite a figure, even as a mummy, and his countenance is recognizable to millions of fans—a spectacular reprise for a once-forgotten conquistador.

Fourteen

Embrace of the Serpent

Explorations into Deeper Meaning

The events portrayed in the film that I will now discuss—*Embrace of the Serpent* (2017)[1]—take place at about the same time Percy Fawcett's decades-long quest for the Lost City of Z was underway in the early twentieth century. However, *Embrace of the Serpent* offers a unique perspective, telling a far more involved story about the reaction that explorers and Indigenous people have when they encounter each other. Directed and co-written by Colombia's Ciro Guerra, it depicts the expeditions of two twentieth-century explorers who arrived at two different times (ca. 1906 and 1940) on two separate quests, but had at least one common objective: to find a rare plant called *yakruna*. The movie is shot on high quality 35mm black and white film that lends a vintage documentary feel, but is so crisp that it shines in high-definition. That film choice gives *Embrace of the Serpent* a retro touch yet modern feel.

Linking both expeditions into this nominally "Amazonian" region is the same Indigenous shaman named Karamakate. He had assisted both expeditions, one as a young man suspicious of outsiders in 1909 (played by Nilbio Torres) and the other as an elderly man full of regret in 1940 (played by Antonio Bolívar). The fact that the Indigenous Karamakate is a central character of the story makes this film unusual. In effect, *Embrace of the Serpent* becomes an Indigenous story, and from the beginning, several tribes in the area of Colombia where it was filmed were involved with the production. Karamakate serves as an intermediary between the outsider explorers and those Indigenous people living in the area.

In an enthusiastic review that makes explicit the connection between South American exploration and filmmaking, *Variety* summarized *Embrace of the Serpent* as "a majestic showcase for its native landscape, and an affirmation that there will always be uncharted realms for cinema to conquer."[2] The term "native landscape" refers to the film's emphasis on the native tribes living in the Amazon basin, particularly the vegetation there that has sustained them, and the rubber trees that were exploited by Europeans in the late nineteenth and early twentieth centuries. The term "uncharted realms" refers to frontiers in cross-cultural communication and personal discovery.

We first encounter Karamakate in the film's opening scenes set in 1906, when he gazes out toward a river and sees a canoe carrying two men. Karamakate is an impressive figure, and his tiger-claw necklace suggests his prowess and social status. Guiding the canoe is an Indigenous man named Manduca, and a seriously ill man lying down in it is his European "travel partner" named Theo von Martius (Jan Bijvoet). Theo is loosely based on the German ethnographer Theodore Koch-Grunberg (1872–1924) of the museum in Stuttgart. As the canoe carrying the ailing Theo edges closer to shore, Kara-makate refuses the guide's plea to help. Although he is a shaman and healer, Karamakate has witnessed white people bringing destruction to the area. However, after becoming convinced of Theo's sincere interest in the region's natural habitats, Karamakate relents and temporarily heals him, decorating his face with sacred markings. After this encounter, all three men continue their journey upriver by canoe, where Theo hopes to discover more about the tribes that live there.

At this point in the film, a series of sequences depicting a huge snake giving birth to numerous offspring dominates the screen. The snake is an anaconda for which the region is well known, largely through its portrayal in a wide range of films. The fluidity with which the newly born snakes emerge from this mother snake and begin slithering away—and the way in which the larger snake soon returns to the river as an underwater camera records it swimming away—underscores a central theme of the film; namely, that the river and the snake are inseparable.

In the next scene, which fast-forwards to 1940, we encounter Karamakate (Antonio Bolívar) as an old man along that same river as he has an encounter with the second explorer called Evan (Brionne Davis). Arriving by himself in a dugout canoe, this explorer is based on American botanist Richard Evans Schultes (1915–2001). Evan is in search of a plant called *yakruna* that can do two things, namely, benefit society by improving rubber production, and help him dream. As Evan puts it, "I've never dreamed, either awake or sleeping." Karamakate holds the key to Evan's success or failure, and recites a tale of woe involving the destruction of his people by the intrusion of European culture. He notes that he is the last of his people, and that he is losing his memory; when he dies, his people will be gone.

One key visual element in the scenes involving the encounter between Karamakate and Evan is a large, mural-like group of pictographs that this shaman is painting on a huge rock outcrop along the river. Like all pictographs, they are rather abstract representations that may have varied meanings, but can be recognized as animals, plants, stars and other objects in nature. One prominent icon throughout the film is the serpent (La Serpiente) central to this story. In Amazonian lore, the serpent is seen as the giver of life descending from the Milky Way onto earth. In the film, serpents appear in many guises.

The film now jumps back in time to the first expedition, when Theo has become well enough to conduct his field research. The audience now becomes part of that exploration journey, on which he collects scientific specimens such as butterflies, and makes many fine illustrations of the flora and fauna. Local tribes are introduced to these and marvel at what they capture. This film emphasizes the reactions that Indigenous people have to the musings and recordings made by scientifically trained outsiders. Theo is also keeping a log of the journey. In this notebook, he makes a drawing that resonates with Karamakate as it contains natural symbols, including a circular motif that suggests interconnectivity. When Karamakate asks Theo where he saw these images, Theo answers from a dream, and the shaman realizes that this European has some powers of his own.

In this film, technology such as photography and navigation are shown in light of the impact they have on the Indigenous peoples. In a movie full of scenes depicting intense inter-cultural encounters, one involving a compass stands out. In it, Theo introduces the compass to a local tribe, noting that it points to the morning star. Momentarily

At the beginning of Ciro Guerra's *Embrace of the Serpent* (2015), which takes place in 1909, the young warrior/shaman Karamakate (Nilbio Torres) already has ample reason to suspect the motives of explorers, for the rubber boom is destroying his people's way of life. Technically speaking, the Colombian film is also unique in that it was shot using 35 mm black and white film, giving it a decidedly retro feel and artistic cachet (Buffalo Films).

In a second sequence in the film *Embrace of the Serpent*, which is set in the same locale only about three decades later (ca. 1940), a now aged Karamakate (Antonio Bolívar) is here pictured as he stands at river's edge near a huge rock surface covered with symbolic pictographs. As the film unfolds, the significance of these symbols becomes clearer to the explorers arriving from the outside world (Buffalo Films).

distracted, Theo loses sight of the compass, but when no one can tell him what happened to it, suspects that it has been stolen. Tensions mount as Theo begins demanding the missing compass, and the tribe's people claim to know nothing about it. The situation threatens to become violent as Theo begins frisking some young men for it. The audience naturally assumes that the compass is extremely important to Theo as it will help

In the 2015 film *Embrace of the Serpent*, a tense moment ensues when a tribal leader refuses to return the navigational compass belonging to Theo von Martius (Jan Bivuoet)—a confrontation that, though defused, has remarkable ramifications. In a sense, the compass is another cartographic device as it can assist users in telling direction (Buffalo Films).

him navigate as he explores this uncharted land. He seems increasingly desperate as the tribe becomes increasingly recalcitrant. Finally, Theo discovers that the chief has it, but is unwilling to part with it. Clearly, the compass is an object conveying power (knowledge) and this is important to the chief. Tensions further mount as Theo tugs it from the chief's hands.

At this point, Karakamate wisely escorts Theo out of the village before the situation further deteriorates. As he does, he asks Theo why he did not simply let them keep the compass. In a surprising answer, Theo states that the natives should not have the compass because they will come to rely on it, and thus lose their ages-old skills of navigating by signs in nature, including the stars and other clues. Karamakate's response to Theo is similarly surprising, for he berates him for denying the tribe something that can help them navigate even more effectively! Unexpected exchanges like this one defy audience expectations and shed light on the inconsistencies that characterize all cross-cultural interaction. This ability to keep the audience off balance—never quite knowing how the explorer and the explored will react—is one of the things that makes *Embrace of the Serpent* such a profound film. Many surprises await the two explorer-discoverers, and the viewer as well.

As this first expedition travels along the river, it encounters a religious mission overseen by a sadistic priest who metes out cruel punishment to his young followers, whose parents were enslaved and killed by rubber barons. It is here that Karamakate's fears of his culture dying are confirmed, for its language and ways of life are being lost in the process of zealous evangelization. The loss can work both ways, for ultimately Theo becomes a martyr who sacrifices his health and forfeits his comfortable family life in Germany in order to record a vanishing way of life. Although he perished somewhere in the Amazon, his ethnographic journals compiled in Brazil and Venezuela would live on, later published in book form in Germany and, most recently, in Cambridge, UK.[3]

The film now returns to the second expedition, on which Evan Schultes embarks with Karamakate to journey in the footsteps of Theo and make additional discoveries. In one remarkable scene, Evan shows a copy of Theo's book to Karamakate, who is amazed by it for two reasons. It appears to be the first published book he has ever seen, and moreover he is moved by the memories this particular book evokes. For Karamakate, so much has changed for the worst since that first expedition. He is truly the last living member of his tribe, and sees ruin encroaching from all sides. As Theo did years earlier, Evan introduces Karamakate to modern technology, in this case a wind-up phonograph on which he plays classical music records. To Evan, the music is restorative but it means nothing to Karamakate, who asks "what story is it telling?" In a cinematic sense, both the photographic images he encountered earlier, and the music from the phonograph in the second exploration, pair up to symbolize the evolution of technology involved in filmmaking itself; picture first, then sound. This slyly self-reflective scene is yet another example of this film's depth.

On that later expedition, the old mission has fallen into near-ruin and is now overseen by a Brazilian madman who thinks he is Jesus the Messiah. His followers are a strange flock indeed—but strangely familiar. Actually, they are the violent, full-grown fanatical acolytes who had learned well from his sadistic predecessor. Symbolically speaking, these mission scenes are an outright condemnation of Christianity imported by outsiders, an institutionalization of depravity. Although the Brazilian messiah is thankful when the visiting team consisting of shaman and explorer helps heal his dying wife, the resulting celebration he oversees degenerates into bacchanalia. Having witnessed quite enough, Karamakate and Evan continue their quest.

Along the way, there is plenty of tension between Karamakate and Evan as well, for this shaman constantly challenges the scientist's perceptions. In one scene, they talk about the river along which they are travelling. For his part, Evan regards the river scientifically, which is to say a geographic feature, the interface between running water and land; however, Karamakate tells him "The river is the anaconda's son." As a metaphor, perhaps, in one darkly-lit scene, a black panther and a snake are locked in mortal combat. Wrapping itself around the panther, the snake will likely win this battle.

As hinted at earlier, vegetation is an especially important element in this story. Karamakate considers plants to be spiritual while Evan simply regards them as a resource. Tellingly, Evan has dedicated his life to finding valuable plants for exploitation, even helping his country win wars, while Karamakate has devoted his life to protecting them for their spiritual value. In one scene they arrive at a location where rubber is being harvested and a yakruna tree is flourishing, but Karamakate regards this too as a desecration, and sets fire to the tree at its base to put an end to a corrupted way of life. Alas, the effort seems futile as civilization has encroached.

For Karamakate the world has crumbled, and he feels compelled to go back to the source of spiritual enlightenment. In structure, this film is very picaresque in several senses. First, a series of encounters in both time and place are involved, but the fact that two Karamakates play roles makes it doubly picaresque. Now on a very primordial quest—Karamakate for the source of life, and Evan for the source of dreams—they depart again. Significantly, Evan finally yields to Karamakate's repeated requests to jettison his cumbersome belongings such as a huge suitcase. Evan tosses the suitcase overboard, symbolically getting rid of the excess baggage of civilization.

They finally arrive at a spectacular locale where several steep bare mountains rise abruptly from the jungle. Filmed on the Inirida River (a tributary of the Orinoco in eastern Colombia) they paddle along until reaching the Cerros de Mavecure. This is a fitting setting for the concluding action in the movie, for it features spectacular views of the surrounding landscape that they had traversed, including the serpentine course of the river. After they climb to the top of the hill, Evan is shown what Karamakate claims is the very last *yakruna* plant in existence. Dismayed by what he has been witnessing, Karamakate becomes angry, threatening to destroy the plant. However, he instead relents, offering it to Evan for its true purpose—spiritual awakening. Evan is soon under the spell of this sacred, mind-altering plant. In a particularly striking scene, Evan hallucinates that fire is emanating from Karamakate's face. This scene is especially significant because it is the younger Karakamate who is incandescent, bringing his life and the film full circle chronologically, and symbolically.

As Evan continues experiencing psychedelic images, the audience comprehends that the symbols he had seen on Karamakate's huge pictographic rock surface are being revealed to him in a dream-like state that finally liberates his mind from the straitjacket of science. On film, these colorful symbols merge into the landscape panorama below, in which the serpentine river and the serpent itself become one. It is a psychedelic epiphany leading to the conclusion that the ultimate exploration occurs within the mind. Cinematically speaking, these scenes make one of the more effective transitions from black and white to color in film history, the most effective being when Dorothy leaves black and white Kansas and enters the polychrome land of the Munchkins in *The Wizard of Oz* (1939)[4]—a story and film that, too, is about exploration into altered states of consciousness.

Adding to the special effects of *Embrace of the Serpent* is something that happened unplanned at the end of the filming, but harkens to an earlier scene in which Karamakate is encircled by butterflies for which the region is famous. In this concluding

Toward the conclusion of *Embrace of the Serpent*, the time period has shifted to the year 1940. After a long journey by canoe, American botanist Evan Schultes and Karamakate (Antonio Bolívar)—seen here as an old man—finally arrive at a sacred locale. Here, in the spectacular Cerros de Mavecure, Karamakate ponders the last *yakruna* plant in existence (Buffalo Films).

scene, as Evan walks along a riverbank, he reaches a point where a rising cloud of butterflies swirls around him. The scene is so perfect and magical that it has the aura of computer-generated imagery. However, it really happened serendipitously, astounding both the actor and the cinematographers—a reminder that South America can live up to its reputation as a land of natural wonders. Ironically, because that scene was shot in black and white, those swirling butterflies are visible in the movie, but virtually disappear when the scene is captured as a still.

Quite beyond its stunning visuals, *Embrace of the Serpent* is rich in social messages and critiques. Ideologically speaking, it takes on the Western scientific and economic system that appropriates Indigenous cultural knowledge and resources. It is a complex film, perhaps a bit too ambitious in that it tackles so many themes and topics, but visionary nevertheless. Its underlying concern about social justice and other progressive causes is typical of movie-making (and movie makers) today, just as more conservative sentiments were the rule about seventy years ago when entrepreneurial outsider heroes were in vogue. Audiences themselves seem to be changing along with political values.

In a recent article in *Terrae Incognitae* that I mentioned in the Preface, Carter Ringle singles out three of the films I have now discussed—*Zama*, *The Lost City of Z*, and *Embrace of the Serpent*—precisely be*cause* they feature seemingly commendable (which is to say progressive) protagonists, whom Ringle calls "White Fanatics." Based on their states of mind, Ringle existentially positions these protagonists' dilemmas on a scale, concluding that there is "…a fine line between the White Fanatic experiencing catharsis, madness, or death." In a literary and cinematic sense, of course, the differences between these alternatives are profound, and could profitably be explored and nuanced.[5]

These protagonists—Zama, the Fawcetts, and Theo—are all white males, but what makes them White Fanatics in Ringle's eyes is that they meet their demise in search of something just out of reach. Although an element of self-sacrifice might be involved, their downfall lies in pursuing something passionately and perhaps even recklessly. However, according to Ringle, they all serve the same ultimate purpose for audiences, namely, "…connect[ing] the dots between these Westerners' assuaging colonial white guilt and Jesus dying for sins." In this scenario, by identifying with each doomed protagonist "…the white viewers can divorce themselves from the colonizers and rubber barons and instead relate to the well-meaning victim of circumstance."[6] This is an intriguing premise and warrants careful research into how monolithic "white viewers" are. Interestingly, some of the biggest fans of *Embrace of the Serpent* are direct descendants of the Indigenous people depicted in it.[7]

A central point explored in *Embrace of the Serpent* involves a fusion of two themes—that plants with magical powers can be found in the heart of South America and that the Indigenous peoples here can help unlock those powers for soul-searching outsiders. This is the premise of a film released at about the same time titled *Icaros: A Vision*.[8] This Peruvian/American production centers on a young woman named Angélica (Ana Cecilia Stieglitz) who seeks a cure for her recently diagnosed breast cancer. Suspicious of modern medicine, which often employs some very potent industrially produced drugs for chemotherapy, Angélica is drawn to the herbal medicinal cures attributed to the Shipibo and other Amazonian tribes. Ayahuasca is among the plants in South America that can induce such spectacular psychotropic effects.

After finding her way to the tribal healing center, Angélica meets two shamans, the elder Guillermo (Guillermo Arevaldo) and his grandson Arturo (Arturo Izquierdo) who are in effect playing themselves. This film's use of special psychedelic effects is stunning, as is the cinematography throughout. Filmed on location in Peru, it has the feel of a mind-bending docudrama. Through a series of intense drug-induced experiences, Angélica learns to confront her fears. Interestingly, the young shaman Arturo similarly comes to grips with blindness, so the two of them have learned from their experiences. In a sense, this film was semi-autobiographical for its director Leonor Caraballo, for she succumbed to her own breast cancer shortly before the film's production was completed.

In a manner of speaking, *Icaros: A Vision* and *Embrace of the Serpent* are bookends—one current, the other historic—that highly respect Indigenous peoples and their traditions. Cinematically speaking, *Icaros: A Vision* is also a tribute to the legacy of legendary director Werner Herzog, who literally put this region of South America on the map for generations of film-lovers. In fact, portions of *Icaros: A Vision* were filmed at the hotel Casa Fitzcarraldo, named in honor of Herzog's film. Writing in *Variety*, film critic Nick Schager observed that "Icaros: A Vision presents the Amazon jungle as a literal and psychological heart of darkness." Angélica's journey takes her into the depths of her soul, and she emerges anew after her experiences with the sacred ayahuasca plant, from which she learns incantations. *Icaros: A Vision* seems conscious that it is charting new territory, or as critic Schager astutely put it using a cartographic metaphor, "… this trippy work maps the intersection of West and East, body and spirit, faith and terror with beguiling grace." He further predicted that although this film was "too uniquely out-there to attract strong theatrical support," it would likely find a good reception on the festival circuit.[9]

In essence, that is how many cult films initially began life and ultimately received recognition. Like Herzog with *Fitzcarraldo*, director Caraballo put her soul into this project set deep in the Amazon. Both of their cinematic works provide audiences with a lasting impression of how this geographic location can magically transform the human spirit, and both are likely to be appreciated well into the future.

FIFTEEN

Anaconda

Cinematic Exploration
of River-Spawned Horrors

South America has long been associated with fictionalized accounts of expeditions that sought vanishing Indian tribes but stumbled onto something quite unexpected. These stories are usually based on the premise that a mysterious and dangerous creature exists in the backcountry, most often somewhere in the Amazon Basin, and that an expedition must suddenly confront it. Among the early cryptozoologically themed films set in South America was the wildly successful 1954 sci-fi classic *The Creature from the Black Lagoon*,[1] in which a geological expedition into the Amazon encounters more than it bargained for. They encounter not only fossils of a piscine amphibious humanoid, but also to their dismay discover it has living relatives. Their efforts to capture one lead to disaster as the creature goes on a deadly rampage. That film not only confirmed that science fiction and horror are two closely related genres, but that their combination can be a box office bonanza. Although this chapter will focus on Latin America's cinematic aquatic terrors, they are not confined to its waters. For example, the 1990 film *Arachnophobia*[2] featured deadly spiders originally found in the jungles of northern South America invading a California town.

The next film I will discuss involves a slightly more plausible creature based on one of the region's fear-inspiring fauna—serpents. The region is home to some of the world's largest snakes, such as boa constrictors and especially the green Anacondas that can reach almost thirty feet (ca. 10 meters) in length. As one might anticipate, these figure in legends. It should be noted here that such huge snakes—forty, fifty, or even sixty or more feet long—have been reported for generations. Explorer Percy Fawcett claimed that he shot and killed a sixty-two footer in 1906,[3] but science has consistently debunked such reports. Nevertheless, they persist. Given widespread fears about snakes in general, it was inevitable that someone would base a movie on an oversize serpent, especially one with a nasty disposition and a hankering for human flesh.

In this category is the part sci-fi, part horror, and part adventure film *Anaconda* (1997).[4] Although its story takes place in the early 1990s, I include it here because it has a 1950s sci-fi premise in that it involves something freakish that scientists would have trouble explaining. That, of course, also puts it in the category of fantasy—a reminder that the boundary between the genres is difficult to set. Above all, it is a film about exploration, or rather what I call "explortation," that is, exploration seemingly exploited for pure thrill and considerable box-office profit. *Anaconda* originated as a tersely co-written screenplay by Hans Bauer, Jim Cash, and Jack Epps, Jr., although it

173

later became available as an e-book by Hans Bauer titled *Anaconda: The Writer's Cut*.[5] The film, which proved wildly successful, was directed by Luis Llosa, a Peruvian with a penchant for tackling edgy projects.

The way the film opens—with a full written statement about the expedition—gives it a decidedly retro feel:

> Our adventure begins one thousand miles from the mouth of the mighty Amazon, deep in the heart of the rain forest. From here we will travel by river barge up through shallow tributaries and unexplored backwaters in search of the elusive people of the mist—the Shirishama tribe, one of the last great mysteries of the rain forest.

Of special note is the perspective from which the story is told, namely, through the eyes (and lenses) of a documentary filmmaking team that sets out to film one story, but winds up filming something quite different, to put it mildly. To my knowledge, this is the first modern adventure film set in South America to use this filming-of-an-expedition perspective, although earlier movies set elsewhere using it (for example, the original 1933 film *King Kong*[6]) have done so to great effect. However, highly unusual is the expedition's remarkable casting diversity as regards the ethnicity and gender—a departure for most exploration films that tend to depict expeditions solidly under the control of white men. In fact, *Anaconda* may be a first in that its hero is not a white man at all, but rather a Latina.

Beautifully filmed in part on the Amazon and its tributaries in the vicinity of Manaus, Brazil, *Anaconda* opens with a tense scene featuring a lone man on small boat that is under attack by an unseen creature so terrible that when he finally sees it, he chooses to shoot himself rather than be killed by it. The film then begins anew with an expedition getting underway on a larger vessel named the *Micaela—1*. Like many predecessors, *Anaconda* involves a boat trip deep into the interior, the suspense mounting with each mile traversed. As hinted at in the written opening lines, the journey begins as a purely anthropological expedition led by Dr. Steven Cale (Eric Stoltz), its goal being to find and document, on film, the elusive "People of the Mist." The fact that they are associated with the "rain forest" in the film's opening written lines suggests that they too are endangered.

On this expedition, the documentary film's director/producer is the energetic Terri Flores (Jennifer Lopez), who commands the film crew of about half a dozen, including her right-hand man—cinematographer Danny Rich (Ice Cube). Her sound engineer Gary Dixon (Owen Wilson) is a jokester with a quirky personality and an odd sense of humor. The relationship between Dr. Cale and Terri is soon revealed to be more than professional. She is romantically involved with him but clearly an independent woman. The captain is a taciturn local named Mateo (Vincent Castellanos) who commands the flat-bottomed, smoke-spewing diesel riverboat.

As with most films about expeditions, this one features a map early on. In this case, Professor Cale shows Terri an official nautical map of the river system they will explore. The map, which also appears later on, works at several levels. First and most obvious, its presence confirms that Cale has done some planning. Next, and a bit deeper, its content being articulated pretty scientifically reaffirms that the region has already been explored to some extent, despite the claim made in the opening written statement that the region is "unexplored." This map, therefore, is perfect for underscoring the premise that anthropology rather than geographic discovery is the goal. Lastly, and most symbolically, is the name of the most important feature on the map, the Rio Negro, which translates as black river. This toponym may suggest the obscurity of the region but, more to the point, may subconsciously alert the audience that the plot will center on something metaphorically darker, and likely more sinister.

The film captures the expedition's progress upriver in stunning wide panoramas alternating with claustrophobia-inducing narrow channels through which the boat barely squeezes. The earlier written wording promised these types of challenges and the cinematography delivers. Adding to the alternating moods are the varied skies—sunny, cloudy, and foggy. A hallmark of jungle films like this one is the overall bluish-greenish-gray tones that accentuate the gloominess of many stories set in this region. *Anaconda* has plenty of them but many bright spots as well.

As the plot progresses, the expedition is on course but takes a turn when the captain stops to help a man whose boat has broken down. As opposed to the bookish anthropologist Dr. Cale, this man named Paul Serone[7] (Jon Voight) states that he is from Paraguay and had trained to become a padre but wanted to see more of the world. That is the public version he relates but his back story is darker. Whereas he was originally youthful and idealistic, he is now middle-aged, cynical, and has a different agenda, one based on revenge. In brooding close ups, he reveals that his extensive experience in the region will help him find and capture a monstrous anaconda that lives farther upstream near a waterfall. Everyone on board thinks this is nonsense, but Serone claims otherwise. In a sense, *Anaconda* is about what and whom to believe in the face of uncertainty.

One specific source of tension in *Anaconda* involves Serone's differences of opinion with the professional academic authority on board. That, of course, is similar to the case of Harry Steele vs. Professor Moorehead in *Secret of the Incas*. The expedition aims to show that the existence of the Shirishama is based on myth as other people live in the region, but Serone disagrees, saying they are still alive and well. Moreover, Serone claims that they are worshippers of that huge snake he hopes to capture. As one might expect, these claims are dismissed on both counts by Professor Cale. Undeterred, Serone adds some gruesome details; for example, after the monster snake swallows its prey, it regurgitates it, and then consumes it again. Small wonder the Indians fear, and worship, this creature. For good measure, Serone points the nasty scar on his own face as proof of an earlier encounter with the serpent. Again, it is real-world experience versus book learning that are at loggerheads here, and the audience will soon learn which claims are true, and which are not.

Like most adventure films, place plays an important role in *Anaconda*. As the film progresses, and the *Micaela 1* moves upstream, the jungle itself becomes a character as it increasingly enshrouds the vessel and its film crew. It soon becomes apparent that this film is a masterful blend of dark comedy and terror, a combination that builds and releases tensions as it takes the audience on an emotional roller coaster ride from one place to another within this huge river basin. In one scene, the clearly flirtatious soundman Gary asks a female film crew member "Is it just me, or does the jungle make you really, really horny?" This may be an insider's reference to Klaus Kinski's statement about the jungle being erotic as Herzog's crew was filming *Fitzcarraldo* more than a decade earlier. However, Herzog's claim that the jungle is not erotic but rather a monstrous deformity of nature is more on target here, for the place is fraught with danger. Gary soon discovers this when a ferocious wild boar interrupts a makeshift tryst in the jungle. With a blast from a rifle, Serone comes to the rescue, proving his skills and putting Gary in his debt.

The rest of the film crew is wary, and with good reason: From the moment they picked up Serone, things have begun to go awry. At about this time, the expedition enters waters marked by a large totem pole with a menacing snake motif—a serpent wrapping around a hapless human figure. The audience sees it through the lenses of pair of binoculars as it emerges out of the mist, barely discernible from dense vegetation. Geographically speaking, it is a wildly out of place feature. In reality, totem poles are found only in northwestern North America. However, as a prop, this one works in the tropics because it proves that the Indigenous people have a tradition of venerating these deadly snakes.

From this point on, the film's action-sequences intensify. Cale becomes incapacitated during a suspicious underwater diving accident, and will be sidelined for much of the film. In short order, one of the huge serpents appears and attacks the boat, causing pandemonium while Serone readies himself for action he seems to crave. With little warning, the captain Mateo becomes the first victim, his death as terrifying as Serone predicted. Mateo is unable to scream as the snake coils around him and crushes the air out of him, then silently drags him under the water. As the DVD cover of this film promises, "it will take your breath away." With the captain "missing," Serone now begins taking charge, while the visibly-shaken crew tries to make sense of what has just happened.

Although the audience now needs no convincing about the veracity of the snake tales, Gary discovers among Serone's possessions some snake-related historical documents that help fill in the back-story. These include an old journal containing a sketch of a snake squeezing a grimacing victim and other material suggesting the impact of the snakes in pre-historic or early modern times by an outsider, possibly a European explorer. Serone is right: the snakes have been a menace for a long time. Also among Serone's papers is a more recent illustrated newspaper article about his reptilian exploits. Clearly, Serone's reputation has been enhanced by the press—something explorers since Columbus have relished.

As seen through a pair of binoculars in *Anaconda* (1997), a documentary film team sets out to record a "lost" Indian tribe deep in the Amazon, but along the way discovers something sinister, as evident in this carved totem pole featuring a huge serpent with its human prey. The genre soon turns to horror as they come under attack by the serpents (Sony Pictures).

Snakes are now not only a clear and present danger, but also an opportunity. Agreeing with Serone that capturing one of these serpents can bring fame and fortune, Gary now sides with him. The crew considers this disloyal, but Gary justifies his actions on the premise that people will pay more to see a film in which a monster snake is caught than one about the search for a lost tribe. Cinematically speaking, this is a brilliant device that subliminally informs the audience why the movie they are watching was made.

As the plot develops, it soon becomes apparent that Serone and the captain had been in cahoots even before the expedition had set out. Dr. Cale's accident was no accident at all, but rather Serone's doing. With Dr. Cale still incapacitated and the snakes running rampant, Serone effectively takes over the entire expedition. His brutishness is evident in a scene in which he uses a big hunting knife to point to the parts of the map where he will now take the expedition. The implication of brute force in this ham-fisted scene is obvious—it's his way or else.

Things go from bad to worse in short order. In jaw-dropping scenes featuring forty-five-foot-long serpents picking off members of the crew, the story becomes one of pure terror. As the action intensifies, Serone manages to escape the snake's wrath, but Gary becomes another of the early casualties as he is attacked by it, squeezed tightly, and pulled under. Shocked silence follows. However, just when the audience thinks they have seen the last of Gary, the camera reveals his fate in a gruesome underwater scene. In the murky darkness, the bloated Anaconda that has just swallowed Gary glides by, revealing the form of his entrapped body, including his face as if covered in a tight snake-skin ski-mask. This scene brings to mind the disquieting 1893 painting titled *The Scream* by Edvard Munch, but of course Gary had never uttered a sound. In this Gothic-like scene, the Amazon becomes the ultimate cradle of horrors. For its part, what Spanish literature scholar Carmen Serrano calls the "Gothic Imagination" has deep roots—and is alive and well—in Latin America.[8]

Serone is now top-dog and in charge of the vessel and the expedition—but has underestimated Terri, who begins plotting ways to take it back. As she defiantly puts it using a metaphorically-charged synopsizing statement that audiences can readily grasp: "I can trap a snake too." The scenes in this film pitting Serone and Terri are intense and well acted. Luckily, the cameraman Danny is on Terri's side, taking turns filming and attempting to keep the rampaging Serone under control. Her faux attempt to sexually seduce Serone in order to let down his guard ends in near disaster as his cynicism and lightning-fast reflexes kick in. Serone is a ferocious adversary, with nearly superhuman strength and a remarkable talent for survival. Terri is remarkably tenacious and vows to stop him.

Continuing upriver, the expedition finally encounters the waterfall that Serone had described—the source area of the snakes. Nearby is an abandoned factory complex likely left over from the rubber boom period, and it is here that the showdown with the anacondas takes place. Viewers with a sharp eye might notice that the environment in this part of the film—especially the sky, vegetation, and lighting—is noticeably different. This entire set, including the waterfalls and old factory, was developed at the Los Angeles (Arcadia) arboretum and gardens. To me as a geographer, those California desert palms (*Washingtonia filifera*) are a dead giveaway, but most terror-stricken viewers would not even notice that detail. In the filmmaker's favor, most people do not normally differentiate one type of palm tree from another. As a student of mine once quipped, "They all look alike to me."

Interpersonal tensions abound in Luis Llosa's smash hit *Anaconda* (1997). In this scene, anxiety mounts as the villainous former Jesuit priest Serone (left, Jon Voight) increasingly confronts documentary filmmaker Terri Flores (Jennifer Lopez). Her role is a breakout for exploration-discovery films: a woman—and a Latina—who takes charge of an expedition (Sony Pictures).

At this point in the film, most of the movie crew has become a meal for the huge anacondas. Only Terri, Danny, Serone and the comatose Dr. Cale remain alive. Fortuitously, Cale now awakens in time to help them subdue Serone, but quickly passes out again. However, once again Serone's strength and cunning puts him back into the action in time for a deadly climax. The animatronic special effects throughout the film are noteworthy, but especially so in this part of the film. No place is safe from these serpents, for they can slither up tall trees next to the waterfall and even scale tall chimneys in search of human prey, hence my placing this film into sci-fi and fantasy genres as well as horror. Terri and Danny manage to hold off the huge snakes, one of which now finishes off Serone using the consumption-regurgitation treatment that he described so well. About halfway through this gruesome process, the slime-covered Serone pops out of the snake's mouth, and winks before being re-consumed—presumably for the last time. This wink is totally unexpected but perfectly in keeping with the filmmakers' edgy playfulness.

Anaconda has some truly iconic moments. One scene involves a close call that Terri and Danny have with a huge serpent that momentarily ensnares them inside the factory. The stunning image featuring Terri facing the camera with her arms at her side as the snake coils around her not only confirms that she is a force of nature. It also mirrors the earlier scene of the snake-worshippers' totem pole, and thus comes full circle, bringing the archeological past and the present together—and confirming veracity of the legend. Something else about this scene is noteworthy. It is strikingly reminiscent of the female figurehead on the steamboat in *Fitzcarraldo*. Here, too, the tension between a strong woman and a large coiling serpent suggest the power of two natural elemental forces, woman and snake; significantly, both are symbols of fertility. Although the images of snake/woman are brief in these two films, they leave a lasting impression.

With Serone now out of the picture, the resourceful Terri and Danny prevail by rapidly devising a plan to set the snakes on fire, thus sending the flaming serpents slithering into film immortality. Of the ten people who started out on the expedition, only

In a remarkable scene carefully "snagged" from the DVD of *Anaconda* (1997), a huge anima-tronic serpent is wrapping around Terri Flores (Jennifer Lopez) and her cinematographer Danny (Ice Cube). This image not only brings to life the content the totem pole seen earlier, but also brings to mind the maidenhead in the similarly Amazon-set film *Fitzcarraldo* (Sony Pictures).

three (Cale, Terri and Danny) have lived to tell the tale. As the film nears its conclusion, Cale fortuitously awakens just in time to discover the Shirishama tribe, whose members paddle toward the *Micaela I.* Terri and Danny see them as well, and smile knowingly. Evidently, the Shirishama are appreciative of their newly gained freedom from the ana-condas. This scene is appropriately filmed in foggy conditions so that the tribe appears to confirm their name "people of the mist." Symbolically, that mistiness underscores the tribe's ephemeral nature and fragility.

Although many viewers no doubt considered this revelation about the Shirishama to be an ethereal moment, to others it could be seen as yet another example of brave American adventurers coming to the rescue of hapless Indians. Regardless, the expe-dition has been successful on all accounts now with the tribe documented for posterity by Terri and Danny. For his part, Dr. Cale will be credited with a new anthropologi-cal discovery, but the viewer knows better: Terri is the real hero. *Anaconda* closes as the *Micaela-1* boat smokes its way into an Amazonian sunset on its way to fame, presumably by [re-]producing the film that the audience has just watched.

In retrospect, music is a very important element in *Anaconda*, and in two scenes appears to make a subliminal nod to two earlier films. In the first, as the *Micaela-1* moves up the river early in the film, strains from Verdi's opera *Dio Che Nill'Almo Infi-dere* bring to mind Herzog's *Fitzcarraldo*, which is also set in the Amazon and features a Verdi opera score as the *Molly Aida* steams along the Pachitea River into the interior.

In a deliberately misty scene at the end of *Anaconda*, (1997), the menacing snakes have been annihilated and the secretive "people of the mist" give silent thanks as they emerge along a fog-shrouded tributary of the Amazon. In this film, director Luis Llosa provided a subtle rendition of the lost tribe trope so common in exploration-discovery quests (Sony Pictures).

In the second, as the credits begin to appear in the film's finale, a moving pan-pipe solo is reminiscent of the haunting solo in *The Mission* and perfectly timed to suggest a successful encounter with Indians, in this case not the Guaraní but the no-longer-mythical Shirishama tribe.

Many critics were very hard on *Anaconda* but missed the boat, or rather the broader picture. Although admittedly over-the-top, this film actually plumbs elements long incorporated in the history of exploration-discovery. These include the need to demystify the unknown, and to re-examine and contextualize it in light of other discoveries. Then, too, the disequilibrium of an expedition being taken over by a madman (e.g., Aguirre) is on full display here. As social commentary *Anaconda* is also a back-handed reference to stories and films in which religious zealots menace the backwaters of South America.

Since their invention, films have not only entertained but have also been rich in deeper meaning.[9] Even a purely entertaining film like *Anaconda* can have deeper messages about the power of the unknown to instill terror, or of a determined character to overcome fear in the face of evil. Tasting success but not taking itself too seriously, *Anaconda* spawned several sequels, although none took place in South America and none matched the original's pure campiness, dark humor, absurdity, and introspection about the liminal zone where science and folklore intersect. Cinematically speaking, some enthusiastic fans consider it a cult classic, and I am now among them.

In the grander scheme of things, anacondas are but one of the animal terrors facing explorers in South America. Well before *Anaconda* and its sequels slithered across the screen, the dreaded flesh-eating piranha achieved cinematic fame in a series of campy films. Likely influenced by Steven Spielberg's 1975 blockbuster *Jaws*,[10] the low budget film *Piranha*[11] was released in 1978. Despite its potent competition in the form of Jaws II,[12] which like its predecessor was a box office hit, *Piranha* became an instant success. It incorporated that unique blend of dark comedy and terror that proved irresistible. Although filmed on a much smaller budget than *Jaws*, it earned a huge return at the box office, about ten dollars for every one expended. It also became part of a series of sequels—in this case four theatrical releases plus a made-for-television version—that kept these pint-size ravenous fishes in the public consciousness.

Just as real piranhas originated in the rivers of South America, namely the Amazon, Paraguay-Paraná, and Orinoco but are now found in south Asia and parts of China, these fish in cinema usually show up in waters closer to home, namely the United States and the United Kingdom. The fear of the once alien piranhas now being in home waters stems from the fear of them accidentally escaping and thus infiltrating, the ultimate in destructive invasive species. They were once sold in pet stores nationwide but this fear resulted in their being outlawed in twenty-five states. Some urban folkloric accounts have a presumed dead piranha being flushed down a toilet, only to survive, breed, and become a menace—a fear that can be found in the UK as well.[13]

In a sense, both the *Jaws* and *Piranha* movies are not exploration films *per se* in that they involve the deadly fishes showing up not in the field, but at home, so to speak. As opposed to the original film *Anaconda*, piranhas are rarely seen in their native habitat on film. The closest that films come to depicting piranhas in their natural habitat is *Killer Fish*.[14] Its 1979 release date suggests that it was filmed in a frenzy to capitalize on its American competition from *Piranha*. Shot on location in Angra das Reis in southern Rio de Janeiro state, Brazil, the plot of *Killer Fish* revolves around the use of piranhas as a deterrent. In this film, they are used to stock a reservoir where stashes of priceless emeralds are hidden. Anyone attempting to steal the gems from this site will be in for a rude awakening.

The title of this film—*Killer Fish*—is noteworthy given that the word "killer" suggests a single perpetrator, whereas "fish" can suggest either one fish or many. When it comes to the piranha, plural fishes are the real menace. In reality, piranhas are small creatures, usually only four to eight inches long, and are omnivorous rather than carnivorous. The bite of a lone piranha, which is painful and can remove a finger or ear, is far from fatal. They become a lethal menace only when they are in great numbers and/or are confined to unusual situations. Then, they can be truly ravenous, able to kill large animals in seconds. As a character in the movie *Piranha 3D* claims, in a classic example of comedy-terror phrasing, "...there are thousands of them, and they're pissed."[15] Further adding to fears are the rare but all too real tragedies involving these ravenous fish. For example, an inebriated 18-year-old man was killed by a school of them in Rosario del Yata, eastern Bolivia in 2011; or even more tragic, a six-year-old girl was devoured after her grandmother's boat capsized in Brazil.[16]

It is often difficult to pinpoint the source of what I call "piranhanoia"—the irrational fear of piranhas—but it is likely that it arrived in early twentieth-century American popular culture in the form of a book and film based on Theodore "Teddy" Roosevelt's much-publicized expedition to South America in 1913–14. Roosevelt (1858–1919) had served two terms as president and was widely known as a political powerbroker, progressive thinker, and outdoorsman-conservationist. His Latin American exploits are normally associated with the Spanish-American War (1898) in which his Rough-Riders liberated Cuba, as well as his advocacy of the Panama Canal project beginning about 1901. However, after he lost his bid for a third term as president in 1912, Roosevelt accepted an invitation from Argentina to visit on behalf of the equally progressive thinking Museo Social. His initial goal on this trip was to study the natural history and hopefully get in some big game hunting; at the time, those two endeavors were not as far

apart as they are today. Teddy's love of nature was well known, and the trip was originally intended to be recreational and educational, with a few diplomatic stops.

However, during Roosevelt's first stop in Brazil, he received an offer too good to
pass up: real exploring in the western portion of that sprawling country. In particular, it
involved an expedition to determine the courses of rivers, a signature type of endeavor
that had long lured explorers, including Humboldt. The area in question was the Rio
Duvida or River of Doubt, which lay beyond the Mato Grosso in what was still terra
incognita. Roosevelt was to be in good hands because the consummate authority of Brazil's geography—Cândido Mariano da Silva Rondon (1865–1958)—was leading it. Born
and raised in the still-wild Mato Grosso and part Indian, Rondon was a highly respected
military leader. Roosevelt enthusiastically accepted, declaring it his "…last chance to be
a boy."

Roosevelt relates this story and expedition in his book *Through the Brazilian Wilderness*, which was initially published in 1914, with many editions thereafter. It is one of
the best-written accounts of a South American expedition; clearly and engagingly presented, factually accurate but also emphasizing the ever-present dangers. Among these
were deadly coral snakes (one of which struck the tip of his boot but whose fangs just
missed his toes), jaguars, anacondas, alligators (caymans), crocodiles, insects, and what
he called "…one of the most formidable genera of fish in the world, the piranha or can-
nibal fish that eats men when it can get the chance." In another passage, Roosevelt even
more emphatically claimed that piranhas were "…the most ferocious fish in the world."
He observed that they "habitually attack things much larger than themselves," adding
that an animal's blood in the water brings them to the scene ravenously to devour animals alive. In macabre passages he describes a man who carelessly held what he thought
was a dead piranha near his mouth, only to have it force its way in and bite off his tongue.
Another relates to the expedition's finding the skeleton of a man picked clean by them.[17]

The silent film version of the expedition—which dates from about 1920 but contains some original footage shot on the expedition—appears to be the first widely shown
motion picture footage of a South American exploration. In it, a quote attributed to
Roosevelt appears on screen, proclaiming "…we jumped at the chance to explore the
so-called River of Doubt and put it on the map." Rivers play a major role in this film,
and they happen to be locales where piranhas thrive. Although these fish are dangerous, they are part of the local diet in this part of South America. In one scene, natives are
shown "fishing for the piranha or cannibal-fish, which abound in these waters." Another
sentence on the screen adds "Note: One of the Roosevelt-Rondon party was badly
bitten by a piranha the day this picture was taken, and men are to be found in every
water-town in Paraguay who have been mutilated by them." One close up of a piranha
is accompanied by the text: "Their ferocity and strength can be seen in the malignant
looking eyes and the formation of their deep bodies with the undershot bulldog jaw." An
ethnographic-like passage observes: "It is said that the natives 'stand in awe of the piranha,' a position which many of our party took."[18]

Of special interest here is that Roosevelt himself is not only a self-conscious
explorer-discoverer on this expedition, but also self-consciously aware of being a late
comer to real exploration which was far more difficult in the past than it was in his day.
In his book, he contextualizes South American exploration, noting that "Humboldt's
work had a profound effect on the thought of the civilized world; his trip was one of
adventure and danger; and yet it can hardly be called exploration proper." Roosevelt

here notes that Humboldt "...visited places which had been settled and inhabited for centuries and traversed places which had been travelled by civilized men for years before he followed in their footsteps." Roosevelt here was not criticizing Humboldt *per se*, but rather reminding readers that first explorations are followed by others that benefit from it. As he put it, "The work done by the original explorers of such a wilderness necessitates the undergoing of untold hardship and danger. Their successors, even their immediate successors, have a relatively easy time." Rondon's Commission expedition featured some of both types of exploration; whereas it took routes and methods of transportation similar to those early explorers used, it also benefited from many modern methods and inventions, including those in mapmaking. Roosevelt himself noted the expedition had "an excellent British map of Brazil."[19] That said, the area around the River of Doubt was still only vaguely known, and they aimed to resolve that. Although Roosevelt did not dwell on it, this expedition almost cost him his life as a cut on his foot sustained whilst he was moving canoes across the rocks became infected. Gripped by fever and at times delirious, he was incapacitated for days and not expected to live; however, thanks to his receiving professional medical attention in the field, he recovered.

Despite setbacks, what biographer Candice Millard calls "Theodore Roosevelt's Darkest Journey" succeeded. In wording that filmmaker Werner Herzog might appreciate, Millard observes that tropical South America amounted to "...the greatest natural battlefield anywhere on the planet, hosting an unremitting and remorseless fight for survival." Despite these conditions, and a sometimes rocky relationship between Rondon and Roosevelt, she observes that efforts of the expedition paid off, revealing in considerable detail the course of a 1500 kilometer long river that had never before appeared on maps. Having pretty much recovered by the time he returned home in 1914, but claiming that the trip may have taken ten years off his life, Roosevelt published his book. It, and the film that was produced about the expedition, brought the Brazilian interior to life for millions in the United States and Europe.

Although some geographical authorities and journalists on both sides of the Atlantic were skeptical about just how much the expedition accomplished, Roosevelt made convincing presentations to the National Geographic Society and the Royal Geographical Society. Of the former, a journalist for the *New York Evening Journal* dispelled the doubters, adding: "With a little piece of chalk, Colonel Roosevelt has put the River of Doubt upon the map of South America." Of the latter presentation in London, Millard concludes: "By the time that Roosevelt had finished his speech—rich with tales of disease-carrying insects and man-eating fish and punctuated by his trademark high-pitched giggle, which sent his audience into roaring waves of laughter—nearly all of England had surrendered."[20] Roosevelt got the last laugh. The expedition's efforts not only resulted in the charting of the River of Doubt, but also in the official changing of its name to the Roosevelt River.

Sixteen

Green Fire

The Prospector
as Explorer-Discoverer

In the late 1940s and 1950s, films about Latin America increasingly involved outsiders—usually men of action who possessed technical savvy and could re-shape the environment. This type of man was personified by the intrepid railroad builder played by John Wayne in *Tycoon* (1947),[1] which is set in a South American mining region but filmed in California, whose towering Sierra Nevada stands in for the Andes. As regards mining itself and the challenges associated with it, the film *Treasure of the Sierra Madre*[2] (1948) is widely regarded as a classic. Based on the 1927 book of the same name by B. Traven, it is a grim tale of three outsiders trying to make a fortune in Mexico by mining gold. These Americans originally arrived in Tampico to work on oil wells, but were swindled out of their wages. By chance, they hear about a promising gold prospect from an old-timer, who takes them up into the Sierra Madre mountain range. Gold is found, but infighting dooms them to catastrophe. In this dark tale, no one gets rich. The greediest miner among them is murdered by bandits, but the others ultimately lose all they earned, philosophically thankful just to be alive. Mexico is portrayed as an edgy place where risks might pay off, but fate usually has the last say. For realism, *Treasure of the Sierra Madre* was partly shot on location in the state of Durango, with a few additional scenes in Tampico.

Mexico has long been a magnet for outsiders hoping to mine its rich deposits of gold and especially silver, but in this chapter I shall focus on another part of Latin America—South America. Since the search for El Dorado began, mineral treasures have played a role in stories set on that continent, which is a storehouse of mineral deposits—gold, silver, copper, tin and other metals, and gems such as diamonds, emeralds, aquamarine and topaz—that have long been developed and romanticized. Given the energy and expertise involved in this process, it is no surprise that they found their way into literature and cinema. The book and film *Green Fire* focus on early twentieth-century developments in Colombian emerald mining, but also make reference to the long history of emerald mining there.

For readers unfamiliar with mining history in Latin America, some deeper historical contextualization may be helpful. From the time of contact in the 1520s, Spanish explorers in northern South America had heard tales of transparent green stones that came from a mountainous and remote area. In 1537, the Spanish explorer Gonzalo Jiménez Quesada (1509?-1579?) began searching for the source area of those tales. Believing that the stories and legends of rich emerald deposits from the Chibcha Indians had some substance, Jiménez dispatched a forty-man team led by Pedro Fernández

Valenzuela to find the mine that the Indians called Somondoco ("god of green stones"). The Spaniards found the source and surface-mined these green stones using Indigenous labor. Emeralds soon proved valuable to the treasury. Additional deposits were discovered, but for the most part the mines at Chivor and Muzo located in the mountainous Andean region of Nueva Granada (Colombia) produced fine stones that wound up in locales as far distant as the Mughal, Persian and Ottoman Empires.[3]

However, through poor administration and neglect, the Spanish emerald mines declined by the late seventeenth century. Some became "lost" mines, so to speak, as erosion took its toll and vegetation encroached. By the later 1800s, the convergence of geological knowledge and free market capitalism led to new efforts to exploit emeralds, the most sensational being the 1896 rediscovery of the lost (since 1675) Somondoco (Chivor) mine by Don Francisco Restrepo, the noted South American mining developer. In the early part of the twentieth century, outsiders flocked to the area, and were part of this new search for emeralds.

Don Restrepo represented a new type of explorer—the professionally trained and well-educated prospector in search of mineral treasures. He was part of a longer prospecting tradition in Latin America. Given the enterprising prospector's ability to find and carry off precious metals and gems without authorities becoming aware, it is no surprise that they had flourished for centuries alongside farming and mercantile enterprises[4]—despite Spain's attempts to regulate all mining activity. Although prospecting became even more common as Spain's ability to control economic activity began to unravel in the late 1700s, it came into its own after political independence, i.e., from the 1820s onward. This watershed political development coincided with the beginnings of aggressive development of mines using outside capital.

In the nineteenth century, the prospector thrived in both North and South America. In the popular culture of the American West, he might discover a mine by luck when trying to retrieve a wayward burro or, as in South America (Chile), a wayward *guanaco*.[5] By century's end, prospecting had become more scientific. Worldwide, mining schools proliferated. In Latin America, two-dozen such schools were created close to mining areas in mineral-rich South American countries such as Brazil, Chile, Colombia, Peru, and Venezuela. These mining schools turned out a special breed of explorer called the mining engineer, who essentially received a college education focused on the practical application of science. Don Restrepo was among them.

Typically, mining engineers were well-trained, well-traveled, and innovative. When they study mining regions they frequently fill the role of explorer-discoverer. And when they write about their experiences, they turn out some compelling travel narratives. That was the case of Anselm Verner Lee Guise, whose book *Six Years in Bolivia: The Adventures of a Mining Engineer* (1922)[6] makes the early twentieth-century search for mineral wealth in the interior of South America come alive. Published two decades later, the book *Green Fire*[7] by South African mining engineer Peter W. Rainier (1890–1945) turned his 1920s and 1930s search for profitable emerald mines into an impressive memoir. The book *Green Fire* demonstrates how literature can help inspire popular interest that can in turn lead to a motion picture. Rainier's book was originally published as a hardback in 1942 and its dust jacket featured a beautiful abstract painting of a mine tucked into some spectacular Andean topography. The book cover itself was embossed, and featured a map of South America showing the location of Colombia, from which a diagonal, arrow-like line led to a close-up of gleaming emeralds.

Rainier's book became popular enough that it was reprinted as a Bantam paperback in 1952 with the original word-for-word text, including the author's fine hand-drawn map of the Colombian emerald mines. However, the paperback's colorful, lurid front and back covers—complete with a heroic, gun-toting white male, two attractive Polynesian-looking topless Indian women, and machete-wielding Indian men—simultaneously sensationalized and popularized the story. With a relatively low price of just 35 cents, it jumped off the bookracks. By the early 1950s, the term "green fire" and emeralds became synonymous in American popular culture.

Despite its titillating cover, *Green Fire* is remarkably well written and an important contribution to the continent's literature. Part travel narrative and part on-site mining exploration saga, it relates Rainier's journey into and through Colombia to reach the emerald bearing districts in the mountains via the Río Magdalena. Rainier contextualizes his explorations in terms of both the company he represents and the international markets that dictate the prices of emeralds, and hence the feasibility of mining in a particular locale. He candidly explains that he was learning about emeralds on this assignment, for very little had been written about their geological environments and their mineralogy. The hexagonal shape of their crystals was one of the clues to identifying these stones, but only those with the correct clarity and deep-green color were valuable enough to mine.

Although his geological explorations were promising, Rainier had nearly constant problems with the American mining company's manipulative and deceitful home office in New York. In the field, he had stumbled into a situation that lasts to this day: the emerald mines are highly contested and often fought over, sometimes violently. Rainier describes his nemesis, the shifty "Joaquin the Bandit" and their escalating confrontations. His stories about what it took to hold onto claims—throwing lighted dynamite sticks and brandishing revolvers—read like fiction, but they are substantiated in the historical record. Rainier was also looking for signs of earlier mining efforts, stating "…it is a matter for exploration to rediscover the spot where hundreds of men had toiled and lived only a few years before."[8]

Rainier's goal was to discover the emeralds that others had missed. Particularly memorable is his finding a vug (small cavity) that he could only reach his hand into, but could feel loose stones that he hoped were emeralds. As he recounts, "My fingers explored them. Hexagons. *Emeralds*, by the miners' god! They must be emeralds…." However, the hole was too small for him to take out a fistful, so he pulled them out one at a time. In the light, he found they were brown-stained and seemingly worthless; the miners thought so as well. However, intuition led him to scrape off that rusty surface, revealing stones of exceptional beauty and value. He was ecstatic.[9]

Like many mining engineers, Rainier was an eager learner who had a strong interest in the region he explored, including its history. In fact, he noted the close linkage between emeralds and the myth of golden El Dorado. Of other mineral treasures, he relates partnering with a man who had found promising gold deposits high in the mountains. Rainier was a quick study: he learned Spanish and communicated in that language, becoming an effective mine boss who could motivate the miners, including Indians. He appreciated the region's Spanish heritage, even relating a colorful folkloric reference to Don Francisco Restrepo's 1890s explorations. He notes a chance discovery that occurred when an Indian in Restrepo's party was chasing a fat *buruga* (groundhog-like animal) for dinner. As Rainier glibly concludes, "It was a *buruga* that found Chivor for Don Pacho."[10]

During the decade he lived in Colombia, Rainier fell in love with the highland area in the vicinity of Chivor, considering it Paradise. Accordingly, he soon brought his wife and family to settle the area. They purchased land and built a home, the children soon forgetting how to speak English. They named their estate after the mine (Las Cascadas), and his enterprising wife developed South America's first commercial tea growing operation there. Beyond this area, he grew to love the entire country of Colombia and its people. His descriptions of its varied landscapes are among the best I've encountered. Interestingly, in the book he reveals that one of his passions was medicine, and the descriptions of makeshift medical procedures in the book are fascinating. The second is no surprise: he confesses that he always wanted to be a writer.

Given the sales of Rainier's book, the growing popular interest in South America, and the pending release of Paramount's *Secret of the Incas*, this tale about emerald mining in Colombia attracted the interest of Hollywood. MGM took the leap, but the big question was how to convert a rather cerebral book punctuated by a few action scenes into something that would hold viewers' attention for just under two hours. The film's screenwriters Ivan Goff and Ben Roberts transformed the book into a story with far more action and far less contemplation. Like W.H. Hudson, who never saw his *Green Mansions* on screen, the same fate awaited Rainier, who had died eight years earlier (1945) in a hotel fire while he was on assignment in Canada.

Green Fire was beautifully filmed in CinemaScope, portions of it on location in the vicinity of the Colombian emerald mines, as well as some related filming in Cartagena and Barranquilla. These are places that Rainier brought to life in the book, and on film the landscape and the towns truly sparkle in Technicolor. Although the cinematographers captured the locations beautifully, one can safely predict that Rainier would have noted wild deviations from the story told in his book. To begin with, he probably would not have recognized himself. On screen, he is played by the robust and virile Stewart Granger, star of other adventure films, including *King Solomon's Mines* (1950),[11] which was also directed by Andrew Marton. In *Green Fire*, the mining engineer is British and named Rian X. Mitchell. The biggest change, though, involves in his personality. The film transforms Rainier the sensitive mining engineer as explorer into Mitchell the mining engineer as insensitive action hero. One might charitably say the movie was a loose adaptation, and let things go at that, but I think it is instructive to show how the film *Green Fire* veers in new directions, with varied results.

Like Rainier's book, the movie *Green Fire*[12] is about efforts to mine Colombian emerald deposits in the twentieth century, and features a male mining engineer protagonist who hopes to develop those deposits. However, that is where the stories diverge. Whereas Rainier had a background in mineralogy and knew that they are a chromium and vanadium rich variety of the mineral beryl, the script writers have Rian ignorant of the basic mineralogy and even misidentifying specimens of low-grade emeralds as "beryllium." As a savvy mining engineer, Rainier would have been appalled by his own character's ignorance.

The film opens with a brief on-screen written reference to emerald exploitation by the early Spanish conquistadors which is accompanied by a romantic, exotic-sounding theme song now justifiably called "exotica." Titled "Green Fire," the song touts the treasure that can be found in remote places, but warns they can lead to temptation and disaster. The visual background behind this opening is a close-up of stratified grayish limestone rock studded with green stone that emits green light. The actual opening scene is especially revealing. Instead of relating how the mining engineer got to the mining area, which was an intriguing part of Rainier's original story, the film opens with mining engineer Rian Mitchell already in the mine; he faces away from the camera as he begins to chip away at the limestone with a geologist's rock pick, exposing more of the green stones. His digging reveals a cluster of glittering emerald crystals that the opening song has just referenced. Through the magic of Hollywood, they glow almost supernaturally, throwing radiant beams of green light onto his gloriously tanned face.

After Rian smiles and stuffs the emerald cluster into the breast pocket of his shirt, he turns to leave. However, on the way out he accidentally discovers an old Spanish conquistador's helmet, which he picks up and momentarily peruses. This artifact/prop is significant because it not only reveals the Spanish past but also subliminally suggests that Spanish identity is a thing of the past now that this new conquistador—the mining engineer—has arrived. Digressing for a moment, I should note that the Kevin Costner film *Dances with Wolves* (1990)[13] used a conquistador helmet to great effect as an artifact possessed by the Plains Indians as a symbol of their outlasting the Spaniards (presumably from Coronado's expedition ca. 1540), which is to say Europeans up until the time depicted in the film (ca. 1865). However, in the film *Green Fire*, the conquistador's helmet means little or nothing to Rian, who dismissively tosses it as he begins to exit the mine. The audience gets the message: he has no interest in the past.

Upon leaving the mine opening, Rian looks back and notes a date carved into the old wooden lintel above it: 1687. Before leaving this mining property, he conceals the opening with brush to deter others from finding it. The film places Rian in the position of a modern-day explorer-discoverer, or rather re-discoverer. Unlike Rainier, though, he has little or no appreciation for the earlier Spaniards' mining efforts, nor the aforementioned Francisco Restrepo, the South American mining engineer who made that

At the beginning of *Green Fire* (1954), in an abandoned mine in Colombia, prospector Rian X. Mitchell (Stewart Granger) finds a cluster of gleaming emeralds in the limestone bedrock. In this scene, he has extracted it with his rock-pick, and ponders it as his flashlight reflects its green light on his face. (Metro-Goldwyn-Mayer).

In the film *Green Fire* (1954), possession and operation of a Colombian emerald mine is central to the drama. Outside the mine that he has now [re]discovered, Rian X. Mitchell (Stewart Granger) quickly becomes a man of action as he gets the drop on a would-be robber (uncredited) (Metro-Goldwyn-Mayer).

re-discovery in 1896. As Rian leaves the now-concealed mine, he notes startled birds flying from a tree, and becomes alarmed. Moving stealthily, he gets the drop on a bandit, commanding him in Spanish, "Do not make a move!" The pistol that Rian wields leaves no doubt that he is a man of action.

Having established that Rian is a take-possession and take-charge guy, the film now throws him into extreme danger. The next few minutes are breathtakingly exciting: Rian is ambushed and shot by the bandit's accomplices, thrown down a steep hillside and left for dead, recovers, groggily finds his way to a river while unknowingly being stalked by a jaguar, is about to take a drink at the river's edge when the huge cat pounces and mauls him, but is dispatched in the nick of time by a rifle-wielding padre, who then takes him to a coffee hacienda where he meets the beautiful co-owner named Catherine Knowland (Grace Kelly), who just happens to know enough about medicine to heal him in one day. When Rian awakens, he retrieves his shirt in hopes of finding the emeralds, but the pocket is empty. Just then, the smiling Father Riparo (Robert Tafur) hands him the emeralds, solemnly informing him that searching for such stones only brings grief. Rian has no intention of heeding that advice, for he is obsessed with emeralds and the wealth they will bring.

The action in the above scenes comes so quickly that the viewer has little time to contemplate what may have inspired them. In the case of the scene in which Rian is about to be pounced upon by the jaguar, it appears to be almost identical to the one in the later (1959) film *Green Mansions* (see again Chapter Ten)—right down to the hero escaping death due to intervention by a stranger who just happens to be there in time to dispatch the man-eating cat in mid-air. Clearly, this was no coincidence but rather yet an example of one film borrowing from another. Truth is, ever since the publication of

Arbuckles' Album of Illustrated Natural History (1890), if not even before that, image makers have influenced society in general, and would-be filmmakers as well. As a result, jaguars have become one of the most recognizable tropes for South America. In most films—for example, *Green Fire* and *Green Mansions*—they signify danger. However, in others they may serve another purpose as incarnations of a character's spirit, as was the case in *The Emerald Forest* and *The Old Man Who Read Love Stories*.[14] For that matter, emeralds can serve symbolically, as in *The Emerald Forest*, where gleaming green stones found in a riverbed are a source of magic. In *Green Fire*, they symbolize wealth on the one hand, and risk-and-reward on the other.

Although these adventure films often involved some shooting on location, they also employed studio sets back in California. In *Green Fire*, the well-tended hacienda where Rian recovers presents a vivid contrast to the gritty mining area in which we first encountered him, and provides a good example of Hollywood's skills in creating memorable places. The film depicts the hacienda as idyllic, and in one view the rows of crops and the distant mountains have a painterly appearance. It, too, seems like something out of an evocative Arbuckles' trading card, notably Brazil, with its coffee plantation featuring obedient women workers and piles of scarlet-colored coffee beans.

Hollywood specialized in creating scenes like this hacienda on large sound-stages, and they did it so effectively that it takes a good eye to see where the stage ends and the background begins. In the case of *The Wizard of Oz*, the yellow brick road appears to go on forever but in reality ends at the point where Dorothy skips down it into the seeming distance but the camera goes to another scene just as she reaches the backdrop. In *Green Fire*, the backdrop appears to begin just behind the hacienda wall and gate. Beautifully painted backdrops and well executed matte scenes (in which a scene is superimposed on another, either as a painting or now digitally) can go a long way in romanticizing a locale—a reminder of filmmaking's magical powers.

To return to this comparison of the book and the film, unlike the happily married Rainier, Rian is a womanizer who now sets his sights on Catherine, though it will

The idyllic coffee plantation and hacienda in *Green Fire* (1954) has a romantic painterly quality, in part because it was filmed on a carefully-constructed sound stage by MGM. Throughout the film, this agrarian operation will be contrasted with the extractive industry of emerald mining, which terraced hillsides and diverted streams. (Metro-Goldwyn-Mayer).

mean spending more time away from the mines. Whereas Rainier's main concern was always keeping the workers motivated and effective, Rian casually voices the arrogant sentiment that "I wouldn't allow a little labor problem to interfere with my social life." Another vast difference between the book and film is how Rian treats his own long-time mining partner, now named Vic Leonard (Paul Mitchell). He too is highly fictionalized. In the film version of Rainier's story, Vic once had the same passion for finding emeralds as Rian still does, but has become jaded. He is leaving to develop a coal mine in Canada but through subterfuge, Rian gets Vic drunk and he misses his boat. Rian should be ashamed, but he does not know the meaning of the word.

In these river port scenes, the place and time of the story is set. On Rian's office wall, a colorful, large scale map showing the various departments (states) of Colombia suggests that he knows the territory and has staked out part of it. This map appears in a pivotal scene in which Rian's amorous Colombian secretary tries to seduce him but he rejects that advance in order to get back to business outside. In that role, the map does more than simply authenticate the film's geographic location. It also defines Rian's more expansive ambitions, which now include not only mining emeralds but also wooing Catherine, who has rural landholdings. Regarding the time or date in which the film is set, Catherine drives a Second World War surplus Jeep in good condition. Further confirming the ca. 1950 era time frame is a slogan painted on the interior wall of a cantina: *Discusión Política Prohibida* (Political Discussion Prohibited), which reinforced the government's strong-arm tactics in the period known as "La Violencia" (1948–1958). In fact, filming *Green Fire* in Colombia at this time was pretty risky. Despite a temporary cease fire in this decade-long civil war, political unrest was one of the complications, along with the weather, that challenged the film's production.[15]

The plot soon thickens. Now forced to stay in Colombia, Vic begins to become infatuated with Catherine. In romance movie style, Rian's interest in Catherine is also growing, as is her interest in him. Nevertheless, Rian jeopardizes his own romance with Catherine when he encourages her brother Donald's budding emerald fever. Donald (John Ericson) joins forces with Rian by helping to finance the mining operations, putting in enough cash to lure the men workers away from the coffee harvest. Now also betrayed by her own brother, Catherine becomes furious. Unlike Rainier, Rian is not only manipulative but also patently sexist, telling Catherine to "stop thinking like a woman." She saves the day when she unites the local women to complete the harvest, one of them claiming they can work many times better than the men. In 1950s films, feminism was seemingly innocent but delightfully subversive.

After a cave-in, Rian's mine more accurately transitions from an underground operation to one using traditional surface mining techniques. The scenes in which Rian applies the terracing technique to create benches that are worked—in effect slowly taking down the entire mountainside—are similar to those described in the book. The scenes are rather well integrated in the film, though they have a different look because they were shot in southern California, where the chaparral vegetation is scrubbier than its counterpart in Colombia. Moreover, the sky has a different coloring, likely due to California's less-humid weather. These spectacular mining scenes were shot after permission was obtained to create huge "steps" in a mountainside near Mulholland Drive in Hollywood. This open face mine plays a major role in the remainder of the film, becoming the site of intense drama and action.

Unexpectedly, tragedy strikes. While working on these mining terraces,

Although portions of *Green Fire* (1954) were filmed on location in Colombia, some scenes involving the operation of an open-face emerald mining operation were shot near Mulholland Drive close to MGM's main production center in Hollywood. In this scene, hundreds of miners extract ore by hand, digging terraces back into the steep mountainside (Metro-Goldwyn-Mayer).

Catherine's brother Donald is accidentally killed by boulders rolling downhill. Making matters even worse, Rian's new mining techniques have diverted the course of a river, whose flow now begins to threaten the Knowland coffee hacienda. Experiencing these setbacks, Catherine now realizes she must act to stop Rian from destroying her way of life. Her plan involves literally turning the tide that is being created due to Rian's ill-considered stream diversion. Sinking to Rian's level as a "gutter fighter," she reluctantly decides to blow up that diversion dam if necessary, even if it means destroying the mine. Hollywood has long relied on spectacular explosions to resolve problems and thrill audiences.

At this point, another problem surfaces: the bandits arrive to claim the site of the mine for themselves. This development is loosely based on the bandit Joaquin as Rainier's nemesis, but in the film he is called El Moro, an Orientalist touch as the name means "the Moor." Like the bandit Joaquin, El Moro (Murvyn Vye) epitomizes duplicity, greed, and cowardice. Earlier scenes that featured tense exchanges between Rian and El Moro emphasized their ethnic differences, and also played on their symbolizing many binaries, including (respectively) handsome vs. ugly; outsider vs. local; enterprise vs. laziness; and above all, future vs. past.

As tension mounts at the mine, El Moro has arrived just in time for a surprise based on a new development. Whereas Rian's egocentricity and obsession had been on collision course with his growing conscience, things have now come to a head. In a two-for-one scenario, Rian realizes the error of his ways and risks life and limb to blow up the mountainside above the new mine terraces in order to divert the waters back to their original location, thus losing the mine but saving Catherine's coffee hacienda, and redeeming his relationship with her. Simultaneously, El Moro and his army of bandits are eliminated as they too are wiped off the face of the earth as tons of loosened debris—a veritable landslide filmed in miniature—cascades down the mountainside.

The film concludes with Rian clutching a superb emerald crystal and the woman he loves. He has lost the mine, but still has his treasure(s). This is the type of a happy ending, similar to that in *Secret of the Incas*, that Hollywood preferred to give audiences in the 1950s. However, it is unlike that in Rainier's book, wherein his wife dies and he moves away in hopes of finding new adventures that will help him forget the beautiful life they had in Colombia. In the movie, Rian's transition to selflessness has not only made him more heroic but also more powerful. He has the power to build and destroy, which is to say, give and take away (and vice versa). On the one hand he has been humbled—the trajectory of the plot all along—but the film itself amounts to a cinematic catharsis. Grace Kelly regretted being in the film, saying she wished she'd have read the script before agreeing. For his part, the devilishly witty Stewart Granger never thought any of his films were very good, but singled out this one in an interview about Kelly, lamenting that he had the misfortune of being "in the only really bad movie she ever made."[16]

Mining remains a potent force in storytelling about South America, as evident in the beautifully filmed Spanish-language saga *Los Andes no Creen en Dios* (*The Andes do not Believe in God*).[17] Shot in the stark Bolivian altiplano in the vicinity of Uyuni, this 2007 film centers on the search for a gold mine. It involves a number of seemingly timeless ingredients typical of mining-related stories on film—including a love triangle; the tension between scientific and ancient traditions; and the discord between insiders (locals) and outsiders (foreigners). However, its being a period piece set in the 1920s during a time when horse-drawn transport and early automobiles coexisted, and steam locomotives ruled, gives it a special appeal. At the same time, that antique character added considerably to its budget. As of this writing, the film has no English subtitle version and remains rather obscure outside of Bolivia—a shame given the poignancy of the story, the quality of the acting, and the majesty of the area's scenery.

For its part, the emerald-mining saga *Green Fire* fits into the category of tropical exploitation films in which outsiders triumph on someone else's native soil. The fact that it is an American film should not be overlooked, because it subliminally celebrates the United States' position as a world power that can move mountains and also create new narratives in the process. In reality, the influx of American capital and expertise helped those mining efforts become more efficient and profitable, but they often built on the bedrock of earlier discoveries by South Americans themselves. Moreover, they often perpetuated social inequalities that had long been in place. With its emphasis on a brash outsider transforming the environment—blasting huge parcels of it to get at minerals while diverting waterways in the process, all the while using Indigenous people to serve that goal of profitable management—*Green Fire* makes its point: free enterprise has superseded archaic and corrupt Latin American business traditions. Like many films, it tells a story that transcends traditional tales. Back in 1954 when *Green Fire* was released, there was relatively little push-back to this economic and cultural jingoism; however, it also nourished the seeds of long-simmering discontent.

At the same time that the book *Green Fire* was about to make its journey to film, South America was beginning to be gripped by the political changes that would culminate in Cuba's communist revolution (1953–1959). Placing that revolutionary movement in historical perspective, it should be noted that American filmmakers such as Walt Disney had tried to put a positive spin on the United States' relationship with Latin America since the early 1940s. At that time, the United States became increasingly concerned that fascist Nazi Germany was courting countries such as Argentina, Chile, and Brazil. In 1942, the film *Saludos Amigos* (Hello Friends)[18] was an attempt to put a good face on Uncle Sam. To that end, the film was well received, thanks largely to Disney's ability to tell engaging stories using vivid animation. By distancing themselves from the present and creating diverting storylines, the cartoon characters in that film showcased Disney as a good-will ambassador.

Two years later, Disney's film *The Three Caballeros*[19] took out all the stops in cementing relationships more broadly throughout all of Latin America. Mexico, in fact, plays a major role in this film, which can best be described as truly Pan-American in focus. It featured Donald Duck forming a bond with other cartoon characters such as José Carioca and Pancho Pistóles. The trio interacted with real actors/performers such as Brazil's Aurora Miranda, and the film is acknowledged as the first time animated cartoon characters played opposite actual actors. The plot of *The Three Caballeros* involved a search for a storied Latin American past and featured several complex sub-plots—though marred by Donald Duck's almost constant gushing over beautiful Latin American women. Then again, in real life and on screen, Latin American women frequently beguiled American men, so Donald Duck may be satirizing a condition that William Walker found himself in a century earlier. On the other hand, Marxist interpretations—including the wildly popular 1971 book *How to Read Donald Duck*—considered Disney and his animators to be sinister forces in spreading capitalism.[20]

That said, there is no denying the appeal of Disney's animated films. Shot in stunning Technicolor, *The Three Caballeros* was a gorgeous film that contained unforgettable images of stylized places and maps that burned their way into the collective subconscious. One unforgettable scene involves the trio high above the Pacific coast of Mexico on a flying carpet bearing not the typical Persian design of Aladdin, but rather the multicolored stripes associated with Latin American textiles. They view Mexico and Central America almost as if gazing down on a colorful relief map whose blue waters, emerald green jungles, and purple mountains set the scene for adventure. As interpreted in the 2008 documentary film *Walt & El Grupo*,[21] these two Disney films went a long way in creating and sustaining relatively inoffensive stereotypes, in part by romanticizing Latin America's peoples and landscapes. They played for years, and as hoped, also helped build considerable international good will—confirming the power of film to shape popular perceptions and attitudes.

With capitalism and the film *Green Fire* in mind, I will close this chapter by noting that it not only inspired other adventure movies such as *Green Mansions*, but in particular two about Colombian emeralds. These included the tense heist caper *Green Ice* (1981), and the literature-based, map-centered blockbuster *Romancing the Stone* (1984). Alas, given the volatile political climate in Colombia, which continued into the 1980s, both of those films were shot largely in photogenic southern Mexico rather than truly on location.

SEVENTEEN

The Motorcycle Diaries
Exploration in Search of Reform

The period immediately following the Second World War witnessed an intensifying interest in Latin America by the United States. Although the defeat of the Axis Powers in 1945 put the brakes on actual German encroachment into the region, former U.S. allies the Soviet Union and China soon joined forces to become adversaries in the Cold War that followed (ca. 1947 to 1990). Readers may recall that part of *Indiana Jones and the Kingdom of the Crystal Skull* is set in this era, which is associated with considerable international political intrigue. Throughout the 1950s, South America tended to be politically conservative with most governments leaning toward the right. Their political corruption was also legendary, and resentment began to build among the people. Cuba was no exception. In 1959, when the U.S.-supported military dictatorship of Fulgencio Batista was deposed by rebellion there, the Eisenhower administration initially hoped it could work with its replacement—the charismatic Fidel Castro. However, when he took power Castro had the support of communist governments and they soon became his staunch allies. In the brinkmanship of the Cuban Missile Crisis (1962), the USSR pulled its nuclear missiles out of Cuba, and the Western Hemisphere breathed a sigh of relief.

With a hot war avoided, communism took a lower profile but continued pursuing its goal of infiltrating Latin America by fomenting rebellion. In turn, the United States redoubled its aid, including military and intelligence support to governments that were deemed pro–American and pro-capitalism. In the 1960s, the hunt for rebels was on throughout South America and it often involved Cuba-inspired and trained insurgents. No figure in South America has been more closely associated with Cuba's communist revolution than Ernesto "Che" Guevara de la Serna (1928–1967). Born in Argentina, Che initially set out to become a doctor, but became a militant supporter of Castro's Marxist Revolution. Although Che was from a white family that traced their ethnic heritage to north-western Europe—in particular Basque and Cantabrian as well as Irish[1]—he identified with struggling Indigenous peoples of color. His involvement in armed rebellions would make him a larger-than-life figure in South American storytelling, and movie making as well.

As an important figure in twentieth-century Latin American history, Che Guevara has been the subject of numerous documentary and docudrama films, including the two-part epic biopic *Che* starring Benicio del Toro and directed by Steven Soderbergh.[2] An insightful synopsis of that film is found in the "Revolutionary Latin America" section of Stewart Brewer's *Latin American History Goes to the Movies*.[3] Moreover, as a character, Che also appears in dramatic films as well. For example, the popular music-infused biopic

Evita (1997)[4] captures some of South America's political turmoil and sweeping geography, and features Antonio Banderas as Che. For her part, Eva Perón was an aspiring actress who found her true calling as the wife of Juan Perón, one of South America's many dictators who had broad popular appeal but many enemies as well.

Che is the subject of a South American film linking personal experiences in twentieth-century exploration—discovery to political consciousness—*The Motorcycle Diaries* (2004).[5] Filmed in locations throughout South America, it is also unquestionably one of the most successful films linking landscapes to character development. In it, Che emerges as a modern-day explorer, and the scenes he experiences are both his inspiration and his call to arms. As with most films, the written word preceded the film. Published several decades after the entries were actually written, Che's so-called Motorcycle Diaries[6] reveal another side of Che often lost amid his charisma as a radical. In places, his prose reveals a gifted writer, as is especially evident in his superb landscape descriptions. Moreover, he is well educated and intensely curious, writing with considerable candor and little concern for what might be called political correctness. He is also a bit ethnocentric as Argentina is the standard by which he measures the countries he visits. His writing reveals traces of the romantic and pragmatic, sometimes in the same passage. As he puts it in one entry: "…I finally felt myself lifted definitively away on the winds of adventure toward worlds I envisaged would be stranger than they were, into situations I imagined would be more normal than they turned out to be."[7]

Alas, little of Che's inner thoughts are related in the film, which is told from the perspective of a fairly lively dialog between the two main characters. Thanks to a fine screenplay by José Rivera, however, *The Motorcycle Diaries* is a delightfully picaresque journey of exploration-discovery focusing on two types of encounters, one involving exploration of place(s) and the other involving discoveries of self and other(s).

This film is a tribute to the optimism of youth and the daring involved in traveling on a shoe-string budget. Because Che and his older friend Alberto Granado journeyed together, the film has a road trip and buddy movie quality. Respectively, they are played by Mexican actor Gael García Bernal and the Argentinian Rodrigo de la Serna. Their steed, so to speak, was a 1939 Norton motorcycle they nicknamed "La Poderosa" (the Mighty One), although it was on its last legs when they bought it. Their goal was to have fun and take a break from their planned career paths. They had little money, so they planned to find work along the way. However, to them the trip would clearly be an adventure and they even make reference to themselves as self-conscious explorers. The movie begins with the pair making preparations for the journey, their stated goal being "to explore a continent we had only known in books."

Geographically speaking, they are determined to see all of South America, or rather much of the western and northeastern part of that vast continent. The film is ever aware of geography and employs a map to chart their course. It is a large map that can be folded, and on it Che and Alberto plot their ambitious 8000 kilometer (ca. 5000 mile) trip at the beginning of the film. Using a pen, Alberto draws the route, which will take them from the temperate south in Argentina, through deserts and mountains along the west coast, up into Peru to Machu Picchu, back over the Andes again into the tropical Amazon basin, and thence to the Guajira Peninsula in Venezuela at "the tip of this grand continent." There, they will bask in tropical pleasure. Romantically, they tell their families that they are about to "…embark on a journey to the farthest reaches of the human spirit where we will encounter new lands, hear new anthems, [and] eat new fruits…."

Bidding farewell to their families, they set out from Rosario and Buenos Aires, careening through the streets of the city as they get the feel of the motorized beast. Heading south, then westward, they traverse the Argentine Pampa, where they unsuccessfully attempt to out-race two gauchos on horseback, and then cross the Andes into southern Chile. Being self-consciously based on the diaries, the film frequently uses a written text to indicate where they are and when they reached those points. This creates the impression that the film is a more or less word-for-word account, but that is not the case. As I shall show, it deviates rather markedly in some places.

Overall, this film frequently embellishes their experiences, a case in point being their crossing of the Andes. It was summer, though the asthmatic Che was particularly susceptible to cold. In one place in the diaries, Che mentions that they experienced some miserably cold and rainy weather. Nevertheless, other days were more pleasant and they even hiked around a bit. He notes that in one of the higher places, he and Alberto were "...joking about in the patch of snow crowning the peak...."[8] and had some fun sliding down it to a stream. In the film however, the snow is far more menacing as they run into a full-blown snowstorm—a virtual white-out—and have to push the motorcycle through it. Sarcastically, Che exclaims: "Some summer we're having!"

On the other hand, the nasty spills they take on the motorcycle for varied reasons—to overcorrect their taking a curve too fast on a gravel road, or to avoid hitting cattle and other hazards—appear to be much as described in Che's own words. In the film they happen occasionally and are spectacular, adding an element of danger. Actually, the film

At the beginning of *The Motorcycle Diaries* (2004), Alberto Granado (Rodrigo de la Serna) is getting the feel of the bike they call "La Poderosa" as Che Guevara (Gael García Bernal) hangs on for dear life while they career through the streets of Buenos Aires (Film Four/BD Cine/Wildwood Enterprises).

seems to show considerable restraint, for in the published version of *The Motorcycle Diaries*, they had nine spills in one day! In addition to its mounting mechanical problems, some of these mishaps help explain the increasingly sorry condition of the bike as they crossed the mountains and headed into southern Chile, where they endeavor to impress the locals with their medical skills and their cachet as adventurers.

Like all explorers whose exploits we know about, they were not above self-promotion. In both the book and film, they seek publicity for their adventures. Upon arriving in Valdivia, a port city in southern Chile, the written Diaries notes that "Ambling around the city, we dropped into the local newspaper, the *Correo de Valdivia*, and they very kindly wrote an article about us." Quite interesting in light of geographical exploration is that Che also notes, "Valdivia was celebrating its fourth centenary and we dedicated our journey to the city in tribute to the great conquistador whose name the city bears." Shortly thereafter, they had another interview with the paper *El Austral* in Temuco. Che considered this part of the country "the land of Pablo Neruda,"[9] a luminary who was a well-known poet and leader of Chile's communist party.

The movie version of Che's diaries does a fine job of recounting these attempts at self-promotion, although it combines them as films tend to do. In one scene, almost as if spontaneously, they happen to pass the office of the newspaper *El Diario de Austral*. Seeing the sign on the door, Che decides to head inside intending to regale them with stories of their medical skills and their epic adventure underway. He evidently did a good

On the epic road trip depicted in *The Motorcycle Diaries* (2004), a regional newspaper in Chile publishes a story about the trip, which Che Guevara (Gael García Bernal) proudly reads to Alberto Granado (Rodrigo de la Serna) as he pushes the ailing bike (Film Four/BD Cine/ Wildwood Enterprises inc.).

job. In the scenes that follow, he proudly reads a copy of the newspaper story about them as Alberto pushes the ailing motorcycle down a narrow street. The plan has worked, and they take great pleasure in reading what others will learn about them. Their ulterior motive is not posterity but rather more immediate. As they observe, readers might offer them places to stay and some cash to continue their trip. With their credentials, including medical skills, and easy ability to make local contacts, the duo is reminiscent of— but a modern incarnation of—Humboldt and Bonpland.

From Temuco, they continue heading north toward Peru after making some mechanical repairs. Along the way, the ease with which they endear themselves to common folk that they meet is noteworthy. Almost seamlessly, the journey becomes less and less about tackling the physical geography and more about getting to know the human geography. Farther north along the highway in Chile, La Poderosa breaks down and they continue on as hitchhikers. By changing modes of transportation, they've now become even closer to the common people they encounter along the way. In the book version, they take a ship from Valparaiso to Antofagasta but the movie downplays this in the interest of time. Also downplayed in the film is their stated mission to see Easter Island, which lies far off the mainland in the South Pacific but is part of Chile.

Upon reaching the austere Atacama Desert of northern Chile, where copper mining dominates the lives of the locals, their lives will be forever changed. It is here, near the mining town of Chuquicamata, that Che will have an epiphany. That evening, they share a campfire and a meager meal with an impoverished Peruvian man and his wife. In the film, Che and Alberto show their map of South America to the couple, who point out the location of their home in Peru. As they do this, the couple notes that a large landholder has swindled that property from them, and they have been forced to work in the mines in Chile. Che comes to the realization that he must side with the impoverished

DESIERTO DE ATACAMA, CHILE
11 de MARZO de 1952
KM 4960

This scene from *The Motorcycle Diaries* (2004) shows Che Guevara (Gael García Bernal) on foot as he and Alberto traipse through the Atacama Desert in northern Chile. In this bleak locale, Che will have an epiphany that ultimately reshapes the political geography of Latin America (Film Four/BD Cine/Wildwood Enterprises Inc.).

and renounce the wealthy. This conversation pinpoints in time and place the beginnings of Che's transformation into a communist revolutionary.

At about the same time in the book, Che also changes his tune about Chile's conquistador explorer. As he now puts it, "Valdivia's actions symbolize man's indefatigable thirst to take control of a place where he can exercise total authority." For good measure, Che notes with some delight the fact that Valdivia met his end "...at the hands of the invincible Araucanian Caupolicán...."[10] The next morning, the now-angry Che becomes infuriated. He witnesses the couple's despair as they seek work in the mines, but are separated as only the man will be hired. In that same scene, after exchanging heated words with mine supervisors at Chuquicamata's open pit copper mine, Che throws a rock at the Anaconda Mining Company truck, a defiant act that pleases audiences but is not mentioned in the book. The date of the event is shown as 15 de Marzo, 1952 and it can viewed as a red-letter day in Latin American history.

This encounter in northern Chile also marks the moment in time that Che becomes a fierce supporter of Indigenous people, which becomes even more evident when they reach the Andean town of Cuzco, Peru. Here, Che and Alberto have a moving conversation with Indian women who have been victimized by the system. In this city, Che develops a strong appreciation for the ingenuity of the Indigenous people as he marvels at the Pre-Columbian architecture. In one scene, they hike up the trail to Machu Picchu, and astute movie goers will immediately recognize it as the same disorienting location used by Herzog (in *Aguirre, the Wrath of God*) to depict the conquistadors' descent into the jungle. This is no coincidence, and can be seen as a subtle homage to filmmaker Werner Herzog—but is far more. Whereas Herzog used it to show an expedition heading downhill bent on conquest, in *The Motorcycle Diaries*, Che and Alberto move up that same path, perhaps symbolically suggesting that they are ascending to a loftier goal, which is to say condemning the colonial past represented by the conquistadors. In this Andean wonderland of spectacular ruins and ancient cities, the movie version of Che asks, "How is it possible to feel nostalgia for a world I never knew?"

After other encounters, the film concludes with their visit to, and volunteer service at, a leper colony on the Amazon. To get there, they built a raft "La Kontikita" which is to say "little Kon Tiki" in reference to Thor Heyerdahl's much larger raft used in his ambitious trans-Pacific expeditions of 1947. This reinforces their claim of being explorers. The more practical side of Che involved his deep interest in leprosy, and he applied his knowledge in helping those afflicted by it. The film nicely showcases this compassion. In both the book and the film, the trip has indeed transformed them, with Granado becoming a dedicated life-long practicing physician and Guevara becoming a passionate life-long revolutionary with medical skills.

At the end of the film, Che and Alberto are parting at an airport, where the developing revolutionary is about to board a DC-3. Che has clearly been changed by the trip, and notes that on it "something happened—something that I'll have to think about for a long time." His next words—"So much injustice"—perfectly summarizes his thoughts. Just before parting, Alberto takes out the folded map and tells Che, "Wait, take this, it may help." Che seems surprised, adding, "You kept it?" Alberto nods, adding, "It's yours," as he hands it over to Che. This is one of the more profound uses of a map in film history. This well-worn map not only documents their life-changing travels but also will serve as a blueprint for the main character's future life's work—freeing the entire continent of his birth from oppression resulting from Spaniards first and their

In a moving scene at the end of *The Motorcycle Diaries*, Alberto Granado (Rodrigo de la Serna) hands over the friends' well-worn map of South America to Che Guevara (Gael García Bernal), who will ultimately use it to foment radical political change throughout the region. (Film Four/BD Cine/Wildwood Enterprises Inc.).

successor after independence—corporate capitalism. Throughout the entire film, from the very beginning to the last frame, that map served as a witness to what the travelers had experienced.

In stories like this one involving transformations in time and place, the medium of film shines because it so compellingly engages both the on-screen actors and the viewers. The expansive cinematography further engages people and locales in ways that written words alone cannot. While watching *The Motorcycle Diaries*, it is easy to believe that we are seeing the real thing, but of course it has been dramatized. The book by Che's traveling companion Alberto titled *Traveling with Che Guevara: The Making of a Revolutionary*[11] provides a different perspective on certain events. Che was idolized by the filmmakers, and that hagiography is on display as certain scenes help give him a more saintly image. One scene finds Alberto gambling in order to make enough money to pay for the services of an enterprising and fetching prostitute they meet along the way. However, it was in fact Che himself who entered into that—dare one say it—capitalistic transaction with that alluring woman. A prudish progressivism is at work in many contemporary films about (and by) leftists, and *The Motorcycle Diaries* personifies it.

Another scene, toward the end of the movie, involves Che swimming across the river at night to help lepers in their quarters on the other side, when in fact he did it on a whim with no social cause in mind. Although taking such liberties with what actually happened might offend some historians, or infuriate those who do not idolize Che, it should be recalled that it comes with the territory. Therefore, it should come as no surprise that we see a more sensitive Che than the one revealed in his printed version of *The Motorcycle Diaries*. For example, regarding the people they met along the way, Che claims in the book that "We were like demigods to these simple people"—a sentiment that had been uttered by European explorers since the time of Columbus, and appears almost verbatim in Cabeza de Vaca's *Relación*. Also noticeably missing from the film are Che's casual asides about "smelly Indians," and Native women's lack of personal hygiene. Needless to say, his lament about the Indian women wearing modern dresses "so you couldn't admire their jugs"[12] is nowhere found in the film. Truth is, Che (and Alberto) had an eye for women, and these explorers were ready for seduction if and when the opportunity presented itself. Although Che was feted with a "Saint Guevara Day" for his commendable work at the San Pablo Leper Colony, a saint he surely was not.

Che's book itself concludes with calls for Pan-American unity and ends on a decidedly militant note: "I feel my nostrils dilate, savoring the acrid smell of gunpowder and blood, the enemy's death; I steel my body, ready to do battle, and prepare myself to be a sacred space within which the bestial howl of the triumphant proletariat can resound with new energy and new hope."[13] Interestingly, if the word "proletariat" were replaced by "Spaniard" it would be the conquistador's call to arms four centuries earlier. Moreover, Che had no way of knowing at the time that his scathing rebuke of conquistadors seizing and holding onto power could be applied, verbatim, to dictator Fidel Castro's vice-like grip over Cuba for forty years.

In the beginning of the book, Che writes with a delightful sense of humor that becomes scarce after he arrives in Antofagasta and receives a letter from his sweetheart, jilting him and souring him on romantic relationships. As with Humboldt and Bonpland, Che's romantic attachments almost threatened to scuttle the expedition at that point. However, he recovered from that funk ready for the life-changing experience with that displaced Peruvian couple in the Atacama Desert. Humor is scarce in the written diaries after that point, but only a hint of this darker trajectory is evident in the movie, which is otherwise more sanguine. Geographically speaking, Che transforms himself from a South American explorer-discoverer into an outspoken advocate for all of Latin America in this far-flung story.

As suggested at the beginning of this book, filmmaking, like exploration itself, involves making a convincing argument about what has been discovered. That process can involve a filmmaker's wishful thinking when it comes to portraying heroes and villains. Conservatives had their day in creating films of the 1940s through the 1950s that lionized take-charge capitalists and regarded Indigenous people dismissively. They too played fast and loose with the facts. However, following the social upheavals in the 1960s, the tide had begun to turn. Currently, stridently progressive portrayals dominate popular filmmaking, which romanticizes left-leaning characters and causes. So be it.

This film helps sustain the heroic image of Che that has predominated, and even increased, since his death. There is no doubt he was a towering figure in the rise of the left, evidenced by his pivotal role in Cuba's communist revolution and its exportation to Africa and Bolivia. One photo that Alberto took of him has become the defining image, an intense and determined Che who gazes upward and symbolizes a man on a selfless mission, to free the world of social and economic repression, even at the cost of his own life. This image was intensified by Irish artist Jim Fitzgerald and appeared in many formats, including a poster that has adorned the office walls of countless professors hoping to inspire students to be willing to die for a political cause that they believe in, preferably one that Che would have endorsed. Engrossed in his role as the revolutionary, actor Gael García Bernal stated that Che "was an amazing character ... a person that changed the world and really forces me to change the rules of what I am."[14] Over the years, that photographic image has become iconic—not only in the sense of being a defining image but also—as with religious icons—to signify a saintly figure worth worshipping.

That said, Che's iconic portrayals on screen demand some deeper critical contextualization, perhaps even some iconoclasm. Films about him often stress his indefatigable passion for his cause, which led to his demise at the hands of American (CIA-U.S. Armed Forces) and Bolivian police in 1967. During Che's life as a revolutionary, however, he was polarizing figure; many described his zeal for revolution in either glowing or unflattering terms, depending on their personal experiences and their political beliefs. On the one hand, he was brave and seemingly selfless in pursuing the cause of global communism. On the other, his ruthlessness and intolerance to opposing political views were well known, and he is still remembered by many in Latin America as "*muy fanático*" (very fanatical). Regardless of which side one remembers, though, Che the movie character presents a dilemma to historians of film: in trading his life for cinematic immortality, and thus passionately inspiring viewers, he too personifies the "White Fanatics" mentioned briefly in the Preface and discussed in more detail in Chapter Fourteen.

Eighteen

Nostalgia for the Light

The Filmmaker as Explorer of Memory

In *The Motorcycle Diaries,* Che Guevara's 1952 epiphany in the Atacama Desert is a turning point in his personal politics, but it reverberated throughout Latin America. About eighteen years later, the left had made significant gains throughout the region despite the grip held by right wing dictators. In the Southern Cone of South America, Chile's political shift toward the left culminated in the election of socialist president Salvador Allende—a relatively rare example of a peaceful transition of power. Fulfilling a campaign promise, Allende nationalized the copper mining industry less than a year later (1971). This proved to be one of the factors that helped plunge the country's economy into a downward spiral and throw its internal politics into chaos.

By 1973, conditions were ripe for the right-wing general Augusto Pinochet to seize power and bring the country under military control. A massive and brutal crackdown followed, leading to the infamous *Batalla de Chile* (Battle of Chile) which lasted from 1975 to 1979. Even outsiders fell prey to it, as immortalized in the poignant film *Missing* (1986).[1] Based on a book of the same name, *Missing* dramatizes the search for a young American journalist, Charles "Charlie" Horman, who was abducted and murdered by Chile's government in 1978. Although the film never names the country in which it occurred, nor names Pinochet, it was banned in Chile by the Pinochet government.

Interestingly, the Chilean flag is shown in one scene of *Missing*, and is so similar (though not identical) to the "Lone Star" flag of Texas that one of my students in a "History and Film" class at UT Arlington asked, "Why is our state flag being shown?" I noted that the similarities appeared to be more than coincidental. As delicately as possible, I mentioned that the Texas flag is actually more recent (dating from the 1830s) and was likely inspired by the Chilean flag, which dates from that country's independence from Spain in 1817. I reminded the students that officials in the Republic of Texas (1836–1845) were enamored by the South American countries' break from Spain, and viewed their break from Mexico with the same enthusiasm. This was one of many examples wherein something seen in a movie can be used educationally.

In Pinochet's Chile, one particularly brutal aspect of the crackdown by the government played out in the austere and politically volatile Atacama Desert region in the country's far north. This part of the Atacama Desert is called *El Norte Grande* by Chileans, and it was originally part of Peru and Bolivia, but Chile wrested it away from them during the War of the Pacific (1879–1884). It was a war fought largely over mineral wealth, namely nitrates but also precious and base metals as well; in the twentieth century copper dominated, and along with other minerals helped Chile become the economic powerhouse of South America. Although the War of the Pacific resulted in Bolivia's becoming a land-locked country, a subsequent early twentieth-century treaty enables it to have access to the booming port cities of Arica and Antofagasta. That said, Bolivia and Peru are still resentful of losing not only territory in the Atacama Desert region, but also the region's mineral-rich areas.

Chilean writers have effectively used the Atacama Desert to reflect on their nation's collective psyche, a very personal and inspirational example being Ariel Dorfman's 2004 memoir *Desert Memories*. Dorfman (b. 1942) is a Marxist Argentine-Chilean-American playwright and academician who had felt the lure of this desert many times since he became a Chilean citizen in the 1960s, but had to rush through it *en route* to his new home in exile after Pinochet's takeover in 1973. Years later, when Dorfman was finally given the opportunity to travel anywhere he wanted in Chile, he chose the Atacama Desert. As Dorfman put it, that part of the country had "...slowly colonized my mind..." and "...emerged ever more mythically inside me like an obsessive mist of sand, calling me to come and see for myself the territory that had decided the fate of the country I had made my own, the territory that had decided in many ways my own fate."[2]

To many movie goers, the Atacama Desert may seem far away and out of mind, and there is good reason for this. Until very recently, few films were made about, or shot within, it. Unknowingly, they have glimpsed its foreboding topography in the second half of the James Bond blockbuster film *Quantum of Solace* (2008).[3] Political intrigue is at the center of this spy-thriller that supposedly takes place in the nearly barren Altiplano of Bolivia, but was shot in the vicinity of Paranal and the town of Baquedano, Chile. The latter locations are in the middle of the Atacama Desert, although the name Atacama is never used in the film. In sweeping views, the Atacama becomes a major character in this energy-charged film. The varied scenes along the Pan American and other highways beautifully reveal the scale and bleakness of this awesome region, although the spectacular aerial combat scenes were filmed over the desert near San Felipe, in northern Baja California.

The "Bond girl" character in this film is named Camille Montes Rivero (Ukrainian born actress Olga Konstiantin Kurylenko). She plays a fetching Bolivian agent who is involved with a duplicitous environmental activist named Dominic Greene (French actor Mathieu Amalric); the character's name is perfect given his purported efforts to save the vast and endangered rainforest in eastern Bolivia and adjacent Peru and Brazil. Associated with the shadowy group Quantum, Greene's real goal is controlling Bolivia's water resources. Near the end of the film, James Bond (Daniel Craig) leaves the nefarious and murderous villain Greene to die in the middle of the desert. As Bond parts with Greene, he cynically gives him an unopened quart-size can of motor oil to slake his thirst—a delightfully ironic fate for a despoiler of the planet.

An interesting back-story to this film relates to the tense situation between Bolivia and Chile that dates from well before the War of the Pacific. Reportedly, Bolivians were none too pleased to have Chile be its stand-in, and for that matter Panama City be the filming locale for the La Paz scenes. Then again, Chile and Panama were far more amenable to outsider filmmakers, especially those from the United States, whose relationship with Bolivia has been strained in the early twenty-first century. Ironically, had the film been made before 1884—a technical impossibility, of course—those desert scenes would indeed have been shot in Bolivia.

Two more recent dramatic exploration-discovery films shot in the Atacama are noteworthy here. The first of them, the oddly titled *Crystal Fairy and the Magical Cactus and 2012*,[4] is about a young American woman (Gaby Hoffmann) who calls herself Crystal Fairy and is on a spiritual search to find herself. It begins in Santiago, Chile's busy capital city, where she has a chance meeting with a cynical and highly opinionated American named Jamie (Michael Cera), and three far more laid-back Chilean brothers who are planning a "psychoactive voyage" northward into the Atacama in their Chevy Suburban. One might call this film a pre–Apocalyptic road trip, their goal being not only to get away from the cities but also to prepare for the end of the world in 2012 according to a prophecy in the Mayan calendar. Filmed in the Atacama in the vicinity of Copiapó and in the Pan de Azúcar national park, *Crystal Fairy* ... epitomizes Chile's nascent film industry, dealing with subjects that had been forbidden by the government for years. With psychedelic inspirations from the San Pedro cactus (*Echinopsis pachanoi*), the group finds their sought-after inspiration in the desert. Above all, this film is a reminder that explorers come in many forms and have varied motivations.

Far fewer movie-goers may have seen the Atacama Desert in the 2014 surreal film *The Dance of Reality*,[5] which is avant-garde Chilean filmmaker Alejandro Jodorowsky's memoir about life in his isolated hometown of Tocopilla during Chile's troubled past. It is a remarkable dramatization of his growing up in this gritty port town on the often fog-shrouded desert coast; here mineral wealth from the desert is loaded onto ships destined for countries around the world. Jodorowsky uses the region's *camanchaca* fogs to great effect as the moods are often sullen. *The Dance of Reality* features characters rarely seen on screen, many of whom are misshapen by accidents and incidents; they include once virile miners now limbless by accidents, as well as other souls psychologically deformed by relentless bullying. Even in these roles, they can—like the dwarf Mala Cosa in *Cabeza de Vaca*—be viewed with awe.

The Dance of Reality involves a deeply personal exploration into the tormented history of Jodorowsky's homeland. Few films have better showcased the monstrous egotism involved in the formation of right-wing and left-wing dictators, both of whom have helped shape the ever-evolving political landscape of Chile, and for that matter, many other parts of Latin America. One scene depicts the arrival of political prisoners into one of the desert mining towns converted into a concentration camp. Jodorowsky is known for his starring role and direction in quirky and edgy movies about father-son relationships, including the wildly surrealistic desert search for spirituality in *El Topo*[6] (1970), which was shot in Mexico. However, as its title implies *The Dance of Reality* is the most compellingly believable of his films, in part because of its autobiographical nature and its being shot on location.

Needless to say, this strikingly graphic film could not have been made nor shown in Pinochet's Chile, but now Jodorowsky can tell his own story unfettered by censorship. That said, one should not be too sanguine about the far left either—a reminder being the Soviet Union's banning both the book and film versions of Boris Pasternak's quintessentially Russian story—*Doctor Zhivago*. Closer to home, Castro's Cuba was notoriously selective about what could and could not be read or seen on film. As a Venezuelan friend colorfully and cynically put it: "Cuando se trata de restringir la libertad de expresión, tanta la izquierda como la derecha son aliados" ("When it comes to curtailing freedom of expression, both the left and the right are allies").

As the movies *Crystal Fairy* ... and *The Dance of Reality* confirm, the Atacama Desert is associated with mind-bending personal experiences. It is worth noting that both these films are ultimately about self-exploration and self-discovery, especially in light of troubled personal pasts. Their bleak settings form the perfect springboard for journeys into the human imagination.

The film that I shall now discuss in detail—the superb 2011 documentary *Nostalgia for the Light*[7]—was directed by Patricio Guzmán. It uses exploration and discovery as major themes in storytelling about the Atacama Desert and its relation to the rest of Chile and the world. The operative terms here are *nostalgia*—the original meaning of which refers to the longing for one's lost home (not past time, per se)—and *light* as a force that is ultimately stellar in origin but also illuminates our existence. It is also another highly personal film, for Guzmán is telling his own story as well as relating a difficult chapter in the history of his beloved but troubled country. That story recounts his childhood love of science and his fascination with astronomy, and it continues into the darker period of political unrest that permanently scarred Chile's history.

Nostalgia for the Light begins with close-up shots of metal gears and tubes, which the moving camera explores to slowly reveal they are part of a precision instrument—a beautiful old German telescope. Significantly, this instrument is a tool used in exploration-discovery, in this case of the heavens. The fact that it is a vintage instrument helps Guzmán segue into the past. Accompanying these introductory scenes, his slow-paced narration is both confessional and mesmerizing. He recalls being a boy when the world was full of wonder and Chile itself seemed young and innocent.

Throughout the film, Guzmán uses a special visual effect that he alludes to as "star dust"—minute particles of matter suspended in the air that sparkle at times—much like the glitter in a snow-globe. At first the effect is a bit distracting, but it soon feels natural

Symbolically, the Atacama Desert-based film *Nostalgia for the Light* (2011) begins with close-ups of an old German telescope that inspired Chilean filmmaker Patricio Guzmán's interest in astronomy. This beautiful scientific instrument will serve as the perfect metaphor for the film's search into infinity (Pyramide International and Icarus Films).

as it mirrors the myriad of stars in the heavens—and the dust that is sometimes suspended in the atmosphere of the desert.

Cartography enhances the narration. Using the oft-seen satellite image of our green and blue earth as seen from outer space, Guzmán zeroes in on what he calls its one brown patch. In a world consisting of oceans and land that is mostly covered by clouds, this brown patch stands out in stark contrast. As the image shows, it lies along the Pacific coast of an often cloud covered continent. There are other deserts in the world, of course, but Guzmán's language lulls the viewer into forgetting those and to regard *his* desert as exceptional. The film contains some vivid footage of the stark desert landscapes, richly colored by mineral oxides and virtually devoid of vegetation.

Guzmán makes such good use of telescopic images that one can also forget that cameras are recording the scenes. Revealed through the telescope, the earth's moon has a fascinating and forbidding surface, not unlike the starkly barren landscape of the Atacama Desert. That lunar image helps Guzmán make the dramatic transition from outer space to northern Chile. In close-ups, his camera reveals that there is life in this desert, but that this land is also hiding terrible secrets as well.

To help tell the desert's human story, Guzmán engages two types of knowledgeable interviewees. The first are authorities such as scientists—particularly astronomers—who use the clear skies in the Atacama to advantage as they peruse the heavens and learn more about the immensity of the universe from the region's many mountain-top observatories. Guzmán notes that "science fell in love with the night sky" that can be seen so clearly in the Atacama. As he then puts it a bit more poetically, "…in the Atacama, one can touch the stars." With little or no humidity, and virtually no light pollution, this desert is renowned for its star-gazing.

It is also considered by some to lie at the doorstep of space travel. Guzmán's statement that man has walked on the moon and will someday walk on mars is noteworthy because the surface of the red planet and the Atacama are visually similar, so much so that astronauts have trained there. Astronomers such as Gaspar Galaz are also philosophical about humankind's place in the cosmos, and they hope that the immensity and potential of deep space can help unify mankind. Galaz observes that we all originated in the same place, which is to say, in outer space. He further notes that when we look out into deep space we are also looking into deep time. Through the telescope we can discover the origins of the universe itself, and the origins of life as well. Guzmán puts it almost poetically when he notes that he used to think our human origins were found in the rocks but now realizes that we originated in outer space as cosmic matter. To the viewer, the pervasive dust particles floating about in the film now make sense: they are no longer inanimate objects but the building blocks of all life—and hence part of us.

Guzmán also interviews archaeologist Lautario Núñez, whose approach is both philosophical and practical. Núñez is knowledgeable about deep antiquity here—which is visible on the desert's surface as well as deep below it. To demonstrate this, he explains the geoglyphs which tell a story about how people got there and lived here thousands of years ago. He is also engaged in forensic archaeology in the desert, for the many crimes the government committed are under investigation. As Núñez puts it in the film, "We've kept our recent past hidden."

Having involved a scientist Galaz and a humanist Núñez—both of whom serve as bookends to the measurement of time—Guzmán now shifts focus to recount the tragic story of the desert in the very recent past. The second type of interviewees that

Guzmán sought out were the actual survivors of Chile's terrible secret war on political dissidents in the 1970s, many of whom were interned far from the cities at a concentration camp-like locale called Chacabuco, a former nitrate mining town in the Atacama. Images of these desert concentration camps have appeared in other Chilean films such as the aforementioned *Dance of Reality* and the superb noir-style film *Neruda,* which involves a ruthless police inspector in the role of explorer searching for the famous poet, who was also leader of Chile's Communist party.[8] As in *Zama,* that zealous quest for an outlaw whose apprehension can redeem a career instead results in a tragic ending.

In a sense, the numerous people interviewed in Guzmán's documentary film are both explorers and detectives, an intriguing topic awaiting further study by scholars. Among those former detainees is Miguel Lawner, called "the Architect of memories" because he paced off the buildings and essentially mapped the Chacabuco complex so that it could described in future investigations into war crimes. Guzmán also interviews the most heart-rending of people associated with Pinochet's abuses, relatives of "Los Desaparecidos" (The Disappeared) whose bodies were disposed of in the vast desert. In a sense, the people who continue to search for the bodies of loved ones are also explorers sifting through the sands for some remnant of them. In another sense, this scene is artistic and has some of the elements of Jean-François Millet's famous 1857 painting titled *The Gleaners.* In the film, and in that painting, the gleaners are standing on bare ground and hoping to find something of value that might remain but has been missed by others. Both convey a sense of desperation as well as hope. Guzmán masterfully uses close-ups at times, one of the more arresting being the top of a skull, which strikingly resembles the pock-marked surface of the moon as seen through a telescope. In one

The Chilean film *Nostalgia for the Light* (2011) is director Patricio Guzmán's tribute to Los Desaparecidos (The Disappeared) who vanished during the political crackdown on dissidents in the 1970s. Like the hopeful souls in the French nineteenth-century painting *The Gleaners,* these modern-day searchers in the Atacama pay attention to the smallest specks that can sustain them (Pyramide International and Icarus Films).

close up, the desert has yielded fragments of human bone that are part of the forensic effort underway.

Two of the searching relatives are Vicky Saavedra and Violeta Berríos, who recount their efforts. After searching for years, Vicky found a shoe that belonged to her brother, his foot still in it. In an almost unimaginable task, she hopes to find the rest of him someday so that he can be complete—and she can finally rest. The close-up of his identification photo-card laid upon the rocky surface of the Atacama in effect helps momentarily preserve his identity. More deeply, the ephemeral nature of the identification paper, and the durability of the stone, underscores the element of time and the urgency of the search. Meanwhile, Violeta continues her epic search as well. In one scene, she gazes out into the desert and mournfully states, "I wish the telescopes didn't just look into the sky, but could also see through the earth so that we could find them." Full of wisdom and pain, it is among the most profound and heart-rending synopsizing statements ever uttered on film—either in a drama or a documentary.

Throughout this moving film, others are interviewed, including Valentina Rodríguez, a relatively young astronomer who was raised by her grandparents after her parents were "detained" by the government. As a scientist, Rodríguez looks upon her shattered family's past philosophically, observing, "It's all part of a cycle" of recycled energy. She thanks science for this perspective, which is in some ways deeply healing. For his part, Guzmán hopes the film will help past wounds heal, but only to a point, and certainly not before far more of the past is unearthed. In one poignant scene, Guzmán assembles the team currently exploring the Atacama for remains of their loved ones.

In a remarkable example of a filmmaker getting deeply involved in a project, Guzmán arranges for the grieving Vicky and Violeta to meet with astronomer Galaz to further assist the process of closure. As the observatory roof opens and the telescope

In this close-up from *Nostalgia for the Light* (2011), a slip of paper with a photograph identifies José Saavedra Gonzáles. He is the brother of Vicky Saavedra, who has spent years searching for his remains in the vast Atacama Desert of Chile. This piece of paper signifies hope in the face of the unrelenting desert where the search for "Los Desaparecidos" (The Disappeared) continues (Pyramide International and Icarus Films).

engages, they peer into it and are awed by what they behold. Galaz beams as he witnesses their awe and joy. As they view the heavens through the telescope, that pervasive stardust swirls around, reaffirming the cycle of life and death. Of course, although it is a highly dramatic scene, it is carefully staged. Nevertheless, only the most jaded film viewer could fail to be moved by it. The scene perfectly epitomizes my earlier statement in the Introduction that even documentary films often involve considerable poetic license.

One of the most remarkable aspects of *Nostalgia for the Light* is the manner in which it palpably involves the filmmaker as explorer of place and time, moving through those dimensions as he encounters and interviews other explorers on their professional and personal journeys of discovery. This film makes clear something that has been pondered for several centuries, was mentioned earlier in this book, and is my credo, namely, that geography and history are inseparable. It also engages the more modern premise that space and time are inseparable as well. For those prone to ponder such philosophical issues, and deeper issues of spirituality, the Atacama is the perfect place. Although this desert has inspired many books and a few documentary and dramatic films, *Nostalgia for the Light* is the first film to tell its story so vividly.

Of all the films discussed in this book, *Nostalgia for the Light* is among the deepest, which is to say (ironically) the darkest despite its title. Metaphorically speaking, film rarely illuminates—that is, shines light on a subject—in the way that this one does. In part, that is because its vision of enlisting science to help humanity out of quagmires is so hopeful. This film also leaves one with a conundrum, for memory is the issue here but Guzmán discovers two forces at work—those of remembering and those of forgetting. When Guzmán made this eloquent film, many Chileans preferred that the past be

In a moving scene from *Nostalgia for the Light* (2011), Vicky Saavedra and Violeta Berríos peer through the telescope as "stardust" floats in the air—a cinematic special effect that underscores humanity's origins in material that arrived from deep space (Pyramide International and Icarus Films).

buried and forgotten; however, he urges otherwise, his premise being that understanding the past is essential to living in the present and responsibly anticipating the future.[9]

Reaching a much wider audience, *The 33* is another fairly recent film that explores the connection between the Atacama Desert and outer space.[10] Directed by Mexican filmmaker Patricia Riggen, it is a dramatized reenactment of the feverish search and rescue of thirty-three miners entombed underground by a massive rock fall that cut off all means of escape. Based on Héctor Tobar's tersely written book *Deep Down Dark*,[11] this film does what film is especially adept at. It compresses sixty-nine days into about two hours, emphasizes some characters as opposed to every single miner, simplifies an otherwise complex event, dramatizes place, and emphasizes the moral of human ingenuity to overcome all. *The 33* epitomizes the way that exploration has turned inward in more recent times. Its cinematography shines and underscores the sci-fi like quality of the rescue by an international team involving NASA. The miners' salvation depended on technology developed for outer space exploration, and also on their inner religious faith. The latter may explain why it was a smash hit in Chile, but performed dismally at the box office in the religiously-jaded United States. Overall, at least, it broke even worldwide.

The 33 and *Nostalgia for the Light* personify one of the Atacama's enduring themes. As I noted in *Imagining the Atacama Desert*,[12] this hyper-arid region provides the key to unlocking some of Latin America's deepest secrets, from the world's most ancient mummies—almost twice as old as ancient Egypt's—to the more recent forensic evidence of politically-inspired brutality. It merges seamlessly into the Peruvian deserts that stretch almost as far north as the equator, and bleeds across the western borders of Bolivia and Argentina. However, the driest and most iconic part of it now lies squarely in Chile, which is developing a vibrant film industry as it awakens from years of political oppression.

The Atacama is the place where one of the world's most poignant sculptures—*Mano del Desierto* (Hand of the Desert) by Chilean sculptor Mario Irarrázabal points skyward, anchored to an arm that disappears into the desert soil like the roots of a tree. Like the film *Nostalgia for the Light*, it serves as a tribute to the disappeared. In all directions, the Martian-like Atacama landscape sweeps toward the horizon of rust-red hills, impressing today's travelers, much as it did those first Spanish explorers who called it *el gran despoblado*—the vast land without people. That impression is lasting, though today we know that it is even more haunting, populated by Los Desaparecidos. Born as visions that inspired authors in numerous genres, including noir and magical realism, many dramatic stories about the Atacama now await the imaginative journey from page to screen.[13]

NINETEEN

Dora and the Lost City of Gold

In Search of New Cultural Frontiers

The last film I will discuss in detail is the most recent (2019) but paradoxically uses some of the oldest South American exploration-discovery tropes—Amazonian El Dorado and Inca Empire treasures—in order to explore new social and cultural frontiers. Symbolically, its female protagonist began life in 2000 as television cartoon character "Dora the Explorer." In episode after episode, this energetic and inquisitive Latina began to rectify gender and cultural imbalances on daytime educational television.[1] Two decades later, she finally made her debut as a "real" explorer in the 2019 film *Dora and the Lost City of Gold*.[2] This partially animated fantasy-adventure saga features a now teenage Dora (American-Peruvian actress Isabela Moner) in the leading role, but cleverly begins with the younger version of Dora (Madelyn Miranda) as a way for two generations of viewers to segue into the action. The casting is very adept for they both look very similar and have big, deep-brown eyes that constantly suggest enthusiasm.

In this cinematic saga, the six-year-old Dora Márquez is living with her mother Elena (Eva Longoria) and father Cole (Michael Peña) in the Amazon basin of eastern Peru. Her parents are well educated and environmentally sensitive, their two goals being to raise their daughter and locate a lost city in the jungle. Dora spends most of her time on adventures accompanied by Boots (a friendly animated monkey) and her seven-year-old cousin Diego (Malachi Barton). Her two imaginary companions are called Backpack and Map, which are of course indispensable to explorers venturing into unchartered regions. Early in the story, Dora reveals that Map is a "map with a mouth," signaling that it can provide Dora the geographic information she needs without her having to consult a paper map. This not only gives map reading a magical quality, but is also a bow to the voice-activated navigation systems of the early twenty-first century. Dora's world is both comfortable and exciting, but she does have a nemesis named Swiper (a troublesome animated kleptomaniac Fox) who plays tricks on her from time to time.

The film begins with the camera view sweeping across a river and toward Dora's rustic home, which sits on stilts at the river's edge. Dora welcomes the audience as imaginary visitors to her world and then begins playing with her cousin Diego, whom she calls "Primo." He calls Dora "Prima," and the audience has already gotten its first subliminal Spanish lesson for the noun "cousin." Elena calls the two of them in for dinner, but they put up some resistance as they are so busy exploring in a cardboard jeep. Reluctantly, they come into the dining area, where primo Diego notices a large map on the wall which bears the mysterious name PARAPATA. As a cinematic device, the map simultaneously reaffirms the seriousness of the parent's search and helps underscore

213

the film's theme of geographic exploration. Like many maps in films, it only appears for a few seconds, and not as a lingering close up, for to do so would demystify the locale rather than stimulate the imagination. So positioned, this big wall map foreshadows where the explorers, and the film, are headed—namely, into the unknown.

Intrigued by the map, Diego asks his uncle Cole, "what is Parapata?" Cole replies that it is the lost city of the Incas. This exotic-sounding name, which rolls off the tongue like Atacama and Alabama, is similarly Indian in origin, but it is apparently derived from the slightly more challenging-to-pronounce Paititi, a lost Inca city that supposedly exists in southeastern Peru, eastern Bolivia, or western Brazil. At any rate, Cole and Elena show Diego and Dora some sketches of the ancient city in a notebook. The sketches are reminiscent of those made by Alexander von Humboldt in Latin America ca. 1802 and subsequent explorers throughout the nineteenth century who combed the region for impressive ancient ruins.

Cinematically, these illustrations are noteworthy. Their being sketches suggests that they are renditions that may have involved considerable imagination. At another level, the sketches not being photographic in nature—which the movie itself is—serves to distance them chronologically from the present. Filmmakers have long known that sketches can stimulate the imagination more than photographs, and the film's director James Bobin uses them to great effect here. Cinematically, the film's animated footage adds another interesting touch, for that medium involves the same kind of imagination as that embodied in sketching. That juxtaposing of imagery—"real" and imaginary—works to great advantage throughout this film.

So, too, does the story line itself, which was written by Tom Wheeler and Nicholas Stoller. Their technique of informing the two cousins about Parapata is also brilliant in that the young audience targeted is learning as well. The cousins being male and female subliminally engages a broader audience. With both of them (and the audience) now excited by the prospect of finding this lost city, they begin asking additional questions. When Diego asks if the city contains any gold, Cole answers that it is said to possess more gold than all the known gold in the world combined. Dora and Diego become excited by this, but Cole informs them that the gold is only secondary to finding and understanding the city itself. Elena drives this point home by telling them that the knowledge about the city, rather than its riches, should be paramount. Elena sums it up by saying, or rather synopsizing, "treasure hunting bad, exploring good."

In a sense, this slogan is the film's mantra. Its sentiment, of course, is similar to the epiphany revealed in *Indiana Jones and the Kingdom of the Crystal Skull*. As this scene at the dinner table proceeds, the audience learns that Diego and his parents will return home to the city the next day. This is a bitter-sweet ending to this part of the film in that the cousins are not only very close but now very sad as well. Before they part, Dora and Diego both vow, "'Til our next adventure,'" another foreshadowing of things to come.

The next scene involves a big leap in time that film is so adept at delivering, especially when the audience is properly informed. In this case, the film relies on the written word as bold lettering bilingually announces, "10 years Later—10 Años Después." The audience now finds a teenage Dora traipsing through the jungle having real and imaginary encounters with animals. The imaginary ones apparently include a herd of elephants (way out of their range in the Old World here) and the real ones include ferocious caymans and rare crocodilians as well as beautifully colored and deadly frogs native to the Amazon. The monkey Boots is still Dora's companion. Dora is so comfortable here that she has a six-foot long pet boa constrictor, which she carries over her shoulders like a shawl.

Out in the jungle, Dora is still in her element, only now even more self-confident and aware of her surroundings. By chance, she and Boots encounter a cave and enter it. Deeper in the cave, Dora first spots ancient Inca petroglyphs and then encounters a large temple flanked by stairs, atop which rests a golden figure. Dora states that it may be the gateway to Parapata. Overly excited, she tries to leap across the chasm to reach the statue, but falls into the abyss. Dora evidently leads a charmed life amid all the dangers, for despite the fall that appears to be about 30 feet (10 meters), she is uninjured. However, because she is unable to climb up the steep walls, she calmly tells Boots to go get her parents.

The next scene finds them all safely back home, with Dora consulting additional sketches of ancient Inca images. Excitedly, she claims that what she encountered represents a map that can help them locate Parapata. The city should be where lines intersect, but her parents already seem to know this. In fact, Dora (and the audience) now learn that Cole has indicated the location of the city as a series of red lines that come together at a large red map-pin. Although we only see this part of the map for a few seconds, it is clear that the converging red lines mark the spot. Cole mentions that the location of Parapata proves that the Inca Empire had a much greater extent than previously thought.

All of this information is good news to Dora, who excitedly tells her folks she is ready to find the lost city with them. However, they have other plans for her. Figuring that the trek will be too dangerous for the rambunctious Dora—after all, they just had to rescue her from a foolhardy miscalculation—they inform her that she will be sent to the city where cousin Diego has been living with his family for the last ten years. Deeply disappointed, Dora tries to convince her parents to let her stay, but to no avail. They have made up their minds, and besides, Elena tells Dora that even more exciting exploration awaits her: Now, she tells Dora, "You have the whole world to explore."

To soften the disappointment, the parents remind Dora that—via their GPS signaling—she can track their progress on her large paper map titled The Valley of the Amazon. It is remarkable how many different kinds of maps figure in this brief part of the film. They include the ancient Inca glyph-map, modern wall maps, and implied satellite mapping. It becomes apparent that this film is hyper aware of spatiality and uses it to great advantage in the plot. A case in point is how Dora's journey to the city is depicted, namely, through yet another map—this one informative but including cartoonlike images of animals such as a hummingbird, parrot, and a black panther. Although the technique of showing how a journey proceeds by having a dot moving (or a line progressing) along a map on screen has been common in cinema for about a century, this map scene has a clearly whimsical quality. In it, a stylized LATAM jet airliner departs from the Amazon area as if flying off of a colorful map of South America that shows (and names) the countries. We know that Dora is aboard, and that her journey is now taking her northwestward over Colombia, then over Central America and Mexico as the plane "flies" over the map. By now it is apparent that reaching her cousin's city involves traveling thousands of miles.

This animated map sequence ends in a Eureka moment, for it now reveals that her destination city is Los Angeles. Up until that time, "the city" that they have talked about was never named, nor its location even hinted at, but now it is shown and immediately

James Bobin's *Dora and the Lost City of Gold* (2019) effectively uses many kinds of maps, including this colorful one showing Dora's air travel from her jungle home in Peru to Los Angeles/Hollywood (Paramount Players/Nickelodeon Movies/Walden Media/Media Rights Capital/Burr! Productions/Screen Queensland).

recognized. Actually, the destination's name on the map is "Hollywood," not only an iconic Southern California destination but also—in yet another subliminal bit of messaging—the locale where so many magical movies (like the one that the audience is watching) are made. This geographic connection broadens both the film's horizons and the audience's base. In a sense, it helps expand the definition of Latin America, or rather a Latinizing America. In real life, Dora's journey to the city would involve at least two flights, likely a change of planes (in Lima), and would consume a total of about twenty-four hours' traveling time. However, through the magic of cinema, this flight is depicted as non-stop and in daylight all the way—another reminder that film often compresses time, which in this case compresses geographical space as well, at least perceptually. Dora the indomitable explorer arrives at LAX as bubbly and as fresh as ever.

At the airport, the gregarious and enthusiastic Dora introduces herself to strangers, skips along energetically, and even slides down the side handrail of an escalator, the message being you can take the girl explorer out of the jungle, but not the urge to explore out of the girl. Relatives have awaited her arrival at LAX. When he sees Dora, cousin Diego (Jeff Wahlberg)—now a tall, slender and handsome teenager who has adjusted to the city—is clearly embarrassed by her innocent but very un-cool behavior. None too pleased, he sarcastically remarks that she still has the same boundless energy he remembered, as if that were a bad thing. Dora being Dora, which is to say hyper-enthusiastic and highly gregarious, is not fazed by Diego's uptight attitude. After all, she is simply heeding her mother's parting advice about adjusting to life in the city: "be yourself."

At the high school that Dora and Diego are now both attending, the cousins' relationship frays as he is socially self-conscious and she is such a carefree spirit who is criticized by other students. Dora feels overwhelmed. As she puts it, "I never felt lonely when I was by myself in the jungle," but now, surrounded by people, she feels a sense of loneliness. Ironically, it is Dora the Explorer from South America's tropical interior who must now "fit in" with what she calls "the Indigenous people" of the new locale she finds so daunting.

Dora has been home-schooled by her professor parents and is much smarter than most of the students. A case in point involves her interaction with Sammy (Madeleine Madden) a haughty, socially climbing girl who regards Dora as a threat. Even being class president is not enough for Sammy. In one scene, a teacher calls on the class to answer the question "who is Moby Dick and why is it important?" Several students, including the socially climbing Sammy, raise their hands. However, the teacher calls on the new student Dora. After introducing herself, Dora answers "...Moby Dick is a whale. The novel exemplifies the Western writer's nostalgic appropriation of colonized Indigenous cultures, which explains its reified status in American fiction today." This answer is not only spot on, but totally unexpected—especially for someone who does not have a Ph.D. (yet). Needless to say, Dora is now on Sammy's radar as a dangerous competitor.

Later, in the school's quad, Sammy is manning a table dedicated to "saving the rain forest." Seemingly confused by that theme, Dora innocently asks the question "which rain forest?" and then names five or six separate ones, including the *yungas*. Alas, Sammy has now again been out-done by Dora, who then proceeds to lecture Sammy about the actual causes of deforestation and how they might be rectified. This scene involves far more than two-high school girls squaring off. It amounts to a wake-up call by the filmmakers about outsiders (like Sammy) who think they know more about issues than local insiders (like Dora). In scene after scene, *Dora and the Lost City of Gold* reveals itself to be much more sophisticated, and far more complicated, than the typical film made for ages 6 through 16. Its PG rating suggests that everyone will understand it, and yet many of its themes and messages will keep adults on their toes. Surprisingly, it is one of the more complex films reviewed in this book. I have watched it four times and still spot something new every time.

A turning point in the film occurs on a class trip to the museum of natural history, which is in fact also a museum of cultural history as it features many archaeological exhibits. Tasked with finding the oldest item on exhibit, the larger group breaks down into sets of four students each. Through a process of elimination, Diego, Sammy, and a nerdy neurotic fellow student named Randy (Nicholas Coombe) are grouped with Dora. The soon-to-be opened Egyptian exhibit would be the best choice, but is not yet ready for tours. Dora persists in her efforts to see the off-limits Egyptian artifacts. A female docent standing near a sign warning no-admittance-beyond-this-point slyly informs Dora that access can be gained surreptitiously. That seemingly sympathetic docent leaves the door ajar, and Dora naturally enters the forbidden area where many artifacts are stored. Diego, Sammy, and Randy also find their way there, but Dora is detected by a surly security guard and hides in the same large crate that the other students have also jumped into to escape detection. Alas, those museum staffers are actually nefarious mercenaries who are searching for Parapata and trying to get Dora's map showing the last whereabouts of her parents. The mercenaries spray a chemical into the crate that renders the four students unconscious, then seal the crate, and fly it to the Amazon, where they awaken.

Thus begins the real South American exploration adventure in this film—not only finding Dora's parents, who are being sought by the mercenaries, but also finding Parapata itself. Recently, Dora had been increasingly concerned that she had not received the promised map updates from her parents, and now she knows why. They may be missing, but then again may have a reason for their cartographic stealth. After all, the very mapping that has helped Dora stay connected to her parents can be used to entrap them and compromise their search for the lost city. This revelation—that maps can be used for good and evil—is not only sobering but also rather nuanced; typically, maps in films made for children are used less multi-dimensionally—for example, to show how to get from point A to point B, to indicate territorial boundaries, or to indicate where lost or stolen treasure may be located. The film, in fact, is truly cartocentric (map-centered).

Escaping from their captors, who have enlisted the efforts of the devious animated fox Swiper, the four students now find themselves on the adventure of their lives. Their escape is assisted by a frenetic professor named Alejandro Gutiérrez (Eugenio Derbez) who tells them he is from the National San Marcos University in Lima. Alejandro informs them that he is actually working with Dora's parents—even shows them one of the parents' sketchbooks to prove it—and they thus have a mutual goal. With the four students in his SUV, Alejandro manages to outrun and outwit the mercenaries. Dora uses the sketchbook to help them navigate.

They soon reach the end of the road where the real jungle begins. Alejandro seems to know where he is going, but as they are about to enter the jungle he seems wary, and urges Dora to take the lead. He then confesses that he is terrified of the jungle, to which Dora responds: "The jungle is perfectly safe. Just don't touch anything, or breathe too deeply." For his part, Alejandro is reminiscent of the cowardly lion in *The Wizard of Oz*, whose lament "…if I only had the nerve" could also be Alejandro's mantra on this dangerous journey in search of a fabulous city. With that analogy drawn, it is easy to conclude that Dora is akin to Dorothy, and that the monkey Boots is the equivalent of Toto, a thought that has probably occurred to more than one viewer or critic.

As their quest continues, Dora and the others reach a campsite that had been occupied by her parents, but has clearly been ransacked. Dora notes that the parents must have escaped, for they left a clue in the form of a red circle painted on a tree trunk. Continuing onward into the jungle, Dora and the searchers find more of these circles. In the broader scope of this film, these symbols are yet another form of spatial positioning, that is, part of the elaborate and nearly continuous cartographic messaging that distinguishes *Dora and the Lost City of Gold* from most films discussed in this book.

On their quest, Dora relies on the visual contents of her parent's notebook for clues regarding how to find Parapata. One of these clues is a sketch of an old opera house that was part of the rubber boom. According to Dora's father Cole, one must pass this place on the way to the lost city. When they arrive, the opera house is a forlorn ruin, its steps leading into the jungle. Alejandro states that "The Europeans may have built it but the jungle has taken it back." As we have seen, an opera house in the jungle is a common trope in films about the Amazon. In *Fitzcarraldo*, Werner Herzog uses it very effectively to convey the opulence of the time and place, while Percy Fawcett and his son Jack encounter one in ruins as they too searched for a lost city, in their case *The Lost City of Z*.

In many stories about tropical colonization, including Latin America, a haunting decadence is part of the appeal. In this film, a ruined ornate building not only reveals hints of a grand historical past, and a present proof of that failure, but also serves as a springboard to move the story into the future. At this ruin, Dora's group meets a mysterious old Indigenous woman who speaks Quechua, which Dora understands perfectly. As they are conversing, the woman produces five small stone figurines, which symbolize the members of the group. Angrily, she then breaks these figurines, for she thinks the

In this scene from *Dora and the Lost City of Gold*, the namesake explorer (center) and her companions have reached the ruins of the rubber boom and are about to continue on toward the fabled city of Parapata. To create these scenes that blend reality and fantasy, director James Bobin used a combination of sets, animation, and outdoor locales (Paramount Players/Nickelodeon Movies/Walden Media/Media Rights Capital/Burr! Productions/Screen Queensland).

group members are treasure seekers aiming to plunder Parapata. When Dora tells the woman about their real, honorable purpose, the woman offers to take the group home (that is, out of the jungle). Dora offers to stay in order to find her parents. Now clearly supporting Dora, Diego also offers to stay. However, although Sammy and Randy initially go with the old woman, they relent and re-join Dora and Diego. Now inseparable, the foursome continues their adventure.

Given its primary viewing market (children and very young adults) this movie has its share of the requisite potty-humor. For example, as the group reaches a swampy area, they note that their boots make a farting sound when pulled out of the mud. Each of them enthusiastically chimes in, creating a veritable symphony of flatulence. Alas, the mud turns out to be quicksand and they all begin sinking in it. Dora—who seems to know everything—teaches them how to avoid being sucked under by lying on their backs and slowly back-stroking their way out of danger. All do this except Alejandro, who panics and goes under. The peril in this scene is palpable, again, not unlike the scarecrow being torn apart in *The Wizard of Oz*. This scene also has a happy ending. In their effort to save Alejandro, Randy discovers that the quicksand lies on a rocky shelf through which Alejandro's feet are dangling; thinking quickly, they scramble to that location and pull Alejandro downward and out of peril. Having nearly died, Alejandro confesses to being "a fraud." Although the four students consider this to be a case of

Alejandro being too hard on himself, one begins to wonder about his real motives as his foolhardy actions imperil the expedition from time to time.

Perhaps the funniest potty humor involves the haughty Sammy, who finally confesses that she has to "poop" after two days of holding it in, or rather holding out. Dora tells her that pooping is perfectly natural, and even digs a hole for Sammy's private use, adding that her poop will make good fertilizer. This has the effect of humanizing Sammy, and bringing her down off her perch. Seen in context of adventure films generally, it is a rare example of one that actually portrays an explorer as a defecator. Of the other films in this book, it is hinted at in *Aguirre, the Wrath of God* (where a small privy on a raft is occupied) and the scatological bantering by Esquivel in *Cabeza de Vaca*—though presumably all explorers defecate on a regular basis to keep their expeditions moving. In the Dora film, Sammy's now-encouraged bowel movement is thwarted as the group is besieged by a myriad of darts and arrows fired by unseen assailants, and run for their lives. These unseen ones may be the dreaded legendary guardians who protect Parapata from intruders.

Other hazards abound, including dangerous animals and menacing plants, but the most troubling of all are the ruthless mercenaries. In some scenes, Dora proves she can trip them up. For example, she constantly carries a yo-yo as any kid might, but is adept at using it much like a bola to ensnare the mercenaries long enough to permit her and the group to escape. One might say it is Dora's boleadora, but it only dissuades rather than cripples. In this good-natured film, lethal violence is not an option.

On their epic trek through the jungle, Dora and her fellow explorers encounter a surreal and startling sight, a veritable grove of the most unusual plants imaginable. Rendered in cartoon-like form, these tall plants have huge magenta-colored flowers atop very tall stems. These peculiar plants actually comprise a low-canopy forest of sorts as they tower above the explorers. The plants also possess hypnotic powers—not unlike the field of poppies in *The Wizard of Oz*. Dora tells everyone not to touch anything, but naturally the bumbling Alejandro does, and the plants seem to come to life. In a remarkable sequence, the spores from these plants render the explorers into animated characters, including the youthful Dora of television fame. This altered state of mind leads to closure, and greater self-awareness, the experience being reminiscent of Evan's psychedelic tripping in *Embrace of the Serpent*. The message here is that plants in the interior of South America have potent psychotropic powers.

As part of these cartoon-like sequences, the young Dora and Diego take a flying leap over a gaping chasm, an obstacle much like the one she fell into earlier in the film. Together, they reach the other side safely. This leap is a symbolic act, proving that if they trust each other, all will end well. More broadly it confirms that teamwork can pay dividends. The spell soon ends and they return to their teenage state, which is to say they are humans again rather than cartoon characters. On this journey, Diego is contemplative and confessional, telling Dora, "I never forgot about the jungle and [that] you were my best friend." This is a sincere sentiment that signals their reconciliation. Diego, though, is growing up in other ways, and it is becoming apparent that he and Sammy are falling in love. For her part, Dora seemingly has no time for such dalliances, being a girl of thought, action, and apparently unburdened by hormones.

The explorers' adventures continue, and the resulting thrills and spills abound. After considerable hiking along a narrow trail chiseled into a nearly vertical cliff, they enter a mountainous region studded with smoking volcanoes and tall peaks much like

In a flashback scene from *Dora and the Lost City of Gold* (2019), animated footage captures a daring move by the young Dora (left) and her cousin Diego. Through teamwork, they are able to leap a deep chasm as they search for the ancient city of Parapata (Paramount Players/Nickelodeon Movies/Walden Media/Media Rights Capital/Burr! Productions/Screen Queensland).

those in the Andes. A scene like this one emphasizes both their peril and their wonder. Just as Randy says he is finally beginning to think everyone will be safe, the trail gives way and the explorers tumble into an underground chamber festooned with Inca symbols. The most impressive artifact is a huge celestial map on the ceiling whose stars are glowing and sending beams to selected constellations on the floor. Randy states that it is a "puzzle" that they need to decipher. When questioned about how he knows this, he says that it is because he has seen several jungle movies in which the stars have to be moved into the correct position to open doors. Of course, much the same kind of devices can be experienced in video games as well. Always one step ahead, literally and figuratively, Dora notes that the stars are already in the correct position, because they are properly depicting the night sky in the southern hemisphere.

In scenes that bring to mind the film *Indiana Jones and the Kingdom of the Crystal Skull* and others in that franchise, the group figures out how to gain access to the lost city by selecting the right doorways to enter, and the correct escape routes to follow, when trouble ensues. Much like a theme-park adventure ride, one takes them to safety down a series of chutes and drops them into a river that happens to be adjacent to the campsite of Dora's parents, who are overjoyed and surprised to see them. When Dora shows them the notebook, they inform her that it had been stolen—apparently by Alejandro, who now arrives to commandeer the expedition as it has reached the outskirts of Parapata.

The plot picks up even more momentum at this point. With help from Boots, they manage to again escape and, through a series of ingenious acts, find the lost city.

Parapata is depicted magically on screen as nestled in a verdant valley surrounded by mountains and basking in the rays of the sun. Upon entering the city, they do not find any treasure, and begin speculating about where it has gone, or rather who may have stolen it. In a remarkable post-colonialist inspired scene, Diego speculates that it may have been looted "by Spanish conquistadores," while Randy adds, "or the British, or the French," and Sammy concludes, "or the Americans and the United Fruit Company"—a sweeping, fill-in-the-blanks indictment of colonial appropriation and its appropriators.

This film has some powerful and subtle messaging about the changing character of cinematic explorers. Significantly, whereas Harry Steele ingeniously used a form of triangulation involving a mirror and his flashlight to locate the golden disk in *Secret of the Incas*, in *Dora and the Lost City of Gold* it takes the combined efforts of its namesake and her fellow explorers to decipher where the treasure will be. In one spectacular scene, they too use light bouncing off mirrors, but the message here is that it takes a team rather than an individual to succeed. The take-away here is that the days of rugged individualism are over.

In the film's climactic scenes, Dora and her group find the treasure, apparently unmolested but guarded by a large statue of a golden monkey. It is worth contextualizing this statue as it seems out of place in a film about the part of South America that Dora and her team are exploring. Statues of monkeys have been found in Asia, notably China (Taoist) and Japan, and also figure in the Hindu religion as the deity Hanuman. In the New World, however, they appear to be confined to Central America, particularly Maya culture in the Yucatán and also in Honduras, where they are associated with the mythical Ciudad Blanca, or White City, said to be the site of fabulous treasures. Aviator Charles Lindbergh is said to have flown over it in the 1920s, and expeditions have been mounted in search of it, most notably one in 1939 by the imaginative Theodore Morde (1911–1954). Most archeologists doubt the existence of this city, and the artifactual evidence supposedly found by Morde is widely regarded as spurious. In 2017, Douglas Preston's best-selling book *The Lost City of the Monkey God: A True Story* popularized this controversial subject.[3] For their part, the screenwriters for Dora's adventure are less interested in fact than fancy, and depict her exploring far south of the Isthmo-Colombian area normally associated with the monkey god. In this regard, *Dora and the Lost City of Gold* provides an example of how popular culture cinema can magically expand the geographical distribution of artifacts, in this case from the far northwestern portion of South America to the central Amazon basin of Peru, a distance of more than 800 miles (ca. 1200 km). Regardless, Dora and her fellow explorers discover the golden monkey statue looming, or rather lording, over a majestic cache of golden objects and gemstones, including a huge jaw-dropping emerald that Sammy observes is "the size of a basketball."

As if on cue, the nefarious Alejandro again arrives and seizes control; however, his greed has put him in danger as he is standing on stones that begin to fall into a fiery pit. Although true-to-form Swiper has swiped the golden statue and departed, Boots quickly retrieves it. There is poetic justice in an animated monkey reclaiming a statue of a regal monkey, but the action comes so fast and furious that the audience is likely to miss it. By this time, the guardians of Parapata have arrived to set things right. They are led by the old Inca woman, who is magically transformed into the stunningly beautiful and powerful Indigenous princess Kawillaka. Played by the statuesque German-born American actress/activist Q'orianka Kilcher (who is also part Peruvian), Kawillaka is a cinematic show-stopper and a take-no-prisoners cosmic law enforcer. Upon her command, the guardians of Parapata vanquish the mercenaries and permit Dora and her group, including her parents, to come out unscathed.

In her final act at the lost city, Dora returns the golden monkey statue to its original place, thus playing a role in restoring the cosmic order. Unlike the lost city in *Indiana Jones and the Kingdom of the Crystal Skull*, Parapata does not self-destruct, but rather is restored to its original form. Of course, this now-found lost city looks like the images in the sketchbook, confirming that Dora's parents were right. This film's plot may resonate as yet another example of non–Indigenous saviors helping out Indigenous peoples by rescuing their culture; however, the fact that the Indigenous Guardians of Parapata played a major role is noteworthy.

Moreover, the fluently Quechua-speaking Dora has now pretty much adopted the persona as an insider, if not an Indigene herself. In a sense, the entire quest has not only validated Dora's credentials as a real explorer, but also one who fully respects and embraces the culture of the place that has been discovered. For her part, the actress Isabela Moner, who plays the teenage Dora, claimed in an interview in *Forbes* that Dora "… doesn't have a defined ethnicity." Some might find this surprising given that her character's Latina identity is made clear throughout the film, from her introductions ("Hola!" to "Yo soy Dora!") to the conclusion where she and her parents speak fluent Spanish. However, it is possible that Moner was referring to Dora's transcultural quality, which is to say her character's adaptability and appreciation of Andean Indian culture. For her part, Moner learned some lines in what she calls an "Indigenous Peruvian language" to play the part so convincingly.[4] Subsequently, she changed her name from Moner to Merced.

In *Dora and the Lost City of Gold* (2019), the teenage namesake explorer (Isabela Moner) follows her mother's credo—"Treasure hunting bad, exploring good"—and returns the statue of a golden monkey to its rightful place in the ancient city of Parapata. Intended for young audiences, this film contains some surprisingly sophisticated, even subversive, messages about exploration and discovery (Paramount Players/Nickelodeon Movies/Walden Media/Media Rights Capital/Burr! Productions/Screen Queensland).

The film closes with Dora's parents praising her. Elena says, "Tú eres la mejor explo-radora" (You are the best explorer) while Cole adds, "La mejor de todo el mundo" (the best in all the world). Dora's parents now tell her that they are ready to continue explor-ing the jungle with her by their side, for she has now proven herself. However, Dora responds that she wants to go back to the city, and especially high school. As she puts it, "I know the jungle pretty well ... but need more time to study that culture and its indigenous people." This rather unexpected ending brilliantly turns exploration upside down as it involves the explorer of the unknown wilderness now endeavoring to under-stand the seemingly known, but in reality very mystifying, modern metropolitan world. This mirrors a theme that I have explored in this non-fiction book and in my own fic-tion writing, namely that the most exciting kind of exploration now involves new fron-tiers that look inward rather than outward. In that sense, it is noteworthy that a movie created primarily for young audiences turns out to be the movie that can also be recom-mended for adults interested in how the theme of exploration-in-new-directions plays out cinematically.

Dora and the Lost City of Gold got generally good reviews, though some dissented. Writing in *National Post*, Angelo Muredda claimed, "Dora and the Lost City of Gold makes for a charmless experience despite all its colour and cheer." Muredda character-ized it as "...a performatively liberal take on the character's adventures that's out of sync with its colonial story...."[5] That criticism may be valid to a point, but then again the art of storytelling often involves use of recognizable tropes that are culturally embedded and thus bound to offend someone. This is especially true in this era of "woke" senti-ments when even well-meaning messages boomerang.

To most viewers, Dora's charm does shine through in this film. In a positive review, Ryan Bordow observed that "'Dora and the Lost City of Gold' is better than it has any right to be," adding that it is surprisingly funny in places and lampoons itself by empha-sizing how ridiculous Dora's behavior is in a realistic, rather than cartoon, setting.[6] An example of this film's subversiveness was hinted at earlier when the character Randy mentions the plot devices used in "jungle films"—a subtle take on just how shop-worn many geographic exploration adventure movies have become. It is also an indication of how self-confident this film is—even daring to challenge its own genre by parodying it. This self-confidence helps make *Dora and the Lost City of Gold* so irreverent—and so relevant.

All the more remarkable is that most of the film's production took place in the Gold Coast area of Queensland, Australia. More to the point, the Village Roadshow's large Sound Stage No. 9 was used for many of the jungle scenes as well as the Inca temple. Some filming was done in the vicinity of Tarapoto, Peru, which gives the film some cachet as Latin American. Doubly ironic is that director James Bobin selected the Aus-tralian Gold Coast locale not only because of its ability to deliver convincing South American jungle scenes but also because the area's Southern California vibe lent authen-ticity to the high school scenes. In retrospect, the cartoon-like mapped flight of Dora's plane traveling from South America to Hollywood perfectly captured Bobin's directo-rial sleight of hand, for he has the audience believing it is connecting two real filming locales. That should serve as a reminder that films are rarely shot where they supposedly take place, but if carefully done can convince the audience otherwise.

Conclusion

Reflections on the Changing Significance of Exploration-Discovery Films

The nineteen films covered in detail in this book, and the other supporting films as well, involve many genres—for example, adventure, horror, biography, romance, crime, war, and science-fiction. Normally, a film is characterized by its genre, but that type of classification may not do it justice. More typically, films tend to combine genres, at least to a point. Thus, a film like *Green Mansions* is said to represent a fusion of romance and adventure. Some films are even more complex. For example, *Walker* involves not only biography but also several other genres such as history, war, and adventure. As is clear from the films reviewed, each involves its own creative way of storytelling that may borrow freely from preconceived notions of genre, but may break new ground and move into unnamed territory.

There is growing ambivalence about genres. On the one hand, they are convenient shorthand and may help contextualize a film. On the other, emphasizing genres involves of a form of typecasting that may cloud, rather than shed light on, any particular film. As Andrew McGregor Olney observed, "…film genres are structured more around ideals than around features of film … and are [a] set of shifting, fuzzy, and highly contextualized psychological categories."[1] Implicit in Olney's argument is that filmgoers (the audience) rather than elite film critics should play a role in determining these ever changing categorizations. Moving away from genre categories can be a refreshing and even productive way to approach cinema—though it involves more work on the part of the viewer, and reviewer, to figure out the nature of a film for themselves.

That said, it is apparent that I may have inadvertently created a new genre under the rubric "exploration-discovery film." Perhaps the term "metagenre," as used by M. Carter, is more apt.[2] At any rate, a number of the films reviewed herein transcend the traditional "Age of Discovery" category that typically has a European origin and a defined time period. In that regard, exploration-discovery films can be set in any time(s) and any place(s). What makes these films distinctive is their structure and focus. The five unifying aspects of such exploration-discovery films is that they:

1. involve a process by which their protagonists *penetrate space and/or time*, the trajectory typically moving spatially from outside to inside (i.e., exterior to interior) or vice versa—and back and forth in time—regardless of whether that space is geographical or psychological, and the time is chronologically measured or less precisely perceptual. Examples include Jaguar Paw's race against time (*Apocalypto*), Dora's quest for the Lost City, and Walker's invasion of Mexico and Central America;

    2. are largely concerned with the *encounter* that occurs when the explorer discovers something such as an object, place, tribe, condition, etc. Examples here include Humboldt and Bonpland encountering new flora and fauna in *Aire Libre*; archaeologists locating lost artifacts in *Secret of the Incas*; or searchers finding relatives' remains in the Atacama Desert in *Nostalgia for the Light*;

    3. involve the explorer-discover being personally impacted or even transformed by the experience, as opposed to being a character who remains the same throughout the story. Examples of this kind of transformation include a finally victorious Fitzcarraldo and a Dora the Explorer who now realizes that exploration involves understanding her own teenage subculture. The transformation may occur almost unnoticed (as an Aguirre or Walker who slowly slips into madness or delusion) or be regarded as an epiphany (for example, in *Green Fire* when Rian realizes that Catherine is more important than emeralds, or when Indiana Jones realizes that the ancient culture he has been tracking was pursuing the same knowledge he seeks);

    4. depend on *allegories* that can be literal and/or symbolic and which not only enhance the story but also give it a chronological and/or spatial texture. For example, in *Green Fire*, emeralds signify temptation and seduction; in *Green Mansions*, birds and their distinctive calls signify both nature and the surreal character Rima; and sexual relationships in films such as *The Other Conquest* and *Walker* may not only signify intercourse between individuals, or even different cultures, but also the power they wield over each other.

    5. are highly *inter-textual*, that is, dependent on varied types of texts such as written narratives and images. These can include historical written and graphic documents as primary sources, their later shaping into screenplays, and even other films that serve as inspiration. Maps, in particular, are a frequent textual device encountered, and are so commonly associated with exploration-discovery that their absence in some films may be noteworthy as well. Moreover, their allegorical use (as in 4, above) attests to their versatility, as in *Fitzcarraldo* and *Dora and the Lost City of Gold*.

All of the films reviewed in this book meet the criteria outlined above, and many more films await deeper analysis. Epitomizing them is Dennis Hopper's enigmatic 1971 rough-cut gem titled *The Last Movie*.[3] It is one of the more prescient Latin American exploration-discovery films, though it seemed to defy categorization. It centers on what occurs when an American Western film project being shot in Chinchero, Peru, but pretending to be Lama, New Mexico, finishes up shooting and goes home to Hollywood. They have left the Indigenous people involved in the shooting to face a new reality: what to do next? Oddly, they begin re-enacting the filming process themselves, creating faux cameras, etc., and disturbingly reenacting the same kind of violence in the film—only for real. One of the actors (Hopper) stays on to document the town's devolution into the Wild West and has a soul-searching epiphany in the process.

    Although *The Last Movie* received some good initial reviews, harsher critics piled on. Completely missing the film's point, critic Roger Ebert called it "a wasteland of cinematic wreckage."[4] This, coupled with its limited release, relegated it to oblivion. The response was so troubling to Hopper that he went into virtual exile for a decade, slowly emerging as people began to see the genius in this film. Hopper later began sharing *The Last Movie* in private showings, and it is now regarded as a cult classic. Part of this film's problem is that it defied convention and fit into no recognizable genre. Many highly creative but easily dismissed films fit into the exploration-discovery category, and await such reconsideration.

When deconstructed, even films that seem to fit perfectly into traditional genres may fit better in the exploration-discovery category Among these is Paul Mazursky's wonderfully watchable 1988 comedy *Moon Over Parador*,[5] which was filmed in Brazil and based on the 1939 movie *Caviar for His Excellency*. Before that, it had begun life as a short story. In Mazursky's version, an American actor (Richard Dreyfuss) reluctantly finds himself serving in the real role of dictator in a fictional Latin American country for a year. It turns out to be the role of his life, and an eye-opening experience in Latin American politics. However, his performance was so true to life that when he returns to New York, his friends do not believe that it was him playing the dictator. Mazursky's film is ultimately about exploration-discovery, in particular self-discovery—as well as a subversive exposé of filmmaking itself. This film also provided Mazursky the opportunity to skewer a right-wing dictator and lambaste the CIA's adventurism in the region, much as Cox did with *Walker*. Mazursky hoped to pull off a surprise box office smash, similar to what Woody Allen did with his 1971 spoof about a fictional Latin American nation's politics cleverly titled *Bananas*.[6] However, times had changed, and Mazursky's otherwise brilliant *Moon Over Parador* only recouped about half of the production costs. Put another way, it lost about nine million dollars.

In reflecting on the films in this book, I have sidestepped the issue of what makes a film successful. True, I occasionally mention how they did at the box office, but whether or not they were successful depended on many factors. Critics often have the last say, but may miss important points. Ultimately, the only person who can make that determination is the filmmaker. In other words, a box office failure may be successful in achieving the goals of a filmmaker—to tell a story a certain way—whether or not the public literally "buys" it. Ditto for critics, who may savage a film and leave a director such as Dennis Hopper wondering what happened, and why.

Much the same thing happened with *Walker*, which fulfilled Alex Cox's vision of creating a surreal interpretation of 1980s American adventurism in Nicaragua but failed on two counts. It not only faltered during final production, but also faced an unrelenting critics' firing squad when released. For the record, Cox claims that he was "blacklisted" by Hollywood—not in the traditional political sense but rather in the form of gangster-like harassment by financier company executives who unfairly questioned the safety of his filming techniques. In the long run, however, those who counted most were the critics, who felt betrayed by *Walker*'s design and execution; they wanted more of the same they had come to expect from Cox, and he disappointed them. There is little doubt that Cox's daring and innovativeness cost him dearly in Hollywood. For his part, Cox has claimed that *Walker* is his best film made for the big studios—and this reviewer completely agrees.[7]

The films reviewed in this book were based on ideas that were funded, came to fruition, and then faced fates running the gamut from commercial success to oblivion. In more recent times, those who advise would-be filmmakers on the most successful genres to pursue use box office data to chart the trajectory of movie preferences. In the ten-year period ending about 2017 (and hence pre-pandemic) the film industry witnessed a decline in those based on romance, history, and biography. On the other hand, horror and sci-fi were increasing in popularity.[8] Whereas that information was provided for would-be writers to more accurately gauge their chances of success, it does not account for how a talented and inspired filmmaker can defy the odds. Robert Zemeckis's 1994 smash hit *Forrest Gump* comes to mind. More typically, though, innovative films do not perform well at the box office, but may be treated more kindly as time passes. Going from art-house status to cult status is a process that can take decades.

In retrospect, exploration-discovery films have a few things in common with the "ethnographic cinema" sought by Jean Rouch, whose biographer, Paul Henley, notes that "…his life project can be conceived as one long and constantly experimental *Aventure*, one that involved the intrepid exploration not only of the exterior world … but also of the recesses of the imaginary, an evocation of the surreal as made manifest in the real."[9] As Henley notes "aventure" is the French word for adventure, but it means far more than its equivalent in English—more poetic in nature and fluid in meaning. It is worth noting that *aventura* means more in Spanish as well, including risk and vicissitude.

Latin America is a natural locale for such stories. On the one hand, it not only beckons some optimistically, but also includes some of the darkest terrain and darkest history imaginable, where utopian dreams can turn into nightmares: Guyana was the locale where the infamous "Jonestown Massacre"—the murder-suicide of over 900 people—took place in 1978. To some outsiders, even normal politics in Latin America is off-putting, given its long and continuing history of political oppression and abuse. In reality, however, political instability personifies the human condition itself; certainly, the Africa that filmmaker Rouch loved also had its challenges. In such places, a struggle between good and evil, individual and society, past and future can result in the most poignant story telling, and filmmaking. Films such as *The Other Conquest*; *Aguirre, the Wrath of God*; *The Mission*; and *Nostalgia for the Light* epitomize this.

The historical and ongoing impact of colonization is one of the enduring themes in Latin American films. A finding hinted at earlier in this book is worth restating. When colonization by Spain ended ca. 1820, it was replaced by a system of outside capital investment that promised to free the individual nations but ultimately wound up being perceived as equally oppressive. In this regard, the political left is now portrayed as the liberator, and the political right the equivalent of the colonial oppressors. In other words, capitalism is now the despised "ism" that replaces colonialism as the villain. This is ironic, because in much of early-to-mid twentieth century, capitalism on film—and in much public discourse—was seen as the engine that would drive away poverty, increase upward mobility, and do away with oppression. Che Guevara threw a monkey wrench in that, although the film *The Motorcycle Diaries* shies away from what his posthumous book of the same name made very explicit: lofty idealism about a cause often leads to bloodshed. As should be clear by now, in making that page-to-screen transition, stories are almost invariably transformed to some extent, sometimes radically by filmmakers hoping to shape popular perceptions.

As I began writing this book, I hoped that it would provide readers with ways of understanding Latin America in a new light, that of place-oriented storytelling making the transition from the page to the screen. That transition is interesting in itself, but the final product (the feature film version) is frequently more engaging than the original book, which takes much more time to get through. This may explain why far fewer people read books than watch movies. Those films have a tremendous impact on perceptions, and may be as close as anyone normally gets to understanding what happened and what the locale looked like. It is humbling to realize that the films covered in this book have shaped far more people's views of Latin America than firsthand experiences ever have, or ever will.

An important film deliberately NOT covered in this book is one I have been saving for last as one I would like readers to see for themselves from start to finish without having been walked through it first. That film is the 2017 Australian gem titled *Jungle*.[10] A dramatization of harrowing events experienced by the Israeli explorer Yossi Ghinsberg in the Amazonian portion of Bolivia in 1981, it neatly brings together virtually every theme and trope discussed in this book. If I had to recommend only one easily accessible and riveting depiction of Latin American exploration-discovery on film, it would be *Jungle*, which features truly stunning cinematography and superb acting. One key element to look for in this film involves the map that sets this jungle quest into motion. Not to be missed on the DVD version of *Jungle* is the bonus feature about the making of this film, a behind-the-scenes look at how the magic of filmmaking works. Starring as explorer Ghinsberg, Daniel Radcliffe gives what may be the finest performance of his career. After watching this film with friends, one of them exclaimed, "Wow! Harry Potter has sure grown up!"

Geographically speaking, the films covered in this book may seem to jump all over the map(s) of Latin America, but there is a pattern. As readers may have gathered by now, regionalism *within* Latin America is evident in the films about its exploration-discovery. Along with the literary works that inspired most of them, the films discussed in detail confirm that some portions of Latin America are more alluring than others to filmmakers. This partly relates to how photogenic those locales might be, but mostly how important and dramatic their historical events were.

I shall begin at the far northern reaches of New Spain—today's American Southwest—where El Dorado's fabled counterparts of Cíbola and Quivira were rumored to

Based on a true story, Greg McLean's tersely-titled film *Jungle* (2017) epitomizes the exploration-discovery genre. The film, set in modern times, features a team of four explorers—left to right, Karl Ruprechter (Thomas Kretschmann); Marcus Stamm (Joel Jackson); Yossi Ghinsberg (Daniel Radcliffe); and Kevin Gale (Alex Russell)—that rely on a hand-drawn map to find a lost tribe in the Amazonian wilderness of Bolivia (Babber Films/Cutting Edge Group/Screen Australia/Screen Queensland).

exist, as related in the tall tales told by the members of the expedition in *Cabeza de Vaca*. Immediately to the south, northern Mexico's mountainous and semi-arid interior are commonly associated risk-taking ventures as depicted in films such as *The Treasure of the Sierra Madre* and *The Wild Bunch*. Today, the drug trade has turned the desert north into the living *Hell*[11] depicted by Mexican director Luis Estrada. After his difficulties with the film *Walker*, Alex Cox turned his attention northward and made the wonderful, contraband-centered film *El Patrullero* (The Highway Patrolman) mentioned earlier—a modern-day exploration-discovery saga (or sorts) set and filmed in Mexico's desert states of Coahuila and Durango. At the conclusion of Roberto Rodriguez's delightfully bizarre film *From Dusk till Dawn*[12] the desert U.S.-Mexican border is home to the wild night-spot "Titty-Twister" which, it turns out, had been built atop the site of an ancient Aztec ruin! That displacement may seem absurd—the Aztec center of power was far to the south—but it keeps alive the popular Mexican-American legend that the Southwest was originally Aztlán, the birthplace of the Aztec empire.

To the south of this northern frontier of present-day Mexico, the surprisingly large ancient city of Tenochtitlan awed the Spaniards and provided the setting for numerous films, including *Captain from Castile* and *The Other Conquest*. Continuing southward, the Mayan region located in extreme southern Mexico lured filmmaker Mel Gibson, whose film *Apocalypto* showcased Pre-Columbian peoples and their rural-urban landscapes—dramatized, of course, for an intense viewing experience. There is something irresistible about the highly photogenic and highly developed city-building Mayans, as today their temples loom out of the jungle. They appear in film genres from traditional exploration to horror/suspense. Among the latter is a thriller titled *The Ruins*.[13] In that map-driven film, an ancient Mayan temple lures modern-day vacationers-as-explorers seeking some authentic archaeological ruins into an out of the way locale. They are warned by locals to stay away from those ruins, but disregard the advice. Their horrifying experiences reprise the premise in *Apocalypto* that Mayan temples have their darker side.

In Carter Smith's thriller *The Ruins* (2008), a group of adventurous American college students on spring break has used a hand-drawn map to find an alternative to popular tourist sites—an ancient, vine-covered Mayan temple. Convincing in appearance for most movie watchers, this stylized Central American temple was constructed in Queensland, Australia, where much of the film was shot (Spyglass Entertainment/Red House Productions).

Clustered in various parts of Latin America, the ruins of advanced cultures are compelling and irresistible subjects for filmmakers. Most are from well-known sites, but in films such as *Dora and the Lost City of Gold* and *Indiana Jones and the Kingdom of the Crystal Skull*, we witness them discovered anew. These are sought in a mysterious region lying east of the Inca realm, and it lures the imagination today much as it did the earliest explorers in search of ancient civilizations in South America. The mythical lost city itself may be of Inca origin, as in *El DORADO: Temple of the Sun*,[14] a televised action/fantasy film shown in 2010 and released on DVD shortly thereafter. That film is built on a fascinating supply-and-demand premise, namely that the treasure really does exit—and is found—but that a nefarious, internationally-based group of evil doers must deliberately destroy it in order to keep current gold prices high. Regardless of plausible or implausible plot devices, the persistence of such mythical cities, both in literature and film, is truly remarkable. On the written page it has endured for five centuries and for over half a century in films ranging from *Aguirre, the Wrath of God* to *Dora and the Lost City of Gold*.

In terms of filmmakers' own personal geographic preferences, cinema's spatial connections to its own past run deep. The Andean-to-Amazonia part of Latin America mentioned immediately above is not only where the Spielberg/Lucas character Indiana Jones got his start as Harry Steele in *Secret of the Incas* (1954), but also where Werner Herzog immortalized the Andean connection to Amazonia in *Aguirre, the Wrath of God* (1972). Both films were seminal, but their influences went in two directions. Whereas *Secret of the Incas* had a powerful effect on popular filmmaking for the masses, Herzog's *Aguirre, the Wrath of God* literally blazed a path that led to art-house showings that in turn inspired future generations of filmmakers seeking to tell deeper stories about the consequences of Amazonian exploration-discovery.

That these cities are not fixed geographically is evident in a recent (2022) satirical comedy film predictably-named *The Lost City*.[15] Interestingly, its lead character (Sandra Bullock) is a writer of romance/adventure novels. Although it is set on an island in the Atlantic rather than in Latin America per se, its tropes of jungle exploration and its on-site filming in the Dominican Republic owe a debt to the films covered in this book. So, too, does its back-story of having been reached by Spanish explorers who named it Isla Hundida (Sunken Island). Geographically speaking, *The Lost City* suggests that the Latin American exploration-discovery film has a remarkably broad reach. Stylistically speaking, this story self-consciously uses theme of exploration-discovery as a bridge between literature and film. Its premise is that a mythical lost place becomes found—and hence becomes real as the story writer arrives there. In a sense, the film itself "proves" the veracity of the story, though it is fictional. Of course, in Latin America itself, the term "mythical" for these cities may be in for some revision: As recent archaeological investigations are confirming, ancient urbanization of the kind sought by Percy Fawcett in *The Lost City of Z* might have existed here long before the arrival of Europeans. In this sense, filmmakers may be helping the public prepare for surprising archaeological discoveries that many authorities once regarded as fictional delusions.

Without a doubt, though, the perennial favorite natural region for filmmakers is South America's vast and mysterious Amazon basin. We tend to associate this region with nature at its wildest and most dangerous—and with "primitive" or "lost" Indian tribes as well—and films depict that in abundance. As hinted at above, part of its appeal is the ancient myth of El Dorado, but later failed enterprises like the more recent rubber extraction also figure in the attraction. Nature itself is the star in most films set in the Amazon. As if this heavily forested region were not claustrophobia-inducing enough, filmmakers sometimes add filters to make it seem even gloomier. It is the perfect locale for moody, thought-provoking films such as *Embrace of the Serpent*. Films set here confirm our culture's deep ambivalence about this vast region, which hides untold troves of treasure yet is fraught with both natural and cultural terrors such as deadly animals and fiercely resistant Indian tribes.

Another popular geographic location in South America, at least in terms of cinematic depictions, is the part of the continent that lies south of the Caribbean and extends inland for several hundred miles. It, too, witnessed some the earlier searches for El Dorado and later adventure journeys also involving considerable fantasy. Like the Amazonian region, it is associated with danger, but also with reward. This region explored by Humboldt and Bonpland in about 1800 (*Aire Libre*) and a century later by the fictional Abel (*Green Mansions*), is a natural wonderland. In addition to fantastic experiences such as those depicted in *The Lost World*, this part of South America is still associated with quick riches and dangerous missions. In the 2017 action film *American Made*,[16] a clueless pilot (Tom Cruise) looking for adventure gets more than he bargained for by unknowingly flying out a fortune in Colombian drugs. How quickly this very good box-office hit fell off the critics' radar is still something of a mystery.

Farther to the south, the land-locked nation of Bolivia has served as the locale for some modern, edgy political satires that put their protagonists in the role of explorer-discoverers. In *American Visa* (2005),[17] a Bolivian professor seeks a new life in the U.S., traveling to La Paz in order to reach the U.S. Embassy. After jumping through hoops and shelling out cash, he discovers that the American staff there is totally corrupt. After this series of disappointments involving considerable travel, he concludes that the American Dream is a lie, and that he should stay in Bolivia. Similarly, the film *Our Brand Is Crisis* (2015)[18] finds an American political consultant advising a conservative political candidate's campaign in La Paz—only to discover that American operatives have rigged things in his favor. Totally disillusioned, she could return to the U.S., but decides to remain and join forces with those who hope to overthrow the government that she just helped gain power. In these films set in modern times, the theme of exploration-discovery results in epiphanies. Significantly, both favor Indigenous/leftist power over imported (American) manipulation—a theme evident in the rise of power by Bolivia's president Evo Morales—the first Indigenous leader in Bolivia to hold that title.

Toward the southern end of this continent, the Argentine Pampa symbolizes liberation, as depicted in *The Motorcycle Diaries* and, in its "western" guise, in *Way of a Gaucho*.[19] To Argentines, and outsiders as well, the vast, semi-arid expanses of Patagonia also play a role in adventures. In the 2005 film *Intimate Stories*[20] three hopeful individuals traverse geographical space in order to achieve their dreams. This film was originally called *Historias Minimas* (Minimal Stories) in that their sagas are concise, but poignant, much like interwoven short stories. The depiction of Patagonia's landscapes in this film, from sweeping pan shots to close-up details, is remarkable. Perfectly captured on film, the austere beauty of Patagonia, and the almost constantly blowing winds there, showcase these individuals' personal exploration-discovery stories.

On the Pacific side of the continent, readers will recall that Chile's Atacama Desert has also been used cinematically to depict characters involved in deeply personal, sometimes desperate, searches. In addition to films such as *Nostalgia for the Light* and *The 33*, fictionalized stories set here await transformation into screenplays. Some of these are classic detective novels, and they are among the more interesting explorer-discoverer prospects for filmmakers.[21] A project currently under consideration by a Hollywood producer is my 2019 novel titled *The Enchantress of Atacama*. In it, the youthful Mexican-American geographer/detective Thomas Williams Mendoza experiences firsthand the varied meanings of exploration-discovery as he interacts with the story's remarkable *protagonista* Carmen Segura.[22] In this story set in 1971, a poem titled "Explorers" takes the traditional exploration in Kipling's poem and re-shapes it into a parable about deeper exploration into interpersonal space. Recently, this novel received Next Generation Indie Books awards in two categories ("Regional Fiction" and "Suspense"), which is akin to being nominated in the Academy Awards process—not an Oscar, but good publicity nevertheless. At this point, how this Atacama noir novel might be reinterpreted by screenwriters, and then filmed without compromising its literary quality, is my biggest concern.[23] Nevertheless, in its favor are its colorful multi-ethnic characters, its storied geographical setting in the driest place on earth, and its time period fraught with abuses of political power.

A major point that needs re-stating here pertains to geography itself, or rather the depiction of it in internationally distributed exploration-discovery films. When we compare films *set* in Latin America with those that were actually *filmed* there, a far greater number were actually shot elsewhere. True, some classics such as *Aguirre, the Wrath of God* and *Fitzcarraldo* were filmed on location, but many others such as *Indiana Jones and Kingdom of the Crystal Skull* and *Dora and the Lost City of Gold* were largely filmed elsewhere. Surprisingly, the lush forests and hilly topography of Queensland, Australia, are far more commonly seen in films about the Amazon than is the real Amazon itself—a reminder that many factors such as labor costs, tax breaks, and political climate enter into these decisions. However, as made clear in this book, Latin American filmmakers who created works such as *Cabeza de Vaca*; *The Other Conquest*; *Zama*; and *Aire Libre* literally shot on location. As a geographer, I have an eye for landscape and can often tell the difference, but the general film-going public is usually blissfully unaware of subtle aspects such as topography, vegetation, soil color, atmospheric conditions, and regional architecture.

Regarding traditional exploration-discovery movies set in Latin America, readers may have gathered that their focus appears to be shifting away from the patently geographical to other themes such as political oppression, environmental protection, and social justice. Truth is, modern exploration-discovery is going deeper into the human mind and spirit than ever before. This may be lamented by some, but is actually an exciting prospect. In the meantime, both types of exploration-discovery sagas—outwardly geographical and inwardly psychological—are not simply coexisting but also helping to sustain each other. As this book suggests, the future of cinematic exploration-discovery films is bright, given their breadth of subject matter.

Cultural/tribal representation and social justice are likely to be big determinants in what will be filmed in the future. In traditional exploration there were winners and losers, and we are unable to go back and change that scorecard. However, one way that reconciliation may begin is by encouraging the telling of geographical exploration-discovery stories more fairly and compassionately. Graciously letting the losers tell their side of the story has proved to be a wise decision resulting in some memorable filmmaking. After all, they managed to survive some horrendous mistreatment and have many compelling stories to tell about it. This is evident in the more recent films about Indigenous-European contact in Latin America. Of these, *Embrace of the Serpent* stands head and shoulders above the rest. Still, some critics are not satisfied with filmmaker's stances, claiming that their films are not de-colonized enough. These critics may attempt to coach or even shame filmmakers into offering more acceptable points of view. That is their prerogative, of course. However, because I value filmmakers' freedom of speech and artistic creativity above all else, I prefer to steer clear of such well-meaning interference.

That said, some imbalances in films about the exploration-discovery of Latin America are worth noting here. The first thing that jumps out is a protagonist who functions as a White Savior. In his book *The White Savior Film: Content, Critic, and Consumption*,[24] historian Matthew W. Hughey focuses on North America and deeply explores films in which a lead character saves peoples of color consigned to slavery and second-class status. However, in the case of Latin America much the same model holds up in the form of a foreigner who arrives to save either the Indigenous peoples or their cultural heritage. Glaring examples include Harry Steele in *Secret of the Incas* but even Theo in *Embrace of the Serpent* embodies some of it. Here, too, the filmmakers are regarded as well-meaning but patronizing, for their films place Indians in a subservient position of being rescued. In a sense, the White Savior seems to be predicated on considerable guilt for past actions by those very foreigners, and in particular their forbearers who may have been far less sensitive. In films like *Green Fire*; *Secret of the Incas*; and *The Emerald Forest,* the audience is treated to lead characters experiencing socially-conscious epiphanies, in effect the selfish becoming selfless, or nearly so—but always increasing their status in the process.

This brings me to a second observation about lead characters. The protagonists in the films interpreted in this book are rarely female, the exceptions being Terri Flores in *Anaconda* and the eponymous *Dora and the Lost City of Gold*. However, even in a few other older films such as *Secret of the Incas* and *Green Fire*, women characters such as Elena Antonescu and Catherine Knowland *do* play determined and intelligent roles. In some ways, their near absence as leaders of expeditions, or their lack of agency when they are present, simply reflects the fact that most real exploration-discovery was in the hands of those most empowered, and hence more active, in these endeavors: men, who tended to write about—and were widely recognized for—their exploits.

That this is changing is evident in the recent (2021) film *Jungle Cruise*,[25] which reveals another trend evident in this book, and which should be made even more explicit—namely that earlier films influence later ones. In this regard, the film *Aguirre, the Wrath of God* has probably been the most influential of all. Like that Herzog film, the much lighter *Jungle Cruise* is largely set in the Amazon basin and begins in the sixteenth century as a Spanish *entrada* is underway. The expedition is not-so-coincidentally headed by Don Aguirre (Edgar Ramírez), an unmistakable reference to Herzog's film, though the actor who plays him is Latino and not German. In *Jungle Cruise*, Aguirre searches for the "Tears of the Moon" tree, which is claimed to cure all illnesses and even lift curses from those afflicted. In this film, Aguirre hopes that the cure will work on his daughter Anna. That type of botanical search, of course, is what drove Evan in *Embrace of the Serpent*. For his part, Aguirre kills a cacique (chief) who refuses to divulge the plant's location, but in the process he and his men are cursed to forever remain in sight of the Amazon River. One might be tempted to see this as a metaphor for what happened cinematically, because filmmakers can't seem to resist returning to this region again and again to bring it into our view—even though *Jungle Cruise*, like *Indiana Jones and the Kingdom of the Crystal Skull*, was filmed on Hawaii.

Jungle Cruise is also about another later (ca. 1916) expedition into the Amazon to search for that mythical plant. It is spearheaded by a British woman named Lily Houghton (Emily Blunt), whose scientific research into the "Tears of the Moon" tree confirms that it really exists. Like Percy Fawcett in *The Lost City of Z*, she has to face hurdles with the fictional Royal Anthropological and Diverse Adventures Society, one clearly parodying the real Royal Geographical Society, which finally admitted women Fellows at about this time.[26] When Lily is not permitted to make the presentation, her brother does it on her behalf. The expedition receives support—though will be in competition with another led by a nefarious German aristocrat. By the way, Lily will bring an early motion picture camera to record the expedition's progress in black and white footage. Bravo!

After Lily and her brother reach South America, they hire riverboat captain Frank Wolff (Dwayne Johnson) to take them deep into the interior. The adventure that follows involves a mash-up of characters and tropes, including the conquistadors, a pet jaguar, a supposedly cannibalistic tribe, and plenty of snakes. The audience has seen these before in many films, from *Green Fire* and *Green Mansions* to *Anaconda*. The biggest surprise in this film is Frank, who turns out be a survivor of the original Aguirre expedition. However, he had a conscience, defied Aguirre, and was spared by the Indians. Interestingly, his name was Francisco Lopez de Heredia, and he was also a cartographer who drew many important maps of the Amazon. In a sense, these maps can be seen as over-compensation for Herzog's including none at all in *Aguirre, the Wrath of God*. Then again, *Fitzcarraldo* had several, and may have served as the inspiration for an explorer who can make his own maps on site. Unsurprisingly, some critics see in Frank's modern (ca. 1916) command of a refurbished river steamboat a sly tribute to Herzog's *Fitzcarraldo*. Overall, *Jungle Cruise* appears to be the most wildly derivative movie discussed in this book. That contributes to its odd charm. Looked at more deeply, though, it is also rather unique in that it brings upbeat *Indiana Jones* type comedic action face to face with moodier *Aguirre* type feel. Plus, it is truly cartocentric.

Upon its release in theaters, critics reflexively bashed *Jungle Cruise* despite expectation-lowering claims by Disney that it was intended to be enjoyable to watch and simply "escapist" entertainment. Of course, most in the audience will never know the rich cinematic territory it plumbed to reach its goal. For a very different reason, scholars should have a field day deconstructing it, unless they become too offended by its "colonialism" or do not approve of its depiction of an openly gay/LGBTQ+ supporting character, who appears to be a first in an exploration-discovery saga set in Latin America. The affirmation of this character is, in a word, heartwarming. For that matter, actor Dwayne Johnson's mixed ethnicity involving some African and Samoan ancestry is unusual—long overdue, and welcome, in a lead explorer.

Of special interest in *Jungle Cruise* is that Francisco/Frank epitomizes an explorer-discoverer's transformation, as does Lily Houghton. For that matter, two high-profile and co-equal explorer-discoverers in one film is rare, but adds considerable interest, as evident in *The Other Conquest* and *Embrace of the Serpent*. Although more than one cynical critic has claimed that the main goal in producing *Jungle Cruise* was to increase ridership at the eponymous ride in Disneyland, that is ironic. When Disney's resident genius Harper Goff originally designed the popular ride, which opened in 1955, he noted that it was based on *The African Queen* (1951).

Like Dora the Explorer, and Terri Flores (*Anaconda*), Lily Houghton is fictional. However, filmmakers seeking real female explorer-discoverers do not have very far to look. The remarkable Isabela Godin des Odonais (born 1728 in Riobamba, Ecuador), whose family traced their heritage to France, immediately comes to mind. Isabela married Jean Godin, a member of the La Condamine Expedition but they became separated as he explored the northeastern portion of South America. Some years passed, and she ultimately mounted her own expedition down into and along the Amazon to reach him. Jean later recounted Isabela's extensive travels into the South American interior, a journey that ruined her health; yet she (and he) fulfilled their goal of ultimately starting life anew, not in the Americas, but in France, where she died in 1792. That reverse-migration twist on the story makes it all the more interesting. Surprisingly, although three versions of Isabela Godin's story have been told in popular books,[27] a movie about her has never been made. Alas, when those stories do not see the light of day on screen, it amounts to an ongoing neglect of strong and determined women in cinema. Ironically, because films about actual geographic exploration seem to be waning in overall popularity, these real women's stories may never be experienced on screen if the current trend continues.

Much the same may be said of the imbalance between white/European vs. Indigenous representations. In the past, Indians appeared in films, though those in leadership roles were often played by well-meaning whites, an example being Christopher Plummer playing Atahualpa in *The Royal Hunt of the Sun*. Equally astounding is the virtual absence of people of African ancestry in locales where they have had a long and storied presence in Latin America.[28] They were (and are) visibly present in much of the *tierra caliente*, especially so in coastal locales, but also could be found far inland, even in Andean cities such as Potosí.[29] Evidently, they do not fit the popular stereotype of Latin America as having only two cultures (Iberian and Indian). On the other hand, they are depicted in many films, including *Cabeza de Vaca*; *Aguirre, the Wrath of God*; *Zama*; and *Fitzcarraldo*—though their speaking roles tend to be minimal with the exception of the latter. Usually, though, their on-screen body language speaks volumes—another example of how film can sometimes tell a story more cogently than literature.

In this regard, it appears high time that Estevanico's account of his own life, hinted at in *Cabeza de Vaca* as a man equal to the others despite his slave title, be told in a biopic. The aforementioned recent book titled *Esteban* by Dennis Herrick would make a good starting point. Since so little is actually known about him, the account is liable to be speculative, but that is to be expected. Given the smashing success of Ryan Coogler's *The Black Panther* in 2018,[30] one can only guess what form it would take; regardless, it is likely to be an exploration-discovery film. An equally interesting possibility is Laila Lalami's novel *The Moor's Account*,[31] which emphasizes Esteban's connection to North Africa and his Muslim heritage in addition to his blackness. Throughout, it peppers its flawless prose with fascinating references to history and geography—and underscores Spain's, and even New Spain's—debt to its Islamic past.

Historically and collectively, slights toward Indigenous and African cultures result in films that disproportionately celebrate exploits and successes of white males. I have already hinted at the gender imbalances in these films but shall conclude this book by pointing to the historical record for inspirational examples of other female explorer-discoverers who await cinematic discovery. Marie Robinson Wright (1853–1914) is among them. After being widowed, Wright realized her calling as a travel writer, and moved into her new profession with unbridled passion. Now free to travel, the adventuresome Wright was exploring, discovering, and describing part of the same territory that Hiram Bingham would traverse a few years later. She is said to have crossed the Andes three times. In 1907—several years before Bingham's book—Wright published a beautifully photographed record of her travels in Bolivia based on "...my journey of a thousand miles on muleback in the interior...."[32] It was a huge format book, and hugely popular. Her work is reminiscent of the *National Geographic* magazines of the period in that it celebrated progress and described colorful Indigenous peoples.

As a remarkable kind of media-savvy explorer—the travel writer[33]—Wright was bent on sharing stories with the public and documenting what she experienced. Her last chapter titled "The Primitive Inhabitants of Bolivia" has a touch of the ethnographic and hints at the enduring role that Indigenous peoples would play as the country modernized. The photographs accompanying that chapter speak volumes about the cultural diversity she encountered.

If Wright's early-twentieth-century story is too modern, or too Anglo-American, one from three centuries earlier beckons as a truly transsexual-centered Latin American saga. It concerns the "Lieutenant Nun," a Basque transvestite named Catalina de Erauso, who pretended to be a man in the very early 1600s and had a series of wild adventures throughout South America while serving as a Spanish soldier. If Catalina's account can be believed, s/he was as hot-tempered and quick to revenge as any macho male. Her picaresque travels left a trail of bloodshed and narrow escapes, some romantic. Today, her uncivil behavior might be seen as too reactionary by some easily offended, but surely many others would love to see this story. The sexual tensions alone would make this story sizzle on screen. In other matters as well, including her brushes with death, her prose is vivid.

For example, as Catalina leaves the desolate coast of Chile and ascends into the mountains (Andes) on her way to Tucumán (Argentina), she notes that "the land grew cold—so cold we were half frozen." They trudge along until a scene arrests their progress: "One day from a distance we saw two men leaning against a rock and this gave us heart." Those men never answered when Catalina and others called out to them, and with good reason: "When we came to the spot, we saw they were dead—frozen through, their mouths hanging open as if they were laughing, and this filled us with terror." If ever a scene cried out to be filmed, this is it. Catalina rarely describes the landscape in the detail that we now expect, especially after scientists raised our expectations beginning about 1700. Nevertheless—from the sultry coastal towns, to the jungles, deserts, coasts and towering mountains—place is still a palpable character in Catalina's story. She gives us just enough information about place to position her many adventures. A filmmaker could too, provided those locales do not steal the show by diminishing her intensely human story. Catalina's tersely written memoir would be the logical starting point.[34]

Positioned historically between these women, the early age of scientific discovery also awaits a woman protagonist. In particular, the story of Maria Sibylla Merian reenacted on the big screen seems a natural. Her stunning natural history illustrations brimming with life would add an especially intriguing element to that movie, as would her recorded interactions with the Indigenous peoples of northern South America. A century before Humboldt, she provides an unparalleled opportunity to bring Latin

America's past and its stunning landscapes to life—and revealed through the eyes of a woman. Like Humboldt and Bonpland a century later, she recognized the importance of Indians in exploration. For that matter, African-origin peoples were also present in significant numbers at that time as well.

Realistically, any of these three noteworthy women explorer-discovers making it to the silver screen would face an uphill climb. The biggest obstacle might be our culture's seemingly growing disinterest in historical exploration sagas, which comes at just the time that such films could help set the record straight. Nevertheless, aside from the colonialist implications of all three stories, intrepid filmmakers could defy trends and make Erauso's, Merian's, and Wright's journeys come to life.

Of course, this is likely to happen only if and when women assume a much greater role off-screen as well as on—including screenwriting and directing. In *Zama*, Argentina's Lucrecia Martel provides a shining example of how this can work. In *The 33*, Mexico's Patricia Riggen did much the same. Both worked with stories originally written by men, but a new type of material is evident in Wright's and Erauso's now-published books, and Merian's own journals and illustrations. Naturally, bringing these women to life in time and place would take considerable research into their back-stories.

However, as is now clear, filmmakers' imaginations are often rich enough to fill in the blanks, no matter how much (or how little) information exists. Ultimately, what really counts is the passion to relate a compelling story, and the skill to make it jump off the page and onto the screen. As was evident in the films reviewed in this book, the essential element is identifying and building on the *character* of two essential elements— *people* and *place*. As screenwriter Diana Ossana (*Brokeback Mountain*) concludes:

"The most important thing to know before sitting down to write is the nature of each of your characters—know them inside and out, through and through, as if they're real. Know them better than you do yourself."[35]

Chapter Notes

Preface and Acknowledgments

1. *Journey to Mecca: In the Footsteps of Ibn Battuta*, directed by Bruce Neibaur, USA: SK Films/National Geographic, 2009.

2. Carter Ringle, "Fear and Loathing in the Americas: White Fanatics and the Cinematic Colonial Mindset," *Terrae Incognitae*, Vol. 51, No. 3, December 2019, pp. 271–280.

3. Richard Weiner, "Special Issue on Exploring Latin America: Travelogues by Alexander von Humboldt, Archduke Maximilian, and James Bryce," *Terrae Incognitae*, Vol. 52, No. 1, April 2020, pp. 1–11.

Introduction

1. See, for example, Stuart C. Aitken and Leo E. Zonn, *Place, Power, Situation and Spectacle: A Geography of Film* (Lanham, MD: Rowman & Littlefield, 1994); and Stuart C. Aitken and Deborah P. Dixon, "Imagining Geographies of Film," *Erdkunde*, Vol. 6, No. 4, 2006, pp. 326–336.

2. *Knives Out*, directed by Rian Johnson, USA: T Street, 2019.

3. These figures were obtained from the Statista website, statista.com/statistics/909289/number-visitors-united-states-latin-america-sub-region/ consulted July 7, 2021.

4. Out of about 300 articles published in the journal's first six decades, only 18 were devoted to South America. Viewed quantitatively, although South America comprises about 12 percent of the world's landmass, only about six percent of *TI*'s articles addressed it. Regarding the journal's coverage of Latin America generally, most articles focus on Mexico, Central America and the Caribbean; that emphasis is understandable, given their proximity to the United States.

5. Tim Creswell and Deborah Dixon, *Engaging Film: Geographies of Mobility and Identity* (Lanham, MD: Rowman & Littlefield, 2002).

6. https:www.brainyquote.com consulted January 29, 2022.

7. Richard Francaviglia and Jerry Rodnitzky, *Lights, Camera, History: Portraying the Past in Film* (College Station: Texas A&M University Press, 2007), p. vii–viii.

8. See Sara Vicuña Guengerich, "The Perceptions of the Bison in the Chronicles of the Northern Spanish Frontier," *Journal of the Southwest*, Vol. 55, No. 3, Autumn 2013, pp. 251–276.

9. *A Cultural History of Exploration*, an in-progress six–volume book project by the Bloomsbury Press, London, UK.

10. Carla Rahn Phillips, "Can We Define Ideal and Idealized Types of Explorers?" A Zoomed presentation to the Society for the History of Discoveries, February 17, 2022.

11. *Natural Encounters in Texas History*, directed by Richard Francaviglia, USA: University of Texas at Arlington, 2005.

12. Ferdinand von Roemer, *The Cretaceous Formations of Texas and their Organic Inclusions* (Bonn, 1852).

13. Tom Conley, "Film and Exploration," in *The Oxford Companion to World Exploration* (New York: Oxford University Press, 2007), pp. 306–307.

14. Tom Conley, "Film and Exploration," pp. 308–309.

15. Stewart A. Weaver, *Exploration: A Very Short Introduction* (New York: Oxford University Press, 2015), pp. 1, 3–6.

16. Goodreads.com/quotes/177137-if-it-can-be-written-or-thought-it-can-be#:~:text=Quotes%20>%20Quotable%20Quote consulted January 29, 2022.

17. Margaret King, "Place Sets the Agenda," *Cultural Intelligence*, Friday June 4, 2021.

18. brainyquote.com/quotes/alfred_hitchcock_141870.

19. Good reads.com/quotes/634604-i-don-t-think-there-s-any-border-between-science-and-art consulted February 5, 2022.

20. Stewart Brewer, *Latin American History Goes to the Movies: Understanding Latin America's Past Through Film* (New York: Routledge, 2016).

21. This venerable statement is undated, but probably dates from about 1610. See Bukrate.com/author/john-smith1quotes consulted January 30, 2022.

22. Jennifer Hayward, "Latin America," Chapter 33, in Carl Thompson, ed., *The Routledge Companion to Travel Writing* (New York: Routledge, 2016), pp. 361–371; p. 361 cited.

23. See Jordana Dym and Karl Offen, eds. *Mapping Latin America: A Cartographic Reader* (Chicago: University of Chicago Press, 2011).

24. For a more detailed and scientific geographical description, see Thomas T. Veblen, Kenneth R. Young, and Anthony R. Orme, *The Physical Geography of South America* (New York: Oxford University Press, 2007).

25. For an example of this close connection in the Andean region of Peru and Bolivia, see anthropologist Joseph W. Bastien, *Mountain of the Condor: Metaphor and Ritual in an Andean Ayllu* (St. Paul/New York/Los Angeles/San Francisco: West Publishing Company, 1978); and *People of the Water: Change and Continuity Among the Uru-Chipayans of Bolivia* (Salt Lake City: University of Utah Press, 2012).

26. These were described and mapped under the direction of editor Wilbur E. Garrett. See the folding map *Indians of South America* (Washington, D.C.: National Geographic Society, 1982).

27. William M. Denevan, "The Pristine Myth: The Landscape of the Americas in 1492." *Annals of the Association of American Geographers*, Vol. 82, No. 3, 1992, pp. 369–385. pp 379–380 quoted

28. See Matthew H. Edney, *Cartography: The Ideal and Its History* (Chicago: University of Chicago Press, 2019.

29. J. B. Harley, *The New Nature of Maps: Essays in the History of Cartography* (Baltimore: Johns Hopkins University Press, 2001), p. 47.

30. Tom Conley, *Cartographic Cinema* (Minneapolis: University of Minnesota press, 2007), p. 1.

31. Ricardo D. Salvatore, *Disciplinary Conquest: U.S. Scholars in South America, 1900–1945* (Durham, NC: Duke University Press, 2016), p. 242.

32. See Byron Wolfe and Scott Brady, *Phantom Skies & Shifting Ground: Landscape, Culture, and Rephotography in Eadweard Muybridge's Illustrations of Central America* (Santa Fe/Philadelphia: Radius Books/Temple University Press, 2015), p. 11 quoted.

33. Christopher Lukinbeal and Laura Sharp, "Geography and Film," Oxford Bibliographies (on-line), 2017, oxfordbibliographies.com/view/document/obo-9780199874002/obo9780199874002-0097.mxl consulted July 20, 2021.

34. *Lawrence of Arabia*, directed by David Lean, UK: Horizon Pictures, 1962.

35. *Doctor Zhivago*, directed by David Lean, UK/Italy: Metro-Goldwyn-Mayer/Carlo Ponti Productions/Sostar SA, 1965.

36. Boyd Tonkin, "Love in the Time of Fame," *New York Times* (Book Section) Saturday-Sunday, July 17–18, 2021, p. C-10.

37. Gabriel García Márquez, *One Hundred Years of Solitude*, translated by Gregory Rabassa (New York: Harper Collins, 1970).

38. Gabriel García Márquez, *Living to Tell the Tale*, translated by Edith Grossman (New York: Alfred A. Knopf, 2003.)

39. "One Hundred Years of Solitude" (faux) movie trailer on youtube.com/watch?v=pv8cklgAjj4 consulted September 6, 2020.

40. Gabriel García Márquez, *Love in the Time of Cholera*, translated by Edith Grossman (New York: Alfred A. Knopf, 1988). The film version is *Love in the Time of Cholera*, directed by Mike Newell, USA: Stone Village Pictures, 2007.

41. "Love in the Time of Cholera (Film)" en.wikipedia.org/wiki/Love_in_the_Time_of_Cholera_(film) consulted July 12, 2020.

42. Daniel Fienberg, "'The Luminaries': TV Review," February 9, 2021 hollywoodreporter.com/review/the-luminaries-tv-review consulted February 21, 2021

Chapter One

1. T.J. Ferguson and Chip Colwell-Chanthaphonh, *History Is in the Land: Multivocal Tribal Traditions in Arizona's San Pedro Valley* (Tucson: University of Arizona Press, 2006), esp. pp. 188–227.

2. John Lloyd Stephens, *Incidents of Travel in Central America, Chiapas, and Yucatan* (Washington, D.C.: Smithsonian Institution Press, 1841).

3. See Richard Francaviglia, *The Mapmakers of New Zion: A Cartographic History of Mormonism* (Salt Lake City: University of Utah Press, 2005), pp. 159–161.

4. *Apocalypto*, directed by Mel Gibson, USA: Touchstone Pictures and Icon Productions, 2006.

5. "American Indians Hail 'Apocalypto' Cast," Associated Press, Sunday, December 3, 2006 oklahoman.com/article/2852566/American-indians-hail-apocaylpto-cast consulted July 26, 2021.

6. Robert W. Welkos, "In 'Apocalypto,' fact and fiction play hide and seek," *Los Angeles Times*, Dec. 6, 2006. Latimes.com/archives/la-xpm-2006-dec-09-et-apocalypto9-story.html consulted June 23, 2021.

7. "*Apocalypto* First Look" http://www.wildaboutmovies.com/movies/ApocalyptoMovieTrailer-PosterMelGibspn.php—as referenced in "Apocalypto" Wikipedia https://en.wikipedia.org/wiki/Apocalypo consulted June 23, 2021.

8. Stewart Brewer, *Latin American History Goes to the Movies* (New York: Routledge, 2016), p. 19.

9. Mark Twain, *Innocents Abroad, or The New Pilgrims' Progress* (Hartford, CT: American Publishing, 1869) p. 441; see also Richard Francaviglia, *Go East, Young Man: Imagining the American West as the Orient* (Logan: Utah State University Press, 2011), pp. 80–81.

10. See Richard D. Hansen, "Relativism, Revisionism, Aboriginalism, and Emic/Etic Truth: The Case Study." Chapter 8, pp. 147–190, in R.J. Chacon and R.G. Mendoza, eds., *The Ethics of Anthropology and Amerindian Research: Reporting on Environmental Degradation and Warfare,* DOI 10.1007/978–14614–1065–2_8. Springer Science+Business Media, LLC 2012/2013 consulted June 23, 2021.

11. Richard Hansen, "Relativism, Revisionism, Aboriginalism...." broadly discusses and contextualizes these issues.

12. "In Apocalypto (2006) a full moon is shown the night after a solar eclipse...." Posted by u/Villanueva92 on reddit.com/r/MovieDetails/comments/g0353z/in_apocalypto_2006_a_full_moon_is_shown_the/ consulted February 1, 2022.

13. Richard Hansen, "Relativism, Revisionism, Aboriginalism....," p. 169.

14. *The Naked Prey*, directed by Cornel Wilde, USA: Paramount Pictures, 1965.

15. Mark Stevenson, "'Maya Culpa?' 'Apocalypto' Reaches Latin America," *Los Angeles Times*, January 16, 2007. latimes.com/archives/la-xpm-2007-jan-16-et-apocalypto16-story.html consulted January 30, 2022.

16. Alex von Tunzelmann, "Apocalypto and the end of the wrong civilisation" *The Guardian*, Reel History: Period and Historical Films section. November 6, 2008 theguardian.com/film/2008/nov/06periodandhistorical-melgibson consulted June 26, 2021.

17. "Mel Gibson criticizes Iraq war at film fest—Troubled filmmaker draws parallels to collapsing Mayan civilization" (http:www.today.com/id/15001985) Associated Press. September 25, 2006.

Chapter Two

1. *1492: Conquest of Paradise*, directed by Ridley Scott, USA: Paramount Pictures, 1992.

2. Carla Rahn Phillips and William D. Phillips, Jr., "Christopher Columbus: Two Films," in Mark C. Carnes, ed., *Past Imperfect: History According to the Movies* (New York: Henry Holt and Company, 1995), pp. 60–65.

3. Enrique Dussell, *The Invention of the Americas: Eclipse of "The Other" and the Myth of Modernity* (New York: Concilium, 1992; 1995), p. 29.

4. *The Other Conquest* (La Otra Conquista), directed by Salvador Carrasco, Mexico: Twentieth Century Fox, 1999/2000.

5. *Captain from Castile*, directed by Henry King, USA: Twentieth Century-Fox Film Productions, 1947.

6. Luis I. Reyes, *Made in Mexico: Hollywood South of the Border* (Lanham, MD: Applause Theatre and Cinema Books, Rowman & Littlefield, 2018).

7. "The Other Conquest," Wikipedia https://en.wikipedia.org/wiki/The_Other_Conquest consulted June 9, 2021

8. Roger Atwood, "CITY POLITICS: In Sixteenth Century Mexico, the democratic city-state of Tlaxcallan thrived in the face of Aztec Imperialism," *Archaeology*, Vol. 75, No. 4, July-August 2022, pp. 34–49.

9. Santiago Juan-Navarro, "Between El Dorado and Armageddon: Utopia and Apocalypse in the Films of the Encounter," *Delaware Review of Latin American Studies*, Vol. 6, No. 2, January 15, 2006, pp. 1–7, p. 5 quoted. ww1.udel.edu/LAS/Vol6-2Juan-Navarro.html

Chapter Three

1. *Cabeza de Vaca*, directed by Nicolás Echevarría, Mexico: Concorde-New Horizons, 1991.

2. Alvar Núñez Cabeza de Vaca, *The Journey and Ordeal of Cabeza de Vaca: His Account of the Disastrous First European Exploration of the American Southwest*, translated by Cyclone Covey (Mineola, NY: Dover Publications, 2003).

3. James C. Martin and Robert Sidney Martin, *Maps of Texas and the Southwest, 1513–1900* (Austin: Texas State Historical Association, 1999), p. 17–19.

4. Lauren Eisner (with additional comments by Alexandra Neumann and Eddie Strumfels), "The Spaniard and the Dwarf" Films>>Cabeza de Vaca>> Scene Analysis>>*Reel American History*. History on Trial, Main Page, Digital.lib.lehigh.edu/tirial/reels/films/list/0_5_8_80, pp. 1–4, p. 2 cited consulted June 1, 2021.

5. Alan J. Silva, "Conquest, Conversion, and the Hybrid Self in Cabeza de Vaca's Relacion." Vol. 2, No. 1, Winter 1999. pp. 4–23, p. 8 cited. http://hdl.handle.net/2027/spo.pid9999.0002.106 consulted July 1, 2021.

6. Dennis Herrick, *Esteban: The African Slave Who Explored America* (Albuquerque: University of New Mexico Press, 2018).

7. Alan Silva. "Conquest, Conversion, and the Hybrid Self....," p. 18.

8. Cabeza de Vaca, *The Journey and Ordeal*....p. 83.

9. See James D. Mauseth, Roberto Kiesling, and Carlos Ostolaza, *A Cactus Odyssey: Journeys into the Wilds of Bolivia, Peru, and Argentina* (Portland, OR: Timber Press, 2002) especially pp 4–14.

10. Cabeza de Vaca, *The Journey and Ordeal...*, pp. 103 and 116.

11. Cabeza de Vaca, *The Journey and Ordeal...*,. pp. 91 and 92.

12. Cabeza de Vaca, *The Journey and Ordeal*...., p. 91.

13. David Weber, *The Spanish Frontier in North America* (New Haven: Yale University Press, 1992) pp. 44–45.

14. Alvar Núñez Cabeza de Vaca, *The South American Expeditions, 1540–1545*, translated with notes by Baker H. Morrow (Albuquerque: University of New Mexico Press, 2011).

Chapter Four

1. *The Royal Hunt of the Sun*, directed by Irving Lerner, UK/USA: Cinema Center Films, 1969.

2. For a lively interpretation of Carvajal and this river's naming, see Victor Wolfgang von Hagen, *South America Called Them: Explorations of the Great Naturalists—La Condamine, Humboldt, Darwin, Spruce* (New York: Duell, Sloan and Pearce, 1955), pp. 249–252.

3. Gaspar de Carvajal, *Discovery of the Amazon According to the Account of Friar Gaspar de Carvajal*. José Toribio Medina; translated by Bertram T.

Lee; edited by H. C. Heaton (New York: American Geographical Society, 1935).

4. According to the source "Aguirre, the Wrath of God," en.wikipedia.org/wiki/Aguirre,_the_Wrath_of_God consulted January 16, 2022.

5. *Aguirre, the Wrath of God*, directed by Werner Herzog, West Germany: Werner Herzog Filmproduktion, 1972.

6. William Bollaert, *The Expedition of Pedro de Ursua & Lope de Aguirre in Search of El Dorado and Omagua in 1560–1*. Translated from Fray Simón's Sixth Historical Notice of the Conquest of Tierra Firme, 1627. (London: Routledge, 2010).

7. Ingrid Galster, *Aguirre o La Posteridad Arbitraria: La Rebellion del Conquistador en Historiografía y Ficción Histórica* (Bogota: Universidad Javeriana and Universidad del Rosario, 2011).

8. "Werner Herzog Reads His Minnesota Declaration: Truth and Fact in Documentary Cinema." *Crosscuts*. Walkerart.org/magazine/minnesota-declaration—truth-documentary-cinema- 1999. Consulted December 12, 2020.

9. Stewart Brewer, *Latin American History Goes to the Movies*, p. 51.

10. Julian Smith, "Mapping a City in the Clouds: Drone-mounted lasers reveal a new view of an ancient Peruvian Citadel." *Archaeology*, Vol. 74, No. 2, March-April 2021, pp. 32–38. p. 36 quoted.

11. Gabriel García Márquez, *One Hundred Years of Solitude*, p. 11–12.

12. "Magic Realism" en.wikipedia.org/wiki/Magic_realism consulted February 7, 2022

13. Gregory A. Waller, "'Aguirre, The Wrath of God': History, Theater, and the Camera." *South Atlantic Review*, Vol. 46, No. 2, May, 1981, pp. 55–69. Pp. 55 and 57 quoted.

14. Ronald Fritze, "Werner Herzog's Adaptation of History in *Aguirre, the Wrath of God*." *Film and History*, Vol XV, No. 4, December 1985, p. 79 quoted.

15. See Penelope Gilliatt, "Gold," *New Yorker*, April 11, 1977, pp. 127–128.

16. Ronald Fritze, "Werner Herzog's Adaptation of History…" p. 85.

17. *El Dorado*, directed by Carlos Saura, Spain: Canal + Chrysalide Film, 1988.

18. *Oro [Gold]*, directed by Augustín Diaz Yanes, Spain: Apache Films/Sony Pictures, 2017.

19. Bart R. Lewis, *The Miraculous Lie: Lope de Aguirre and the Search for El Dorado in the Latin American Novel* (Lanham; Boulder; New York; Oxford: Lexington Books, 2003).

Chapter Five

1. Carol Delaney, *Columbus and the Quest for Jerusalem* (New York: Simon and Schuster, 2011).

2. Nigel Cliff, *The Last Crusade: The Epic Voyages of Vasco Da Gama* (New York: Harper Perennial, 2011).

3. David Block, *Mission Culture on the Upper Amazon: Native Tradition, Jesuit Enterprise, & Secular Policy in Moxos, 1660–1880* (Lincoln:

University of Nebraska Press, 1994), 6. It is worth noting that on page 10 Block astutely frames his study as "between 1660 and 1880, cinematographically between *The Mission* and *Fitzcarraldo*."

4. Robert H. Jackson, *Frontiers of Evangelization: Indians in the Sierra Gorda and Chiquitos Missions* (Norman: University of Oklahoma Press, 2017), pp. 54–55.

5. *The Mission*, directed by Roland Joffé, UK: Goldcrest Films, 1986.

6. Philip Caraman, *The Lost Paradise: The Jesuit Republic in South America* (New York, 1976).

7. Richard M. Morse, *The Bandeirantes: The Historical Role of the Brazilian Pathfinders* (New York: Alfred A. Knopf, 1965).

8. James Schofield Saeger, "*The Mission* and Historical Missions: Film and the Writing of History," *The Americas*, Vol. 51, No. 3, January 1995, pp. 393–415; p. 399 quoted.

9. See Gustavo Gutiérrez, *A Theology of Liberation: History, Politics, and Salvation* (New York: Orbis Books, 2004; originally published 1998; Translated and edited by Sister Caridad Inda and John Eagleson).

10. James Saeger, "*The Mission* and Historical Missions," pp. 41–411.

11. *End of the Spear*, directed by Peter R. de Vries, USA: Rocky Mountain Pictures, 2006.

Chapter Six

1. Ernesto Sabato, *El Túnel* (Buenos Aires: Editorial Sur, 1948); also published in English as *The Tunnel* (New York: Penguin Group, 1988).

2. Antonio Di Benedetto, *Zama* (New York: New York Review Books, 2000).

3. *The Secret in Their Eyes*, directed by Juan José Campanella, Argentina: Hadock Films/100 Bares/Tornasol Films, 2009.

4. *Wild Tales*, directed by Damián Szifron, Argentina/Spain: Kramer & Sigman Films, 2014.

5. Benedict Anderson, *Imagined Communities: Reflections on the Origins and Spread of Nationalism* (London: Verso, 1983), p. 57. See also Ralph Bauer, *The Cultural Geography of Colonial American Literatures: Empire, Travel, Modernity* (Cambridge: Cambridge University Press, 2003), p. 118.

6. *Zama*, directed by Lucrecia Martel, Argentina: Bananeira Filmes LTDA, 2017.

7. The Order of Pedro Gregorio, Valdivia, August 19, 1779, as related in David J. Weber, *Bárbaros: Spaniards and Their Savages in the Age of the Enlightenment* (New Haven: Yale University Press, 2005), p.239, n143.

8. David Weber, *Bárbaros*, pp. 233–260.

9. Antonio di Benedetto, *Zama*, pp 197–198.

Chapter Seven

1. Mary Louise Pratt, *Imperial Eyes: Travel Writing and Transculturation* (New York: Routledge, 1992), p.9.

2. This quote is from the preface of Merian's *Metamorphosis*. See Victoria Dickenson, *Drawn from Life: Science and Art in the Portrayal of the New World* (Toronto: University of Toronto Press, 1998), p. 148

3. Mark A. Burkholder, "Humboldt, Alexander von," *The Oxford Companion to Exploration* (Oxford: Oxford University Press, 2007) Vol. 1, A-L, pp, 394–396; p. 394 quoted.

4. Stephen Bell, *A Life in Shadow: Aimé Bonpland in Southern South America, 1817–1858* (Palo Alto: Stanford University Press, 2010).

5. *Aire Libre*, directed by Luis Armando Roche, France/Canada/Venezuela: Bleu Blanc Rouge, 1997 (DVD 2006).

6. Mary Louise Pratt, *Imperial Eyes,* p. 120.

7. Mary Louise Pratt, *Imperial Eye*s, p. 120.

8. Victor Wolfgang Von Hagen, *South America Called Them: Exploration of the Great Naturalists; La Condamine, Humboldt, Darwin, Spruce* (New York: Duel, Sloan and Pearce, 1955); Gerard Helferich, *Humboldt's Cosmos: Alexander von Humboldt and the Latin American Journey that Changed the Way We See the World* (New York: Gotham Books, 2004); and Edward J. Goodwin, *The Explorers of South America* (Norman: University of Oklahoma Press, 1972).

9. Alexander von Humboldt and Aimé Bonpland, *Essay on the Geography of Plants*, edited with an Introduction by Stephen T. Jackson, translated by Sylvie Romanowski (Chicago: University of Chicago Press, 2009).

10. Alexander von Humboldt and Aimé Bonpland, *Personal Narrative of a Journey to the Equinoctial Regions of the New Continent During the Years 1799–1804,* Vols. 1, 2 and 3 (Oxford, UK: Benediction Classics, 2012).

11. Karl S. Zimmerer, "Humboldt's Nodes and Modes of Interdisciplinary Environmental Science in the Andean World," *The Geographical Review*, Vol. 96, No. 3, July 2006, pp. 335–360; p. 343 quoted.

12. Alexander von Humboldt, *Personal Narrative of Travels to the Equinoctial Regions of the New Continent During the Years 1799–1804* (London, 1814), vol. III, pp. 34–35.

13. Anne Buttimer, "Bridging the Americas: Humboltian Legacies," *The Geographical Review*, Vol. 96, No. 2, April, 2006, pp. xvi–ix; p. vii quoted.

14. *Cabo Blanco*, directed by Lee Thompson, USA: 1980.

Chapter Eight

1. Joseph A. Stout, *Schemers and Dreamers: Filibustering in Mexico, 1848–1921* (Fort Worth: Texas Christian University Press, 2002).

2. See Michael Gobat, *An Empire by Invitation: William Walker and Manifest Destiny in Central America* (Cambridge, MA: Harvard University Press, 2018).

3. *Walker*, directed by Alex Cox, USA and Spain: In-Cine Compañia/Industrial Cinematográfia/Northern/Walker Film Ltd, 1987.

4. William Walker, *The War in Nicaragua* (New York: S. H. Goetzel, 1860).

5. Rudolph Wurlitzer, *Walker: The True Story of the First American Invasion of Nicaragua* (New York: Harper & Row Publishers, 1987).

6. It is also widely claimed that the film character's own use of both the first and third person supports this, but it should be recalled that Walker's own book *The War in Nicaragua* uses the third person (e.g., "him" and "Walker") consistently.

7. Rudolph Wurlitzer, *Walker: The True Story of the First American Invasion of Nicaragua*, p.28.

8. See Stephen Prince, *Savage Cinema: Sam Peckinpah and the Rise of Ultraviolent Movies* (Austin: University of Texas Press, 1998).

9. "*Walker*" booklet with the DVD *The Criterion Collection, Walker: A Film by Alex Cox*, n.d. p. 37.

10. Patrick Goldstein, "Hollywood Invades Nicaragua," *Los Angeles Times*, April 19, 1987. latimes.com/archives/la-xpm-1987–04–19-ca-1690-story.html. consulted July 27. 2021.

11. Walker (film) Wikipedia, https://en.wikipedia.org/wiki/Walker_(film) p. 3, consulted July 11, 2021.

12. Graham Fuller, "*Walker*: Apocalypse When?" The Current/The Criterion Collection. Essays—Feb 18, 2008. https://www.criterion.com/current/posts/558-walker-apocalypse-when consulted July 10, 2012.

13. Robert Houston, foreword to William Walker, *The War in Nicaragua* (Tucson: University of Arizona press, 1985), pp. 1–12; p. 1 quoted.

14. Rudolph Wurlitzer, *The True Story of the First American Invasion of Nicaragua.* p. 36.

15. "*Walker*" booklet with the DVD *The Criterion Collection, Walker: A Film by Alex Cox*, pp. 40 and 41.

16. See Scott Martelle, *William Walker's Wars: How One Man's Private American Armies Tried to Conquer Mexico, Nicaragua, and Honduras* (Chicago Review Press, 2019), p. 265; and Robert Houston, Foreword to William Walker, *The War in Nicaragua*, p. 12.

17. *El Patrullero* (The Highway Patrol Man), directed by Alex Cox, Mexico, 1991.

18. *Burn!*, directed by Gillo Pontecorvo, Italy: Produzioni Europee Associati, Les Productions Artistes Associés. 1969.

19. *Viva Zapata!*, directed by Elia Kazan, USA: 20th Century Fox, 1948.

20. See Stewart Brewer, *Latin American History Goes to the Movies*, esp. Chapter 7, "Revolutionary Latin America," pp. 80–98, which includes analyses of *Burn!* and *Viva Zapata!* p. 80 quoted.

Chapter Nine

1. *Fitzcarraldo*, directed by Werner Herzog, West Germany: Werner Herzog Filmproduktion, 1982.

2. "Carlos Fitzcarrald" en.wikipedia.org/wiki/

Carlos_Fitzcarrald consulted July 19, 2020; also Alfonso Cueva Sevillano, "Carlos Fermin Fitzcarrald," *Diccionário Histórico Biográfico: Peruanos Ilustres* (AFA Editores Importadores, p.222; and Dan James Pantone, "The Myth of Fitzcarraldo," Iquitos News and Travel Guide, 2004–2006, iquitosnews.com/page14a.html consulted October 22, 2020.

3. Werner Herzog, *Fitzcarraldo: The Original Story*; translated from the German by Martje Herzog and Alan Greenburg (San Francisco: Fjord Press, 1982), Foreword (p. 9).

4. "Isthmus of Fitzcarrald" en.wikipedia.org/wiki/Isthmus_of_Fitzcarrald consulted July 22, 2020.

5. Richard John Ascárate, "'Have You Ever Seen a Shrunken Head?': The Early Modern Roots of Ecstatic Truth in Werner Herzog's 'Fitzcarraldo'" *PMLA*, Vol. 122, No. 2, March 2007, pp. 483–501; p. 487 quoted

6. Richard John Ascárate, "Have You Ever Seen a Shrunken Head?" p. 497.

7. Werner Herzog, *Conquest of the Useless: Reflections from the Making of Fitzcarraldo* (New York: HarperCollins, 2009). p 121.

8. Les Blank, *Burden of Dreams*, a 77-page booklet distributed with the DVD of Les Blank's film of the same name. n.d., p. 24. This booklet notes that "These journals were originally edited by James Brogan and published in 1984 by North Atlantic Books in Berkeley, California. Les's journals are excerpted from letters home to Chris Simon."

9. Les Blank, *Burden of Dreams*, p. 28.

10. "Fitzcarraldo" https://en.wikipedia.org/wiki/Fitzcarraldo consulted July 15, 2020.

11. Wade Davis, "Foreword" to *Tracks in the Amazon: The Day-to-Day Life of the Workers on the Madeira-Mamoré Railroad*, by Gary Neeleman and Rose Neeleman (Salt Lake City: University of Utah Press, 2014), p. x.

12. *Burden of Dreams*, directed by Les Blank. USA: Flower Films, 1982.

13. Cobra Verde, Wikipedia https://en.wikipedia.org/wiki/Cobra_Verde consulted February 27, 2022.

14. *Cobra Verde*, directed by Werner Herzog, West Germany: Werner Herzog Film Produktion, 1987. This film is also known as *Slave Coast*.

15. *Mein Liebster Feind* (My Best Fiend), directed by Werner Herzog, Germany: Werner Herzog Produktion, 1999.

Chapter Ten

1. W. H. Hudson, *The Purple Land: Being the Narrative of One Richard Lamb's Adventures in the Banda Oriental, in South America, as told by Himself* (New York: E.P. Dutton & Co., 1916). According to Hudson in the Preface to that edition, it was originally published as *The Purple Land That England Lost* (in two slim volumes: London: Messrs. Sampson Low, 1885).

2. W. H. Hudson, *Green Mansions: A Romance of the Tropical Forest* (originally published in

1904); subsequently in numerous editions and reprints, including an illustrated edition with an introduction by Margaret Atwood (New York: London & New York: Duckworth Overlook, 2018).

3. W.H. Hudson, *Green Mansions*, pp. 16–17.

4. *Green Mansions*, directed by Mel Ferrer, USA: Metro-Goldwyn-Mayer, 1959.

5. W. H. Hudson, *Green Mansions*, p. 17.

6. W. H. Hudson, *Green Mansions*, p. 22.

7. Joseph Conrad, *Heart of Darkness*; originally published as a two-part serialized story in *Blackwood's Magazine* (1899) and as a book three years later (Edinburgh: William Blackwood, 1902).

8. David Miller, *W.H. Hudson and the Elusive Paradise* (New York: St. Martin's Press, 1990), pp. 136–37.

9. W. H. Hudson, *Green Mansions*, pp. 27–28.

10. W.H. Hudson, *Idle Days in Patagonia* (New York: E.P. Dutton & Co., 1917), pp. 140–41 and 156–57.

11. Jason Wilson, *W.H. Hudson: The Colonial's Revenge* (London, 1981) as cited in David Miller, *W.H. Hudson and the Elusive Paradise*, pp. 147–48.

12. David Miller, *W.H. Hudson and the Elusive Paradise*, pp. 154–155.

13. W.H. Hudson, *Green Mansions*, p. 83.

14. W.H. Hudson, *Green Mansions*, p. 41.

15. *Avatar*, directed by James Cameron, USA: 20th Century Fox, 2009.

16. Linda Williams, "Film Bodies: Gender, Genre, and Excess," *Film Quarterly*, Vol. 44, No. 4, Summer 1991, pp. 2–13; p. 10 quoted.

17. W. H. Hudson, *Green Mansions*, pp. 234–235.

18. David Miller, *W.H. Hudson and the Elusive Paradise*, pp. 157, 158–9.

19. *The Emerald Forest*, directed by John Boorman, UK: Christel Films, 1985.

Chapter Eleven

1. *The Lost City of Z*, directed by James Gray, USA: Plan B Entertainment, 2016.

2. David Grann, *The Lost City of Z* (New York: Doubleday, 2009).

3. Rudyard Kipling, "The Explorer" (1898 poem), in *Collected Verses of Rudyard Kipling* (New York: Doubleday, Page, and Company, 1915), pp. 19–22.

4. Richard Francaviglia, *Mapping and Imagination in the Great Basin: A Cartographic History* (Reno: University of Nevada Press, 2005), especially the chapter titled "Maps in the Sand," 97–121.

5. Juliet Wiersema, "The Map of the Yurumanguí Indians: Charting the Erasure of the Pacific Lowlands' Indigenous Inhabitants, 1742–1780, *Terrae Incognitae*, Vol. 52, No. 2, August 2020, pp. 160–194.

6. D. Graham Burnett, *Masters of all they Surveyed: Exploration, Geography, and a British El Dorado* (Chicago: University of Chicago Press, 2000), pp. 183 and 186.

7. Richard F. Burton, *Explorations of the Highlands of the Brazil* (2 vols.) (London: Tinsley Bros, 1869).

8. For a comprehensive view of explorer Burton, see Dane Kennedy's *The Highly Civilized Man: Richard Burton and the Victorian World* (Cambridge, MA: Harvard University Press, 2005).

9. An informative overview the film's generally laudatory reviews can be found at en.wikipedia.org/wiki/The_Lost_City_of_Z_ (film) consulted August 6, 2020.

10. Eliza Berman, "The True Story Behind *The Lost City of Z*," *Time*, April 14, 2017 time.com/4735505/the-lost-city-of-z-true- story consulted September 6, 2020.

11. *Spectator*, April 1, 2017; see spectator.co.uk/article/lost-city-of-fantasy

12. A. Conan Doyle, *The Lost World* (London: Hodder & Stoughton, 1912).

13. For a definitive review of these films, see Mark F. Berry, *The Dinosaur Filmography* (Jefferson, NC and London: McFarland & Company, Inc., Publishers, 2002), pp. 240–264.

14. See, for example, *The Lost World*, directed by Stuart Orme, UK: BBC and A&E Network, 2001.

15. *The Lost World*, directed by Timothy Bond, Canada: Harry Alan Towers, 1992.

16. *Explorer: The Last Tepui*, directed by Renan Ozturk, Drew Pulley, and Taylor Freesolo Rees, USA: Disney Plus films, 2022.

Chapter Twelve

1. Jordana Dym, "In the footsteps of Simón Bolívar: Hiram Bingham from Caracas to Bogotá, 1906–1907." A Zoomed presentation to the Society for the History of Discoveries, June 17, 2021.

2. Hiram Bingham, *Across South America: An Account of a Journey from Buenos Aires to Lima by Way of Potosí* (Boston & New York: Houghton Mifflin Company, 1911).

3. James Bryce, *South America: Observations and Impressions* (New York: The Macmillan Company, 1913), p. 113.

4. Hiram Bingham, "In the Wonderland of Peru," *National Geographic Magazine*, Vol. XXIV, No. 4, April 1913.

5. Ricardo Salvatore, *Disciplinary Conquest: U.S. Scholars in South America, 1900–1945* (Durham, NC: Duke University press, 2017), pp. 4–5, 237.

6. Hiram Bingham, *Lost City of the Incas: The Story of Machu Picchu and its Builders* (New York: Simon & Schuster, 1948).

7. *Tintin and the Temple of the Sun*, directed by Eddie Lateste, France, Belgium, Switzerland: Belvision, 1969.

8. *Secret of the Incas*, directed by Jerry Hopper, USA: Paramount Pictures, 1954.

9. *The Naked Jungle*, directed by Byron Haskin, USA: Paramount Pictures, 1954.

10. *Secret of the Andes*, directed by Alejandro Azzani, Argentina/USA: National Institute for Cinema and Audiovisual Arts, 1998/1999.

Chapter Thirteen

1. *Indiana Jones and the Kingdom of the Crystal Skull*, directed by Steven Spielberg, USA: Lucasfilm Ltd. and Paramount Pictures, 2008.

2. *Raiders of the Lost Ark*, directed by Steven Spielberg, USA: Lucasfilm Ltd. and Paramount Pictures, 1981.

3. See Steve Neale, "Action-Adventure as Hollywood Genre," in Yvonne Tasker, Action and Adventure Cinema (London: Routledge, 2004), pp. 71–83.

4. Karl Brugger, *The Chronicle of Akatar* (New York: Delacorte Press, 1977).

5. "Myths and Mysteries Surround Chile's Desert Drawings," www.nbcnews.com/science/weird-science/myths-mysteries-surround-chiles-desert-drawings-n27651 accessed April 4, 2016.

6. Linda Williams, "Motion and e-motion: lust and the 'frenzy of the visible,'" *Journal of Visual Culture*, Vol. 18, No. 1, 2019, pp. 97–129, p. 97 cited.

7. Linda Williams, "Motion and e-motion: lust and the frenzy of the visible," pp. 97–129, p. 1 quoted.

8. James Kendrick, Action Cinema, Oxford Bibliographies oxfordbibliographies.com/view/document/obo-9780199791286/obo-9780199791286-0157.xml consulted September 12, 2021

9. indianajones.fandom.com/wiki/Orellana%-27s-grave consulted March 3, 2021.

Chapter Fourteen

1. *Embrace of the Serpent*, directed by Ciro Guerra, Colombia: Buffalo Films, 2015.

2. In addition to the Variety review on the DVD, others equally positive are found at Embrace of the Serpent https://en.wikipedia.org/wiki/Embrace_of_the_Serpent consulted July 15, 2020.

3. These are in German, and include "Two Years among the Indians: Travels in Northwest Brazil (1903–1905)," "Indian Types of the Amazon Basin (1906)." His "Vom Roraima zum Orinoco: Ergebnisse einer Reise in Nordbrasilien und Venezuela in den Jahren 1911–1913" was recently republished (Cambridge, UK: Cambridge University Press, 2009).

4. *The Wizard of Oz*, directed by Victor Fleming, USA: Metro-Goldwyn-Mayer, 1939.

5. Carter Ringle, "Fear and Loathing…" p. 279.

6. Carter Ringle, "Fear and Loathing…" p. 279.

7. "Embrace of the Serpent," Reception/Response from the Indigenous Community; p. 5 https://en.wikipedia.org/wiki/Embrace_of_the_Serpent consulted July 15, 2020.

8. *Icaros: A Vision*, directed by Leonor Caraballo and Matteo Norzi, Peru/USA: Conibo Productions, Nice Dissolve, 2017.

9. Nick Schager, "Film Review: 'Icaros: A Vision'" *Variety*, April 25, 2016, https://variety.com/2016/film/reviews/icaros-a-vision-film-review-1201759828/ consulted February 6, 2021.

Chapter Fifteen

1. *The Creature from the Black Lagoon*, directed by Jack Arnold, USA: Universal Pictures, 1954.

2. *Arachnophobia*, directed by Frank Marshall, USA: Hollywood Pictures, 1990. Although most of the film was shot in California, the jungle scenes were reportedly filmed on location in Venezuela.

3. See, for example, "Percy Fawcett" en.wikipedia.org/wiki/Percy_Fawcett, p. 1, consulted September 1, 2020; and "Giant Anaconda at CryptoWiki at crytpzoology.fando.com/wiki/Giant_Anaconda consulted September 8, 2020.

4. *Anaconda*, directed by Luis Llosa, USA: Sony Pictures, 1997.

5. Hans Bauer, *Anaconda: The Writer's Cut* goodreads.com/book/show/20730048-anaconda consulted September 1, 2020.

6. *King Kong*, directed by Merian Cooper and Ernest Schoedsack, USA: Radio Pictures, 1933; and a later version directed by Peter Jackson, USA: Wing Nut Films/Universal Pictures, 2005.

7. In some written sources, this character's surname is variously spelled Sarone and Sirone.

8. Carmen Serrano, *Gothic Imagination in Latin American Fiction and Film* (Albuquerque: University of New Mexico Press, 2019).

9. See, for example, Stephen Prince, *Movies and Meaning: An Introduction to Film* (Boston: Pearson, Allyn and Bacon, 2007.

10. *Jaws*, directed by Steven Spielberg, USA: Zanuck/Brown and Universal Pictures, 1975.

11. *Piranha*, directed by Joe Dante, USA: Piranha Productions, 1978.

12. *Jaws 2*, directed by Jeannot Szwarc, USA: Zanuck/Brown, 1978.

13. See, for example, "Piranhas in the Chichester Sewers (& Associated Urban Legends)" no1984.org/2018/03/30piranhas-in-the-chichester-sewers-associated-urban-legends/ consulted January 11, 2021

14. *Killer Fish*, directed by Antonio Margheriti. Italy, France, and Brazil: Fawcett-Majors Productions/Victoria Productions and Filmar do Brasil, 1979.

15. *Piranha 3D*, directed by Alejandro Aja, USA: The Weinstein Company, Atmosphere Entertainment, Chako Film Co, Mark Canton/IPW, 2010.

16. These were noted in the "attacks" section of the Wikipedia Website "Piranha." en.wikipedia.org/wiki/piranha consulted January 14, 2021.

17. Theodore Roosevelt, *Through the Brazilian Wilderness* (Sagamore Hill, New York, September 1, 1914) and published in many editions, including (New York: Charles Scribner's Sons, 1914; 1920 and others) Author's copy a digitally printed facsimile obtained January 8, 2021. pp. 34–36, 42–43 quoted.

18. *The River of Doubt*, original film 1920, available online at the Library of Congress in two parts titled part 1 and part 2. Part 1 quoted. Loc.gov/item/mp76000367

19. Theodore Roosevelt, *Through the Brazilian Wilderness*, pp. 228 and 272 quoted.

20. Candice Millard, *The River of Doubt: Theodore Roosevelt's Darkest Journey* (New York: Anchor Books, 2005), pp. 148 and 341.

Chapter Sixteen

1. *Tycoon*, directed by Richard Wallace, USA: RKO Pictures, 1947.

2. *Treasure of the Sierra Madre*, directed by John Huston, USA: Warner Brothers-First National, 1948.

3. See Thomas P. Moore and Wendell E. Wilson, "The Emerald Mines of Colombia" *The Mineralogical Record*, vol. 47, No. 1, January-February, 2016. pp. 12–16.

4. for an informative interpretation of these activities, see Ann Twinam, *Miners, Merchants, and Farmers in Colonial Colombia* (Austin: University of Texas Press, 1982).

5. A deer-size camel-like animal common in parts of Andean South America; see Lieut. James J. M. Gilliss, *The U.S. Naval Astronomical Expedition to the Southern Hemisphere in the Years 1849-'50-'51-'52, Vol. 1, Chile*. Washington: A.O.P. Nicholson, Printer, 1855, pp. 256–257.

6. Anselm Verener Lee Guise, *Six Years in Bolivia: The Adventures of a Mining Engineer* (West Lafayette, IN: NotaBell Books, an imprint of Purdue University Press, 1998).

7. Peter Rainier, *Green Fire* (New York: Random House, 1942); republished by Bantam Books, 1953.

8. Peter Rainier, *Green Fire*, p. 10.

9. Peter Rainier, *Green Fire*, p. 128.

10. Peter Rainier, *Green Fire*, p. 32.

11. *King Solomon's Mines*, directed by Compton Bennett and Andrew Marton, USA: Metro-Goldwyn-Mayer, 1950.

12. *Green Fire*, directed by Andrew Marton, USA: Metro-Goldwyn-Mayer, 1954.

13. *Dances With Wolves*, directed by Kevin Costner, USA: Tig Productions/Orion Pictures, 1990.

14. *The Old Man Who Read Love Stories*, directed by Rolf de Heer, Australia: 2001.

15. *Green Fire*, wikipedia site.p.3, https://en.wikipedia.org/wiki/Green_Fire consulted August 25, 2020.

16. Aljean Harmetz, "Hollywood's Lovely but Lonely Lady," *New York Times*, September 16, 1982.

17. *Los Andes no Creen en Dios* (The Andes do not Believe in God), directed by Antonio Eguino, Bolivia: Laboratores Sonido Filmoso do Santiago de Chile, Imagen Technicolor Montreal Canada, 2007.

18. *Saludos Amigos*, directed by Norman Ferguson, Wilfred Jackson, Jack Kinney, Hamilton Luske, and Bill Roberts, USA: Walt Disney Productions, 1942.

19. *The Three Caballeros*, directed by Norman Ferguson, Clyde Geronomi, Jack Kinney, Bill Roberts and Harold Young, USA: Walt Disney Productions, 1944 (Mexico) and 1945 (USA).

20. Ariel Dorfman and Armand Mattelart, *Para Leer el Pato Donald* (Chile, 1971); later released in

English as *How to Read Donald Duck* (1976) and subsequent printings and editions (2018).

21. *Walt & El Grupo*, directed by Theodore Thomas, USA: Walt Disney Family Foundation Films/Theodore Thomas Productions, 2008.

Chapter Seventeen

1. See for example "The fascinating history of Ché Guevara's Irish ancestry," *Irish Central* irishcentral.com/roots/genealogy/history-che-guevara-irish-ancestor#:~:text=Ernesto%20Raphael%20Guevara%20de%20la,and%20Celia%20de%20la%Serna.&text consulted February 9, 2022

2. *Che* (Part 1: "The Argentine" and Part 2, "Guerrilla"), directed by Steven Soderberg, Telecinco Cinema, Wild Bunch, Section 8 Productions, 2008–2009.

3. Stewart Brewer, *Latin American History Goes to the Movies: Understanding Latin America's Past Through Film* (New York: Routledge, 2016), pp. 96–98.

4. *Evita*, directed by Alan Parker, USA: Hollywood Pictures; Cinergy Pictures; RSO Films; Dirty Hands Productions, 1996.

5. *The Motorcycle Diaries*, directed by Walter Salles, Argentina/Brazil/USA/Chile/Peru/UK/Germany/France: Film Four; BD Cine; Wildwood Enterprises, Inc., 2004.

6. Ernesto Che Guevara, *The Motorcycle Diaries: A Journey Around South America* (San Francisco: Analytical Club of San Francisco, 1995).

7. Che Guevara, *The Motorcycle Diaries*, p. 36.

8. Che Guevara, *The Motorcycle Diaries*, p. 49.

9. Che Guevara, *The Motorcycle Diaries*, pp. 57–58.

10. Che Guevara, *The Motorcycle Diaries*, p. 85.

11. Alberto Granado, *Traveling with Che Guevara: The Making of a Revolutionary* (New York: Newmarket Press, 2004).

12. Che Guevara, *The Motorcycle Diaries*, pp. 91 and 149.

13. Che Guevara, *The Motorcycle Diaries*, p. 165.

14. "Che Guevara in Popular Culture," en.wikipedia.org/wiki/Che_Guevara_in_popular_ culture consulted February 7, 2022.

Chapter Eighteen

1. *Missing*, directed by Costa-Gavras, USA: PolyGram Filmed Entertainment; Universal Pictures, 1982.

2. Ariel Dorfman, *Desert Memories: Journeys through the Chilean North* (Washington, D.C.: National Geographic, 2004), p. 9

3. *Quantum of Solace*, directed by Marc Forster, UK/USA: Eon Productions/Metro-Goldwyn-Mayer, Sony Pictures, 2008.

4. *Crystal Fairy and the Magical Cactus and 2012*, directed by Sebastián Silva, Chile: Content Media, 2013.

5. *The Dance of Reality*, directed by Alejandro Jodorowsky, Chile/France: Camera One/Le Soleil Film, 2013/2014.

6. *El Topo*, directed by Alejandro Jodorowsky, Mexico: Producciónes Panical, 1970.

7. *Nostalgia for the Light*, directed by Patricio Guzmán, France/Chile/Germany/Spain/USA: Pyramide International and Icarus Films, 2011.

8. *Neruda*, directed by Pablo Larraín, Chile/Argentina/France/Spain/USA: 2016.

9. Guzmán made this clear in a number of early interviews on *The Sanctuary for Independent Media*; see also "Nostalgia for the Light" wikipedia https://en.wikipedia.org/wiki/Nostalgia_for_the_ Light consulted September 4, 2020.

10. *The 33*, directed by Patricia Riggen, USA, Chile, and Colombia: Phoenix Pictures, 2015.

11. Héctor Tobar, *Deep Down Dark: The Untold Story of 33 Men Buried in a Chilean Mine, and the Miracle That Set Them Free* (New York: Farrar, Straus, and Giroux, 2014).

12. Richard Francaviglia, *Imagining the Atacama Desert: A Five-hundred-Year Journey of Discovery* (Salt Lake City: University of Utah Press, 2018).

13. See for example, Hernán Rivera Letelier, *El Vendedor de Pájaros* (The Birdseller) (Santiago: Alfaguara, 2014) for a magically inspired story; and for a noir example, see *El Alemán de Atacama* (Santiago: Editorial Planeta, 1997).

Chapter Nineteen

1. "Dora the Explorer," a long-running American television series, created by Chris Gifford, Valerie Walsh Valdes, and Eric Weiner in 2000. See https://en.wikipedia.org/wiki/Dora_the_Explorer consulted September 12, 2020.

2. *Dora and the Lost City of Gold*, directed by James Bobin, USA: Paramount Players, Nickelodeon Movies, Walden Media, Media Rights Capital, Burr! Productions, Screen Queensland, 2019. See also en.wikipedia.org/wiki/Dora_and_the_Lost_City_of_Gold.

3. Douglas Preston, *The Lost City of the Monkey God: A True Story* (New York: Grand Central Books, 2017).

4. Rosy Cordero, "Isabela Moner Learned Indigenous Peruvian Language to Play 'Dora the Explorer.'" *Forbes*, March 7, 2019, https://www.forbes.com/sites/rosycordero/2029/03/07/isabela-moner-learned-indigenous-peruvian-language-to-play-dora-the-explorer/ consulted January 4, 2021.

5. Angelo Muredda, "Dora and the Lost City of Gold Makes for a Charmless Experience Despite all its Colour and Charm," *National Post*, August 6, 2019, nationalpost.com/entertainment/movies/dora-and-the-lost-city-of-gold-makes-for-a-charmless-experience-despite-all-its-colour-and-cheer consulted January 2, 2021.

6. Ryan Bordow, "'Dora and the Lost City of Gold' is Better Than it Has Any Right to Be."

Lifestyle, AZBigMedia, August 9, 2019. azbigmedia.com/lifestyle/consumer.-news/movie-reviews/dora-and-the-lost-city-of-gold-is-better-than-it-hs-any-right-to-be/ consulted January 2, 2021.

Conclusion

1. Andrew McGregor Olney, "Predicting film genres with implicit ideals." *Frontiers in Psychology*, January 7, 2013, p.1 fronteirsin.org/articles/10.3389/fpsyg.2012.00565/full consulted July 14, 2021.

2. M. Brown, "Ways of Knowing, Doing, and Writing," *College Composition and Communication*, Vol. 58, No. 3, 2007; pp. 385–418.

3. *The Last Movie*, directed by Dennis Hopper, USA: Alta-Light, 1971.

4. Roger Ebert, "The Last Movie/Chinchero," January 1, 1971, rogerebert.com/reviews/the-last-movie-chinchero-1971 consulted August 5, 2021.

5. *Moon Over Parador*, directed by Paul Mazursky, USA: Universal Studios, 1988.

6. *Bananas!*, directed by Woody Allen, USA: United Artists, 1971.

7. Harry Sword, "Visionary Director Alex Cox on Joe Strummer, Punk, and Getting Blacklisted by Hollywood." VICE Entertainment. December 8, 2015, vice.com/en/article/ppxv5b/alex-cox-acid-punk-visionary-022 consulted May 5, 2022.

8. See, for example, Stephen Follows Film Data & Education, stephenfollows.com/genre-trends-global-film-production/ consulted July 14, 2021.

9. Paul Henley, *The Adventure of the Real: Jean Rouch and the Craft of Ethnographic Cinema* (Chicago: University of Chicago Press, 2009). p. xiv.

10. *Jungle*, directed by Greg McLean, Australia: Babber Films/Cutting Edge Group/Screen Australia/Screen Queensland, 2017.

11. *Hell* (aka El Infierno), directed by Luis Estrada, Mexico: Bandidos Films, 2010.

12. *From Dusk Till Dawn*, directed by Robert Rodríguez, USA: Dimension Films/A Band Apart/Los Hooligans Productions, 1996.

13. *The Ruins*, directed by Carter Smith, Australia and USA: Spyglass Entertainment and Red House Productions, 2008.

14. *EL DORADO: Temple of the Sun*, directed by Terry Cunningham, USA: American Cinema International, 2010.

15. *The Lost City*, directed by Adam Nee and Aaron Nee, USA: Fortis Films/3dot Productions/Exhibit A, 2022.

16. *American Made*, directed by Doug Linman, USA: Cross Creek Pictures/Imagine Entertainment/Hercules Film Fund/Quadrant Pictures/Vendian Entertainment, 2017.

17. *American Visa*, directed by Juan Carlos Valdivia, Bolivia: Bola Ocho Producciones, 2005.

18. *Our Brand Is Crisis*, directed by David Gordon Green, USA: Participant Media/RatPac-Dune Entertainment/Smokehouse Pictures/Fortis Films, 2015.

19. *Way of a Gaucho*, directed by Jacques Tourneur, USA: Warner Bros, 1947.

20. *Intimate Stories*, directed by Carlos Sorin, Argentina/Spain: Guacamole Films, 2002/2005.

21. Notable among these is the Cuban detective Cayetano Brulé in Roberto Ampuero's *El Alemán de Atacama* (Santiago: Editorial Planeta, 1997), which has been published in several subsequent editions, e.g., by Random House, 2012.

22. Richard Francaviglia, *The Enchantress of Atacama* (Newport and Bend, OR: Dancing Moon Press, 2019).

23. See Richard Francaviglia, "Writing Regional Fiction: A Cultural Geographer's First-Hand Account," *Journal of Cultural Geography*, Vol. 39, Issue 2, 2022, pp. 293–305.

24. Matthew W. Hughey, *The White Savior Film: Content, Critics, and Consumption* (Philadelphia: Temple University Press, 2014).

25. *Jungle Cruise*, directed by Jaume Collet-Serra, USA: Walt Disney Pictures/Davis Entertainment/Seven Bucks Productions/Flynn Picture Company, 2021.

26. See Morag Bell and Cheryl McEwan, "The Admission of Women Fellows to the Royal Geographical Society, 1892–1947; the Controversy and the Outcome," *The Geographical Journal*, Vol. 162, No. 3, November 1996, pp. 295–312.

27. See Celia Wakefield, *Searching for Isabel Godin* (Berkeley, CA: Creative Arts Book Co, 1994); Anthony Smith, *The Lost Lady of the Amazon: The Story of Isabela Godin and Her Epic Journey* (Cambridge, MA: Da Capo Press, 2003); and Robert Whitaker, *The Mapmaker's Wife: A True Tale of Love, Murder, and Survival in the Amazon* (New York: Basic Books, 2016).

28. Henry Louis Gates, *Black in Latin America* (New York: NYU Press, 2011).

29. See Kris Lane, *Potosí: The Silver City that Changed the World* (Oakland: University of California Press, 2019), especially pp. 5–7, 34, 55, 63–66, 78, 94–95, 103–105, 128 and 130.

30. *The Black Panther*, directed by Ryan Coogler, USA: Marvel Studios, 2918.

31. Laila Lalami, *The Moor's Account* (New York: Vintage Books, 2014).

32. Marie Robinson Wright, *Bolivia: The Central Highway of South America, A Land of Rich Resources and Varied Interest* (Philadelphia: George Barrie & Sons, 1907), p. 14.

33. See Tim Youngs, *Travel Writing: A Very Short Introduction* (New York: Oxford University Press, 2020); and Nandini Das and Tim Youngs, *The Cambridge History of Travel Writing* (Cambridge: Cambridge University Press, 2019).

34. Catalina de Erauso, *Lieutenant Nun: Memoir of a Basque Transvestite in the New World*; translated from the Spanish by Michele Steptoe and Marjorie Garber (Boston: Beacon Press, 1996), pp. 26–27.

35. http://www.azquotes.com>39687-Diana_Ossana consulted April 12, 2022.

Bibliography

Aguirre, the Wrath of God. Directed by Werner Herzog. Werner Herzog Filmproduktion, 1972.

Aire Libre. Directed by Luis Armando Roche. Bleu Blanc Rouge, 1997.

Aitken, Stuart, and Leo E. Zonn. *Place, Power, Situation and Spectacle: A Geography of Film.* Lanham: MD: Rowman & Littlefield, 1994.

American Made: Directed by Doug Linman. Cross Creek Pictures; Imagine Entertainment; Hercules Film Fund; Quadrant Pictures; Vendian Entertainment, 2017.

American Visa. Directed by Juan Carlos Valdivia. Bola Ocho Producciones, 2005.

Anaconda. Directed by Luis Llosa. Sony Pictures, 1997.

Apocalypto. Directed by Mel Gibson. Touchstone Pictures and Icon Productions, 2006.

Ascárate, Richard John. "'Have You Ever Seen a Shrunken Head?': Early Modern Roots of Ecstatic Truth in Werner Herzog's Fitzcarraldo." *PMLA* [Publications of the Modern Language Association] Vol. 122, No. 2, March 2007, pp. 483–501.

Avatar. Directed by James Cameron. Twentieth Century-Fox, 2009.

Bauer, Ralph. *The Cultural Geography of Colonial American Literatures: Empire, Travel, Modernity.* Cambridge: Cambridge University Press, 2005.

Bell, Stephen. *A Life in Shadow: Aimé Bonpland in Southern South America, 1817–1858.* Palo Alto: Stanford University Press, 2010.

Berry, Mark F. *The Dinosaur Filmography.* Jefferson, NC: McFarland, 2002.

Bingham, Hiram. *Across South America: An Account of a Journey from Buenos Aires to Lima by Way of Potosí.* Boston: Houghton Mifflin Company, 1911.

Bingham, Hiram. "In the Wonderland of Peru." *National Geographic Magazine,* Vol. 24, No. 4, April 1913.

Bingham, Hiram. *Lost City of the Incas: The Story of Machu Picchu and its Builders.* New York: Simon & Schuster, 1948.

Block, David. *Mission Culture on the Upper Amazon: Native Tradition, Jesuit Enterprise, & Secular Policy in Moxos, 1660–1880.* Lincoln: University of Nebraska Press, 1994.

Bollaert, William. *The Expedition of Pedro de Ursua & Lope de Aguirre in Search of El Dorado and Omagua in 1560–1. Translated from Fray Simón's Sixth Historical Notice of the Conquest of Tierra Firme, 1627.* London: Routledge, 2010.

Brewer, Stewart. *Latin American History Goes to the Movies: Understanding Latin America's Past Through Film.* New York: Routledge, 2016.

Bryce, James. *South America: Observations and Impressions.* New York: The Macmillan Company, 1913.

Burden of Dreams. Directed by Les Blank, Flower Films, 1982.

Burn! (aka Quemado!). Directed by Gillo Pontecorvo. Produzioni Europee Associati/Les Productions Artistes Associés, 1969.

Burnett, D. Graham. *Masters of All They Surveyed: Exploration, Geography, and a British El Dorado.* Chicago: University of Chicago Press, 2000.

Burton, Richard F. *Exploration of the Highlands of Brazil* (two volumes). London: Tinsley Bros., 1869.

Buttimer, Anne. "Bridging the Americas: Humboldtian Legacies." *The Geographical Review,* Vol. 96, No. 2, April 2006, pp. xvi-ix.

Cabeza de Vaca. Directed by Nicolás Echevarría. Concorde-New Horizons, 1991.

Cabeza de Vaca, Alvar Núñez. *The Journey and Ordeal of Cabeza de Vaca: His Account of the Disastrous First European Exploration of the American Southwest,* translated by Cyclone Covey. Mineola, NY: Dover Publications, 2003.

Cabeza de Vaca, Alvar Núñez. *The South American Expeditions, 1540–1545,* translated with notes by Baker H. Morrow. Albuquerque: University of New Mexico Press, 2011.

Cabo Blanco (aka *Caboblanco*). Directed by Lee Thompson. Lance Hool, 1980.

Captain from Castile. Directed by Henry King, Twentieth Century-Fox Film Productions, 1947.

Caraman, Philip. *The Lost Paradise: The Jesuit Republic in South America.* Westville FL: Allenson, Inc. 1976.

Cliff, Nigel. *The Last Crusade: The Epic Voyages of Vasco de Gama.* New York: Harper Perennial, 2011.

Cobra Verde. Directed by Werner Herzog. Werner Herzog Film Produktion, 1999.

Conley, Tom. *Cartographic Cinema.* Minneapolis: University of Minnesota Press, 2007.

Conley, Tom. "Film and Exploration," in *The Oxford Companion to World Exploration*. New York: Oxford University Press, 2007, pp. 306–309.

The Creature from the Black Lagoon. Directed by Jack Arnold. Universal Pictures, 1954.

Creswell, Tim, and Deborah Dixon. *Engaging Film: Geographies of Mobility and Identity*. Lanham, MD: Rowman & Littlefield, 2002.

Crystal Fairy and the Magical Cactus and 2012. Directed by Sebastián Silva. Content Media, 2013.

The Dance of Reality. Directed by Alejandro Jodorowski. Camera One; Le Soleil Film, 2013/2014.

Delaney, Carol. *Columbus and the Quest for Jerusalem*. New York: Simon & Schuster, 2011.

Di Benedetto, Antonio. *Zama*. New York: New York Review Books, 2000.

Dickenson, Victoria. *Drawn from Life: Science and Art in the Portrayal of the New World*. Toronto: University of Toronto Press, 1998.

Dora and the Lost City of Gold. Directed by James Bobin. Paramount Players; Nickelodeon Movies; Walden Media; Media Rights Capital; Burr! Productions; Screen Queensland, 2019.

Dorfman, Ariel. *Para Leer el Pato Donald*. Chile: Siglo Veintiuno, 1971.

Doyle, A. Conan. *The Lost World*. London: Hodder & Stoughton, 1912.

Dussell, Enrique. *The Invention of the Americas: Eclipse of "The Other" and the Myth of Modernity*. New York: Concilium, 1992/1995.

Dym, Jordana, and Karl Offen, eds. *Mapping Latin America*. Chicago: University of Chicago Press, 2011.

Edney, Matthew H. *Cartography: The Ideal and Its History*. Chicago: University of Chicago Press, 2019.

El Dorado. Directed by Carlos Saura, Canal + Chrysalide Film, 1988.

El Dorado: Temple of the Sun. Directed by Terry Cunningham. American Cinema International, 2010.

El Patrullero (aka The Highway Patrolman). Directed by Alex Cox, Lorenzo O'Brien, 1991.

Embrace of the Serpent. Directed by Ciro Guerra. Buffalo Films, 2015.

The Emerald Forest. Directed by John Boorman. Christel Films, 1985.

End of the Spear. Directed by Peter R. de Vries. Rocky Mountain Pictures, 2006.

Erauso, Catalina de. *Lieutenant Nun: Memoir of a Basque Transvestite in the New World,* translated from the Spanish by Michele Steptoe and Gabriel Steptoe. Boston: Beacon Press, 1996.

Evita. Directed by Alan Parker. Hollywood Pictures; Cinergy Pictures; RSO Films; Dirty Hands Productions, 1996.

Explorer: The Last Tepui. Directed by Renan Ozturk, Drew Pulley, and Taylor Freesolo Rees. Disney Plus Films, 2022.

1492: Conquest of Paradise. Directed by Ridley Scott. Paramount Pictures, 1992.

Francaviglia, Richard. *The Enchantress of Atacama*. Newport and Bend, OR (digital and print version Amazon.com books), 2019.

Francaviglia, Richard, and Jerry Rodnitsky. *Lights, Camera, History: Portraying the Past in Film*. College Station: Texas A & M University Press, 2007.

Fritze, Ronald. "Werner Herzog's Adaptation of History in *Aguirre, the Wrath of God*." *Film and History*, Vol. XV, No. 4, December 1985, pp. 74–86.

Gates, Henry Louis, Jr. *Black in Latin America*. New York: NYU Press, 2011.

Gobat, Michael. *An Empire by Invitation: William Walker and Manifest Destiny in Central America*. Cambridge, MA: Harvard University Press, 2018.

Goulding, Michael, Ronaldo Barthem, and Efrem Ferreira, *The Smithsonian Atlas of the Amazon*. Washington, D.C.: Smithsonian Books, 2003.

Granado, Alberto. *Traveling with Che Guevara: the Making of a Revolutionary*. New York: Newmarket Press, 2004.

Grann, David. *The Lost City of Z*. New York: Doubleday, 2009.

Green Fire. Directed by Andrew Marton. Metro-Goldwyn-Mayer, 1954.

Green Mansions. Directed by Mel Ferrer. Metro-Goldwyn-Mayer, 1959.

Guevara, Ernesto Che. *The Motorcycle Diaries: A Journey Around South America*. San Francisco: Analytical Club of San Francisco, 1995.

Hansen, Richard D. "Relativism, Revisionism, Aboriginalism, and Emic/Etic Truth: The Case Study," in R.J. Chacon and R.G. Mendoza, eds. *The Ethics of Anthropology and Amerindian Research: Reporting on Environmental Degradation*. Springer Science + Business Media, LLC, 2012/2013) pp. 147–190.

Harley, J.B. *The New Nature of Maps: Essays on the History of Cartography*. Baltimore: Johns Hopkins University Press, 2001.

Hayashida, Frances; Andrés Troncoso; and Diego Salazar. *Rethinking the Inka: Community, Landscape, and Empire in the Southern Andes*. Austin: University of Texas Press, 2022.

Herrick, Dennis. *Esteban: The African Slave Who Explored America*. Albuquerque: University of New Mexico Press, 2018.

Herzog, Werner. *Conquest of the Useless: Reflections from the Making of Fitzcarraldo*. New York: HarperCollins, 2009.

Herzog, Werner. *Fitzcarraldo: The Original Story,* translated from the German by Martje Herzog and Alan Greenburg. San Francisco: Fjord Press, 1982.

Hudson, W.H. *Green Mansions: A Romance of the Tropical Forest* (1904 and subsequent editions). New York; Duckworth Overlook, 2018.

Hudson, W.H. *Idle Days in Patagonia*. New York: Dutton & Co., 1917.

Hughey, Matthew W. *The White Savior Film: Content, Critics and Consumption*. Philadelphia: Temple University Press, 2014.

Humboldt, Alexander von, and Aimé Bonpland. *Personal Narrative of a Journey to the Equinoctial Regions of the New Continent During the Years 1799–1804.* London, 1814.

Icaros: A Vision. Directed by Leonor Carraballo and Mateo Norzi. Conibo Productions, Nico Dissolve, 2017.

Indiana Jones and the Kingdom of the Crystal Skull. Directed by Steven Spielberg. Lucasfilm Ltd. and Paramount Pictures, 2008.

Jackson, Robert H. *Frontiers of Evangelization: Indians in the Sierra Gorda and Chiquitos Missions.* Norman: University of Oklahoma Press, 2017.

Juan-Navarro, Santiago. "Between El Dorado and Armageddon: Utopia and Apocalypse in the Films of the Encounter." *Delaware Review of Latin American Studies,* Vol. 6, No. 2, January 15, 2006, pp. 1–7.

Jungle. Directed by Greg McLean. Babber Films; Cutting Edge Group; Screen Australia; Screen Queensland, 2017.

Jungle Cruise. Directed by Jaume Collet-Serra. Walt Disney Pictures; Davis Entertainment; Seven Bucks Productions; Flynn Picture Company, 2021.

Knives Out. Directed by Rian Johnson. T Street, 2019.

Lane, Kris. *Colour of Paradise: The Emerald in the Age of Gunpowder Empires.* New Haven: Yale University Press, 2010.

The Last Movie. Directed by Dennis Hopper. Alta-Light, 1971.

Lewis, Bart R. *The Miraculous Lie: Lope de Aguirre and the Search for El Dorado in the Latin American Novel.* Lanham, MD: Lexington Books, 2003.

Los Andes no Creen en Dios. Laboratores Sonido Filmoso do Santiago de Chile; Imagen Technicolor Montreal Canada, 2007.

The Lost City. Directed by Adam Nee and Aaron Nee. Fortis Films; 3dot Productions; Exhibit A, 2022.

The Lost City of Z. Directed by James Gray. Plan B Entertainment, 2016.

The Lost World. Directed by Stuart Orme. BBC and A&E, 2001.

Love in the Time of Cholera. Directed by Mike Newell. Stone Village Pictures, 2007.

Lovell, W. George. "Latin America on Screen: Film as a Complement to Teaching Regional Geography," *Journal of Latin American Geography,* Vol. 18, No. 2, June 2019.

Lukinbeal, Christopher, and Laura Sharp. "Geography and Film," *Oxford Bibliographies* (on-line), 2017.

Márquez, Gabriel García. *One Hundred Years of Solitude,* translated by Gregory Rabassa. New York: Alfred A. Knopf, 1970.

Mauseth, James D; Roberto Kiesling; and Carlos Ostolaza. *A Cactus Odyssey: Journeys in the Wilds of Bolivia, Peru, and Argentina.* Portland, OR: Timber Press, 2002.

Medina, José Toribio. *Discovery of the Amazon According to the Account of Friar Gaspar de Carvajal,* translated by Bertram T. Lee. New York: American Geographical Society, 1935.

Mein Liebster Feind (My Best Friend). Directed by Werner Herzog, Werner Herzog Film Produktion, 1999.

Millard, Candace. *The River of Doubt: Theodore Roosevelt's Darkest Journey.* New York: Anchor Books, 2005.

Miller, David. *W.H. Hudson and the Elusive Paradise.* New York: St. Martin's Press, 1990.

Missing. Directed by Costa-Gavras. Polygram Filmed Entertainment; Universal Pictures, 1982.

The Mission. Directed by Roland Joffé. Goldcrest Films, 1986.

Moon Over Parador. Directed by Paul Mazursky. Universal Studios, 1988.

The Motorcycle Diaries. Directed by Walter Salles. Film Four; BD Cine; Wildwood Enterprises, Inc., 2004.

The Naked Jungle. Directed by Byron Haskin. Paramount Pictures, 1954.

The Naked Prey. Directed by Cornel Wilde, Paramount Pictures, 1965.

Natural Encounters. Directed by Richard Francaviglia, University of Texas at Arlington, 2002.

Neeleman, Gary, and Rose Neeleman. *Tracks in the Amazon: The Day-to-Day Life of Workers on the Madeira-Mamoré Railroad.* Salt Lake City: University of Utah Press, 2014.

Nostalgia for the Light. Directed by Patricio Guzmán. Pyramide International and Icarus Films, 2011.

The Old Man Who Read Love Stories. Directed by Rolf de Heer. 2001.

Oro (Gold). Directed by Augustín Diaz Yanes. Apache Films/Sony Pictures.

The Other Conquest. Directed by Salvador Carrasco. Twentieth Century Fox, 1999/2000.

Our Brand Is Crisis. Directed by David Gordon Green. Participant Media; RatPac-Dune Entertainment; Smokehouse Pictures; Fortis Films, 2015.

Piranha. Directed by Joe Dante. Zanuck/Brown and Universal Pictures, 1975.

Pratt, Mary Louise. *Imperial Eyes: Travel Writing and Transculturation.* New York: Routledge, 1992.

Quantum of Solace. Directed by Marc Foster. Eon Productions; Metro-Goldwyn-Mayer; Sony Pictures, 2008.

Rainier, Peter. *Green Fire.* New York: Random House, 1942.

Reyes, Luis I. *Made in Mexico: Hollywood South of the Border.* Lanham, MD: Applause Theater and Cinema Books, Rowman & Littlefield, 2018.

Ringle, Carter. "Fear and Loathing in the Americas: White Fanatics and the Cinematic Colonial Mindset," *Terrae Incognitae,* Vol. 51, No. 3, December 2019, pp. 271–280.

Roosevelt, Theodore. *Through the Brazilian Wilderness.* Sagamore Hill, NY, 1914.

The Royal Hunt of the Sun. Directed by Irving Lerner. Cinema Center Films, 1969.

The Ruins. Directed by Carter Smith. Spyglass Entertainment and Red House Productions, 2008.

Sadlier, Darlene J. *A Century of Brazilian Documentary Film: From Nationalism to Protest.* Austin: University of Texas Press, 2022.

Saeger, James Schofield. "*The Mission* and Historical Missions: Film and the Writing of History." *The Americas,* Vol. 51, No. 3, January 1995, pp. 393–415.

Saludos Amigos. Directed by Norman Ferguson. Wilfred Jackson, Jack Kinney, Hamilton Luske and Bill Roberts. Walt Disney Productions, 1942.

Salvatore, Ricardo. *Disciplinary Conquest: U.S. Scholars in South America, 1900–1945.* Durham, NC: Duke University Press, 2016.

Secret of the Andes. Directed by Alejandro Azzani. National Institute for Cinema and Audiovisual Arts, 1998/1999.

Secret of the Incas. Directed by Jerry Hopper. Paramount Pictures, 1954.

Serrano, Carmen. *Gothic Imagination in Latin American Fiction and Film.* Albuquerque: University of New Mexico Press, 2019.

Smith, Amanda M. *Mapping the Amazon: Literary Geography After the Rubber Boom.* Liverpool, UK: Liverpool University Press, 2021.

Stout, Joseph A. *Schemers and Dreamers: Filibustering in Mexico, 1848–1921.* Fort Worth: Texas Christian University Press, 2002.

The 33. Directed by Patricia Riggen. Phoenix Pictures, 2015.

The Three Caballeros. Directed by Norman Ferguson, Clyde Geronomi, Jack Kinney, Bill Roberts, and Harold Young. Walt Disney Productions, 1944 (Mexico) and 1945 (USA).

Tintin and the Temple of the Sun. Directed by Eddie Lateste. Belvision, 1969.

Treasure of the Sierra Madre. Directed by John Huston. Warner Brothers-First National, 1948.

Tycoon. Directed by Richard Wallace. RKO Pictures, 1947.

Viva Zapata! Directed by Elia Kazan. 20th Century-Fox, 1952.

Walker. Directed by Alex Cox. In-Cine Compania/Industrial, 1987.

Walker, William. *The War in Nicaragua* [originally New York: S.H. Goetzel, 1860]. Tucson: University of Arizona Press, 1985.

Waller, Gregory A. "Aguirre, the Wrath of God: History, Theater, and the Camera." *South Atlantic Review,* Vol. 46, No. 2, May 1981, pp. 55–69.

Walt and El Grupo. Directed by Theodore Thomas. Walt Disney Family Foundation Films; Theodore Thomas Productions, 2008.

Weaver, Stewart A. *Exploration: A Very Short Introduction.* New York: Oxford University Press, 2015.

Weber, David. *Bárbaros: Spaniards and Their Savages in the Age of Enlightenment.* New Haven: Yale University Press, 2005.

Weber, David. *The Spanish Frontier in North America.* New Haven: Yale University Press, 1992.

Wiersema, Juliet. "The Map of the Yurumangí Indians: Charting the Erasure of the Pacific Lowlands' Indigenous Inhabitants, 1742–1780." *Terrae Incognitae,* Vol. 52, No. 2, August 2020, pp. 160–194.

The Wild Bunch. Directed by Sam Peckinpah. Warner Bros.-Seven Arts, 1969.

Wild Tales, Directed by Damián Szifron, Kramer & Sigman Films, 2014.

Williams, Linda. "Motion and e-motion: lust and the 'frenzy of the visible.'" *Journal of Visual Culture,* Vol. 18, No. 1, 2019, pp. 97–129.

Wilson, Jack. *W.H. Hudson: The Colonial's Revenge—A Reading of His Fiction and His Relationship with Charles Darwin.* London: University of London, 1981.

The Wizard of Oz. Directed by Victor Fleming. Metro-Goldwyn-Mayer, 1939.

Wolfe, Byron, and Scott Brady. *Phantom Skies & Shifting Ground: Landscape, Culture, and Rephotography in Eadweard Muybridge's Illustrations of Central America.* Philadelphia: Radius Books/Temple University Press, 2017.

Wright, Mary Robinson. *Bolivia: The Central Highway of South America, A Land of Rich Resources and varied Interest.* Philadelphia: George Barrie & Sons, 1907.

Wurlitzer, Rudolph. *Walker: The True Story of the First American Invasion of Nicaragua.* New York: Harper & Row, 1987.

Index

Numbers in *bold italics* indicate pages with illustrations